TWENTIETH-CENTURY EVANGELICALISM

GARLAND REFERENCE LIBRARY
OF SOCIAL SCIENCE
(VOL. 521)

TWENTIETH-CENTURY EVANGELICALISM
A Guide to the Sources

Edith L. Blumhofer
Joel A. Carpenter

GARLAND PUBLISHING, INC. • NEW YORK & LONDON
1990

Library of Congress Cataloging-in-Publication Data

Blumhofer, Edith L., 1950–
Twentieth-century evangelicalism: a guide to the sources / Edith L. Blumhofer, Joel A. Carpenter.
p. cm. — (Garland reference library of social science; vol. 521)
Includes bibliographical references.
ISBN 0–8240–3040–0
1. Evangelicalism—United States—Study and teaching. 2. Evangelicalism—United States—Bibliography. 3. United States—Church history—Study and teaching. 4. United States—Church history—Bibliography. I. Carpenter, Joel A. II. Title. III. Series: Garland reference library of social science; v. 521.
BR1644.U6B48 1990
227.3'082'07—dc20 90–31842
CIP

Printed on acid-free, 250-year-life paper
Manufactured in the United States of America

ACKNOWLEDGMENTS

We acknowledge with thanks the help of Cassandra Niemczyk, Candace Wegner, Mary Noll, Kristin Helmer and Teri Kondo, research assistants at the Institute for the Study of American Evangelicals at Wheaton College, in preparing the manuscript and compiling bibliography. James Wilhoit, Lyle Dorsett and Robert Coleman, colleagues at Wheaton College, reviewed the chapters on education and evangelism, and we are grateful for their comments. The editors also express their gratitude to the staffs of the Billy Graham Center Library and Buswell Library at Wheaton College for the support they provided throughout this project.

Edith L. Blumhofer
Wheaton, IL

Joel A. Carpenter
Philadelphia, PA

CONTENTS

INTRODUCTION
RESEARCHING AMERICAN EVANGELICALS

This book is designed to assist people who are doing research on evangelicals, especially the ones who have inhabited twentieth-century America. Learning more about fundamentalists, pentecostals, holiness Wesleyans, Southern Baptists, and other varieties of modern American evangelicals has had obvious relevance in recent years. These groups, which have long been considered marginal to the mainstream of American public life, have reasserted their presence in a variety of ways. The rise of a New Christian Right with links to the Reagan Administration in the early 1980s and the highly publicized misdeeds of several televangelists in the late 1980s are only two of the more infamous indications that evangelicals have reentered the public arena. Now acknowledged to be the more dynamic, growing wing of American Protestantism's "two-party system," evangelicals are forcing leaders of Protestantism's more liberal party to recognize that "old-line" is a more accurate label for themselves than "mainline." Evangelicals seem to crop up in many other spheres of life also, with varying degrees of winsomeness: on both sides of Senate foreign policy debates, on the pop music charts, as volume leaders in religious publishing, alongside Catholics in anti-abortion demonstrations, in appointments to the Cabinet and to major university posts, and in major league baseball interviews. It is becoming increasingly obvious that whatever impressions one might have of evangelicals, they comprise a vigorous and enduring segment of the American populace. To avoid attending to them is to leave much unknown about modern American religion and about contemporary America.

DEFINING "EVANGELICAL"

Discussions about evangelicals or "evangelicalism" cannot proceed very far before they run headlong into the problem of definition. It would be presumptuous, then, to present a guide to the study of evangelicals without at least attempting to clarify our use of these terms. What constitutes evangelicalism? And who are the evangelicals? Are Southern Baptists evangelicals? Are fundamentalists evangelicals? How about pentecostals? Charismatic Roman Catholics? Mennonites? Lutherans? "Evangelical" has been bandied about much these days, often by those who are transparently ignorant of its meaning. It remains an elusive concept that has rarely been used with any precision. Nevertheless, it is possible to give a careful description of what constitutes the evangelical branch of American Christianity and to demonstrate the senses in which the term can be used with the most accuracy in a contemporary American context.

Any definition of evangelical must go back to the New Testament, since the term is derived from the Greek word euangelion, which is translated as good news, or gospel. The first groups to use evangelical as their label in more recent history were the sixteenth-century followers of Martin Luther. For them, "evangelical" implied that their movement had recovered the gospel, the good news of salvation by grace through faith. So in Europe today, and especially in Germany, evangelical is virtually synonymous with Protestant. This was the case in nineteenth-century America also, but for a different reason--because of the domination of revivalism in the Protestant churches. As late as the 1920s, even liberal Protestants such as Harry Emerson Fosdick customarily referred to themselves as evangelicals. Catholics also use the term evangelical, usually as an adjective, though, not as a noun. By it they refer to the gospel-proclaiming or evangelistic functions in the church, such as an evangelical sermon or preaching mission.

Another common twist in the use of the term evangelical is to place it in reference to another term, fundamentalism. Some people, especially those in the news media, use the two interchangeably. Others, who are trying to show a bit more sophistication, distinguish between the two terms by putting conservative Protestants into two categories: the moderates and the militants. In this case, an evangelical is an uptown fundamentalist, with perhaps more education and nicer manners. I think that some conservative evangelicals are tempted to use the term in this way also, by being very eager for people to know that they are not fundamentalists. Hard-line fundamentalists throw this back at them by suggesting that an evangelical is a fundamentalist who has gone bad and has compromised his or her convictions. Bob Jones, Sr. is reported to have said: "I'll tell you what an evangelical is: it's someone who says to a liberal, 'I'll call you a Christian if you call me a scholar.'[1]

Despite all of this confusing variance in usage, it is possible to get a clearer picture of what constitutes the evangelical wing of Christianity. Be warned, however, that clarity does not in this case equal simplicity or uniformity. Indeed, historians refer to this complex cluster of movements and traditions as the American evangelical mosaic.[2] One of the best attempts at explanation and definition of "evangelical" comes by way of George Marsden. He points out that there are three senses in which the term is used today, and by identifying and distinguishing between them, we can eliminate much of the confusion.[3]

The first sense of the term is to identify a conceptual unity, to label as "evangelical" all Christians who match up with a few fundamental theological beliefs and religious concerns. I would propose that there are about five of these: 1) the divine inspiration, complete trustworthiness and final authority of the Bible; 2) salvation only through personal trust in Christ; 3) an emphasis on a distinct and personal experience of saving faith; 4) the importance of living a morally and spiritually transformed life; 5) and the importance of evangelism, that is, proclaiming the gospel to all people and calling them to faith in Christ. There is a problem with defining evangelical in this way alone, however, especially in the United States. Evangelicalism has been so pervasive in American culture that its tenets often show up in folk piety here; many people who rarely practice the Christian faith can emerge as "evangelicals" on opinion polls according to these criteria.

Any definition of evangelical, then, needs to pay attention to an important second sense in which the term is understood, as an organic family of movements and traditions that comprise the American evangelical mosaic. There have been more than a dozen different faith families in this nation that express, albeit with tremendous internal variety and nuance, common evangelical beliefs and practices. Evangelical movements and traditions of many kinds have emerged from the waves of revivals and awakenings that have occurred since the days of the Pietists and the Puritans, and some groups, whose heritage is older and different, have been influenced as well. Just to name some of these different groups is to suggest the mosaic's diversity: Black Baptists and Methodists, Mennonites and Brethren, restorationists of the Disciples of Christ/ Christian Church/ Churches of Christ tradition, German and Scandinavian ethnic pietist-evangelicals, pentecostals--both black and white, Southern Baptists, fundamentalist Baptist and Bible churches, holiness Wesleyans such as the Nazarenes, Dutch Reformed evangelicals, evangelical Friends, charismatics--both Catholic and Protestant, proliferating Hispanic evangelical and pentecostal communities, and the varied Asian-American congregations of the born-again.

There is a problem in using the evangelical label this broadly, however. Not all of these groups readily identify themselves as "evangelicals," much as they might share some basic traits. And as the mosaic image suggests, there is a great deal of fragmentation and isolation among these groups.

One reason why these parties do not all self-identify as evangelicals is because the term is most often used in a third, more narrow sense, as the self-ascribed label for a movement or coalition that has arisen since World War II. Marsden calls the people in this movement "card-carrying" evangelicals. "Evangelicalism" in this sense was envisioned and organized by a progressive, reforming party within fundamentalism that sought to bring together all conservative Protestants in America under a common agenda. They never fully succeeded, for a variety of reasons, including the fact that some, especially the Black and Hispanic churches, were never fully invited; that others were simply too self-absorbed and protective to get involved; and that yet others saw remnants of a fundamentalist agenda behind the coalition and did not accept it. One last reason is that the evangelical mosaic keeps adding new forms, and in this culture's "free enterprise" religious economy the newcomers are often perfectly content to accentuate their uniqueness and go their own way.

Nevertheless, this narrower fellowship of "card-carrying" evangelicals is large and internally complex. One might expect that the "card-carrying" evangelicals would find their primary identity and centers of operation in the nation's conservative Protestant denominations, but that is not really the case. This loose coalition that calls itself "evangelicalism" is in fact less dependent on denominations than on a network of parachurch agencies such as InterVarsity Christian Fellowship, Christianity Today magazine, World Vision, Campus Crusade for Christ, Moody Bible Institute, Seattle Pacific University, Trinity Evangelical Divinity School, The 700 Club, and the Billy Graham Evangelistic Association. As Marsden describes it, "evangelicalism" was dominated until about the mid-1970s by post-fundamentalist theologians and ministry leaders, but it also includes some people from all of the other movements and traditions that have embodied evangelical beliefs and emphases. Perhaps the key test for membership in this new evangelical coalition is to find out whether someone identifies more with his or her home denomination or with this parachurch network. In this sense, Senator Mark Hatfield is more an evangelical than a Conservative Baptist; former Surgeon

General C. Everett Koop is more an evangelical than a Presbyterian; and both Pat Robertson and Billy Graham identify more as evangelicals than as Southern Baptists.

In sum, whether evangelicals are defined in the "mosaic" sense or the "card-carrying" sense, they are a radically diverse lot, despite their common convictions. This book will attempt to give a sense of the evangelical mosaic's breadth, especially in Section II, where it treats the religious traditions that feed into and comprise the American evangelical mosaic. In Sections III through VI, however, the focus will be on the new evangelical coalition of post-World War II vintage. Contending with its internal complexity and kaleidoscopic changing patterns has proven to be challenge enough for the contributors.

STUDYING EVANGELICALS

In the past few years the study of American evangelical Christianity, like its practice, has been flourishing. That was not always the case, for until fairly recently, many students of American religion and culture shared the opinion confessed by one eminent sociologist of religion, that

> "The point of view variously called evangelical, fundamentalist, holiness, Pentecostal, or millenarian was moribund in America . . . . The whole conservative religious scene . . . was out of step with the America I knew. Therefore it could be dismissed. And dismiss it I did until recently."[4]

This lack of attention led historian Ernest Sandeen to quip: "the fate of Fundamentalism in historiography has been worse than its lot in history."[5]

To a certain extent, however, scholarship, like art, tends to imitate life. The persistent popular support for evangelical Christianity and its resurgence as a cultural force have prompted scholars to question some of their assumptions about the relationship between religion and modernity that had persuaded them that the evangelical kind of Christianity was not terribly important to study. The American religious scene has been particularly puzzling because the formula that has worked so well in analyzing trends in almost every other western nation--modernization equals secularization--does not fit the situation here.

Sociologists are perhaps the most agitated about this issue, since they have been most concerned with theories of secularization.[6] "Evangelicalism," with its surprising vitality and persistence in the world's most modern nation, has become a hot topic in the sociology of religion. James Hunter's American Evangelicalism (1983) and Evangelicalism: the Coming Generation (1987), Nancy Ammerman's Bible Believers (1987) and R. Stephen Warner's New Wine in Old Wineskins (1988) have set new standards for careful attention to the interior character of evangelicalism and its ecological niche in the larger culture. The latter subject is also a central concern of Robert Wuthnow's major treatise, The Restructuring of American Religion (1988).

Historians have been concerned with evangelicals' cultural role for a bit longer, thanks in part to the work of Perry Miller, who led the resurgence of interest in the New England Puritans. At the time of his death in the early 1960s, Miller was working on nineteenth-century America, and pointing out that evangelical revivalism was "a central mode of this culture's search for national identity."[7] A harvest of scholarship on religion in pre-twentieth-century America has appeared in the last two-and-a-half decades, and the crop seems to improve in volume and quality every year. The excellent bibliographic essay by Leonard I.

Sweet in his book, The Evangelical Tradition in America (1984), and the book notices and bibliographic essays published in the Evangelical Studies Bulletin since then show the richness of this literature and the message that it reflects: to know the evangelicals is to know a great deal about the heart and soul of America.

Historians have been less interested in assessing religion's role in twentieth-century America. Like the sociologists, many assumed that fundamentalism and other kinds of evangelicalism were momentary reactions to America's irresistible march toward cosmopolitan, secular maturity. Furthermore, they tended to see such beliefs as obstacles to enlightened and rational public discourse. As radical historian R. Laurence Moore put it, this bias prompted historians to attempt to "write Americans beyond their religious backwardness as quickly as possible."[8] Nevertheless, Ernest Sandeen's Roots of Fundamentalism (1970) helped launch a new interest in America's premier popular religion, "born-again" Christianity; and George Marsden's magisterial Fundamentalism and American Culture (1980) seems to have brought legitimacy to the study of twentieth-century evangelicals in much the same way that Perry Miller's work rehabilitated the Puritans. Since Marsden, a number of excellent treatments of twentieth-century evangelical movements' varied careers have appeared. James Bratt's Dutch Calvinism in Modern America (1984), David Edwin Harrell, Jr.'s Oral Roberts (1985), Mark Noll's Between Faith and Criticism (1986), and not least, Marsden's "sequel," Reforming Fundamentalism (1987) are but a few of the more exemplary offerings in a growing body of solid historical literature.

THIS BOOK'S DESIGN

This book comes, then, at a time when the study of twentieth-century American evangelicals is still expanding and maturing. No doubt there are many avid readers, as well as students and more established scholars who would like to be introduced to this literature. Others are seeking some assistance in getting started with research in some aspect of this field. The more seasoned researchers may wish to have at hand, for quick reference, a selection of the scholarly studies now available, plus a large assortment of materials created by evangelicals themselves. This book is designed to fulfil these needs.

It is also formulated to help researchers know where to look for sources. Evangelicals, as we have seen, are scattered across at least a dozen different movements or traditions, and each of these faith families is actually a cluster of denominations, movements, and parachurch agencies. Some of these agencies have libraries, archives, or museums, but they are not all that easy to locate. So in order to make a solid start at studying twentieth-century evangelicalism, it is important that the researcher get a broader view of the sources and their location than can be provided by a bibliography alone.

The first section of this book, then, is designed to help the researcher find good collections of sources. It contains a chapter on reference works which includes both generalized bibliographies on religion in America and specialized research handbooks such as Charles Edwin Jones's monumental Guide to the Study of the Pentecostal Movement (2 vols., 1983). As an added feature, this chapter includes a selection of reference books published by evangelicals. They cover a variety of religious subjects and introduce the researcher to evangelical perspectives and the scholars who hold them in such areas as church history, theology, biblical studies, and missions.

Another feature of the first section is its annotated lists of libraries, archives, and museums with significant collections on evangelicals. Twentieth-century evangelicals have produced mountains of books and magazines, and they have excelled at creating other media, including pamphlets, fliers, tracts, postcards, photographs, audio recordings, and motion pictures--as well as their highly publicized radio and television ventures. In addition, the unpublished records and papers of a variety of their leaders and organizations have been preserved. Section I will aim the researcher at the location of these materials. Some of these sites are well-known and distinguished research libraries, but many strategic caches of sources are far from researchers' common haunts. Special attention has been devoted to collections of artifacts, pictorial resources, and electronic media. These sources are not often included in research guides but they are of obvious importance when studying evangelicals. Finally, Section I includes annotated lists of periodicals and publishing houses and their locations. Throughout the section, then, are many leads to help researchers negotiate the organizational mazes that constitute evangelicalism.

Sections II-VI constitute a more traditional bibliography. They contain annotated lists of books, chapters and articles (and a very few theses) by and about evangelicals. Section II offers a historical context; its first chapter locates discussions of evangelicalism in the more general literature of American religious history. Next comes a chapter on the historical literature of the various traditions and movements that comprise or feed into the American evangelical mosaic. The bulk of the section, organized into chapters covering chronological periods, samples the works on the salient issues, movements, and leaders that characterized evangelicals' history from the Great Awakening to the present.

Sections III through VI focus on the post-World War II era, and especially on the years since 1970, when evangelicals' notoriety and apparent influence began to surge. The contributors are most intent on documenting the history and character of the evangelicals of the "card-carrying" variety. These sections illustrate the variety of interests with which evangelicals concerned themselves: from scholarship in the natural sciences to marriage and family matters, and from political action to devotional life. Care has been taken to represent something of the variety of convictions that evangelicals have expressed on any given interest or issue. These chapters show that whatever adjectives might describe American evangelicals' opinions, "unanimous" is not one of them.

In closing, a few words of contrition seem fitting. Bibliography-making is both a labor of love and, unfortunately, a sure-fire way to lose friends and antagonize colleagues in the profession. We probably have written some things in our annotations that will offend or perplex some authors. Please rest assured that "malice toward none" has been our motto. Without a doubt we have also committed sins of omission that authors who peruse these pages will notice immediately. The growing volume of published work on our subject means that every section of the bibliography has had to be extremely selective, and certainly our selections are flawed by our limited knowledge and fallible judgment. We beg the pardon of authors whose writings have been omitted; to you we offer, as a weak compensation, this last word. Attention, readers: many of the books cited herein contain extensive bibliographies. These should allow the industrious researcher to dig deeper into the field, where more treasures lie.

JOEL A. CARPENTER
Philadelphia, PA

NOTES

1. Bob Jones, Corn Bread and Caviar: Reminiscences and Reflections (Greenville, SC: Bob Jones University Press, 1985), 104, offers a rendition of this characterization which his father, Bob Jones, Sr., made famous.

2. The first to develop this concept was Timothy L. Smith. See his "The Evangelical Kaleidoscope and the Call to Christian Unity," Christian Scholar's Review 15 (1986): 125-40; and Cullen Murphy, "Protestantism and the Evangelicals," Wilson Quarterly 5 (Autumn 1981): 105-16, which was written in consultation with Smith.

3. George Marsden, "Introduction: The Evangelical Denomination," in Evangelicalism and Modern America, ed. Marsden (Grand Rapids; Eerdmans, 1984), vii-xvi. The definition that follows below depends most heavily on Marsden's thoughts.

4. Phillip E. Hammond, "In Search of a Protestant Twentieth Century: American Religion and Power since 1900," Review of Religious Research 24 (March 1983): 281.

5. Sandeen, The Roots of Fundamentalism: British and American Millenarianism, 1800-1930 (Chicago: University of Chicago Press, 1970), 285.

6. See R. Stephen Warner, "Theoretical Barriers to the Understanding of Evangelical Christianity," Sociological Analysis 40 (Spring 1979): 1-9.

7. Miller, The Life of the Mind in America: From the Revolution to the Civil War (New York: Harcourt, Brace & World, 1965), 6.

8. Moore, "Insiders and Outsiders in American Historical Narrative and American History," American Historical Review 87 (April 1982): 406.

Twentieth-Century Evangelicalism

SECTION I: LOCATING SOURCES

CHAPTER 1
REFERENCE WORKS

The titles in this section represent a selection of reference sources which provide access to the body of information available for the study of evangelicalism in America.

The resources are divided into three categories: works about evangelical activities and traditions, works on religion in North America containing information about evangelicals and works reflecting an evangelical perspective.

The first category includes sources which focus directly on the movement as a whole or specific segments or aspects of the movement. These provide the researcher with the primary information sources documenting the movement. The second category contains key sources of a more general nature which commit significant portions of their content to evangelicalism.

The last category provides the researcher with a different perspective. It includes a selection of key reference sources used by evangelicals themselves as they conduct their scholarly pursuits. These allow the investigator to look at the evangelical perspective from the inside and obtain an orientation to the general mindset. The researcher is cautioned that because of the diversity of the movement what may be acquired by using this method is a caricature. However, careful scholars will find their understanding much enhanced by these resources.

(A) Reference Works About Evangelical Activities and Traditions

1. Burgess, Stanley M. and Gary B. McGee, eds. _Dictionary of Pentecostal and Charismatic Movements_. Grand Rapids: Zondervan, Regency Reference Library, 1988.

   A mixture of information on historical and current people, places and organizations relating to the movement. Heavily slanted toward Anglo-American pentecostalism, but includes representative entries for ethnic America and other parts of the world.

2. Dayton, Donald W., ed. _The Higher Christian Life: A Bibliographical Overview_. New York: Garland Publishing, 1985.

   A reprint of three bibliographical essays published by the B. L. Fisher Library, Asbury Theological Seminary. Includes: Donald W. Dayton, _The American Holiness Movement: A Bibliographic Introduction_; David W. Faupel,

The American Pentecostal Movement: A Bibliographical Essay; and David D. Bundy, Keswick: A Bibliographic Introduction to the Higher Life Movements.

3. Directory of Religious Broadcasting. Morristown, NJ: National Religious Broadcasters, 1967-. Annual.

Provides information about religious radio and television stations, program producers and the various agencies and auxiliary services connected with religious broadcasting. Published by the National Religious Broadcasters Association for its membership.

4. DuPree, Sherry Sherrod, ed. Biographical Dictionary of African-American, Holiness-Pentecostals, 1880-1990. Washington, DC: Middle Atlantic Regional Press, 1989.

Provides information on more than 1,000 religious leaders, religious educators, lay leaders, missionaries and musicians. The bibliography includes numerous dissertations as well as published sources.

5. Ehlert, Arnold D., comp. A Bibliographic History of Dispensationalism. Grand Rapids: Baker, 1965.

Discusses the people who promoted dispensationalism over the years and describes their major publications. Attempts to show that dispensationalism is consistent with the faith and practice of the primitive church.

6. Encyclopedia of Southern Baptists. 3 vols. Nashville: Broadman Press, 1958.

Contains over 4,000 articles about Southern Baptists written by themselves. It is intended as a source book for members of the denomination as well as a source of information for outsiders.

7. Jones, Charles Edwin. Black Holiness: A Guide to the Study of Black Participation in Wesleyan Perfectionist and Glossolalic Pentecostal Movements. Metuchen, NJ: Scarecrow Press, 1987.

Includes materials relating to Black-led religious organizations as well as the participation of Black minorities in other groups. While the scope includes Africa, the West Indies and parts of Europe, the bulk of the information is about North America.

8. Jones, Charles Edwin. A Guide to the Study of the Pentecostal Movement. 2 vols. Metuchen, NJ: Scarecrow Press, 1983.

The most comprehensive resource available for publications in western languages. Refers the reader to Walter J. Hollenweger, Handbuch der Pfingstbewegung for material in non-western languages.

9. Jones, Charles Edwin. A Guide to the Study of the Holiness Movement. Metuchen, NJ: Scarecrow Press, 1974.

This work has become the standard bibliography for researching the holiness movement. Includes sections on the Keswick Movement and holiness denominations which later became pentecostal.

10. Keeley, Robin, ed. Christianity in Today's World. Grand Rapids: Eerdmans, 1985.

A global portrait of contemporary Christianity from an international evangelical perspective. A good source to discover how evangelicals think about themselves.

11. National Evangelical Directory: A Directory Serving the Evangelical Community. Wheaton, IL: National Association of Evangelicals, 1977-. Biennial.

Includes agencies of the National Association of Evangelicals, member organizations and those applying for membership. Types of organizations include camping, counseling, education, media, missions, outreach and service.

12. Peterson, Paul D., ed. Evangelicalism and Fundamentalism: A Bibliography Selected From the ATLA Religion Database. Rev. ed. Chicago: American Theological Library Association, 1983.

A selected bibliography produced from the Religion Index computer files. Entries are arranged under the same subject headings used in ATLA Religion Indexes.

(B) Reference Works on Religion in North America Containing Information About Evangelicals

13. The Brethren Encyclopedia. 3 vols. Philadelphia: Brethren Encyclopedia Inc., 1983.

Provides information on the religious bodies which trace their origins to the Brethren movement. While the movement as such would not be described as evangelical, it includes groups such as the Grace Brethren which were heavily influenced by evangelical movements.

14. Brunkow, Robert deV., ed. Religion and Society in North America: An Annotated Bibliography. Santa Barbara, CA: ABC-Clio Press, 1983.

A selected bibliography based on America: History and Life, a guide to periodical literature published by ABC Clio- Press. Citations are from about 600 periodicals published from 1973-1980.

15. Burr, Nelson R. Religion in American Life. Volume 4: A Critical Bibliography of Religion in America. Princeton, NJ: Princeton University Press, 1961.

A comprehensive bibliography which includes all aspects of evangelicalism. Intended to provide a general review of the history of religion in the United States and illustrate the numerous influences religion has had on American life.

16. Burr, Nelson R., comp. Religion in American Life. New York: Appleton-Century-Crofts, 1971.

Much more selective and yet more current than the entry above. Emphasizes twentieth-century research.

17. Carroll, Jackson W., Douglas W. Johnson and Martin E. Marty. Religion in America, 1950 to the Present. San Francisco: Harper & Row, 1979.

Attempts to analyze trends in American religious life during a period beginning in 1950. Considers social, cultural, economic, scientific and technological factors are considered. Includes statistics on church attendance, born again experiences, witnessing and interpretation of the Bible.

18. Directory of Religious Organizations in the United States. 2nd ed. Falls Church, VA: McGrath Publishing Co., 1982.

Includes general organizations such as departments of national churches, professional associations, volunteer groups, government agencies, businesses, foundations and fraternal societies. An attempt was made to include many smaller more obscure organizations.

19. Fraker, Anne T., ed. Religion and American Life: Resources. Urbana, IL: University of Illinois Press, 1989.

Concentrates on the influence of religion on American life. Following a cross-disciplinary approach this resource cites selected sources with extensive annotations.

20. Hill, George H. and Lenwood G. Davis. Religious Broadcasting, 1920-1983: A Selectively Annotated Bibliography. New York: Garland Publishing, 1984.

Designed to cover the entire scope of religious broadcasting in the United States and intended for the serious researcher. Annotations are provided for book and thesis entries.

21. Hill, Samuel S., ed. Encyclopedia of Religion in the South. Macon, GA: Mercer University Press, 1984.

Intended as a quick reference source to identify specific items, topics and people. The only contemporary leaders included are those who are older and already considered historically significant.

22. Jacquit, Constant H., ed. Yearbook of American and Canadian Churches. Nashville: Abingdon Press, 1986. Annual.

Combines sixteen directories of varying types of organizations which provide detailed information about each group. Also contains a statistical section. Only major religious bodies, both Christian and non-Christian, are included. Prepared and edited by the Communication Unit of the National Council of Churches.

23. Lippy, Charles H. Bibliography of Religion in the South. Macon, GA: Mercer University Press, 1985.

A comprehensive listing of information sources. The material is arranged under broad topics with an introduction in each section which discusses the significance of the topic and the major sources.

24. Lippy, Charles H. Twentieth-Century Shapers of American Popular Religion. Westport, CT: Greenwood Press, 1989.

Contains biographical and bibliographical information on over sixty evangelists and religious communicators who have significantly influenced popular religion in America during the twentieth-century.

25. Lippy, Charles H. and Peter W. Williams, eds. Encyclopedia of the American Religious Experience: Studies of Traditions and Movements. 3 vols. New York: Charles Scribner's Sons, 1988.

Covers the entire North American continent with emphasis on the United States. Attempts to address the entire scope of religious activity and its impact on American life.

26. Mead, Frank S. and Samuel S. Hill, eds. Handbook of Denominations in the United States. 8th ed. Nashville: Abingdon Press, 1985.

Entries are grouped by tradition. Provides brief background information and the address of the headquarters for each denomination. Includes all denominations about which information could be verified.

27. Melton, J. Gordon. The Encyclopedia of American Religions. 2nd ed. Detroit: Gale Research Co., 1987.

Provides information on about 1350 organizations and classifies them according to their religious tradition or family. The traditions are discussed in general in part one. Part two lists each organization and describes its unique characteristics.

28. Melton, J. Gordon, ed. The Encyclopedia of American Religions, Religious Creeds: A Compilation of More Than 450 Creeds, Confessions, Statements of Faith, and Summaries of Doctrine of Religious and Spiritual Groups in the United States and Canada. Detroit: Gale Research Co., 1988.

A companion volume to The Encyclopedia of American Religions. Reprints the creeds substantially as they are written by the various religious groups.

29. Mills, Watson E. Charismatic Religion in Modern Research: A Bibliography. Macon, GA: Mercer University Press, 1985.

Provides a selected list of materials relating to the pentecostal/charismatic movement in the United States. Entries were selected on the basis of their usefulness in understanding the movement; thus, most polemical material has been excluded.

30. Mission Handbook: North American Protestant Ministries Overseas. Samuel Wilson and John Siewert, eds. 13th ed. Monrovia, CA: MARC, 1986.

Provides statistical and analytical information about North American Protestant missions. Attempts to include all agencies committing significant resources overseas.

31. Parker, Harold M., comp. Bibliography of Published Articles on American Presbyterianism, 1901-1980. Westport, CT: Greenwood Press, 1985.

Covers publications in both religious and secular periodicals. House organs of the Presbyterian churches have been omitted. A topical index is included to enhance access to the entries.

32. Piepkorn, Arthur Carl. Profiles in Belief: The Religious Bodies of the United States and Canada. 4 vols. New York: Harper & Row, 1977-1979.

Categorizes the organizations into religious families and gives a brief description/justification for each division. Provides a concise narrative on the individual denominations which includes historical development and distinctives. Volumes three and four cover holiness, pentecostal, evangelical and fundamentalist denominations.

33. Prince, Harold B., comp. and ed. A Presbyterian Bibliography: The Published Writings of Ministers Who Served in the Presbyterian Church in the United States During Its First Hundred Years, 1861-1961, and Their Locations in Eight Significant Theological Collections in the U.S.A. Metuchen, NJ: Scarecrow Press, 1983.

The title says it all.

34. Quinn, Bernard, Herman Anderson, Martin Bradley, Paul Goetting and Peggy Shriver. Churches and Church Membership in the United States, 1980: An Enumeration by Region, State, and County, Based on Data Reported by 111 Church Bodies. Atlanta: Glenmary Research Center, 1982.

An informative collection of information on Judeo-Christian religious bodies in the United States. The study is heavily slanted toward large denominations. Independent churches, which are often evangelical, were not invited to participate in the survey.

35. Religion in America. The Gallup Report. Princeton, NJ: Gallup Organization, 1971-. Irregular.

Published as an issue of The Gallup Report. Formerly an annual, this report is now published irregularly. Contains a statistical analysis of religion in America.

36. Rowe, Kenneth E. Methodist Union Catalog, Pre-1976 Imprints. Metuchen, NJ: Scarecrow Press, 1975-. In progress.

Represents the Methodist holdings of about 200 libraries in an alphabetical arrangement. Six volumes are available to date which include A-I.

37. Sandeen, Ernest R. A. and Frederick Hale. American Religion and Philosophy: A Guide to Information Sources. Detroit: Gale Research Co., 1978.

Intended as a general introduction to the topic and supplement to Nelson Burr, Critical Bibliography of Religion in America. Brief annotations are included.

38. Schuller, David S., Merton P. Strommen and Milo L. Brekke, eds. Ministry in America: A Report and Analysis, Based on an In-Depth Survey of 47 Denominations in the United States and Canada, with Interpretation by 18 Experts. San Francisco: Harper & Row, 1980.

An impressive collection of statistical and analytical information regarding ministry in the United States and Canada. Five thousand clergy and laity participated in the survey which formed the raw data upon which the volume is based. The results are summarized by denominational family.

39. Shupe, Anson D., David G. Bromley and Donna L. Oliver. The Anti-Cult Movement in America: A Bibliography and Historical Survey. New York: Garland Publishing, 1984.

Includes the publications of numerous evangelical organizations and individuals who have written against cults.

40. Starr, Edward C. A Baptist Bibliography: Being a Register of Printed Material By and About Baptists; Including Works Written Against the Baptists. 25 vols. Rochester, NY: American Baptist Historical Society, 1947-1976.

Includes a chronological register and index to joint authors, translators, Baptist publishers, distinctive titles and subjects.

41. Who's Who in Religion. 3rd ed. Chicago: Marquis Who's Who, 1985.

Provides biographical information on more than 7,000 religious leaders and religion professionals in North America.

42. Wilson, John F. Church and State in America: A Bibliographical Guide. 2 vols. Westport, CT: Greenwood Press, 1986-87.

Designed to survey the historiographical resources that relate to the church-state issue in American culture. Each of its twenty-two chapters constitutes a signed bibliographical essay on a particular aspect of the subject. A bibliography of sources cited is found at the end of each chapter.

(C) Reference Works Reflecting an Evangelical Perspective

43. Barber, Cyril J. The Minister's Library. 3 vols. Grand Rapids: Baker, 1974-1989.

A standard evangelical guide to religious literature designed for ministers. Includes a section on how to organize a library collection.

44. Branson, Mark Lau. The Reader's Guide to the Best Evangelical Books. San Francisco: Harper & Row, 1982.

A bibliography of books selected from lists compiled by noted evangelicals. The lists reflected the books considered to be most influential in the person's professional and personal life. The Bible and reference tools for Bible study were omitted.

45. Douglas, J. D., ed. The New International Dictionary of the Christian Church. Rev. ed. Grand Rapids: Zondervan, 1978.

Attempts to present selected facts of church history in a readable, yet scholarly format. Most of the articles were written by well-known evangelical scholars.

46. Dowley, Tim. Eerdmans' Handbook to the History of Christianity. Grand Rapids: Eerdmans, 1977.

A popular presentation of the highlights of the history of Christianity. Places the evangelical movement within the context of the Christian church.

47. Drummond, Lewis A., comp. "Bibliography of Works on Evangelism." Unpublished list, 1973. 55 leaves. Photocopy.

The most extensive list of books about evangelism. Most of the titles are held in the Southern Baptist Theological Seminary Library, Louisville, Kentucky. Call numbers for the library's holdings are provided.

48. Elwell, Walter A., ed. Evangelical Dictionary of Theology. Grand Rapids: Baker, 1984.

Succeeds Baker's Dictionary of Theology published in 1960. Analyzes 1200 subjects from an evangelical theological perspective. Written in non-technical language for popular appeal, yet has scholarly articles with bibliographies.

49. Ferguson, Sinclair B. and David F. Wright, eds. New Dictionary of Theology. Downers Grove, IL: InterVarsity Press, 1988.

Intended to be a basic introduction to the world of theology. The editors and contributors share a common allegiance to the supreme authority of the Bible.

50. Henry, Carl F. H., ed. Baker's Dictionary of Christian Ethics. Grand Rapids: Baker, 1978.

A topical treatment of the subject covering a broad range of issues. The contributors reflect the diversity and sometimes contradictory theological traditions within the evangelical movement.

51. Keeley, Robin, ed. Eerdmans' Handbook to Christian Belief. 1st American ed. Grand Rapids: Eerdmans, 1982.

Attempts to give a clear and comprehensive account of Christian belief in a non-technical format. A broad topical arrangement of material is used. Significant emphasis is given to the comparison of Christian and non-Christian belief to demonstrate what Christianity is not.

52. Kerr, Ronn, comp. Directory of Bible Resources: A Comprehensive Guide to Tools for Bible Study. Nashville: Thomas Nelson Publishers, 1983.

Resources listed in the catalogs of more than 200 publishers, producers and distributors in the United States. The project was organized by the National Committee for the Year of the Bible.

53. McDowell, Josh and Don Douglas Stewart. Handbook of Today's Religions. San Bernardino, CA: Here's Life Publishers, 1983.

Provides information about religious groups in America considered to be non-Christian by most evangelicals. Attempts to demonstrate the incompatibility of these groups with Christianity.

54. Reid, Daniel G., ed. Dictionary of Christianity in America. Downers Grove, IL: InterVarsity Press, 1990.

This is an impressive publication which brings together both evangelical and non-evangelical scholars to provide one of the most significant reference tools for the study of religion in America. Two of its major strengths are the emphasis on popular religion which molded religious life in America and the enlightened evangelical scholarship reflected in the project.

55. Smith, Wilbur M. Good Books and the Good Book: Reading Lists by Wilbur M. Smith, Fundamentalist Bibliophile. Volume 1. Fundamentalism and American Religion, ed. Joel A. Carpenter. New York: Garland Publishing, 1988.

Reprints four bibliographic essays and annotated reading lists compiled by prominent theologian and journalist Wilbur M. Smith, during the 1930s and 1940s. Includes: Profitable Bible Study (1939), Some Much Needed Books in Biblical and Theological Literature (1934), 55 Best Books on Prophecy (1940), and "Reading for Christians" (1946).

56. Turnbull, Ralph G., ed. Baker's Dictionary of Practical Theology. Grand Rapids: Baker, 1967.

Treats the areas of practical theology under broad general topics. Intended as a reference source for pastors, students and lay person.

57. Unreached Peoples. Elgin, IL: David C. Cook, 1978-. Irregular.

One of several publications spawned by the Lausanne Committee for World Evangelization. It fulfills one of the tasks of the Committee--to identify and describe the world's unreached peoples. Each edition of the series includes an accumulative list of identified unreached people groups and articles related to the evangelical perspective on the task of world evangelization. Publisher varies.

CHAPTER 2
LIBRARIES

The published sources for the study of twentieth century evangelicalism are spread across the United States in both religious and secular libraries. Through the National Union Catalog and national inter-library loan databases such as OCLC and RLIN, it is easy, though time-consuming, to identify, locate and obtain specific works authored by well-known figures in the evangelical or fundamentalist traditions. Libraries making concerted efforts to build special collections around major movements and persons usually report these in such frequently-updated directories as The Directory of Special Libraries and Information Centers and the American Library Directory.

More difficult to identify are the rich resources contained in the general collections of many libraries. As new educational institutions developed in response to theological differences, librarians built collections which supported the doctrinal positions, philosophies of education and ministry concerns of their respective institutions. Because the research value of these resources to outsiders is often underestimated by the institutions, specific library holdings are often not listed in the standard guides to special collections.

This section focuses primarily on selected libraries of evangelical and fundamentalist institutions. Materials documenting evangelical movements within mainline denominations may be found in the denominational seminaries, universities, and historical libraries. Only a few will be noted here.

It is best to contact a library before making a visit. A special collections or reference librarian can be more helpful if given some time to meet the specific research request. Most libraries are open to the public for reference use, but some may require special permission to use all or part of their collections.

(A) Interdenominational Collections

58. Asbury Theological Seminary
B. L. Fisher Library
N. Lexington Ave. SPO 152
Wilmore, KY 40390
606/858-3581, Ext 229

Background: Interdenominational within the Wesleyan-Arminian tradition; Henry Clay Morrison, President of Asbury College, served as the founding leader in 1923.

Subject strengths: Biblical studies; the Holiness movement; Methodism; missions; theology; Alfred E. Price Healing Collection; World Council of Churches Faith and Order Papers Collection.

59. Biola University
Rose Memorial Library
(includes Rosemead School of Psychology, Talbot Theological Seminary, and the School of Intercultural Studies)
13800 Biola Ave.
La Mirada, CA 90639-0001
213/944-0351, Ext 3255

Background: founded in 1908 as the Bible Institute of Los Angeles by those who promoted the publication of The Fundamentals; initially supported by Lyman Stewart; published The King's Business.

Subject strengths: Bible; Bible versions; evangelical Christianity; intercultural studies; psychology; theology; Lyman Stewart Papers.

60. Bob Jones University
J.S. Mack Library
Greenville, SC 29614
803/242-5100, Ext 6010

Background: Interdenominational; founded in 1927 by Methodist Bob Jones, Sr.

Subject strengths: Art; Christian education; music; religious studies; Bob Jones University Press Publications; Fundamentalism File; G. Archer Weniger File (editor of the Blue-Print); W. O. H. Garman Papers (Associated Gospel Churches).

61. Columbia Bible College and Graduate School of Bible and Missions
Learning Resources Center
7435 Monticello Road, P.O. Box 3122
Columbia, SC 29230
803/754-4100, Ext 276

Background: founded in 1923 by Robert C. McQuilkin; school promoted Keswick movement; library supports M.A. in missions.

Subject strengths: Bible; missions; theology; Visual Aids for Religious Education and Christian Service Collection; Missionary Curios Collection.

62. Dallas Theological Seminary
Turpin Library
3909 Swiss Ave.
Dallas, TX 75204-6411
214/841-3750, Ext 285

Background: founded in 1924 as Evangelical Theological College with Lewis Sperry Chafer as first president; second president, John F. Walvoord; provides support for strong Th.M. and Th.D. programs.

Subject strengths: Bible; Biblical languages; Christian education; Christian literature; church history; devotional literature; missions; practical theology; theology; especially dispensationalism and premillennialism.

63. Fuller Theological Seminary
McAlister Library
135 North Oakland Ave.
Pasadena, CA 91182
818/584-5218

Background: Interdenominational; founded by Charles E. Fuller and Harold John Ockenga; charter members of the faculty were Edward John Carnell, Everett F. Harrison, Carl F. H. Henry, Harold Lindsell, and Wilbur M. Smith; supports Ph.D. programs in theology, missions, and psychology.

Subject strengths: Biblical studies; feminism; missiology; philosophy; psychology; religion; social and behavioral sciences; theology; David J. du Plessis Collection; holdings include the libraries of Professors Everett Harrison, Robert Bower and George Eldon Ladd.

64. Gordon College: The United College of Gordon and Barrington
Jenks Learning Resource Center
255 Grapevine Road
Wenham, MA 01984-1895
508/927-2300, Ext 4342

Background: Interdenominational; Gordon College was founded in 1889 as the Boston Bible and Missionary Training Institute with Adoniram Judson Gordon as chief among its founders; Harold J. Ockenga served as president between 1969 and 1976; Barrington College was founded in 1900 as Bethel Bible Training School; Paul Rader served briefly as president of the school when it was called the Dudley Bible Institute; in 1985 the two schools joined forces to become the "leader in New England Christian higher education."

Subject strengths: Biblical studies, education, humanities, social and behavioral sciences; Bible Collection.

65. Gordon-Conwell Theological Seminary
Burton L. Goddard Library
130 Essex Street
South Hamilton, MA 01982
508/468-7111, Ext 585

Background: Interdenominational; Conwell School of Theology joined Gordon Divinity School in 1969 with Harold John Ockenga as first president.

Subject strengths: Biblical studies; Christian education; Christianity and society; church history; church ministry; evangelism pastoral psychology and counseling; preaching and the communication arts; theology; world missions; Mercer Collection of Assyro-Babylonian Materials; Roger Babson Collection of Rare Bibles (especially early English Bibles).

66. Howard University
School of Divinity Library
1400 Shepherd St., NE
Washington, D.C. 20017
202/636-8914

Background: Howard University traces its roots to 1866 when plans were laid for the founding of the Howard Normal and Theological Institute for the Education of Teachers and Preachers. Today "the Divinity School emphasizes (1) the preparation of professional religious leaders ... for service in the urban, underserved, poor black communities; (2) an international cross-cultural inquiry into humane values; and (3) further graduate study primarily in the cultural and religious heritage of Afro-Americans." -- Howard University Bulletin.

Subject strengths: Biblical studies; Christianity and society; church history; ethics; ministry studies; theology; Black Religious Studies Collection.

67. King's College Library
Briarcliff Manor, NY 10510
914/944-5543

Background: Interdenominational; founded in 1936, its first president was evangelist and youth leader Percy B. Crawford.

Subject strengths: Religious studies, Social and behavioral science.

68. Miami Christian College Library
2300 NW 135th St.
Miami, FL 33167
305/953-1130

Background: Interdenominational; founded in 1949 as Miami Bible Institute, the school is now affiliated with Trinity Evangelical Divinity School (Deerfield, IL).

Subject strengths: Bible, pastoral studies, religious studies, and theology; the general collection incorporates the Winona Lake School of Theology collection, including William Biederwolf's personal library.

69. Moody Bible Institute Library
820 N. LaSalle Dr.
Chicago, IL 60610
312/329-4138

Background: Interdenominational; past presidents of Moody include R. A. Torrey, James M. Gray, Will H. Houghton, William Culbertson, and George Sweeting.

Subject strengths: Bible; Christian education; evangelism; missions; music; pastoral studies; theology; Moodyana Collection, Moody Bible Institute Archives, including biographical data of notables connected with MBI; Rare Book Collection includes early Bibles and rare theology works.

70. Northwestern College
McAlister Library
3003 North Snelling Ave.
Roseville, MN 55113
612/631-5241

Background: Interdenominational; founded in 1902 by William Bell Riley as a Bible and Missionary Training School in the First Baptist Church of Minneapolis; Billy Graham served as second president.

Subject strengths: W. B. Riley Collection.

71. Philadelphia College of the Bible Library
200 Manor Ave.
Langhorne, PA 19047
215/752-5800, Ext 230

Background: Interdenominational; result of merger of two Bible schools, National Bible Institute and Philadelphia School of the Bible, co-founded by C. I. Scofield and William L. Pettingill.

Subject strengths: Bible; Christian education; missions; music; social work; theology; Hymnals Collection; C.I. Scofield Library of Biblical Studies; Jamieson Missionary Research Collection.

72. Taylor University
Zondervan Library
Upland, IN 46989-1022
317/998-5241

Background: Interdenominational; began in 1846 as the Fort Wayne Female College; present name chosen to honor the Bishop William Taylor, missionary of the Methodist Episcopal Church.

Subject strengths: Protestant theology; Wesley Collection, African, Oriental, and Rare Book Collections.

73. Trinity Evangelical Divinity School
Rolfing Memorial Library
2065 Half Day Road
Deerfield, IL 60015
708/945-8800, Ext 317

Background: Sponsored by the Evangelical Free Church of America; in 1963 made special effort to expand curriculum and add outstanding scholars from many denominations, who were "noted for their defense of orthodox Christianity and committed to earnest piety and the evangelical faith;" supports doctoral programs in ministry, missiology, and education.

Subject strengths: Biblical studies; Christian education; church history; counseling psychology; evangelicalism and fundamentalism; ministry; missions; philosophy of religion; theology; Evangelical Free Church of America Archives; Divinity School Archives; holdings include the personal libraries of Carl F. H. Henry and Wilbur M. Smith.

74. Westminster Theological Seminary
Montgomery Library
Location: Willow Grove Ave. & Church Rd., Glenside, PA
Mailing address: Chestnut Hill, P.O. Box 27009
Philadelphia, PA 19118
215/572-3821

Background: Interdenominational within the Reformed tradition; founded by former Princeton Divinity School faculty: Robert Dick Wilson, J. Gresham Machen, Oswald T. Allis, and Cornelius Van Til.

Subject strengths: Biblical studies; church history, especially of the Reformation; patristics; systematic theology; the Rare Book Room houses a strong collection of early Reformed theology and an extensive collection of Latin, Greek, and English Bibles; holdings include portions of the libraries of Wilson, Machen, Allis, Caspar Wistar Hodge, Geerhardus Vos, Edward J. Young, and Ned B. Stonehouse.

75. Westmont College
Roger John Voskuyl Library
955 La Paz Road
Santa Barbara, CA 93108-1099
805/565-6000, Ext 522

Background: Interdenominational; founded in 1940 by Ruth W. Kerr of Kerr Manufacturing Company, the school is an "enthusiastically evangelical Christian college." -- Westmont College Bulletin.

Subject strengths: History, religious studies; Christ and Culture Collection focuses on the interaction of Christian faith and culture.

76. Wheaton College
Billy Graham Center Library
500 E. College Ave.
Wheaton, IL 60187-5593
708/260-5194

Background: Interdenominational research center developed to study and promote world evangelization.

Subject strengths: American church history, with emphasis on evangelicalism and fundamentalism; evangelism; missions and intercultural studies; revivalism; Billy Graham Collection; Moravian Missions to the Indians (microfilm); Missionary Children Collection; Prison Ministry Collection.

77. Wheaton College
Buswell Memorial Library
Franklin & Irving
Wheaton, IL 60187-5593
708/260-5169

Background: Interdenominational; past presidents included Jonathan and Charles Blanchard, J. Oliver Buswell, V. Raymond Edman, and Hudson T. Armerding; supports M.A. programs.

Subject strengths: Bible; church history; communications; counseling psychology; education; religion; theology; American Scientific Affiliation Papers; Keswick Collection; Mormonism Collection; Hymnal Collection; Faculty and Alumni Collection; Wade Collection (C.S. Lewis materials).

(B) Baptist Collections

78. Bethel Theological Seminary
Carl H. Lundquist Library
3949 Bethel Dr.

St. Paul, MN 55112
612/638-6184
Denominational affiliation: Baptist General Conference.

Subject strengths: Baptistica; Biblical studies; church history; evangelicalism; practical theology; theology; Skarstedt Collection of Pietistic Literature; Carl Nelson Collection of Devotional Books; Klingberg Puritan Collection.

79. Cedarville College
Centennial Library
P.O. Box 601
Cedarville, OH 45314-0601
513/766-2211, Ext 207

Denominational affiliation: General Association of Regular Baptists.

Subject strengths: Baptist history; religious studies.

80. Denver Conservative Baptist Seminary
Carey S. Thomas Library
Location: 3401 S. University Blvd., Englewood, CO 80110
Mailing address: P.O. Box 10,000, Denver, CO 80210
303/781-8691

Denominational affiliation: Conservative Baptist; founded in 1950.

Subject strengths: Bible; Christian education; church history; homiletics; missions; philosophy; pastoral theology; theology; Baptistica Collection; holdings include Vernon Grounds' library.

81. Liberty University Library
Lynchburg, VA 24506
804/582-2220

Denominational affiliation: Independent Baptist, founded in 1971 under the auspices of the Thomas Road Baptist Church.

Subject strengths: Jerry Falwell Collection.

82. Northern Baptist Theological Seminary
Seminary Library
Butterfield & Meyers Roads
Oak Brook, IL 60521
708/620-2214
**Combined library with Bethany Theological Seminary (see 88).

Denominational affiliation: American Baptist; founded in 1913

Subject strengths: Baptist history, especially the conservative wing of the Northern Baptist Convention; religious studies; Norwegian Theological Seminary Archives; holdings include the Biblical archaeology collection of A. T. Olmstead and the collections of William Mefford Fouts and Roland E. Turnbull.

83. Southern Baptist Theological Seminary
James P. Boyce Centennial Library
2825 Lexington Rd.
Louisville, KY 40280
502/897-4807

Denominational affiliation: Southern Baptist; supports doctoral programs in Christian education, church music, and theology.

Subject strengths: Bible; church history; comparative religions; music; philosophy; religious education; theology; Baptist Historical Collection; Billy Graham Collection; Everett Helm Music Collection; William F. Albright Archaeology Collection; Converse Hymnology Collection; R. Pierce Beaver Missions Collection; Ingersoll Music Collection.

84. Southwestern Baptist Theological Seminary
Roberts Library
2001 W. Seminary Drive, PO Box 22,000-2E
Fort Worth, TX 76122
817/923-1921, Ext 277

Denominational affiliation: Southern Baptist; presidents include: B. H. Carroll, L. R. Scarborough; supports doctoral programs in theology, religious education, and church music.

Subject strengths: Baptist history; Bible; missions; music and hymnology; religious education; theology; Baptist History Collections (James M. Carroll, George W. Truett, and M. E. Dodd); Texas Baptist Historical Collections.

85. Sunday School Board of the Southern Baptist Convention
E. C. Dargan Research Library
127 Ninth Ave., N.
Nashville, TN 37234
615/251-2124

Denominational affiliation: Southern Baptist.

Subject strengths: Baptist history; education; publishing; religious education; religion; theology; Southern Baptist History Community Archives and Collection.

86. Tennessee Temple University
Cierpke Memorial Library
1815 Union
Chattanooga, TN 37404
615/493-4250

Denominational affiliation: Independent Baptist; founded in 1946 by Highland Park Baptist Church under the leadership of Lee Roberson; supports an M.S. in Education, with a major in Christian School Administration and Supervision.

Subject strengths: Christian education; education; religious studies; Religious Education Collection; Educational Curriculum Collection.

87. Western Conservative Baptist Seminary
Cline-Tunnell Library
5511 SE Hawthorne Blvd.
Portland, OR 97215
503/233-8561, Ext 323

Denominational affiliation: Conservative Baptist.

Subject strengths: Bible; ministry; psychology; religion; theology; Oregon Baptist History Collection.

(C) Brethren Collections

88. Bethany Theological Seminary
Seminary Library
Butterfield & Meyers Roads
Oak Brook, IL 60521
708/620-2214
**Combined library with Northern Baptist Theological Seminary (see 83).

Denominational affiliation: Church of the Brethren; founded in 1905 as the Bethany Bible School, in 1931 officially became Bethany Biblical Seminary.

Subject strengths: Church of the Brethren history; intentional and Utopian communities; missions; pacifism; Cassel Collection (religion and history of the 16th-19th centuries); Huston English Bible Collection; holdings include libraries of D. W. Kurtz and D. L. Miller.

89. Grace Theological Seminary
Morgan Library
200 Seminary Dr.
Winona Lake, IN 46590

219/372-5177

Denominational affiliation: Fellowship of Grace Brethren Churches; founded in 1937.

Subject strengths: Archeology; Bible; Christian education; missions; Billy Sunday Papers; Grace Brethren Archives.

(D) Evangelical Covenant Church Collection

90. North Park Theological Seminary
Mellander Library
3225 W. Foster Ave.
Chicago, IL 60625
312/583-2700, Ext 5285

Denominational affiliation: Evangelical Covenant Church.
Subject strengths: Biblical studies; pietism; theology; Evangelical Covenant Church History; supplemented by The Covenant Archives and Historical Library.

(E) Holiness Collections

91. Anderson University School of Theology
Anderson University Library
Anderson, IN 46012-3462
317/641-4280

Denominational affiliation: Church of God (Anderson, Ind.); established in 1917 as Bible Training School; graduate division added in 1950.

Subject strengths: Bible; Christian education; church history; pastoral psychology; preaching; theology; The Archives of the Church of God; University; and Charles E. Wilson are housed in the library.

92. Azusa Pacific University
Marshburn Memorial Library
929 E. Alosta Street
Azusa, CA 91702-7000
818/969-3434, Ext 3272

Denominational affiliation: Interdenominational, designated as official college of Free Methodist Church, Church of God (Anderson, Ind.), and five other denominations.
Subject strengths: American church history; John Hess Memorial Holiness Collection; Clifford M. Drury Collection on the Missionary in the American

West; the Monsignor Francis J. Weber Collection of American Catholic Church History.

93. Houghton College
Willard J. Houghton Library
Houghton, NY 14744
716/567-9240

Denominational affiliation: The Wesleyan Church; founded in 1883.

Subject strengths: Christian education, missions, theology; John Wesley Collection, Science and Christian Faith Collection.

94. Messiah College, Grantham, PA - (See Archives entry for Brethren in Christ Church, 129)

95. Nazarene Theological Seminary
William Broadhurst Library
1700 E. Meyer Blvd.
Kansas City, MO 64131
816/333-6254, Ext 41

Denominational affiliation: Church of the Nazarene seminary established in 1944.

Subject strengths: Biblical studies; Christian education; church history; missions; philosophy; theology, especially on the doctrine of holiness; History of the Church of the Nazarene Collection; Wesleyana-Methodistica Collection; History of the Holiness Movement Collection.

96. Nyack College and Alliance Theological Seminary Library
Nyack, NY 10960-3698
914/358-1710, Ext 750(Seminary Library), 103(College Library)

Denominational affiliation: Christian and Missionary Alliance.

Subject strengths: Bible; church history, especially of the Christian and Missionary and Alliance; cultural anthropology; missions; music; religious studies.

97. Point Loma Nazarene College
Ryan Library
3900 Lomaland Drive
San Diego, CA 92106-2899
619/221-2312

Denominational affiliation: Church of the Nazarene college, founded in 1902.

Subject strengths: Church history; Arminianism and Wesleyana Collection; 19th and 20th Century Christian Holiness Movement Collection.

98. Salvation Army Archives and Research Center, New York, NY - (See Archives entry, 125)

99. Seattle Pacific University
Weter Memorial Library
3307 Third Ave. West
Seattle, WA 98119
206/281-2228

Denominational affiliation: Free Methodist Church.

Subject strengths: Religious studies; Free Methodism Collection.

(F) Lutheran Collections

100. Concordia Seminary Library
801 DeMun Ave.
St. Louis, MO 63105-3199
314/721-5934, Ext 292

Denominational affiliation: Lutheran Church-Missouri Synod.

Subject strengths: Biographical information on Lutheran pastors, teachers & laypersons; congregational histories; Lutheranism in America; theology; Lutheran Foreign Mission Resources Collection; The Lutheran Hour Collection (Walter A. Maier).

(G) Methodist Collections

101. Drew University Library
Madison, NJ 07940
201/377-3000, Ext 322

Denominational affiliation: United Methodist.

Subject strengths: Biblical archeology; church history; Methodistica; music; patristics; religion; theology; Tyerman Collection of Methodist Pamphlets; Tipple and Maser Collections of Wesleyana; Methodist Manuscript Collection; David Creamer Hymnology Collection; Walter Koehler Collection in Reformation History.

(H) Pentecostal Collections

102. Assemblies of God Theological Seminary
Cordas C. Burnett Library
1445 Boonville Ave.
Springfield, MO 65802
417/862-3344, Ext 5505

Denominational affiliation: Assemblies of God.

Subject strengths: Anthropology; Assemblies of God history; Bible; communications; Holy Spirit; missions; pastoral counseling; pentecostalism; philosophy; theology.

103. Lee College and the Church of God School of Theology
William G. Squires Library
260 11th Street NE, PO Box 3448
Cleveland, TN 37320-3448
615/478-7438

Denominational affiliation: Church of God (Cleveland, TN).

Subject strengths: Pentecostalism; religious studies; Pentecostal Research Library Collection.

104. Oral Roberts University
John Messick Learning Resources Center
7777 S. Lewis Ave.
Tulsa, OK 74171-0007
918/495-6723

Denominational affiliation: Pentecostal/ Interdenominational.

Subject strengths: Biblical literature; Christianity and culture; Pentecostalism and charismatic renewal; practices of ministry; theological studies; Holy Spirit Research Center; Oral Roberts Ministry Archives.

(I) Plymouth Brethren Collection

105. Emmaus Bible College Library
2570 Asbury Road
Dubuque, Iowa 52001-3096
319/588-8000, Ext 240

Denominational affiliation: Plymouth Brethren.

Subject strengths: Biblical studies; Plymouth Brethren Collection.

(J) Presbyterian and Reformed Collections

106. Calvin College and Seminary Library
3207 Burton St., SE
Grand Rapids, MI 49546-4301
616/957-6297

Denominational affiliation: Christian Reformed Church.

Subject strengths: Philosophy; religion; Calvin and Calvinism Collection; The Colonial Origins Collection consists of resources on the Christian Reformed Church, its leaders, its Dutch origins, and closely related institutions.

107. Covenant Theological Seminary
J. Oliver Buswell, Jr. Library
12330 Conway Road
St. Louis, MO 63141
314/434-4044

Denominational affiliation: Presbyterian Church in America; founded in 1956 as an agency of the Evangelical Presbyterian Church.

Subject strengths: Bible; church history; practical theology; theology; Blackburn Library Collection; Presbyteriana Collection; English Puritans Collection; supplemented by the Presbyterian Church in America Historical Archives.

108. Princeton Theological Seminary
Speer Library
Mercer Street & Library Pl., PO Box 111
Princeton, NJ 08542-0111
609/497-7940

Denominational affiliation: Presbyterian Church/USA.

Subject strengths: Biblical studies; church history; Presbyterianism; Semitic philology; theology; Benson Collection of Hymnology; Grosart Library of Puritan and Nonconformist Theology; Agnew Collection on the Baptism Controversy; Sprague Early American Theological Pamphlets; holdings include portions of Benjamin B. Warfield's library.

109. Reformed Theological Seminary Library
5422 Clinton Blvd.
Jackson, MS 39209-3099
601/922-4988, Ext 252

Denominational affiliation: Independent serving various Presbyterian and Reformed denominations; founded in 1964.

Subject strengths: Biblical studies; Christian education; marriage and family counseling; religion; Southern Presbyterianism; theology; Blackburn Memorial Collection (Southern Presbyterian history and theology).

(K) Restoration Movement Collections - (See Archives section, 130)

(L) Society of Friends (Evangelical Quaker) Collections

110. George Fox College
Murdock Learning Resource Center
Newberg, OR 97132-2698
503/538-8383, Ext 303

Denominational affiliation: Northwest Yearly Meeting of Friends.

Subject strengths: Society of Friends Collection.

111. Malone College
Everett L. Cattell Library
515 25th St. NW
Canton, OH 44709-3897
216/489-7393

Denominational affiliation: Evangelical Friends Church-Eastern region.

Subject strengths: Society of Friends (Quakers); Evangelical Friends church - Eastern Region Archives.

(M) Finding Other Collections:

The following religious reference works identify many other educational institutions which have excellent libraries:

112. Melton, J. Gordon. The Encyclopedia of American Religions. 2nd. ed. Detroit: Gale Research, 1987.

Lists educational facilities supported or approved by each denomination. Excellent indexes facilitate its use.

113. National Evangelical Directory. Carol Stream, IL: National Association of Evangelicals. Annual.

In section "Education/Christian Education," lists seminaries and graduate schools, Christian liberal arts colleges, and Bible colleges.

The following library reference works assist in locating special collections:

114. American Library Directory. New York: R. R. Bowker Co. Annual.

Provides current directory information for most libraries in the United States and Canada.

115. Ash, Lee. Subject Collections. New York: R. R. Bowker. Most recent edition.

Arranges and describes special collection under specific subject headings. Useful for searching specific topics such as names of denominations, persons, etc. Coverage is uneven for broad subjects such as "Fundamentalism" or "Holiness and Pentecostal Movement."

116. Directory of Special Libraries and Information Centers. Detroit: Gale Research. Most recent edition.

Describes special libraries and some special collections in the United States and Canada; arranged by institutional or library name.

117. Howell, J. B., ed. Special Collections in Libraries of the Southeast. Jackson, MS: published for the Southeastern Library Association by Howick House, 1978.

Typical of regional and state guides to special collections; arranged by state and city.

118. Subject Directory of Special Libraries and Information Centers, v. 4: Social Sciences and Humanities Libraries. Detroit: Gale Research. Most recent edition.

The section on "Religion/Theology Libraries" provides a broad overview of special libraries and special collections. Entries arranged alphabetically by institutional or library name.

CHAPTER 3
THE ARCHIVES OF CONSERVATIVE PROTESTANTISM

There are rich archival and manuscript resources in the United States for the study of evangelicalism, pentecostalism and fundamentalism, but they are in widely scattered and, in some cases, obscure locations. In many instances, documents are not heavily used because few people know of their existence. What follows is not a comprehensive description of all that is available, but rather a sampling of some of the more important repositories for the study of the denominations, organizations and leaders of these traditions. This should provide the diligent researcher with a starting point for his or her investigations, including developing leads to other sources. Only archival and manuscript holdings will be described here, not book, periodical or newspaper collections. The names of repositories will be underlined and, at their first appearance, their address and phone number will be given in parentheses. It is always a good idea, before visiting an archives or manuscript repository, to call ahead and discuss the project with the staff. The researcher will want to find out if the archives has enough relevant material to make a trip worthwhile as well as information about restrictions on specific collections, photocopying facilities, hours and other matters.

(A) Denominational Holdings

Religious archives in the United States, as in other countries, usually means denominational archives. The archives are usually a department of the denominational headquarters or seminary and include such record groups as the minutes and other documents of the governing body of the denomination; the files of its executive officers; the files of such major divisions as the foreign mission board, the radio and television commission; personnel department, etc. Often the archives will also have records from individual churches that have been sent to them, the private papers of influential pastors, missionaries and laypersons, and miscellaneous artifacts gathered over the years. Not all denominations mentioned below would be described by their membership as "evangelical", but the documents in the archives of all are relevant to the study of evangelical movements and traditions.

119. Baptists are the nation's largest Protestant family, and are mostly evangelical. Baptists are most prevalent in the South, where there are several fine archival collections featuring this tradition. Of Baptist denominations, the largest is the Southern Baptist Convention (SBC), which also has one of the finest denominational archives in the country. The Southern Baptist Historical Library and Archives (901 Commerce Street, Suite 400, Nashville, TN 37203-3620, tel. 615/244-0344) has, besides the official records of the SBC, the papers of prominent individuals, such as J. Franklyn Norris (1877-1952). In the same city is the Free Will Baptist Historical Collection (Free Will Baptist College, 3606 West End Baptist Avenue, Nashville, TN 37205, tel. 615/383-1340). Other Free Will Baptist materials can be found at the Ohio Historical Society (Archives and Manuscript Division, I-71 and 17th Avenue, Columbus, OH 43211, tel. 614/466-1500). The Missouri Baptist Convention has placed its records in the William E. Partee Center for Baptist Historical Studies (William Jewell College, Liberty, MO 64068, tel. 816/781-7700, ext. 5490 or 5341). Also at the Partee Center are some records about Southern, Primitive, and American Baptists.

120. In both North Carolina (North Carolina Baptist Historical Collection, Room 207, Z. Smith Reynolds Library, Wake Forest University, Winston-Salem, NC 27109, tel. 919/761-5472) and South Carolina (South Carolina Baptist Historical Society, Special Collections Department, University Library, Furman University, Greenville, SC 29613, tel. 803/294-2194) are important Baptist collections that include documents of churches, organizations and individuals. Southwestern Baptist Theological Seminary (A. Webb Roberts Library, P.O. Box 22000-2E, Fort Worth, TX 76122, tel. 817/923-1921, ext. 3330) includes in its collection materials from Texas Baptist churches and individuals.

121. Baptists in the North offer several fine collections as well. The American Baptist Archives Record Center (P.O. Box 851, Valley Forge, PA 19482-0851, tel. 215/768-2373 or 2378) is the official repository for past and present national organizations of American Baptists as well as the Baptist World Alliance. The Record Center also has some Free Will Baptist materials. American Baptist Historical Society (1106 South Goodman Street, Rochester, NY 14620, tel. 716/473-1740) has the papers of many prominent Baptists. The Bethel Theological Seminary Library (3949 Bethel Drive, St. Paul, MN 55112, tel. 612/638-6400) includes among its holdings the records of the Baptist General Conference (formerly the Swedish Baptist General Conference). Some of the records of the once predominantly German ethnic North American Baptist General Conference are housed at the North American Baptist Archives (North American Baptist Seminary, 1321 W. 22nd Street, Sioux Falls, SD 57105, tel. 605/335-9071).

122. Certainly the largest Presbyterian repository in the United States is the Office of History, Presbyterian Church (USA) (425 Lombard Street, Philadelphia, PA 19147, tel. 215/627-1852). The archives of numerous Presbyterian denominations are kept here as well as the files of the National Council of Churches and the papers of many individuals. The Presbyterian Study Center (Box 849, Montreat, NC 28757, tel. 704/669-7061) has the

records of the Presbyterian Church (Southern) and its antecedents as well as those of the Associate Reformed Presbyterian and Cumberland Presbyterian Churches. A more recently started collection, the Presbyterian Church in America Historical Archives (12330 Conway Road, St. Louis, MO 63141, tel. 314/469-9077) preserves the records of the Presbyterian Church in America plus numerous other Presbyterian denominations and organizations.

123. Other denominational archives in the Presbyterian-Reformed family include those of the Reformed Church in America (Reformed Church in America Archives, New Brunswick Theological Seminary, Gardner A. Sage Library, 21 Seminary Place, New Brunswick, NJ 08901, tel. 201/246-1779; and The Joint Archives of Holland, Hope College, Holland, MI 48109, tel. 616/394-7798) and the Christian Reformed Church (Calvin College and Seminary Archives, Grand Rapids, MI 49506, tel. 616/957-6313).

124. The Archives and History Center of the United Methodist Church (36 Madison Avenue, Madison, NJ 07940, tel. 201/822-2787 or 822-2826) is the chief repository for the records of United Methodism and its antecedents. There are many others. A large documentary collection of Methodist leaders and organizations for a single state can be found at the Archives of DePauw University and Indiana United Methodism (Roy O. West Library, DePauw University, Greencastle, IN 46135, tel. 317/653-4501).

125. Several denominations which grew out of the Wesleyan/holiness movement have developed archives. The Marston Memorial Historical Center (Free Methodist World Headquarters, 901 College Avenue, Winona Lake, IN 46590, tel. 219/267-7656) has the files of the Free Methodist Church. The papers of the founder of the denomination, Benjamin Roberts, are in the Library of Congress (Manuscript Division, James Madison Memorial Building, First Street and Independence Avenue, S.E., Washington, DC 20540, tel. 202/707-5387). The Salvation Army grew out of the Methodist tradition and the records of the Army's United States branch are preserved at the Salvation Army Archives and Research Center (145 West 15th Street, New York NY 10011, tel. 212/337-7428). Other holiness denominations sponsoring archives of note are the Church of the Nazarene (Nazarene Archives, Church of the Nazarene International Headquarters, 6401 The Paseo, Kansas City, MO 64131, tel. 816/333-7000, ext. 437), and the Church of God (Archives, Byrd Memorial Library, School of Theology, Anderson University, Anderson, IN 46012-3462, tel. 317/641-4274 or 4526), and the Christian and Missionary Alliance (Archives, P.O. Box 3500, Colorado Springs, CO 80935-3500, tel. 719/599-5999).

126. The pentecostal movement is also developing a growing number of archives. One of the oldest and best of these is the Archives of the Assemblies of God (1445 Boonville Avenue, Springfield, MO 65802, tel. 417/862-2781, ext. 4400). The files of the Pentecostal Fellowship of North America and the Pentecostal World Conference are also stored here. Also in Missouri is the Historical Center of the United Pentecostal Church International (8855 Dunn Road, Hazelwood, MO 63042-2299, tel. 314/837-7300). Another pentecostal denominational archives documents the

Pentecostal Holiness Church (Archives, P.O. Box 12609, Oklahoma City, OK 73157, tel. 405/787-7110).

127. Following the amalgamation of their denominations, several Lutheran archives have combined recently to form the Archives of the Evangelical Lutheran Church in America (8765 Higgins Road, Chicago, IL 60631-4198, tel. 312/380-2818). Besides the records of the ELCA, the American Lutheran Church, the Lutheran Church in America and the Association of Evangelical Lutheran Churches, this archives also preserves the records of dozens of Lutheran organizations and material on the history of Seminex (Seminary in Exile). Another archives of high quality with very valuable collections is the Concordia Historical Institute (801 DeMun Avenue, St. Louis, MO 63105, tel. 314/721-5934, ext. 297 or 351), which is the repository of the Lutheran Church-Missouri Synod.

128. Pietist and evangelical movements emanating from European Protestant traditions having significant archives include the Evangelical Covenant Church (North Park College and Seminary, Archives, 5121 Spaulding Avenue, Chicago, Illinois, tel. 312/583-2700, ext. 5267), the Evangelical Free Church (Trinity Evangelical Divinity School, Archives 2065 Half Day Road, Deerfield, IL 60015, tel. 708/945-8800), the Moravians (Moravian Archives, 41 West Locust Street, Bethlehem, PA 18018, tel. 215/866-3255 and the Archives of the Moravian Church in America, Southern Province, 4 E. Bank Street, Winston-Salem, NC 27101, tel. 919/722-1742), and the United Brethren (United Brethren Archives, Richard Lyn Library, Huntington College, 2303 College Avenue, Huntington, IN 46570, tel. 219/356-6000, ext. 1064).

129. Churches in the Anabaptist tradition have produced an unusually large number of archives. Among the repositories in the United States are those of the Church of the Brethren (Brethren Historical Library and Archives, 1451 Dundee Avenue, Elgin, IL 60120, tel. 708/742-5100), the Grace Brethren (Grace College and Theological Seminary Library, 200 Seminary Drive, Winona Lake, IN 46590, tel. 219/372-5177), the Brethren in Christ (Archives of the Brethren in Christ Church and Messiah College, Messiah College, Grantham, PA 17027, tel. 717/766-2511), the Mennonite Brethren (Center for Mennonite Brethren Studies, 4824 E. Butler, Fresno, CA 93727-5097, tel. 209/453-2225), the Mennonite Church (Archives of the Mennonite Church, 1700 South Main, Goshen, IN 46526, tel. 219/535-7477; the Archives of the Lancaster Mennonite Historical Society, 2215 Mill Stream Road, Lancaster, PA 17602-1499, tel. 717/393-9745; and Menno Simons Historical Library, Eastern Mennonite College, Harrisonburg, VA 22801, tel. 703/433-2770, ext. 153) and the General Conference Mennonites (Mennonite Library and Archives, North Newton, KS 67410, tel. 316/283-2500, ext. 305; and the Mennonite Historical Library, Bluffton College, Bluffton, OH 45817, tel. 419/358-8015, ext. 271).

130. Another important American evangelical tradition is the restorationist movement. Important archives documenting various wings of the movement include those on the Disciples of Christ (Disciples of Christ Historical Society, 1101 19th Avenue, South, Nashville, TN 37601, tel. 615/926-1186),

the Christian Church-Disciples of Christ (Christian Theological Seminary, Manuscript Collection, 1000 West 42nd Street, Indianapolis, IN 46208, tel. 317/924-1331), and the Churches of Christ which grew out of the Campbell/Stone movement (Center for Restoration Studies, Abilene Christian University, Margaret and Herman Brown Library, ACU Station, Box 8177, Abilene, TX 79699, tel. 915/674-2344).

131. The Seventh-day Adventist tradition is documented in several archives, especially General Conference of Seventh-day Adventists, Office of Archives and Statistics, (6840 Eastern Avenue, Washington DC 20012, tel. 202/722-6372). Other major repositories include the Jenks Memorial Collection, (Aurora University, Aurora, IL 60507, tel. 708/844-5445) which has the records of the Advent General Conference as well as some of the papers of William Miller and an extensive collection of early Millerite materials; and the Adventist Heritage Center (James White Library, Andrews University, Berrien Springs, MI 49104, tel. 616/471-3274), which includes early Millerite materials and documents about SDA evangelists and pastors.

132. Many of the archives already mentioned, particularly the larger denominational collections, include documents about the ministry of black Baptists, Methodists and Pentecostals. Wilberforce University (Archives and Special Collections, Rembert E. Stokes Learning Resources Center, Wilberforce, OH 45384-1003, tel. 513/376-2911, ext. 628) contains many records of the African Methodist Episcopal Church, as well as papers of bishops and prominent laypersons. Other major repositories to check include Moorland-Spingarn Research Center (Howard University, Manuscript Division, 500 Howard Place, N.W., Washington, D.C. 20059, tel. 202/636-7480); Talladega College Historical Collections (Talladega, AL 35160, tel. 205/362 0206, ext. 283); thc Amistad Research Center (Old U.S. Mint Building, 400 Esplanade Avenue, New Orleans, LA 70116, tel. 504/522-0432); and the Interdenominational Theological Center (Archives and Special Collections, 671 Beckwith Street, S.W., Atlanta, GA 30314, tel. 404/522-8980).

(B) Educational Institutions

Independent Bible colleges, and liberal arts colleges and seminaries have played a particularly important part in conservative Protestant traditions, often serving as central communication points for movements with few other large organizations. Leaders of these institutions were also regarded as leaders of the larger movements. In addition, of course, the schools served as the training ground for generations of pastors, evangelists, missionaries, teachers, scholars and other Christian workers. It is not uncommon for these institutions to have a corner of the library designated as an archives where records of the institution are kept. The nature of these archives can vary widely, from a few file cabinets whose contents are a mystery to everyone on staff, to well- organized departments which systemically collect the files of the school and prepare finding aids to help researchers find what they are looking for. Among the types of useful records that might be preserved are minutes of the board of trustees, files of the president's office, documentation of student activities, records of academic departments, and private papers of prominent administrators, faculty and alumni.

133. There are a few that deserve special mention. Among Bible schools, preeminent is Moody Bible Institute (Library, 820 North LaSalle Street, Chicago, IL 60610, tel. 312/329-4140). Other influential schools with organized collections include the Bible Institute of Los Angeles, now called Biola University (Archives, Rose Memorial Library, 13800 Biola Avenue, La Miranda, CA 90639, tel. 213/944-0351, ext. 3255); Fuller Theological Seminary (Du Plessis Center); Wheaton College (Archives and Special Collections, Buswell Memorial Library, Wheaton, IL 60187, tel. 708/260-5705); Westminster Theological Seminary (Archives, Chestnut Hill, P.O. Box 27009, Philadelphia, PA 19118, tel. 215/887-5511); Bob Jones University (J.S. Mack Library, Greenville, SC 29614, tel. 803/242-5100); Columbia Bible College, (P.O. Box 3122, Columbia, SC 29230, tel. 803/754-4100, ext. 372); and CBN University (Special Collections, Library, 1000 Centerville Turnpike, Virginia Beach, VA 23464-9882, tel. 804/523-7473).

(C) Leaders

134. Evangelicals, and particularly pentecostals and fundamentalists, minimize the authority of tradition, and emphasize the authority of Scripture and of biblical and evangelistic preaching. Therefore, individual leaders who are gifted with powers of teaching, preaching and/or administration have been particularly influential. The personal papers of such leaders can include correspondence, sermon manuscripts, newspaper scrapbooks about important events, films and tapes, and photographs. When the ministry of an individual is incorporated, such as the Billy Graham Evangelistic Association, the records of the corporation are a major source for documenting the work and influence of an individual. It is not uncommon for the papers of a person to be scattered between two or more repositories. Thus documents by and/or about Dwight L. Moody can be found at Yale University Divinity School (Library, 409 Prospect Street, New Haven, CT 06510, tel. 203/432-5301); the Library of Congress, Moody Bible Institute, and Northfield Mount Hermon School (Pentecost Road, Northfield, MA 01360, tel. 413/498-5311). This doesn't include several other institutions which have a few scattered Moody letters.

135. All or some of the papers of several major evangelists have been preserved: J. Wilbur Chapman (Office of History, Presbyterian Church (USA) and the Archives of the Billy Graham Center, Wheaton College, Wheaton, IL 60187, tel. 708/260-5910, hereafter referred to as the BGC/A); Charles Grandison Finney (Oberlin College Archives, 320 Mudd Learning Center, Oberlin, OH 44074, tel. 216/775-8285, ext. 247); Charles E. Fuller (Du Plessis Center at Fuller Theological Seminary), Billy Graham (the BGC/A, Billy Graham Room, Southern Baptist Theological Seminary,

Louisville, KY 40206, tel. 800/626-5525, and A. Webb Roberts Library, Southwestern Baptist Theological Seminary, P.O. Box 22000-2E, Fort Worth, TX 76122, tel. 817/923-1921, ext. 3330); Bob Jones, Sr. (J.S. Mack Library, Bob Jones University, Greenville, SC 29614, tel. 803/242-5100); Sam Porter Jones (Atlanta Historical Society, 3101 Andrews Drive, N.W., Atlanta, GA 30355, tel. 404/261-1837 and University of Georgia Libraries, Hargrett Rare Book and Manuscript Library, Athens, GA 30602, tel. 404/542-7123); Kathryn Kuhlman (BGC/A), Walter Maier (Concordia Historical Institute), Aimee Semple McPherson (BGC/A), Ford Philpot (Asbury Theological Seminary, B.L. Fisher Library, Wilmore Kentucky 40390, tel. 606/858-3581), William Bell Riley (Northwestern College, Library, 3003 N. Snelling Road, Roseville, MN 55113 and the BGC/A), Oral Roberts (Oral Roberts University, Archives, 7777 South Lewis, Tulsa, OK 74171, tel. 918/495-6750), Oswald J. Smith (BGC/A), and Billy Sunday (Grace College and Seminary and the BGC/A).

136. The papers of many other types of leaders have been preserved as well. These include theologians, scholars, educators, businesspersons, musicians, controversialists and church administrators. Only a few collections of the better known or more influential individuals can be mentioned here: William Jennings Bryan (Library of Congress); David Du Plessis, (Du Plessis Center), Victor Raymond Edman (Wheaton College), Jerry Falwell, (Liberty University, Archives, Box 20000, Lynchburg, VA, tel. 804/582-2000), Jonathan Goforth (BGC/A), J. Gresham Machen (Westminster Theological Seminary, Archives), John Perkins (BGC/A), Pat Robertson (CBN University, Special Collections), Wilbur M. Smith (Trinity Evangelical Divinity School), Herbert J. Taylor (BGC/A), Robert LeTourneau (LeTourneau College, Mary Estes Library, Longview, TX 75607, tel. 214/753-0231), Mel Trotter (BGC/A), George Truett (Southwestern Baptist Theological Seminary), and Ethel Waters (Library of Congress).

(D) Parachurch Organizations

137. Nondenominational organizations have played a very influential part in the fundamentalist, evangelical and pentecostal traditions. Evangelistic associations, faith missions, rescue missions, support groups for individuals engaged in similar ministries, publishing houses, relief and development agencies are among the types of groups that have provided leadership outside of denominational boundaries. The records of these groups are perhaps the least well preserved of all the different types of evangelical movement documentation. But there has been some improvement in the last few years. In some cases, organizations have started their own archives, such as World Vision, which has separate archives for its United States and International branches (Archives, 919 West Huntington Drive, Monrovia, CA 91016, tel. 818/357-7979).

138. Other parachurch group archives which are being preserved are Africa Inland Mission (the BGC/A), the American Bible Society (Archives, 145 West 15th Street, New York, NY 10011, tel. 212/337-7428), the Billy

Graham Evangelistic Association (the BGC/A), Christianity Today, Inc., (BGC/A), Evangelical Foreign Misionary Association (BGC/A), Interdenominational Foreign Missions Association (BGC/A), InterVarsity Christian Fellowship (BGC/A), the Christian Holiness Association (Asbury Theological Seminary), OMS International (Asbury Theological Seminary), the Oral Roberts Evangelist Association (Oral Roberts University), Pentecostal Fellowship of North America (Assemblies of God Archives), Voice of Calvary (the BGC/A), and Youth for Christ (BGC/A).

139. A few special thematic archives have sprung up that document a type of activity or a tradition and include the records of nondenominational organizations in their collecting policy. In this category are Asbury Theological Seminary which is documenting the individuals and organizations of the holiness movement; the BGC/A which is collecting material about nondenominational evangelical Protestant efforts to spread the Gospel; and the Du Plessis Center which is collecting, among other types of material sources on spiritual renewal and records of pentecostalism and the charismatic movement.

(E) Radio and Television

Electronic broadcasting developed in the twentieth century as a means for regularly sending religious messages to worldwide audiences in the tens of millions every day. The types of documentation generated by religious broadcasting include (besides recordings of the programs themselves) scripts, production records, photos of broadcasting activities, audience response in the form of correspondence, magazine and newspaper clippings about specific programs or about religious broadcasting generally. Some of the larger denominations mentioned above, such as the Southern Baptist Convention and the Lutheran Church-Missouri Synod have radio/television departments which produce programming, and the denominational archives might have copies of the programming and the production records. The interested researcher should check with the archives' staff for an accurate idea of relevant holdings.

140. Several of the major independent broadcasters have already been referred to above, such as Jerry Falwell, Charles E. Fuller (besides the Du Plessis Center, a few copies of his radio broadcasts are at the BGC/A), Billy Graham (besides the originals of television and radio broadcasts at the BGC/A, duplicate copies of some radio broadcasts are also at Southern Baptist Seminary and Southwestern Baptist Theological Seminary), Kathryn Kuhlman, Walter A. Maier, Oral Roberts and Pat Robertson.

141. Many of the nondenominational groups mentioned, such as World Vision and Youth for Christ, also do regular broadcasting, and this activity is reflected in their archives. Two early pioneers of interest are Paul Rader for radio and Percy Crawford for television. Rader's papers are at the BGC/A and copies of Crawford's broadcasts can be found at the school he founded, The King's College (Briarcliff Manor, NY 10510, tel. 914/944-

5605) as well as at the BGC/A. A third pioneer was Clarence Jones, who helped develop the missionary use of radio. His papers are also at the BGC/A. The major professional association for those who use television and radio to preach is National Religious Broadcasters. The NRB's records are at the BGC/A, as well as the private papers of past president Eugene R. Bertermann. Of related interest is the Vanderbilt Television News Archives (Jean and Alexander Heard Library, Vanderbilt University, Nashville, TN 37240-0007, tel. 615/322-2927). The staff of this archives have been recording the major television evening news broadcasts every night since 1968, as well as other selected programming. These programs are indexed and stories about particular subjects, including religion, can be viewed. This is a valuable source of information on public perceptions of evangelicals, evangelism, missions, and kindred topics.

CHAPTER 4
PERIODICALS

For both historical and current research, serial literature provides a rich source of contemporary views. They document new movements, the rise (and demise) of popular religious leaders, and the growth of networks and institutions with independent bases and strong editorial lines; evangelical magazines reveal the pulses of the varied movements for which they spoke.

The serial titles in this section are divided chronologically. The first part lists those from the first half of the century, with special attention given to the fundamentalist position during the fundamentalist-modernist Controversy. The second part presents the literature published since 1950 or continuously published since the turn of the century.

The entries include the following elements: title changes, publisher, editor, international standard serial number (ISSN), and OCLC number. The ISSN and OCLC numbers will facilitate searching for locations in national library databases.

For the older titles, primary holding libraries are identified. A few entries will include "Lippy" as a heading. This refers to a more complete description of the item which appears in Lippy, Charles H., ed. Religious Periodicals of the United States: Academic and Scholarly Journals (New York: Greenwood Press, 1986).

(A) Evangelical and Fundamentalist Serials, 1900-1950

Introduction

Between 1900 and 1950, theological and ecclesiastical controversies raged in the press as well as in classrooms and church courts. As key pastors such as J. Frank Norris, John Roach Straton, and William Bell Riley led the fundamentalist cause, they expressed their concerns in church and school magazines and newspapers. Journals such as Our Hope and Revelation promoted premillennialism and other theological views shared by many fundamentalists. The selection of a few Baptist and Presbyterian titles will assist in understanding the turmoil in some denominations before the fundamentalists decided to withdraw and form new denominations.

The Serials

142. The American Fundamentalist

Volume and Issue data:
The Faith: Fundamentalist 1:1 (Nov. 9, 1924) - 2:18 (Aug. 30, 1925)
The American Fundamentalist 2:19 (Sept. 25, 1925) - 2:20 (Oct. 25, 1925)
Publisher: New York: Calvary Baptist Church.
Editor: John Roach Straton.
Notes: Absorbed by the Crusaders' Champion, Clearwater, FL. (OCLC #9451119).
OCLC number:
The Faith: Fundamentalist: #9449429
The American Fundamentalist: #9450720
Primary holding library: Union Theological Seminary (New York)

143. The Baptist Fundamentalist of Texas - (See The Fundamentalist, Fort Worth, TX, et al)

144. The Bible Champion

Volume and issue data:
The Bible Student and Teacher 1:1 (Jan. 1904) - 15:12 (Apr. 1913)
The Bible Champion 16:1 (May 1913) - 36:12 (Dec. 1930)
Publisher: New York and New Brunswick, NJ, etc.: Bible League of North America.
OCLC number:
The Bible Student and Teacher: #2471884
The Bible Champion: #2471945
Primary holding libraries: New Brunswick Theological Seminary; Asbury Theological Seminary; Garrett - Evangelical Theological Seminary; United Library, Gordon-Conwell (v. 1-15; 17-36, incomplete)

145. The Bible Student and Teacher - (See The Bible Champion)

146. The Christian Fundamentalist

Volume and issue data: 1:1 (July 1927) - 6:3/4 (Sept./Oct. 1932)
Publisher: Minneapolis: World's Christian Fundamentals Association.
Editor: William Bell Riley.
Notes: Continues Christian Fundamentals in School and the Church; absorbed the The Pilot.
OCLC number: #17246365; #1554446.
Primary holding libraries: Northwestern College, Bethany/Northern Baptist Seminary Library, Calvin College, Moody Bible Institute.

147. Christian Fundamentals in School and Church

Volume and issue data:
Church and School 1:1 (Sept. 1916)
School and Church 1:2 (Oct. 1916) - 2:13 (Apr.-June 1920)
Christian Fundamentals in School and Church 2:14 (July-Sept. 1920) - 9:2 (Apr.-June 1927)
Publisher: Minneapolis: Northwestern Bible and Missionary Training School.
Editor: William Bell Riley.
Notes: Continues School and Church; continued by The Christian Fundamentalist.
OCLC number:
Church and School: none
School and Church: none
Christian Fundamentals in School and Church: #13211195
Primary holding library: Northwestern College.

148. Christianity Today: A Presbyterian Journal Devoted to Stating, Defending and Furthering the Gospel in the Modern World

Volume and issue data:
1:1 (May 1930) - 11:3 (Spring 1941), (-May 1949, unnumbered)
Publisher: Philadelphia: Presbyterian and Reformed Pub. Co.
OCLC number: #1781870, #9297957 (microform)
Primary holding library: Billy Graham Center Library (microfilm)

149. Church and School - (See Christian Fundamentals in School and Church)

150. The Crusaders' Champion - (See The American Fundamentalist)

151. The Faith: Fundamentalist - (See The American Fundamentalist)

152. The Fence Rail - (See The Fundamentalist, Fort Worth, TX, et. al.)

153. The Fundamentalist (New York)

Volume and issue data:
The Religious Searchlight 1:1 (Jan. 1, 1922) - 1:7 (Oct. 1, 1922).
The Fundamentalist (New York) 2:1 (Dec. 1, 1922) - 3:3 (July 15, 1924).
Publisher: New York: Calvary Baptist Church, Baptist Fundamentalist League of Greater New York and Vicinity, etc.

Editor: John Roach Straton.
Notes: Continued by The Faith: Fundamentalist, then The American Fundamentalist.
OCLC number:
The Religious Searchlight: #9447345
The Fundamentalist (New York): #9449096
Primary holding library: Union Theological Seminary (New York)

154. The Fundamentalist (Fort Worth, TX, et al)

Volume and issue data:
The Fence Rail [1:1] (Jan. 1917)? - 1:6 (Feb. 16, 1917)
The Searchlight 1:1 (Mar. 2, 1917) - 10:22 (Apr. 8, 1927)
The Fundamentalist (Fort Worth, TX: 1927) - 10:23 (Apr. 15, 1927) - 10:24 (Apr. 22, 1927)
The Baptist Fundamentalist of Texas 10:25 (Apr. 29, 1927) - 11:11 (Jan. 20, 1928)
The Fundamentalist of Texas 11:12 (Jan. 27, 1928) - 13:20 (Sept. 6, 1935)
The Fundamentalist (Fort Worth, TX: 1935) - 13:21 (Sept. 20, 1935) - 13:25 (Oct. 18, 1935)
The Fundamentalist of Fort Worth, Texas, and Detroit, Michigan 13:25 (Oct. 25, 1935) - 14:5 (July 3, 1936)
The Fundamentalist (Detroit, MI, etc.) 14:6 (July 10, 1936) - ?
Publishers: Various, including First Baptist Church and Fundamentalist Pub. Co., Fort Worth.
Editor: J. Frank Norris.
ISSN: 0016-2744.
OCLC number:
The Fence Rail: #17446785, #10176420 (Microform)
The Searchlight: #8707254, #10176547 (Microform)
The Fundamentalist (Fort Worth, TX: 1927): #10176659 (Microform)
The Baptist Fundamentalist of Texas: #10176609 (Microform)
The Fundamentalist of Texas: #10176733 (Microform)
The Fundamentalist (Fort Worth, TX: 1935): #10176782
The Fundamentalist of Fort Worth, Texas, and Detroit, Michigan: #10176858
The Fundamentalist (Detroit, MI, etc.): #8816543
Primary holding libraries: Dargan-Carver Library, Nashville; New Orleans Baptist Seminary; Billy Graham Center Library (microfilm)

155. King's Business

Volume and issue data: 1:1 (Jan. 1910) - 61:11 (Dec. 1970)
Publisher: Bible Institute of Los Angeles (later Biola University)
Notes: Superseded by Biola Broadcaster in 1971.
OCLC number: #1776477
Primary holding libraries: Biola University, Samuel Colgate Library of the American Baptist Historical Society, Mooody Bible Institute.

156. Missionary Review of the World

Volume and issue data:
Missionary Review 1:1 (Jan./Feb. 1878) - 10:12 (Dec. 1887)
Missionary Review of the World 11:1 (Jan. 1888) - 62:12 (Dec. 1939)
Publisher: New York: Funk & Wagnalls.
OCLC number:
Missionary Review: #6060419
Missionary Review of the World: #6060424
Primary holding libraries: Andover Newton Theological School, Billy Graham Center Library, Moody Bible Institute, Southern Baptist Theological Seminary, Westminster Theological Seminary.

157. Our Hope: A Testimony for our Lord Jesus Christ

Volume and issue data: 1:1 (July 1894) - 64:6 (Dec. 1957)
Publisher: Waretown NJ, etc.: Arno C. Gaebelein, Inc.
Editor: July 1900-June 1921, Arno C. Gaebelein.
Notes: Absorbed by Eternity.
OCLC number: #1714681
Primary holding libraries: Moody Bible Institute (some in microform).

158. The Presbyterian

Volume and issue data:
The Presbyterian (Philadelphia) 1:1 (Feb. 16, 1831) - 95:24 (June 11, 1925)
The Presbyterian and Herald and Presbyter [95:25] (June 18, 1925) - [96:19] (May 13, 1926)
The Presbyterian (Chillicothe, MO) [96:20] (May 20, 1926) - 118:15 (June 26, 1948)
Publisher: Philadelphia: Russell & Martien, Presbyterian Pub. Co.
Notes: Absorbed by Presbyterian Life.
OCLC number:
The Presbyterian (Philadelphia): #4163914; #8624834 (Microform)
The Presbyterian and Herald and Presbyter: #10200728
The Presbyterian (Chillicothe, MO): #4634689
Primary holding libraries: Microfilm - Auburn University, Harvard Divinity School; Louisville Presbyterian Theological Seminary; McCormick Theological Seminary - Jesuit-Krauss-McCormick Library; Union Theological Seminary (New York), Westminster Theological Seminary

159. The Presbyterian and Herald and Presbyter - (See The Presbyterian)

160. The Religious Searchlight - (See The Fundamentalist, New York)

161. Revelation

Volume and issue data: 1:1 (Jan. 1931) - 20:3 (Mar. 1950)
Publisher: Philadelphia: American Bible Conference Association; Bible Magazine.
Editor: 1931-1939, Donald Grey Barnhouse.
Notes: Superseded by Eternity.
OCLC number: #1776686
Primary holding libraries: Gordon-Conwell Theological Seminary; Moody Bible Institute; Wheaton College-Buswell Memorial Library.

162. School and Church - (See Christian Fundamentals in School and Church)

163. The Searchlight - (See The Fundamentalist, Fort Worth, TX, et al)

164. The Sunday School Times (also, The Sunday-School Times)

Volume and issue data: 1:1 (Jan. 1, 1859) - 108:48 (1966)
Publisher: Philadelphia: J. D. Wattles.
Notes: Continued by Sunday Times, then The Sunday School Times and the Gospel Herald.
OCLC number: #1606027
Primary holding library: Wheaton College-Buswell Memorial Library (some in microform)

165. The Watchman-Examiner

Volume and issue data: 1:1 (Sept. 4, 1913) - 58:6 (Mar. 19, 1970)
Publisher: Somerset, NJ, etc.: Watchman Examiner Foundation.
Editors: 1913-1939, C. L. Laws, et al.; Jan. 1940- J. W. Bradbury.
Notes: Vol. 1, no.1 was published only in the New England edition.
OCLC number: #1773597; #6934507; #8252872 (Microform)
Primary holding libraries: Andover Newton Theological Seminary; University of Chicago.

(B) Evangelical and Fundamentalist Journals, 1950-

Introduction

The following selections emphasize the interdenominational press. These are the most difficult to identify through standard denominational sources. They cover both the scholarly literature and popular publications, ranging from the journals of learned societies and professional associations to The Fundamentalist Journal, Moody Monthly and Charisma and Christian Life.

Only a few titles represent mission agencies and evangelistic associations. For other titles, the researcher may consult the membership list of the Evangelical Press Association which is available in the National Evangelical Directory (Carol Stream, IL: National Association of Evangelicals, annual) or contact an agency directly. In addition to the National Evangelical Directory, most evangelical mission agencies list their addresses in the Mission Handbook: North American Protestant Ministries Overseas (Monrovia, CA: MARC). The eleventh edition, copyrighted in 1976, lists periodical titles along with other agency information.

The titles of most currently-published denominational periodicals do not appear in this volume. They are listed under the name of the denomination in the Yearbook of American and Canadian Churches (Nashville: Abingdon Press, annual). The information for the yearbook is prepared and edited in the Office of Research and Evaluation of the National Council of the Churches of Christ in the U.S.A.

The Christian Periodical Index (West Seneca, NY: Association of Christian Librarians, 1956-) indexes the most important evangelical and fundamentalist journals of interest to Bible school and Christian college libraries.

The Serials

166. AIM International

Volume and issue data:
Inland Africa (New York) 1:1/2 (Jan./Feb. 1917) - 66:4 (1982)
AIM International 67:1- (Winter 1983-)
Current publisher: Pearl River, NY: Africa Inland Mission.
Notes: Inland Africa supersedes Hearing and Doing.
ISSN: Aim International: 0884-6316, Inland Africa: 0020-1464
OCLC number:
Inland Africa (New York): #1585861, #12186818 (Microform)
Inland Africa (London): #5719668
AIM International: #9599989

167. American Baptist Quarterly

Volume and issue data: 1:1- (Oct. 1982-)
Current publisher: Rochester, NY: American Baptist Historical Society.
ISSN: 0745-3698
OCLC number: #8960423
Lippy: pp. 14-18.

168. American Presbyterians

Volume and issue data:

Journal of the Presbyterian Historical Society (1901) 1:1 (May 1901) - 14:2 (June 1930)
Journal of the Department of History (The Presbyterian Historical Society) of the Presbyterian Church in the USA 14:3 (Sept. 1930) - 20:4 (Dec. 1942)
Journal of the Presbyterian Historical Society (1943) 21:1 (Mar. 1943) - 39:4 (Dec. 1961)
Journal of Presbyterian History 40:1 (Mar. 1962) - 63:2 (Spring/Summer 1985)
American Presbyterians 63:3- (Fall 1985-)
Current publisher: Philadelphia: Presbyterian Historical Society.
ISSN:
Journal of the Presbyterian Historical Society (1901): none.
Journal of the Department of History (The Presbyterian Historical Society) of the Presbyterian Church in the USA: 0149-2330
Journal of the Presbyterian Historical Society (1943): 0147-3735
Journal of Presbyterian History: 0022-3883
American Presbyterians: 0886-5159
OCLC number:
Journal of the Presbyterian Historical Society (1901): #7957341
Journal of the Department of History (The Presbyterian Historical Society) of the Presbyterian Church in the USA: #3453900
Journal of the Presbyterian Historical Society (1943): #7957592
Journal of Presbyterian History: #1776473
American Presbyterians: #12900413
Lippy: pp. 281-285.

169. Andrews University Seminary Studies

Volume and issue data: 1:1- (1963-)
Current publisher: Berrien Springs, MI: Andrews University Press.
ISSN: 0003-2980
OCLC number: #1780045

170. Anglican and Episcopal History

Volume and issue data:
Historical Magazine of the Protestant Episcopal Church: 1:1 (Mar. 1932) - 55:4 (Dec. 1986)
Anglican and Episcopal History: 56:1- (Mar. 1987-)
Current publisher: Austin, TX: The Historical Society of the Episcopal Church.
ISSN:
Historical Magazine of the Protestant Episcopal Church: 0018-2486
Anglican and Episcopal History: 0896-8039
OCLC number:
Historical Magazine of the Protestant Episcopal Church: #1752125
Anglican and Episcopal History: #15349617
Lippy: pp. 234-238.

171. The Asbury Theological Journal

Volume and issue data:
The Asbury Seminarian 1:1 (Spring 1946) - 40:2 (Winter 1985)
The Asbury Theological Journal 41:1- (Spring 1986-)
Current publisher: Wilmore, KY: Asbury Theological Seminary.
ISSN:
The Asbury Seminarian: 0004-4253
The Asbury Theological Journal: none.
OCLC number:
The Asbury Seminarian: #1644771
The Asbury Theological Journal: #14472115

172. Assemblies of God Heritage

Volume and issue data: 1:1- (Fall 1981-)
Current publisher: Springfield, MO: Assemblies of God Archives.
ISSN: 0896-4394.
OCLC number: #11014406

173. Baptist History and Heritage

Volume and issue data: 1:1- (Aug. 1965-)
Current publisher: Nashville, TN: Historical Commission of the Southern Baptist Convention.
ISSN: 0005-5719.
OCLC number: #1776384
Lippy: pp. 45-47.

174. Baptist Review and Expositor - (See Review and Expositor)

175. The Biblical Evangelist

Volume and issue data: 1:1- (May 1966-)
Current publisher: Ingleside, TX: Biblical Evangelism.
ISSN: 0740-7998
OCLC number: #5933837

176. Bibliotheca Sacra (1876)

Volume and issue data: 91:1- (Jan. 1934-)
Current publisher: Dallas: Dallas Theological Seminary (formerly Evangelical Theological College).

Notes: See Lippy for a full description of titles, volumes, publishers, and editors.
ISSN: 0006-1921
OCLC number: #5950719 (1864-), #1532843, #5467184 (microfiche)
Lippy: pp. 62-67.

177. Calvin Theological Journal

Volume and issue data: 1:1- (Apr. 1966-)
Current publisher: Grand Rapids, MI: Calvin Theological Seminary.
ISSN: 0008-1795
OCLC number: #1774859, #5462617 (microfiche), #4526087 (microfilm)

178. Campus Life

Volume and issue data:
Youth for Christ 1:1? (1944?) - 23:4 (Sept. 1965)
Campus Life 23:5- (Oct. 1965-)
Current publisher: Carol Stream, IL: Christianity Today, Inc.
ISSN: Campus Life: 0008-2538; Youth for Christ: 0513-3327
OCLC number:
Youth for Christ: #11082401
Campus Life: #1552667

179. CAPS Bulletin - (See Journal of Psychology and Christianity)

180. Charisma & Christian Life

Volume and issue data:
Charisma 1 (Aug.-Sept. 1975) - 12:10 (May 1987)
Charisma & Christian Life 12:11- (June 1987-)
Current publisher: Altamonte Springs, FL: Strang Communications.
ISSN:
Charisma: 0279-0424
Charisma & Christian Life: 0895-156X
OCLC number:
Charisma: #6126408
Charisma & Christian Life: #16502324

181. China's Millions - (See East Asia's Millions)

182. Christian Beacon

Volume and issue data: 1:1- (Feb. 13, 1936-)
Current publisher: Collingswood, NJ: Christian Beacon.

Editor: Carl McIntire.
ISSN: 0009-5265
OCLC number: #1776541, #17267652 (microform), #17270336 (microform)

183. Christian Education Journal

Volume and issue data:
Journal of Christian Education 1:1 (Fall 1980) - 3:1 (Fall 1982)
Christian Education Journal 3:2- (Jan. 1983-)
Current publisher: Glen Ellyn, IL: Scripture Press Ministries in cooperation with the National Association of Professors of Christian Education.
ISSN: Christian Education: 0739-8913; Journal of Christian Education: 0277-9935
OCLC number:
Journal of Christian Education: #7667108
Christian Education Journal: #9809735

184. Christian Herald

Volume and issue data: 25?- (1901-)
Current publisher: Chappaqua, NY: Christian Herald Association.
Notes: Continues Christian Herald and Signs of Our Times, vol. 1 (Oct. 24, 1878) - vol. 24? (1901).
ISSN: 0009-5354
OCLC number:
Christian Herald and Signs of our Times: #1781778
Christian Herald (Chappaqua, NY, etc.): #1554447

185. Christian History

Volume and issue data: 1:1- (1982-)
Current publisher: Carol Stream, IL: Christianity Today, Inc.
ISSN: 0891-9666
OCLC number: #8540047

186. Christian Life

Volume and issue data: 11:1 (July 1948) - 49:1 (May 1987)
Most recent publisher: Altamonte Springs, FL: Strang Communications.
Notes: Continued Sunday; merged with Charisma in June 1987.
ISSN: 0009-5427
OCLC number: #5739829

187. Christian Scholar's Review

Volume and issue data: 1:1- (Fall 1970-)
Current publisher: Grand Rapids, MI (Calvin College): Christian Scholar's Review
ISSN: 0017-2251
OCLC number: #1554486
Lippy: pp. 118-123.

188. Christianity & Literature

Volume and issue data:
Newsletter of the Conference on Christianity and Literature - Oct. 1956 - 22:1 (1972)
Christianity & Literature 22:2- (Winter 1973-)
Current publisher: Seattle, WA (Seattle Pacific University): Conference on Christianity and Literature.
ISSN: 0148-3331
OCLC number:
Newsletter of the Conference on Christianity and Literature: #3591134
Christianity & Literature: #3128374

189. Christianity Today

Volume and issue data: 1:1- (Oct. 15, 1956-)
Current publisher: Carol Stream, IL: Christianity Today, Inc.
ISSN: 0009-5753
OCLC number: #1554505
Lippy: pp. 134-140.

190. Contemporary Christian Music (CCM)

Volume and issue data:
Contemporary Christian Music (1978): 1:1 (July 1978) - 5:12 (June 1983)
Contemporary Christian Magazine: 6:1 (July 1983) - 9:4 (Oct. 1986)
Contemporary Christian Music (1986): 9:5- (Nov. 1986-) **Current publisher**: Nashville, TN: CCM Publications, Inc.
ISSN: 0746-0066; Contemporary Christian Music (1978): 0164-6664
OCLC numbers:
Contemporary Christian Music: #4425969
Contemporary Christian Magazine: #9670881
Contemporary Christian Music: #17938622

191. Cornerstone

Volume and issue data: 1:1- (Apr. 1972-)

Current publisher: Chicago, IL: Jesus People USA.
ISSN: 0275-2743
OCLC number: #7106672

192. Creation Research Society Quarterly

Volume and issue data: 1- (1964-)
Current publisher: Terre Haute, IN: Creation Research Society
ISSN: 0092-9166
OCLC number: #1791775

193. Decision

Volume and issue data: 1:1- (Nov. 1960-)
Current publisher: Minneapolis: Billy Graham Evangelistic Association.
ISSN: 0011-7307
OCLC number: #929428

194. Discipliana

Volume and issue data:
Discipliana 1:1 (Mar. 1941) - 13:1 (Apr. 1953)
Harbinger and Discipliana 13:2 (July 1953) - 19:4 (Dec. 1959)
Discipliana 20:1- (Mar. 1960-)
Current publisher: Nashville, TN: Disciples of Christ Historical Society.
ISSN:
Discipliana (1941): none.
Harbinger and Discipliana: none.
Discipliana (1960): 0732-9881
OCLC number:
Discipliana: #8089928, #2446412, #10524996 (microform)
Harbinger and Discipliana: #8090018, #10523349 (microform)
Discipliana: #8090077, #10523441

195. The Door

Volume and issue data:
The Wittenburg Door #1 (1971) - 103 (June/July 1988)
The Door #104- (Mar./Apr. 1989-)
Current publisher: El Cajon, CA: Youth Specialties.
ISSN: 0199-8295
OCLC number:
The Wittenburg Door: #1781170
The Door: #19357555

196. East Asia's Millions

Volume and issue data:
China's Millions (Council for North America), new series: [1:1] (Jan. 1893) - 60:3 (Mar. 1952)
The Millions 60:4 (Apr. 1952) - 69:4 (Apr. 1961)
East Asia Millions 69:5 (May 1961) - 95:1 (Jan./Feb. 1987)
East Asia's Millions 95:2- (Mar./Apr. 1987-)
Current publisher: Robesonia, PA: Overseas Missionary Fellowship (formerly China Inland Mission).
ISSN:
The Millions: 0740-400x
East Asia Millions; East Asia's Millions: 0012-8406
OCLC number:
China's Millions: #7626696; #1554339 (London)
The Millions: #7626657
East Asia Millions: #3866583; #1696788 (London)
East Asia's Millions: #20555328

197. ESA Advocate

Volume and issue data:
ESA Update, Mar./Apr. 1980 - Oct. 1982, 5:1 (Jan./Feb. 1983) -10:2 (Apr. 1988)
ESA Advocate, Oct. 1988-
Current publisher: Philadelphia: Evangelicals for Social Action.
Notes: Also published ESA Parley and ESA Public Policy Report.
ISSN: None.
OCLC number:
ESA Update: #12181059
ESA Advocate: #20555371

198. Eternity

Volume and issue data: 1:1 (Apr. 1950) - 40:1 (Jan. 1989)
Most recent publisher: Philadelphia: Foundation for Christian Living.
Notes: Superseded Revelation; absorbed Our Hope.
ISSN: 0014-1682
OCLC number: #1568297

199. Evangelical Missions Quarterly

Volume and issue data: 1:1- (Fall 1964-)
Current publisher: Wheaton, IL: Evangelical Missions Information Service.
ISSN: 0014-3359
OCLC number: #1783538

200. Evangelical Newsletter

Volume and issue data: 1:1 (Nov. 5, 1973) - 13:5 (Feb. 14, 1986)
Most recent publisher: Philadelphia: The Evangelical Ministries, Inc.
Notes: Published by the same organization as Eternity.
ISSN: 0744-8783
OCLC number: #1431275

201. Evangelical Studies Bulletin

Volume and issue data: 1:1- (Jan. 1984-)
Current publisher: Wheaton, IL: Institute for the Study of American Evangelicals.
ISSN: 0890-703X
OCLC number: #10511474

202. Faith and Philosophy

Volume and issue data: 1:1- (Jan. 1984-)
Current publisher: Wilmore, KY (Asbury College): Society of Christian Philosophers.
ISSN: 0739-7046
OCLC number: #9801750

203. Faith for the Family

Volume and issue data: 1:1 (Mar./Apr. 1973) - 14:4 (Apr. 1986)
Most recent publisher: Greenville, SC: Bob Jones University.
ISSN: 0099-1759
OCLC number: #2243544

204. Fides et Historia

Volume and issue data: 1:1- (Fall 1968-)
Current publisher: Grand Rapids, MI (Calvin College): Conference on Faith and History.
ISSN: 0884-5379
OCLC number: #1780884

205. Freedom Now - (See The Other Side)

206. Foundations

Volume and issue data: 1:1 (Jan. 1958) - 25:2 (Apr./June 1982)
Current publisher: Rochester, NY: American Baptist Historical Society.

ISSN: 0015-8992
OCLC number: #1569924, #7673811 (microfilm), #4391473 (microfiche)

207. Fundamentalist Journal

Volume and issue data: 1:1- (Sept. 1982-Dec. 1989)
Current publisher: Lynchburg, VA: Old-Time Gospel Hour.
ISSN: 0736-1963
OCLC number: #8819678

208. The Gordon Review

Volume and issue data: 1:1 (Feb. 1955) - 11:5 (Spring 1970)
Publisher: Wenham, MA: Gordon College and Divinity School.
ISSN: 0436-1644
OCLC number: #1695686
Lippy: pp. 118-123.

209. Grace Theological Journal

Volume and issue data:
Grace Journal 1:1 (Spring 1960) - 14:3 (Fall 1973)
Grace Theological Journal 1:1- (Spring 1980-)
Current publisher: Winona Lake, IN: Grace Theological Seminary.
ISSN:
Grace Journal: none.
Grace Theological Journal: 0198-666X
OCLC number:
Grace Journal: #1777003
Grace Theological Journal: #6203551

210. Harbinger and Discipliana - (See Discipliana)

211. Heritage - (See Assemblies of God Heritage)

212. His

Volume and issue data:
His 1:1 (Oct. 1941) - 47:3 (Dec. 1986)
U 47:4 (Jan. 1987) - 48:7 (Apr./May 1988)
Most recent publisher: Downers Grove, IL: InterVarsity Christian Fellowship.
Notes: After change to U, absorbed by World Christian.
ISSN: His: 0018-2095; U: 0893-0201
OCLC number:

His: #1608066
U: #15151626

213. Historical Magazine of the Protestant Episcopal Church - (See Anglican and Episcopal History)

214. Inland Africa - (See AIM International)

215. Journal of Christian Education - (See Christian Education Journal)

216. Journal of Presbyterian History - (See American Presbyterians)

217. Journal of Psychology and Christianity

Volume and issue data:
The Bulletin/Christian Association for Psychological Studies 1 (Summer 1975) - 7 (1981)
Journal of Psychology and Christianity 1:1- (1982-)
Current publisher: Blue Jay, CA: Christian Association for Psychological Studies.
ISSN: The Bulletin/Christian Association for Psychological Studies: 0147-7978; Journal of Psychology and Christianity: 0733-4273
OCLC number:
The Bulletin/Christian Association for Psychological Studies: #3268748
Journal of Psychology and Christianity: #8404774

218. Journal of Psychology and Theology

Volume and issue data: 1:1- (Jan. 1973-)
Current publisher: La Mirada, CA: Rosemead Graduate School of Professional Psychology.
ISSN: 0091-6471
OCLC number: #1787711

219. Journal of the American Scientific Affiliation - (See Perspectives on Science and Christian Faith)

220. Journal of the Department of History of the Presbyterian Church in the USA - (See American Presbyterians)

221. Journal of the Evangelical Theological Society

Volume and issue data:
Bulletin of the Evangelical Theological Society 1:1 (Winter 1958) - 11:4 (Fall 1968)
Journal of the Evangelical Theological Society 12:1- (Winter 1969-)
Current publisher: Jackson, MS: Evangelical Theological Society.
ISSN: Bulletin of the Evangelical Theological Society: 0361-5138; Journal of Evangelical Theological Society: 0360-8808
OCLC number:
Bulletin of the Evangelical Theological Society: #1776411
Journal of the Evangelical Theological Society: #2244860
Lippy: pp. 305-309.

222. Journal of the Presbyterian Historical Society - (See American Presbyterians)

223. Leadership

Volume and issue data: 1:1- (Winter 1980-)
Current publisher: Carol Stream, IL: Christianity Today, Inc.
ISSN: 0199-7661
OCLC number: #5956624

224. The Mennonite Quarterly Review

Volume and issue data: 1:1- (Jan. 1927-)
Current publisher: Goshen, IN: Mennonite Historical Society.
ISSN: 0025-9373
OCLC number: #1638991
Lippy: pp. 343-346.

225. Methodist History

Volume and issue data: 1:1- (Oct. 1962-)
Current publisher: Madison, NJ: General Commission on Archives and History of The United Methodist Church.
ISSN: 0026-1238
OCLC number: #1714380, #4054824 (microfilm), #4363717 (microfiche)
Lippy: pp. 350-352.

226. The Millions - See (East Asia's Millions)

227. Mission Frontiers

Volume and issue data: 1:1- (Jan. 1979-)
Current publisher: Pasadena, CA: US Center for World Mission.
ISSN: 0889-9436

OCLC number: #8630362

228. Moody Monthly

Volume and issue data:
Institute Tie, new series 1:1 (Sept. 1900) - 9:7 (Mar. 1909)
Institute Tie-Christian Worker's Magazine 9:8 (Apr. 1909) - 11:1 (Sept. 1910)
Christian Worker's Magazine 11:2 (Oct. 1910) - 20:12 (Aug. 1920)
Moody Bible Institute Monthly 21:1 (Sept. 1920) - 38:6 (Feb. 1938)
Moody Monthly 38:7- (Mar. 1938-)
Current publisher: Chicago: Moody Bible Institute.
ISSN: 0027-0806
OCLC number: #1758685;
The Institute Tie: not available
The Christian Worker's Magazine: #6427533
Moody Bible Institute Monthly: #1781727, #7619175 (microform)
Moody Monthly: #1758685, #3880359 (microform)
Lippy: pp. 368-371

229. New Covenant

Volume and issue data: 1:1- (July 1971-)
Current Publisher: Ann Arbor, MI: Servant Publications.
ISSN: 0744-8589
OCLC number: #1773468

230. The Other Side

Volume and issue data:
Freedom Now 1 (Jan./Feb. 1965) - 5:5 (Sept./Oct. 1969)
The Other Side 5:6- (Nov./Dec. 1969-)
Current publisher: Philadelphia: The Other Side.
ISSN: 0145-7675
OCLC number:
Freedom Now: #10595002
The Other Side: #2250527

231. Perspectives on Science and Christian Faith

Volume and issue data:
Journal of the American Scientific Affiliation 1:1 (Jan. 1949) - 38:4 (Dec. 1986)
Perspectives on Science and Christian Faith 39:1 (Mar. 1987-)
Current publisher: Ipswich, MA: American Scientific Affiliation.

ISSN: Journal of the American Scientific Affiliation: 0003-0988; Perspectives on Science and Christian Faith: 0892-2675
OCLC number:
Journal of the American Scientific Affiliation: #1480716
Perspectives on Science and Christian Faith: #15139894

232. Pneuma

Volume and issue data: 1:1- (Spring 1979-)
Current publisher: Pasadena, CA: Society for Pentecostal Studies.
ISSN: 0272-0965
OCLC number: #5198011

233. Post-American - (See Sojourners)

234. The Presbyterian Journal

Volume and issue data:
The Southern Presbyterian Journal 1:1 (May 1942) - 18:22 (Sept. 1959)
The Presbyterian Journal 18:23 (Oct. 7, 1959) - 45:16 (March 18, 1987)
Most recent publisher: Asheville, NC: God's World Publications.
Note: Continued by World.
ISSN:
The Southern Presbyterian Journal: 0146-7727
The Presbyterian Journal: 0032-7549
OCLC number:
The Southern Presbyterian Journal: #2057044, #2620822
The Presbyterian Journal: #1777073, #6272615 (microfilm), #8636833 (microfilm)

235. Radix

Volume and issue data:
Right On: 1 (1969/1970) - 7:9 (June 1976)
Radix: 8:1- (July/Aug. 1976-)
Current publisher: Berkeley, CA: Radix Magazine.
ISSN:
Right On: none.
Radix: 0275-0147
OCLC number:
Right On: #1777742
Radix: #4800301, #4930328 (microfilm)

236. Reformed Journal

Volume and issue data: 1:1- (March 1951-)

Current publisher: Grand Rapids, MI: Eerdmans.
ISSN: 0486-252X
OCLC number: #1605740
Lippy: pp. 450-454.

237. Religious Broadcasting

Volume and issue data: 1- (1969-)
Current publisher: Morristown, NJ: National Religious Broadcasters.
ISSN: 0034-4079
OCLC number: #3448651

238. Restoration Quarterly

Volume and issue data: 1:1- (Winter 1957-)
Current publisher: Abilene, TX: The Restoration Quarterly Corp.
ISSN: 0486-5642
OCLC number: #1776685

239. Review and Expositor

Volume and issue data:
Baptist Review and Expositor: 1:1 (Apr. 1904) - 3:3 (Apr. 1906)
Review and Expositor 3:4- (Oct. 1906-)
Current publisher: Louisville, KY: Southern Baptist Theological Seminary.
ISSN:
Baptist Review and Expositor: none.
Review and Expositor: 0034-6373
OCLC number:
Baptist Review and Expositor: #3876993, #1779564
Review and Expositor: #1696862, #4364099 (microfiche), #3827485 (microfilm), #9521045 (microfilm)

240. Right On - (See Radix)

241. Sojourners

Volume and issue data:
Post-American 1:1 (Fall 1971) - 4:8 (Oct./Nov. 1975)
Sojourners 5:1- (Jan. 1976-)
Current publisher: Washington, DC: John Roos.
ISSN: 0364-2097; Post-American: 0361-2422
OCLC number:
Post-American: #1968386
Sojourners: #1995372

Lippy: pp. 479-482

242. The Southern Presbyterian Journal - (See The Presbyterian Journal)

243. The Southwestern Journal of Theology

Volume and issue data:
The Southwestern Journal of Theology (1917): 1:1 (Apr. 1917) - 8:3 (July 1924)
The Southwestern Journal of Theology (1958): 1:1 - (Oct. 1958 -)
Current publisher: Fort Worth, TX: Southwestern Baptist Theological Seminary.
ISSN:
The Southwestern Journal of Theology (1917): 0273-0952
The Southwestern Journal of Theology (1958): 0038-4828
OCLC number:
The Southwestern Journal of Theology (1917): #4646657
The Southwestern Journal of Theology (1958): #1776710, #5654353 (microfiche), #11083493 (microfilm), #3528077 (microfilm)

244. Sword of the Lord

Volume and issue data: 1:1- (Sept. 28, 1934-)
Current publisher: Murfreesboro, TN: Sword of the Lord Foundation.
Editor: John R. Rice.
ISSN: 0039-7547
OCLC number: #1776715, #10946937 (microform)

245. Theology News & Notes

Volume and issue data: 1:1- (Apr. 1954-)
Current publisher: Pasadena, CA: Fuller Theological Seminary.
ISSN: none.
OCLC number: #4619469

246. Trinity Journal

Volume and issue data:
Trinity Studies 1-2 (1971-1972)
Trinity Journal 3:1 (Spring 1974) - 7:2 (Fall 1978); new series 1:1- (Spring 1980-)
Current publisher: Deerfield, IL: Trinity Evangelical Divinity School.
ISSN:
Trinity Studies: 0360-2915
Trinity Journal: 0360-3032

OCLC number:
Trinity Studies: #2243859
Trinity Journal: #2243858

247. Today's Christian Woman

Volume and issue data: Fall/Winter 1978/1979-
Current publisher: Carol Stream, IL: Christianity Today, Inc.
ISSN: 0163-1799
OCLC number: #4324198

248. Today's mission - (See World Christian)

249. TSF Bulletin

Volume and issue data:
TSF News and Reviews, Fall 1977 - 3:5 (Apr. 1980)
TSF Bulletin 4:1 (Oct. 1980) - 10:5 (May/June 1987)
Most recent publisher: Madison, WI: Theological Students Fellowship.
ISSN: TSF Bulletin: 0272-3913: TSF News and Reviews: 0272-040X
OCLC number:
TSF News and Reviews: #3620307
TSF Bulletin: #6831580

250. U - (See His)

251. United Evangelical Action

Volume and issue data: 1:1- (Aug. 1, 1942-)
Current publisher: Wheaton, IL: National Association of Evangelicals.
ISSN: 0041-7270
OCLC number: #1768007

252. The Voice

Volume and issue data:
The Pioneer of a New Era, 1922? - 11:12 (June 1933)
The Voice: 12:1- (July 1933-)
Current publisher: Grandville, MI: Independent Fundamental Churches of America.
ISSN: 0049-6669
OCLC number:
The Pioneer of a New Era: #14988782
The Voice of the Independent Fundamental Churches of America: #14988963; #3956727

253. Wesleyan Theological Journal

Volume and issue data: 1:1- (Spring 1966-)
Current publisher: Wilmore, KY: Wesleyan Theological Society.
ISSN: 0092-4245
OCLC number: #1789816
Lippy: pp. 532-534.

254. The Westminster Theological Journal

Volume and issue data: 1:1 - (Nov. 1938-)
Current publisher: Philadelphia: Westminster Theological Seminary.
ISSN: 0043-4388
OCLC number: #1715830, #56544596 (microfiche)
Lippy: pp. 534-539.

255. The Wittenburg Door - (See The Door)

256. World

Volume and issue data: 1:1-(Jan. 1986-)
Current publisher: Asheville, NC: God's World Pub. Inc.
ISSN: 0888-157x
OCLC number: #13492496, #18850353 (microfilm)
Notes: absorbed Eternity

257. World Christian

Volume and issue data:
Today's Mission 1 (1979, 1982)
World Christian [2:1]- (Jan./Feb. 1983-)
Current publisher: Pasadena, CA: World Christian, Inc.
ISSN: 0743-2399, 0743-2339
OCLC number:
Today's Mission: #8167505
World Christian: #9245267

258. World Evangelization

Volume and issue data:
Information Bulletin of the Lausanne Committee for World Evangelization #1 (Apr. 1975) - #7 (May 1977)
World Evangelization Information Bulletin #8 (Nov. 1977) - #[40] (Sept. 1985)

World Evangelization #41- (Dec. 1985-)
Current publisher: Pasadena, CA: Lausanne Committee for World Evangelization.
ISSN: None.
OCLC number:
Information Bulletin of the Lausanne Committee for World Evangelization: #9797610
World Evangelization Information Bulletin: #9505903

259. World Vision

Volume and issue data:
World Vision Magazine 1:1 (June 1957) - 15:12 (Dec. 1971)
World Vision 16:1- (Jan. 1972-)
Current publisher: Monrovia, CA: World Vision International.
ISSN: World Vision Magazine: 0043-9215
OCLC number:
World Vision Magazine: #1716370
World Vision: #3172234

260. Youth for Christ - (See Campus Life)

CHAPTER 5
PUBLISHERS

This section is intended to provide a general orientation to evangelical publishing in America. Publishers were selected for inclusion on the basis that they were either a primary evangelical publisher or representative of publishers who produce evangelical material. Both quantity and quality of publishing were taken into account in the selection process. A publisher's historical role in the evangelical movement and its current influence were also considered. This list is by no means exhaustive.

A few key evangelical publishers from the past such as Van Kampen Press, Wilde of Boston and Channel Press were significant during the early part of the twentieth century but are no longer in existence. Only publishers currently in business have been included.

Some university presses are now publishing major works by evangelical authors. Other presses produce isolated publications by evangelicals. These are too numerous to list and have been excluded.

(A) Major Evangelical Publishers of Scholarly Books

Selected publishers that produce a significant number of scholarly books. These include reference works and titles intended for use in an academic setting.

261. Baker Book House, P.O. Box 6287, Grand Rapids, MI 49516-6287. Founded 1939.

Strong academic tradition covering a broad range of topics. Emphasis on biblical studies and contemporary evangelical issues. Produces a significant number of reference books.

262. Hendrickson Publishers, P.O. Box 3473, Peabody, MA 01961-3473. Founded 1981.

A newcomer to the publishing field specializing in pentecostal/charismatic studies. Has reprinted a number of classic academic works.

263. InterVarsity Press, P.O. Box 1400, Downers Grove, IL 60515. Founded 1947.

Well-known for its titles on practical Christian living. Has also established a tradition of academic publishing with key reference books and studies addressing contemporary evangelical issues.

264. Kregel Publications, P.O. Box 2607, Grand Rapids, MI 49501-2607. Founded 1949.

Emphasis on biblical studies including Bible commentaries and study guides. Reprints the works of earlier evangelical authors such as F. B. Meyer and Andrew Murray.

265. Moody Press, 820 N. LaSalle Drive, Chicago, IL 60610. Founded 1894.

Carries a complete line of religious literature for all age levels. The academic line emphasizes biblical studies and conservative evangelical publications.

266. Presbyterian & Reformed Publishing Co., P.O. Box 817, Phillipsburg, NJ 08865. Founded 1931.

Publishes the work of many evangelical scholars. Provides educational resources for the college and seminary level as well as the local church.

267. Wm. B. Eerdmans Publishing Co., 255 Jefferson Avenue, S.E., Grand Rapids, MI 49503. Founded 1911.

Produces standard evangelical reference books and academic titles. Provides the most complete coverage of the various aspects of Christian theology by any evangelical publisher.

268. William Carey Library, P.O. Box 40129, Pasadena, CA. Founded 1969.

A fairly new press, this publisher has become an important publisher of evangelical works about missions and related areas. Many of the early titles were the products of the School of World Mission at Fuller Theological Seminary.

269. Zondervan Publishing House, 1415 Lake Drive, S.E., Grand Rapids, MI 49506. Founded 1931.

Publishes reference works and scholarly texts. Attempts to provide material for all levels of ministry with emphasis on pastoral aids. Recently acquired Francis Asbury Press to add a Wesleyan track to its publishing interests.

(B) Major Evangelical Publishers of Popular Literature

A selection of publishers that produce books for the general evangelical community. While they may publish a few scholarly or semi-scholarly titles, their target audience is the lay reader.

270. Banner of Truth, P.O. Box 621 Carlisle, PA 17013. Founded 1955.

Provides mainly reprints of selected Christian authors. Reprints include the works of historical figures such as Calvin and Knox and the works of evangelicals such as B. B. Warfield and D. Martyn Lloyd-Jones.

271. Bethany House Publishers, 6820 Auto Club Road Minneapolis, MN 55438. Founded 1946.

Provides popular literature for all ages. Specializes in novels and Christian self-help books.

272. Christian Literature Crusade, P.O. Box 1449, Fort Washington, PA 19034. Founded 1952.

Publishes mostly non-fiction literature on popular topics. Reprints popular editions of evangelical authors such as Amy Carmichael, Oswald Chambers and F. B. Meyer. Also produces a series of Christian biography for young people.

273. Crossway Books, Division of Good News Publishers, 9825 W. Roosevelt Rd., Westchester, IL 60154. Founded 1938.

Specializes in Christian fiction and fantasy novels and books on practical Christian living and current evangelical issues.

274. David C. Cook Publishing Co., 850 N. Grove Ave., Elgin, IL 60120. Founded 1875.

Best known for Sunday school materials and teaching aids. Also produces books on popular Christian topics.

275. Fleming H. Revell, Subsidiary of Zondervan Corp., 184 Central Ave., Old Tappan, NJ 07675. Founded 1870.

Wide variety of non-fiction books for practical Christian living. Some academic titles and reference books.

276. Gospel Light (see Regal Books)

277. Harold Shaw Publishers, P.O Box 567, Wheaton, IL 60189. Founded 1966.

Concentrates on Christian self-help books and personal Bible study aids. Produces the Wheaton Literary Series which includes the works of Madeleine L'Engle, Flannery O'Connor and C. S. Lewis.

278. Loizeaux Brothers, P.O. Box 277, Neptune, NJ 07754-0277. Founded 1876.

Publishes books on popular evangelical concerns and doctrinal issues. Reprints the works of evangelical authors such as H. A. Ironside and Arno C. Gaebelein.

279. Multnomah Press, 10209 S.E. Division Street, Portland, OR 97266. Founded 1969.

Publishes non-fiction by popular evangelical authors. Concentrates on issues of practical importance to evangelicals such as abortion and interacting with a hostile secular culture. Also produces a series of children's books.

280. Regal Books, Division of Gospel Light Publications, P.O. Box 3875, Ventura, CA 93003. Founded 1933.

Produces non-fiction for all ages. Emphasizes personal growth and devotional literature. Publishes a significant number of books on evangelism, missions, comparative religions and contemporary evangelical issues.

281. Scripture Press (see Victor Books)

282. Servant Publications, P.O. Box 8617, Ann Arbor, MI 48107. Founded 1972.

A Roman Catholic charismatic press which publishes both Protestant and Catholic evangelical books. Concentrates on the publications of Charismatic authors.

283. Standard Publishing, 8121 Hamilton Ave., Cincinnati, OH 45231. Founded 1866.

Produces a broad range of literature for use in local church ministry. Specializes in children's literature.

284. Thomas Nelson Publishing Co., P.O. Box 141000, Nashville, TN 37214. Founded 1961.

Best known for publishing quality Bibles. Also provides a selection of popular evangelical literature.

285. Tyndale House Publishers, P.O. Box 80, Wheaton, IL 60189. Founded 1962.

Produces a variety of practical Christian living and self-help books. Also publishes a number of books on current evangelical issues and devotional literature.

286. Victor Books, Division of Scripture Press, P.O. Box 1825, Wheaton, IL 60189. Founded 1934.

An assortment of practical Christian living, self-help, devotional and general interest material. Includes a few popular reference works and some fiction.

287. Word Books, Inc., P.O. Box 2518, Waco, TX 76702. Founded 1951.

Publishes a wide variety of books from reference books and Bible commentaries to fiction and devotional literature. Emphasis is on non-fiction literature for adults, but includes a significant number of titles for children.

(C) Ministry Oriented Publishers

Includes representative publishers that grew out of evangelistic ministries. They produce literature to promote evangelism and discipleship of new converts.

288. Back to the Bible, Distributed by Spring Arbor, P.O. Box 985, Belleville, MI 48111. Founded 1948.

Publishing arm of Back to the Bible radio broadcast. Features the publications of Theodore H. Epp and Warren W. Wiersbe. Includes a variety of tracts, children's literature and recorded messages and music on audio cassettes.

289. Here's Life Publisher, P.O. Box 1576, San Bernardino, CA 92402. Founded 1978.

An outgrowth of Campus Crusade for Christ. Features the works of Bill Bright, Josh McDowell and other Crusade staff. Focuses on evangelistic literature and practical Christian living for new converts.

290. NavPress, Division of the Navigators, P.O. Box 6000, Colorado Springs, CO 80934. Founded 1933.

Founded by the Navigators. Publishes self-help books and practical ministry guides. Emphasizes evangelistic and discipleship oriented literature.

291. World Wide Publications, 1303 Hennepin Ave., Minneapolis, MN 55403. Founded 1952.

The wholesale publishing branch of the Billy Graham Evangelistic Association specializing in evangelism resources and devotional literature. Includes audio and video cassettes and the proceedings of gatherings such as the Amsterdam conferences. Materials are available to the public through the Grason Company, the retail publishing branch of the Association.

(D) Denominational Publishers

This section includes a selection of denominational publishers that produce a significant number of Evangelical books.

292. Abingdon Press, Division of the United Methodist Publishing House P.O. Box 801, Nashville, TN 37202. Founded 1789.

293. Beacon Hill Press of Kansas City, Subsidiary of the Nazarene Publishing House, P.O. Box 419527, Kansas City, MO 64141. Founded 1912.

294. Brethren Press, Division of the Church of the Brethren, 1451 Dundee Ave., Elgin, IL 60120. Founded 1897.

295. Broadman Press, Division of the Southern Baptist Convention, Sunday School Board, 127 Ninth Ave. North, Nashville, TN 37234. Founded 1891.

296. Concordia Publishing House, 3558 S. Jefferson Ave., St. Louis, MO 63118. Founded 1869. (Lutheran Church--Missouri Synod)

297. Gospel Publishing House, Division of Publication of the General Council of the Assemblies of God, 1445 Boonville Ave., Springfield, MO 65802. Founded 1914.

298. Herald Press, Division of the Mennonite Publishing House, 616 Walnut Ave., Scottdale, PA 15683. Founded 1908.

299. Judson Press, P.O. Box 851, Valley Forge, PA 19482-0851. Founded 1824. (American Baptist)

300. Knox/Westminster Press, 100 Witherspoon St., Louisville, KY 40202-1396. Founded 1988 as a merger of Westminster Press (1838) and John Knox Press (1865).

301. Light and Life Press, 999 College Ave., Winona Lake, IN 46590. Founded 1886. (Free Methodist)

302. Warner Press, P.O. Box 2499, Anderson, IN 46011. Founded 1881. (Church of God)

(E) Fundamentalist

303. Bob Jones University Press, Bob Jones University, Greenville, SC 29614. Founded 1974.

Produce a full range of curriculum support for grades 1-12 written from a conservative Christian perspective. Also provides a wide range of Christian literature. Reprints works of Bob Jones, Sr.

304. Sword of the Lord Publishers, P.O. Box 1099, Murfreesboro, TN 37130. Founded 1934.

Concentrates on doctrinal and evangelistic material. Also publishes commentaries and devotional and Christian living materials. Reprints the works of John R. Rice.

CHAPTER 6
ARTIFACTS AND PICTORIAL RESOURCES

Museums are not often thought of as important resource centers for serious researchers in the humanities and social sciences. They are known as places that present artifacts for the public's enjoyment and learning, usually in the form of exhibits. To the public, that is all there is to a museum, although exhibits usually represent only a small fraction of the materials housed in the institution. Museums are in fact meant for researchers to use; they are generally defined as collections of objects in a particular field that are assembled for the purpose of study within that field. And yet, outside of the fields that are most attuned to the study of artifacts, such as archaeology and anthropology, few scholars make use of artifacts in their work.

That has been changing in recent years, as historians, area studies specialists, and other humanists and social scientists have been playing closer attention to the material culture that the people they study create, and in which they live, move, and have their being. Social, cultural, and even intellectual historians, for example, are paying closer attention to the material context in which their subjects worked, since it obviously reflected and came to bear upon their thoughts, motives, and actions.

Religions can create a wealth of material artifacts, but some produce more than others. Protestant Christianity, with its heritage of iconoclasm, has been relatively spare and objectless compared to other faiths. And revivalistic, evangelical Christianity has been even less interested in creating objects that aid in worship or express religious feeling. Furthermore, the text-centeredness of Protestantism has abetted the bias toward textual research among scholars. And yet, as social historians, anthropologists and folklorists have turned to the study of American popular culture, they have found plenty of artifacts related to grass-roots Christianity and have discovered that these materials provide striking documentation and insights.This section is designed to assist the researcher in locating artifacts that can both illustrate and illumine the story of evangelical Christianity in America. Its categories follow the rough outlines of the various faith families that comprise the evangelical mosaic, plus entries under a grouping for southern religion, one for revivalism and foreign missions, and a "general" category for collections that have items relating to several religious groups.

(A) Adventists

305. Adventist Heritage Center
Andrews University
Berrien Springs, MI 49104

Artifacts, photographs, postcards, prints, slides and prophetic charts relating to the Seventh-day Adventist Church and the Millerite movement.

306. Aurora University Library
The Jenks Memorial Collection of Advental Materials
347 S. Gladstone Avenue
Aurora, IL 60506
708/844-5445

Artifacts, ephemera, photographs, postcards, slides and prophetic charts relating to the Advent Christian Church, the American Advent Mission Society, Woman's Home and Foreign Mission Society, the Millerite movement, and the American Millenial Association.

307. General Conference of Seventh-day Adventists
Office of Archives and Statistics
6840 Eastern Ave., N.W.
Washington, DC 20012
202/722-6372

Evangelistic charts, prophetic charts, photographs, stereoptican slides, transparencies and films relating to Seventh-day Adventists.

308. Heritage Room
Loma Linda University
Dept. of Archives and Special Collections
Loma Linda, CA 92350
714/824-4942

Artifacts, ephemera, photographs, postcards, prints, slides, video tapes and film relating to the Seventh-day Adventist Church.

(B) Baptists

309. American Baptist Historical Society
American Baptist Archives Center
P.O. Box 851
Valley Forge, PA 19482-0851
215/768-2378

Artifacts, photographs and slides relating to Baptists, especially the American Baptist Church, the Baptist World Alliance, and the Freewill Baptist movement.

310. Free Will Baptist Historical Collection
Mount Olive College
Moye Library
Mount Olive, NC 28365
919/658-2502 ext. 126

Artifacts, ephemera, photographs, postcards, prints, slides and film relating to the Free Will Baptists, English General Baptists, and the Continental Anabaptists.

311. Seventh-day Baptist Historical Society
P.O. Box 1678
Janesville, WI 53547
608/752-5055

Artifacts, ephemera, photographs, postcards, prints and slides relating to the Seventh-day Baptist General Conference, USA and Canada, the American Sabbath Tract Society, and sabbath-keeping Baptists.

312. North American Baptist Archives
North American Baptist Seminary
1605 S. Euclid Avenue
Sioux Falls, SD 57105

Artifacts, photographs, prints and slides relating to the North American Baptist Conference.

313. American Baptist/Samuel Colgate Historical Library
1106 S. Goodman Street
Rochester, NY 14620
716/473-1740

Artifacts, ephemera, photographs and slides relating to the American (Northern) Baptist Churches, USA, and their missions.

314. Southern Baptist Historical Library & Archives
901 Commerce Street, Suite 400
Nashville, TN 37203-3620
615/244-0344

Artifacts, ephemera, photographs, postcards, slides, videotapes and films relating to the Southern Baptist Convention.

315. Women's Missionary Union
P.O. Box C-10
Birmingham, AL 35283-0010

Ephemera and photographs relating to the women's mission societies of the Southern Baptist Convention.

(C) Black Evangelicals

316. The Amistad Research Center
Tilton Hall, Tulane University
New Orleans, LA 70118
504/865-5535

(D) Fundamentalists

317. Biola University Archives
13800 Biola Avenue
La Mirada, CA 90639

Photographs and memorabilia relating to the history of the Bible Institute of Los Angeles and fundamentalism in southern California.

318. Wheaton College Archives
Buswell Library
Wheaton, IL 60187
708/260-5705

Photographs and memorabilia relating to the history of Wheaton College.

319. Christian and Missionary Alliance Archives
P.O. Box 3500
Colorado Springs, CO 80935-3500
719/599-5999

Artifacts and photographs relating to the Christian and Missionary Alliance, and its operations both in the United States and in its many foreign missions.

320. Moody Bible Institute
Library, Moodyana Room
820 North LaSalle Drive
Chicago, IL 60610
312/329-4140

Photographs and slides relating to D.L. Moody and especially to the Moody Bible Institute and its contributions to Chicago-area fundamentalism.

321. J.S. Mack Library
Bob Jones University
Greenville, SC 29614

803/242-5100 ext. 6000

Ephemera and published materials related to separatist fundamentalism and evangelists Bob Jones, Sr. and Bob Jones, Jr.

(E) Holiness Movement

322. Anderson University
Church of God Archives
Byrd Memorial Library
School of Theology
Anderson, IN 46011
317/649-9071 ext. 2077

Ephemera, memorabilia and photographs relating to the Church of God.

323. Church of the Nazarene International Headquarters
6401 The Paseo
Kansas City, MO 64131
816/333-7000 ext. 437

Photographs relating to the Church of the Nazarene.

324. Salvation Army Archives & Research Center
145 W. 15th Street
New York, NY 10011
212/337-7428

Artifacts, ephemera, photographs, postcards, prints, slides, videotapes, films and posters relating to the Salvation Army, late 19th-20th century.

(F) Lutherans, Pietists

325. Evangelical Lutheran Church in America Archives
8765 W. Higgins Road
Chicago, IL 60631
312/380-2700 ext. 2818, 2813

Artifacts, ephemera, photographs, postcards, prints, slides, architectural drawings, video tapes and film relating to the Evangelical Lutheran Church of America, the American Lutheran Church, the Association of Evangelical Lutheran Churches, and the Lutheran Church in America.

326. Concordia Historical Institute
801 De Mun Avenue
St. Louis, MO 63105
314/721-5934

Artifacts, ephemera, photographs, prints, audio-visual material and works by Lutheran artists, focused on the Lutheran Church, Missouri Synod.

327. Perry County Lutheran Historical Society, Inc.
Altenburg, MO 63732
314/824-5906

Artifacts, Bibles, photographs and slides relating to the Lutheran Church, Missouri Synod.

328. North Park College & Seminary
Archives & Historical Library
5125 North Spaulding Avenue
Chicago, IL 60625
312/583-2700 ext. 5267

Artifacts, ephemera, photographs, postcards, prints, slides and film relating to the Evangelical Covenant Church of America and its pietistic background.

(G) Mennonites, Brethren

329. Brethren Historical Library & Archives
1451 Dundee Avenue
Elgin, IL 60120
708/742-5100 ext. 294

Artifacts, ephemera, photographs, postcards, prints, slides, videotapes and films relating to the Church of the Brethren.

330. Grace Theological Seminary & College
200 Seminary Drive
Winona Lake, IN 46590
219/372-5177

Artifacts, ephemera, photographs, postcards and slides dealing with Billy Sunday, Winona Lake Assembly, Winona Lake Christian Assembly, Winona Lake Bible Conference, and the Grace Brethren denomination.

331. Mennonite Library & Archives
Bethel College
North Newton, KS 67117
316/283-2500 ext. 305

Photographs, ephemera, paintings, prints, slides and film on Anabaptist-Mennonite history.

332. Mennonite Church Archives
1700 South Main
Goshen, IN 46526
219/535-7477
219/535-7476

Artifacts, ephemera, photographs, postcards, prints, slides, videotapes, films, oil paintings and watercolors relating to the Mennonite Church, the Mennonite World Conference, and the Mennonite Central Committee's relief work.

333. Mennonite Historians of Eastern Pennsylvania
24 Main Street
Souderton, PA 18964
215/723-1700

Artifacts, ephemera, photographs, postcards, prints, slides, videotapes, and films relating to the Mennonite Church, Anabaptists, the Brethren Church, the Reformed Church, and the Lutheran Church.

(H) Methodists, United Brethren

334. St. George's United Methodist Church
235 N. Fourth Street
Philadelphia, PA 19106
215/925-7788

Artifacts, memorabilia, photographs, prints and slides relating to the United Methodist Church, especially the Eastern Pennsylvania Conference.

335. Huntington College
Richlyn Library
Huntington, IN 46750
219/356-6000

Artifacts, ephemera, photographs, postcards, prints and slides relating to the Church of the United Brethren in Christ, the International Society of Christian Endeavor, and the National Association of Evangelicals.

336. Commission on Archives & History
Minnesota Annual Conference
The United Methodist Church
122 W. Franklin Avenue, Room 400
Minneapolis, MN 55404
612/870-3657

Artifacts, ephemera, photographs, prints and slides relating to the United Methodist Church in Minnesota.

337. United Methodist Archives Center
Beeghly Library
Ohio Wesleyan University
Delaware, OH 43015
614/369-4431 ext. 214

Artifacts, ephemera, photographs, prints, slides and maps relating to the United Methodist Church in Ohio from 1797 to present.

338. Barratt's Chapel and Museum
R.D. 2, Box 25
Frederica, DE 19946-9501
302/335-5544

Artifacts, ephemera, photographs, postcards, prints, slides, paintings and maps relating to the United Methodist Church and its antecedents.

339. United Methodist Historical Center
Nebraska Wesleyan University
50th & St. Paul Streets
Lincoln, NE 68504
402/465-2175

Artifacts, photographs, prints and slides relating to the United Methodist Church and its antecedents in Nebraska.

340. Commission on Archives and History
United Methodist Church
P.O. Box 127
Madison, NJ 07940
201/822-2787
201/822-2826

Photographic collections of the United Methodist Church.

341. The Methodist Museum
Arthur J. Moore
Box 407
St. Simons Island, GA 31522
912/638-4050

John and Charles Wesley memorabilia, letters, land grants. History of the Methodist Church.

342. Upper Room Chapel Museum
P.O. Box 189
Nashville, TN 37202
615/340-7207

Museum established by publishers of popular devotional booklets includes art objects having religious significance. Governed by the United Methodist Church.

343. Lovely Lane Museum
United Methodist Historical Society
2200 St. Paul Street
Baltimore, MD 21218
301/889-4458

Artifacts, ephemera, photographs, postcards, prints and slides relating to Methodism and the United Brethren.

344. Archives and Special Collections
Roy O. West Library
Depauw University
Greencastle, IN 46135
317/658-4500

Artifacts, ephemera, photographs, postcards, prints and slides relating to United Methodism in Indiana.

(I) Pentecostals, Charismatics

345. Du Plessis Center for Christian Spirituality
Fuller Theological Seminary
Box K
Pasadena, CA 91182
818/584-5308

Ephemera and photographs relating to the pentecostal and charismatic movements.

346. Assemblies of God Archives
1445 Boonville Avenue
Springfield, MO 65802
417/862-2781 ext. 4400

Artifacts, ephemera, photographs, postcards, slides, videotapes and films relating to the Assembly of God Church and the pentecostal movement.

347. International Church of the Foursquare Gospel
1100 Glendale Boulevard
Los Angeles, CA 90026

Items relating to the Church of the Foursquare Gospel and Aimee Semple McPherson.

348. Pentecostal Holiness Church Archives
P.O. Box 12609
Oklahoma City, OK 73157
405/787-7110

(J) Presbyterians, Reformed

349. Presbyterian Historical Society
425 Lombard Street
Philadelphia, PA 19147
215/627-1852

Oil portraits; communion tokens; silver; pewter; pictures; maps; manuscripts; early Bibles; archives; numismatics.

350. Evangelical & Reformed Historical Society
Lancaster Theological Seminary
555 W. James Street
Lancaster, PA 17603
717/393-0654

Photographs, postcards, prints and slides relating to the United Church of Christ, formerly the German Reformed and Evangelical Reformed Churches.

351. The Historical Foundation of the Presbyterian & Reformed Churches
Box 847
Montreat, NC 28757
704/669-7061

Artifacts, ephemera, photographs, prints and slides relating to the Presbyterian Church, U.S., the Reformed Church in America, and their missions.

352. Presbyterian Church in America Historical Archives
12330 Conway Road
St. Louis, MO 63141
314/469-9077

Artifacts, ephemera, photographs, prints and slides relating to the Presbyterian Church in America and its antecedents, and the conservative Presbyterian and Reformed movement.

353. Historical Society of the Reformed Church in America
21 Seminary Place
New Brunswick, NJ 08901
201/246-1779

Photographic collection of the Reformed Church in America.

(K) Restorationists

354. Disciples of Christ Historical Society
1101 19th Avenue, South
Nashville, TN 37212
615/327-1444

Artifacts, ephemera, photographs, prints, slides, videotapes and films relating to the religious heritage, backgrounds, origins, development and general history of the Disciples of Christ, Christian Churches, Churches of Christ, and related groups of the Campbell-Stone restorationist movement.

(L) General Collections

355. Biblical Arts Center
P.O. Box 12727
Dallas, TX 75225
214/691-4661

16th century to present American sculpture, paintings and drawings pertaining to the Bible.

356. American Antiquarian Society
Department of Graphic Arts
185 Salisbury Street
Worcester, MA 01609
508/755-5221

Black & white original and copy photographs, daguerreotypes, stereograms, postcards, ephemera, architectural drawings, illustrated maps, illustrated books and prints on the history of the United States, including oil paintings of clergymen. Colonial times to 1876.

357. Dr. J. Gordon Melton
Institute for the Study of American Religions
P.O. Box 90709
Santa Barbara, CA 91390-0709

Materials on non-conventional religions.

358. Time-Life Picture Agency
Time-Life Building
1271 Avenue of the Americas
New York, NY 10020
212/556-4800

Black and white original and copy photographs, color transparencies of all subjects and people photographed for Time, Life, Fortune, Time-Life Books, personalities, religion.

359. United Press International
Compix Division
220 East 42nd Street
New York, NY 10017
212/682-0400

Black and white original and copy photos, color photo prints, color transparencies, glass negatives, unprinted film negatives, illustrated maps and art reproduction on world-wide news features including religion.

360. Wide World Photos, Inc.
50 Rockefeller Plaza
New York, NY 10020
212/262-6300

Black and white original photos, unprinted film negatives and color transparencies on news events, personalities, human interest (all Associated Press material).

361. New York Public Library
Prints Division
Fifth Avenue and 42nd Street
New York, NY 10018
212/790-6208

Fine prints, original cartoons, illustrated books and clippings on all subjects, including religion.

362. Religious News Service
P.O. Box 1015
Radio City Station
New York, NY 10101
212/315-0870

Photographs, drawings and illustrative works of religious news and personalities, major churches and religions of the world, social issues, holiday and seasonal graphics, and human interest.

363. Granger Collection
1841 Broadway
New York, NY 10023
212/586-0971

Portraits of famous people, American history. Includes religious subjects.

364. Library of Congress
Prints and Photographs Division

Annex Building Room A 1051
Washington, DC 20540
202/426-6394
202/426-6395

Fine prints, historical prints, posters, drawings and photographs of 19th-20th century religious subjects.

365. Library of Congress
Rare Book Division
Main Building, Room 256
Washington, DC 20540
202/287-5434

Early American pictorial material is represented extensively in the more than 40,000 items in the broadside and American imprint collections.

366. Smithsonian Institution
National Portrait Gallery
F Street at 8th, NW
Washington, DC 20560
202/357-2688

Permanent portrait collection of persons who have made significant contributions to the history of the United States. Study collection of photographs of portraits, portrait engravings and lithographs, chiefly from the 19th century. Includes religious notables.

367. New York Historical Society
170 Central Park West
New York, NY 10024
212/873-3400

Ephemera, photographs, postcards, prints and certificates relating to early American history, including: portraits of clergymen; views of church buildings; illustrations of revivals and camp meetings; specializing in New York state.

368. The Center For Western Studies
Augustana College
P.O. Box 727
Sioux Falls, SD 57197
605/336-4007

Artifacts, photographs and prints relating to the history of the Episcopal Church, the United Church of Christ, and the American Lutheran Church, especially in South Dakota.

369. New York Public Library
Picture Collection
Fifth Avenue & 42nd Street

New York, NY 10018
212/790-6101

Prints from 15th-20th century, sheet music, photographs, paintings, maps and portraits. Includes religious materials.

370. Underwood and Underwood News Photos, Inc.
3 West 46th Street
New York, NY 10036
212/586-5910

Black and white original photos, glass negatives, unprinted film negatives and stereograms on U.S. and world social and political history. Some religion.

371. Historical Pictures Service
Suite 320
Humboldt Building
2753 West North Avenue
Chicago, IL 60647
312/486-6575

Black and white original and copy photographs, glass negatives, daguerreotypes, stereograms, prints, posters, drawings, cartoons and caricatures, postcards, illustrated maps, art reproductions, clippings and tear sheets, and illustrated books on U.S. cultural history and social life. Includes religious materials.

372. Lake County Museum
Curt Teich Postcard Collection
Lakewood Forest Preserve
Wauconda, IL 60084
708/526-8638

Publications and pictoral archives of the Curt Teich Postcard Collection. Includes ephemera, photographs and postcards of church interiors and exteriors, evangelists, religious education, church camps and retreats, religious societies, and religious music. 1898-1974.

373. Huntington College
Richlyn Library
Huntington, IN 46750
219/356-6000

Artifacts, ephemera, photographs, postcards, prints and slides relating to the Church of the United Brethren in Christ, the International Society of Christian Endeavor, and the National Association of Evangelicals.

374. National Association of Evangelicals
P.O. Box 28
450 E. Gundersen

Wheaton, IL 60189
708/665-0500 ext. 104

Photographs depicting current news events of interest or relating to evangelicals, and the history of the association since 1942.

375. Boston Public Library
Print Department
666 Boylston Street
Boston, MA 02117
617/536-5400

Ephemera, photographs, postcards, prints, slides, caricatures, illustrated music sheets and illustrated maps on American people, history and views (1700-1900s). Includes religious subjects.

376. Massachusetts Historical Society
1154 Boylston Street
Boston, MA 02215
617/536-1608

Black and white copy photos, clippings, postcards and old prints on the history of Massachusetts and New England; portraits; historical sites. Colonial period - present. Includes religious subjects.

377. U.S. Army Chaplain Museum
USACHCS-ATSC-SEC-M
Watters Hall, Building 1207
Fort Monmouth, NJ 07703-5000
201/532-5809

Artifacts, ephemera and photographs relating to the U.S. Army Chaplaincy and depicting the religious military heritage of our country.

378. Bettmann Archives
136 E. 57th Street
New York, NY 10022
212/758-0362

UPI news photos collection, including religious events and personages.

(M) Revivalism and Foreign Missions

379. Northfield/Mt. Hermon Schools
Northfield, MA 01360
413/498-5311

Artifacts, ephemera, photographs, postcards and slides relating to the Northfield Summer Conferences founded by D.L. Moody and involving international evangelists from the 1880s-1940s, the founding of the Student Volunteer Movement on the Northfield Campus, D.L. Moody's birthplace, memorabilia, furniture and photographs.

380. Russ Busby
World Wide Pictures
2520 W. Olive
Burbank, CA 91505
818/843-1300
818/845-6953

Photographs relating to the Billy Graham Evangelistic Association, Christianity and other religions around the world, and church buildings around the world.

381. Day Missions Library
Yale Divinity School
409 Prospect Street
New Haven, CT 06510
203/436-5301

Photographs of early 20th century organizations: Student Volunteer Movement for Foreign Missions; World Student Christian Federation; YMCA, Student Division.

382. Roselawn Museum
P.O. Box 128
Cartersville, GA 30120
404/386-1081

Historic house c. 1880, Victorian mansion, former house of evangelist Samuel Porter Jones; furniture; documents; clothing & costumes; silver memorabilia belonging to Jones.

383. Billy Graham Center Archives & Museum
500 E. College Avenue
Wheaton, IL 60187
708/260-5909
708/260-5910

Artifacts, ephemera, photographs, postcards, prints, slides, video tapes and film relating to 18th - 20th century evangelism, revivalism and missions.

384. Grace Theological Seminary & College
200 Seminary Drive
Winona Lake, IN 46590
219/372-5177

Artifacts, ephemera, photographs, postcards and slides dealing with Billy Sunday, Winona Lake Assembly, Winona Lake Christian Assembly, Winona Lake Bible Conference, and the Grace Brethren denomination.

385. American Bible Society
1865 Broadway
New York, NY 10023
212/581-7400 ext. 495

Ephemera, photographs and slides relating to the translation work of the society and its history of transmission of the Bible, historic and unusual scriptures in 1,785 languages from pre-15th century to the present.

386. Summer Institute of Linguistics, Inc.
Route 4, Box 145
Waxhaws, NC 28173
704/843-3168

Photographs, slides and videotapes of Wycliffe Bible Translators.

387. Oberlin College
Archives/Art Library
Oberlin, OH 44074
216/774-1221 ext. 7295, 3117

Items relating to evangelist Charles G. Finney.

388. J. S. Mack Library
Bob Jones University
Greenville, SC 29614
(803) 242-5100 ext. 6000

Ephemera and published materials related to separatist fundamentalism and evangelists Bob Jones, Sr. and Bob Jones, Jr.

(N) Religion in the American South

389. Center for the Study of Southern Culture
The University of Mississippi
University, MS 38677
601/232-5993

Artifacts, ephemera, photographs, postcards, slides, and film documenting Southern popular culture. Many items relating to Southern religion.

390. Harris Swift Museum of Religious and Ceremonial Arts and Library of Rare Books
526 Vine Street
Chattanooga, TN 37403
615/265-3491

Objects of art in silver, ivory, wood, brass and pewter; religious and ceremonial arts; objects pertaining to all religions; rare books.

391. Smithsonian Institution
National Museum of History
14th & Constitution Avenue NW
Washington, DC 20560
202/381-5164

Eleanor Dickinson's collection of artifacts on American religious culture in the South.

SECTION II: HISTORY AND CHARACTER

Mark A. Noll

7. General
8. Denominations and Movements
9. Revival Matrix, 1730-1865
10. The Challenges of Modernity, 1865-1915
11. Conflict, Alienation and Regrouping, 1920-1945
12. Resurgence, 1945-1988

CHAPTER 7
GENERAL

(A) Texts and Surveys in American Religion

Given the prevalence of evangelical Protestantism in American history and its domination for much of the nineteenth century, most surveys of American religious history contain a great deal about the varieties of evangelical experience. Occasionally, evangelical features of the past escape authors who have themselves no use for evangelicals, just as evangelicals return the compliment for groups they disdain. Standards of scholarship for the writing of religious history are now so high, however, that much less blatant partisanship, whether from evangelicals or those in other traditions, is being published now than in earlier decades. The works that follow represent only some of the more notable efforts to chart broad themes in, or the whole of, America's religious history.

392. Ahlstrom, Sydney E. A Religious History of the American People. New Haven, CT: Yale University Press, 1972.

"Ahlstrom" remains the most comprehensive, and in many ways the most satisfying, one-volume history of Christianity in America. Although Ahlstrom's own sympathies ran to romantic and transcendental religion, his text provides a solid background for evangelical themes as well.

393. Askew, Thomas A. and Peter W. Spellman. The Churches and the American Experience: Ideals and Institutions. Grand Rapids: Baker, 1984.

This short text excels at integrating the story of evangelicals, including blacks, into the main narrative of American religious history.

394. Baird, Robert. Religion in the United States of America. Glasgow and Edinburgh: Blackie and Sons, 1844.

Baird, an outward-looking Presbyterian, wrote the first general survey of Christianity in America. The book still reads very well. It contains much information on the main Protestant denominations, most of which were evangelical throughout the nineteenth century, as well as on Catholics and more obscure groups. And it offers fruitful reflections on the way the

American environment shaped the development of the churches in this continent.

395. Dolan, Jay. Catholic Revivalism: The American Experience, 1830-1900. Notre Dame, IN: University of Notre Dame Press, 1978.

Dolan, who heads the Cushwa Center for American Catholicism at Notre Dame, shows how Catholic preachers and members of religious orders adopted popular practices more often associated with Protestant revivalists to encourage a Catholic community that in the nineteenth century was still largely made up of immigrants.

396. Fairbank, John K., ed. The Missionary Enterprise in China and America. Cambridge, MA: Harvard University Press, 1974.

The American missionary presence in China was extensive and long-lasting. What that presence meant for the Chinese, and even more for American sending groups, is the subject of the essays in this magisterial collection.

397. Farina, John. Sources of American Spirituality. Mahwah, NJ: Paulist Press.

This series, which by 1989 had reached nearly twenty volumes, presents well-introduced texts of important spiritual writing from American history. Among books already published in the series are these presenting the work of evangelical figures: Henry Alline (ed. George A. Rawlyk), Charles Hodge (ed. Mark A. Noll), and Phoebe Palmer (ed. Thomas C. Oden).

398. Gaustad, Edwin S., ed. A Documentary History of Religion in America. 2 vols. Grand Rapids: Eerdmans, 1982, 1983.

Gaustad's two volumes of carefully chosen documents include many items relevant to evangelical history. In contrast to the earlier (but also excellent) collection by Smith, Handy and Loetscher (see below), Gaustad's selections focus more on the day-to-day life of ordinary believers.

399. Gaustad, Edwin S. Historical Atlas of Religion in America. Rev. ed. New York: Harper & Row, 1976.

With its maps and extensive charts, especially of denominational families, this is a most helpful resource for plotting the growth and spread of the Christian faith in America.

400. Handy, Robert T. A History of the Churches in the United States and Canada. New York: Oxford University Press, 1977.

Handy, who is now retired after long service as a church historian at Union Seminary in New York, provides here a judicious, balanced, and fact-filled history. Its greatest virtue is its inclusion of significant sections on Canada's church history, a history about which residents of the United States are (in general) scandalously ignorant.

401. Hatch, Nathan O. and Mark A. Noll, eds. The Bible in America: Essays in Cultural History. New York: Oxford University Press, 1982.

Eight authors describe the way the Bible has been important as a cultural force in American life. Several of the essays in this book are mentioned elsewhere in this bibliography. Those that are not include "Word and Order in Colonial New England" (Harry Stout); "The Image of the United States as a Biblical Nation, 1776-1865" (Mark Noll); "Sola Scriptura and Novus Ordo Seclorum" (Nathan Hatch); and "The Bible in Twentieth-Century Protestantism: A Preliminary Taxonomy" (Richard Mouw).

402. Holifield, E. Brooks. A History of Pastoral Care in America: From Salvation to Self-Realization. Nashville: Abingdon, 1983.

This study offers information on major trends in pastoral care, as well as cautious comment on the dangers of abandoning God-focused for human-centered coordinates in dealing with troubled hearts.

403. Hudson, Winthrop S. American Protestantism. Chicago: University of Chicago Press, 1961.

Hudson's volume is a standard, and deservedly so. It is especially valuable in its account of how Protestant denominations adapted European, and largely evangelical, convictions to American notions of freedom and the separation of church and state.

404. Hudson, Winthrop S. Religion in America. 4th ed. New York: Macmillan, 1987.

After Ahlstrom's Religious History of the American People, this is one of the very best texts. And since it is quite a bit shorter than Ahlstrom (its text is about as long as the Eerdmans Handbook), it is a good place to begin the study of American church history.

405. Hughes, Richard T., ed. The American Quest for the Primitive Church. Urbana: University of Illinois Press, 1988.

This well-edited anthology looks at how the desire to restore Christian life and practice to the standards of the New Testament has influenced many groups of American believers, including Puritans, Methodists, Baptists, restorationists and fundamentalists.

406. Hutchison, William. Errand Into the World: American Protestant Thought and Foreign Missions. Chicago: University of Chicago Press, 1987.

Hutchison, who writes with the questions of Protestant liberals uppermost in his mind, nonetheless offers a satisfying general history of how American religious convictions (most often evangelical of some sort) fueled and interpreted the American missionary movement.

407. Lotz, David W., Donald W. Shriver, Jr. and John F. Wilson, eds. Altered Landscapes, Christianity in America: Essays in Honor of Robert T. Handy. Grand Rapids: Eerdmans, 1989.

This very useful collection of essays on the past half century is filled with essays by experts on different aspects of its subjects. Among the chapters most relevant to evangelical history are those by George Marsden ("Unity and Diversity in the Evangelical Resurgence"), Albert Raboteau ("The Black Church: Continuity within Change"), William Hutchison (" Americans in World Mission: Revision and Realignment") and John F. Wilson ("Religion at the Core of American Culture"). The scholar honored through this book has also contributed numerous learned evaluations of religion in America, including evangelicals.

408. Lundin, Roger and Mark Noll, eds. Voices from the Heart: Four Centuries of American Piety. Grand Rapids: Eerdmans, 1987.

The fifty-five selections in this book range widely, from the colonial period to the 1980s, in the effort to illustrate the diversity of piety in American experience. Major evangelical figures like Jonathan Edwards, Charles Finney, Catherine Marshall, and Elisabeth Eliot are included.

McLoughlin, William G. Revivals, Awakenings and Social Reform: An Essay in Religion and Social Change in America, 1607-1977. Chicago: University of Chicago Press, 1978.
(see 1386)

409. Marty, Martin E. "The American Religious History Canon." Social Research 53 (Autumn 1986): 513-528.

Marty asked twenty-nine students of American religious history to select the most important of recent books "that have had a determining influence on the field of American religion." Far in front were Sydney Ahlstrom's Religious History of the American People and George Marsden's Fundamentalism and American Culture. Other oft-mentioned titles relevant to evangelical history were Raboteau's Slave Religion, Mathews' Religion in the Old South, Dolan's Catholic Revivalism, Marty's Protestantism in the United States, Hutchison's Modernist Impulse, and May's Enlightenment in America, all of which are listed separately in this bibliography.

410. Marty, Martin E. A Nation of Behavers. Chicago: University of Chicago Press, 1976.

Marty, who has read everything ever written on the history of religion in America, here argues that the crucial divisions in American religion are behavioral. Two of his six clusters of "behavers," the "Evangelical-Fundamentalist" and the "Pentecostal-Charismatic," are descendants of the nineteenth-century evangelical hegemony. Two others,

"Ethnic Religion" and "Civil Religion," also share broadly in the history of evangelicalism.

411. Marty, Martin E. Pilgrims in their Own Land: 500 Years of Religion in America. Boston: Little, Brown, 1984.

This readable narrative often focuses on out-of-the-way and neglected religious groups or individuals, but also contains a full account of evangelical strands within American history.

412. Marty, Martin E. Protestantism in the United States: Righteous Empire. 2nd ed. New York: Charles Scribner's Sons, 1986.

With Hudson's American Protestantism, this is the best general history of its subject. The book offers particular insight into the great forces unleashed upon the world (for good and for ill) by nineteenth-century evangelical energies.

413. Mead, Sidney E. The Lively Experiment: The Shaping of Christianity in America. New York: Harper & Row, 1963.

Mead's essays focus perceptively on the tensions in American history between revivalistic evangelicalism (which regularly encourages separatism and dogmatic particularism) and the civil religion of the Enlightenment (which seeks to promote unity and shared national purpose).

414. Miller, William Lee. The First Liberty: Religion and the American Republic. New York: Knopf, 1986.

This book arises out of the controversies of the 1970s and 1980s over the role of religion in American public life. Miller concentrates on Roger Williams and James Madison to make his case for the need to separate scrupulously religious and political spheres.

415. Moore, R. Laurence. Religious Outsiders and the Making of Americans. New York: Oxford University Press, 1986.

Moore argues provocatively that contemporary observers have lost sight of the diversity, fragmentation, and near chaos of American religious life. His "outsiders," whom Moore sees as more important than a staid tradition of mainline Protestantism, include premillennialists, fundamentalists, and black Christians.

416. Noll, Mark A. One Nation Under God? Christian Faith and Political Action in America. San Francisco: Harper & Row, 1988.

American Christians, according to this book, have followed "revivalistic" and "Reformed" (as opposed to Lutheran, Catholic, or Anabaptist) strategies in their approach to politics. The results have been productive of much good (like the ending of slavery), but also of considerable damage (as when momentary political goals are confused with the universal truths of Christianity).

417. Noll, Mark A., ed. Religion and American Politics: From the Colonial Period to the 1980s. New York: Oxford University Press, 1989.

Seventeen essays chart connections between religious and political life, with evangelicals often at center stage. Chapters include Ruth Bloch on the Revolutionary era, Daniel Walker Howe on evangelicals and Whigs in the antebellum period, David Wills on blacks, and George Marsden on the place of evangelicals in the persistent search for religious-political consensus.

418. Numbers, Ronald L. and Darrel W. Amundsen, eds. Caring and Curing: Health and Medicine in the Western Religious Traditions. New York: Macmillan, 1986.

Several of the essays in this outstanding book describe the attitudes of American evangelical groups (e.g., Lutherans, Reformed, Anabaptists, Baptists, Methodists, Adventists, Disciples, fundamentalists, pentecostalists) to issues of health, medical care, sexuality, and related matters.

419. Pierard, Richard V. and Robert D. Linder. Civil Religion and the Presidency. Grand Rapids: Zondervan, 1988.

Separate chapters on some of America's best-known presidents (including Washington, Lincoln, Wilson, Eisenhower, Nixon, Carter, and Reagan) assess the way presidents have used religious (including evangelical) themes to define, apply, or exploit a civil faith in the discharge of their official duties.

420. Smith, Hilrie S., Robert T. Handy and Lefferts Loetscher. American Christianity: An Historical Interpretation With Representative Documents. 2 vols. New York: Scribner's, 1960.

For a generation, this was the standard collection of documents for American church history. Now somewhat out of fashion because of its concentration on the pronouncements and actions of white male denominational leaders, the two volumes are still immensely useful (and also better balanced than much work from the avant garde).

421. Turner, James. Without God, Without Creed: The Origins of Unbelief in America. Baltimore: Johns Hopkins University Press, 1985.

Turner's well written treatise argues that unbelief came primarily from the choices of believers. The decision to recast the faith in scientific and moralistic terms, in order to enhance its acceptability in a culture swooning after science and fixated on questions of morality, created, according to the author, a utilitarian faith that opened the way to agnosticism.

422. Wells, David F., Nathan O. Hatch, George M. Marsden, Mark A. Noll and John D. Woodbridge. Eerdmans Handbook to the History of Christianity in America. Grand Rapids: Eerdmans, 1983.

Extensive use of charts, time-lines, and pictures add an extra dimension to this volume. Over sixty contributors add short essays to the narratives provided by the authors, who are evangelicals but who write generally about the history of Christianity in America.

423. Wells, Ronald A., ed. The Wars of America: Christian Views. Grand Rapids: Eerdmans, 1981.

Evangelicals have been an active presence in all of the United States' armed conflicts from the Revolution to Vietnam. One essay examines the Christian factor in each of America's major wars in this carefully conceived and well introduced book.

(B) General or Thematic Studies on Evangelicals

The 1970s and 1980s witnessed a flourishing of history-writing on evangelicals, even as it saw a resurgence of evangelical and fundamentalist political activism. Was history following " real life," or vice versa? In some cases, scholars who had been at work in splendid isolation on fundamentalist or evangelical topics since as early as the 1950s now published their material to totally unexpected attention. In other cases, enterprising scholars and journalists leapt speedily on the bandwagon of interest. Whatever the motives, the result was an outpouring of books and articles--many of them sterling, most of them useful in one way or another--on evangelical history. Many of the books treating recent aspects of that history are mentioned in Chapter 12. This section lists writings that treat broader aspects of evangelical history, or of themes closely related to evangelicals.

424. Abraham, William J. The Coming Great Revival: Recovering the Full Evangelical Tradition. San Francisco: Harper & Row, 1984.

Abraham, an Irish Methodist who has taught at Seattle Pacific College and Southern Methodist University, suggests that if evangelicals could recapture the insights of John Wesley, they could move beyond the pettiness, fascination with separatism, and arid dogmatism that he sees as bedeviling the movement.

425. Barr, James. Fundamentalism. Philadelphia: Westminster, 1978.

Barr, a distinguished professor of Old Testament who as a student took part in the activities of British InterVarsity, here levels both barrels at what he considers the imbecilities of evangelical biblical scholarship. By "fundamentalists" Barr means British "conservative evangelicals" from the Church of England, the Plymouth Brethren, and other groups. His shotgun blasts inevitably hit a target or two, but a rifle would have been better.

426. Bebbington, David. Evangelicalism in Modern Britain: A History from the 1730s to the 1980s. London: Unwin Hyman, 1989.

This comprehensive survey draws upon extensive reading in sources and a comprehensive grasp of secondary literature. Among many other items of interest to those who study American evangelicals are informative accounts of how British evangelicals pioneered voluntary organizations for missionary service and moral reform and how they developed networks of summer meetings for spiritual renewal, devices that would also have a wide use on this side of the Atlantic.

Boylan, Anne M. Sunday School: The Formation of an American Institution, 1790-1880. New Haven, CT: Yale University Press, 1988. (see 1337)

427. Bradley, Ian. The Call to Seriousness: The Evangelical Impact on the Victorians. New York: MacMillan, 1976.

Britain's evangelicals in the Victorian period shared many of the religious and cultural aspirations of their counterparts across the Atlantic, even as they often pointed the way to their American cousins in missions and the organization of voluntary societies. This book has the story.

428. Cairns, Earle E. An Endless Line of Splendor: Revivals and their Leaders from the Great Awakening to the Present. Wheaton, IL: Tyndale, 1986.

In contrast to McLoughlin's Revivals, Awakenings and Social Reform, Cairns here keeps alive the providential approach to revivals, which sees them first and foremost as outpourings of God's spirit. An extra feature is the author's examination of awakenings overseas that have followed the American evangelical pattern.

429. Carpenter, Joel A. and Wilbert Shenk, eds. Earthen Vessels: American Evangelicals and Foreign Missions, 1880-1980. Grand Rapids: Eerdmans, 1990.

Missionary service has long been an ideal among evangelicals. This collection gathers recent and often innovative research to suggest the many dimensions of evangelical missionary outreach, including what the missionary ideal has meant for evangelical churches in the United States.

430. Dayton, Donald W. Discovering an Evangelical Heritage. Peabody,MA: Hendrickson, 1988; orig., 1976.

Dayton's stimulating book, which grew out of essays that originally appeared in Sojourners, takes dead aim at stereotypes. Evangelicals should not be regarded as descendants simply of the Presbyterians, as social conservatives, or as theological dogmatists. Rather a prominent part, if not the prominent part, of evangelical history is a Wesleyan tradition of social activism that cares much more about service and personal holiness than doctrinal precision. This book marked a first effort by Dayton to open the historiography of evangelicalism beyond traditional reliance upon Reformed and dogmatic perspectives.

431. Dayton, Donald W. and Robert K. Johnston, eds. Varieties of American Evangelicalism. Knoxville: University of Tennessee Press, 1990.

The essays in this book examine how the members of individual Protestant traditions have responded to the notion of a pan-evangelicalism linking various denomination families. The traditions include Anabaptism, Adventism, the Holiness Movement, black religion, restorationism, premillennialism, Reformed orthodoxy, Baptists, fundamentalism, pietism and Lutheran orthodoxy.

432. Ellingsen, Mark. The Evangelical Movement: Growth, Impact, Controversy, Dialog. Minneapolis: Augsburg, 1988.

What does evangelicalism look like to a sympathetic Lutheran? The answer is this book, in which Ellingsen provides a competent history of evangelicals and a bracing examination of key evangelical principles, with the larger purpose of bringing American evangelicals into ecumenical dialog with Lutherans (the original European "evangelicals"), Catholics, and mainline Protestants.

433. "Evangelicalism." dialog: A Journal of Theology 24 (Summer 1985): 169-205.

This special issue of a Lutheran theological journal offered several stimulating essays on its themes, including essays by Robert Jenson on Jonathan Edwards and by Erling Jorstad, Harold O. J. Brown, John E. Benson, and Mark Ellingsen on aspects of twentieth-century evangelicalism.

434. Hale, Frederick. Trans-Atlantic Conservative Protestantism in the Evangelical Free and Mission Covenant Traditions. New York: Arno, 1979.

Although not as influential as the British-American links studied by Richard Carwardine, in Transatlantic Revivalism (see 571), Scandinavian-American pietism, here expertly surveyed, is a significant tributary to the evangelical stream.

435. Handy, Robert T. A Christian America: Protestant Hopes and Historical Realities. 2nd ed. New York: Oxford University Press, 1984.

One of the key notions of America's culture-shapers from the Puritans to the late nineteenth century was that God had selected this country for special purposes in the world. Handy's is the most comprehensive treatment of how and why that conviction developed.

436. Hardman, Keith J. The Spiritual Awakeners: American Revivalists from Solomon Stoddard to D. L. Moody. Chicago: Moody Press, 1983.

Hardman, a historian at Ursinus College with a specialty in Charles G. Finney, has mined archives and scoured libraries to present this history. Its strength is the effort to link spiritual and objective historical accounts of what he describes.

437. Hatch, Nathan O. "Evangelicalism as a Democratic Movement." In Evangelicalism and Modern America, ed. George Marsden. Grand Rapids: Eerdmans, 1984.

Hatch traces evangelicalism's propensity for a market-driven, personality-centered, populist-oriented style back to the American Revolution. And he shows why this democratic drive still dominates evangelical life in the age of televangelists as much as it did in the era of circuit-riding preachers.

438. Jester, Arthur M., ed. "The Evangelicals." Union Seminary Quarterly Review 32 (Winter 1977): 67-116.

One year after Newsweek, under the inspiration of Jimmy Carter, proclaimed 1976 "the year of the evangelical," Union Seminary in New York assembled a team of four scholars to explain the movement to its cultured despisers. The result was thought-provoking articles on why recent evangelicals had become socially conservative (Donald Dayton), on the way a literal hermeneutic preserved evangelical boundaries (Gerald Sheppard), on how evangelicals both promoted and undercut the status of women (Virginia Mollenkott), and on how evangelical Protestantism (often inadvertently) informed the ethical reflections of black Bible believers (James Washington).

439. Kantzer, Kenneth S., ed. Evangelical Roots: A Tribute to Wilbur Smith. Nashville: Nelson, 1978.

Wilbur Smith was a bibliophile who taught at Moody Bible Institute, Fuller Theological Seminary, and Trinity Evangelical Divinity School. The diversity of essays in this volume (which include recent history, biblical inerrancy and interpretation, missions, and preaching) and of essayists (Billy Graham, Harld Ockenga, J. I. Packer, John Stott, and many more) were fitting tributes to the range of Smith's own concerns.

440. Lovelace, Richard. Dynamics of Spiritual Life. Downers Grove, IL: InterVarsity Press, 1979.

Lovelace uses the history of evangelicalism, especially the multi-faceted ministry of Jonathan Edwards, as a guide for contemporary religious renewal. This book is the outstanding example in recent decades of evangelical history put to use for spiritual development.

441. Marsden, George, ed. Evangelicalism and Modern America. Grand Rapids: Eerdmans, 1984.

Most important of the essays in this volume is the editor's introduction, which seeks to untangle the knotty question of definition by arguing for different levels for the word "evangelical." The essays of this book concern the self-conscious network of individuals who use the term about themselves; they are those who make up "the evangelical denomination." Other essays include studies of evangelical publishing networks, evangelicals in relationship to fundamentalists, evangelical women, and evangelical participation in the New Religious Right.

442. McLoughlin, William G., ed. The American Evangelicals, 1800-1900: An Anthology. New York: Harper Torchbooks, 1968.

This excellent anthology includes writings to illustrate the range of personalities (e.g., Lyman Beecher, Charles G. Finney, Dwight L. Moody) and themes ("The Battle Hymn of the Republic," "Personal Consecration," "Our Country: Its Possible Future and Present Crisis") of nineteenth-century evangelical life.

McLoughlin, William G. Modern Revivalism: Charles Grandison Finney to Billy Graham. New York: Ronald Press, 1959.
(see 1385)

443. Moberg, David O. Inasmuch: Christian Social Responsibility in the Twentieth Century. Grand Rapids: Eerdmans, 1965.

444. Moberg, David O. The Great Reversal: Evangelism Versus Social Concern. Philadelphia: J. B. Lippincott, 1972.

Moberg, a sociologist who has taught at Bethel College and Marquette University, is a pioneering sociologist among evangelicals. These books chart the evolution of evangelicals from active social engagement to passive withdrawal and also appeal for a discriminating re-engagement.

445. Murch, James D. Cooperation Without Compromise: A History of the National Association of Evangelicals. Grand Rapids: Eerdmans, 1956.

The National Association of Evangelicals came into existence in 1942 as an alternative to the Federal (later National) Council of Churches. This early, celebratory history chronicles its organization and early activities.

446. Murphy, Cullen. "Protestantism and the Evangelicals." Wilson Quarterly 5 (Autumn 1981): 105-116.

Murphy, drawing on the insights of the Johns Hopkins historian Timothy L. Smith, provides a "map" for the various sub-groups within evangelicalism and their relationship to other Protestant traditions.

447. Nash, Ronald H. Evangelicals in America: Who They Are, What They Believe. Nashville: Abingdon, 1987.

This book, aimed at a popular audience, defines evangelicals according to beliefs and customary practices. In this respect, it shares more with the theological tradition of Ramm's Evangelical Heritage than with the historical focus of Dayton's Discovering an Evangelical Heritage or Marsden's Evangelicalism and Modern America.

448. Nash, Ronald H. The New Evangelicalism. Grand Rapids: Zondervan, 1963.

With this volume Nash provided one of the first comprehensive accounts of the group of former fundamentalists (e.g., E. J. Carnell, Carl F. H. Henry, Harold Ockenga) who took the name "evangelical" for themselves in the effort to maintain traditions of theological orthodoxy while setting aside the cultural blinders of the tradition in which they had been reared.

449. Neuhaus, Richard John and Michael Cromartie, eds. Piety and Politics: Evangelicals and Fundamentalists Confront the World. Washington, DC: Ethics and Public Policy Center, 1987.

The diverse essays that Neuhaus and Cromartie assembled treat the recent emergence of evangelicals and fundamentalists in the political arena. A few of the pieces reflect back on the cyclical history of evangelical involvement and non-involvement in politics. That the editors make room for convinced proponents, sympathetic nit-pickers, and flat out opponents provides for an entertaining, as well as instructive book.

450. Noll, Mark A., Nathan O. Hatch and George M. Marsden. The Search for Christian America. Rev. ed. Colorado Springs: Helmers and Howard, 1989; orig., 1983.

The authors, who are themselves evangelicals, write here to convince fellow-evangelicals that neither historical scholarship nor theological reasoning justify the notion that America enjoys a special relationship with God.

451. Ramm, Bernard. The Evangelical Heritage. Waco, TX: Word Books, 1973.

Ramm defines "evangelicalism" as the faith of the Protestant Reformation and then traces its history to the American present. As might be expected from a good theologian, the best sections concern the internal life of doctrine, the weakest treat developments related to the special circumstances of American history.

452. Rawlyk, G. A. Ravished by the Spirit: Religious Revivals, Baptists, and Henry Alline. Kingston and Montreal, Canada: McGill-Queen's University Press, 1984.

Until recently there was little literature on Canadian evangelicals. Rawlyk, a historian at Queen's University, is a leader in remedying that situation. This book draws upon the example of Henry Alline, a revivalist in Nova Scotia in the 1770s and 1780s, to illuminate Canadian Baptist history and to help contemporary Baptists recover at least some aspects of their heritage.

453. Shelley, Bruce. Evangelicalism in America. Grand Rapids: Eerdmans, 1967.

Shelley's history was written to observe the twenty-fifth anniversary of the National Association of Evangelicals. It provides a sketch of Puritan, revivalistic, and voluntaristic themes in evangelical history and a longer account of the NAE, its largely white and northern constituency, and its general association with the work of Billy Graham.

454. Smith, Timothy L. "The Evangelical Kaleidoscope and the Call to Christian Unity." Christian Scholar's Review 15 (1986): 125-140.

This essay provides a full statement of Smith's categorization of evangelical families that was earlier adumbrated in Murphy's "Protestantism and Evangelicalism." The larger point to which Smith directs his historical survey is the potential among the diverse evangelical strands for unity in faith and for ministry in society.

455. Sweet, Leonard I., ed. The Evangelical Tradition in America. Macon, GA: Mercer University Press, 1984.

The centerpiece of this collection is the editor's bibliographical essay of over 80 pages, in which many of the vital strands of evangelical life from the nineteenth century and before receive succinct, but always provocative, comment. Other essays not mentioned elsewhere in this bibliography treat slavery (Jon Butler), millennialism (Nathan Hatch), Charles G. Finney (Garth Rosell), Indian missions (Henry Bowden), women (Carroll Smith-Rosenberg, Nancy A. Hewitt), and the transition from fundamentalism to evangelicalism (Joel Carpenter).

456. Webber, Robert E. Common Roots: A Call to Evangelical Maturity. Grand Rapids: Zondervan, 1978.

This book contains a helpful classification of the many sub-groupings of evangelicals, but its main concern is to persuade evangelicals that greater understanding and appropriation of the early church would greatly strengthen their movement.

457. Webber, Robert and Donald Bloesch, eds. The Orthodox Evangelicals: Who They Are and What They Are Saying. New York: Thomas Nelson, 1978.

A conference in 1977, organized by evangelicals distressed with aspects of the fundamentalist and evangelical past as well as intrigued by a more Catholic spirituality, led to this book. Since 1977, some of its contributors have returned to more traditional forms of evangelicalism while others have gone on to embrace Episcopalianism, Eastern Orthodoxy, or Roman Catholicism.

458. Weber, Timothy P. Living in the Shadow of the Second Coming: American Premillennialism, 1875-1982. Rev. ed. Chicago: University of Chicago Press, 1987.

Belief in a literal return of Christ to the earth in order to establish the thousand-year kingdom mentioned in Revelation 20 has been a central conviction of American evangelicals since the mid-nineteenth century. This careful book explains both the internal religious structure of that belief and the external effects among those who have held it.

459. Wells, David and John Woodbridge, eds. The Evangelicals. Rev. ed. Grand Rapids: Baker, 1977.

This path breaking assessment includes chapters from those inside the evangelical tradition as well as those writing from outside. Notable essays include assessments by "outsiders" Paul Holmer, Martin Marty, and Sydney Ahlstrom; and by "insiders" George Marsden (on the transition from fundamentalism to evangelicalism), Robert Linder (on the history of evangelical social concern), and William Pannell and William Bentley (on black "Bible-believers").

460. Woodbridge, John D., Mark A. Noll and Nathan O Hatch. The Gospel in America: Themes in the Story of America's Evangelicals. Grand Rapids: Zondervan, 1979.

The authors' "themes" are theological development, the Bible, revival, americanization, schisms, the nation, and social concern.

CHAPTER 8
DENOMINATIONS AND MOVEMENTS

(A) Adventist

Adventists arose in response to the proclamation of the New York farmer-preacher, William Miller (1782-1849), that Jesus would return to the earth on March 21, 1844. The dedicated publicity of colleagues like Joshua V. Himes attracted thousands to Miller's views. After "the disappointment," when Jesus did not physically return, other leaders, like Ellen Gould White (1827-1915), reinterpreted the return as a spiritual event and on that basis defined a new variation of Christianity. It made much of both health reform and the observance of Saturday as the Christian sabbath. From the start, the Advent Christian Church (which did not follow Ellen White) bore the marks of an evangelical denomination. In recent decades, the larger Seventh-day Adventist movement has increasingly emphasized characteristics it shares with other evangelicals.

461. Doan, Ruth Alden. The Miller Heresy, Millennialism, and American Culture. Philadelphia: Temple University Press, 1987.

Doan shows expertly how close the apocalyptic message of William Miller was to the more ordinary messages of nineteenth-century evangelicals. She also argues the interesting thesis that the perceived oddities of Millerism created a backlash away from biblical literalism that paved the way for theological liberalism among American Protestants.

462. Gaustad, Edwin Scott, ed. The Rise of Adventism: Religion and Society in Mid-Nineteenth-Century America. New York: Harper & Row, 1974.

Eleven expert interpreters define the broad contexts in which William Miller proclaimed his message of Christ's advent. Discussions include questions of social reform (Timothy Smith), science and religion (John C. Greene), communitarianism (Robert V. Hine), millennialism (Ernest Sandeen), as well as the results of Miller's work itself (David Arthur, Jonathan Butler).

463. Land, Gary, ed. Adventism in America. Grand Rapids: Eerdmans, 1986.

The seven chapters of this book focus on the Seventh-day Adventists. Historical essays carry the story into the 1980s and include a careful, but objective treatment of Ellen White, whose writings and leaderships institutionalized the movement into a church.

464. Numbers, Ronald and Jonathan Butler, eds. The Disappointed: Millerism and Millennialism in the Nineteenth Century. Bloomington: University of Indiana Press, 1987.

This book, one of the finest collections assembled on a single religious body in America, includes essays by Adventists and non-Adventists, all directed toward the end of situating the work of William Miller in its proper historical context. Several of its studies--like David Arthur on publicist Joshua V. Himes, Ronald and Janet Numbers on accusations that Millerism produced insanity, and David Rowe on a profile of the Millerites--are landmark pieces.

(B) Baptists

Baptists appeared in North America early in the colonial period, but it was not until the First Great Awakening of the 1740s that they began to grow, and not until the Second Great Awakening that they became a major force in the nation's religious life. By the twentieth century, however, Baptists had become the largest Protestant family and the Southern Baptist Convention the largest Protestant denomination. Baptists' emphasis on congregational independence, and the Southern Baptist Convention's isolation (before the Second World War) in the South has meant that connections with other evangelicals have been intermittent. Yet with their stress on the authority of the Bible, the new birth, and the need for personal holiness, the Baptists more than any other group have defined the territory of evangelicalism (and fundamentalism) in America.

465. Baker, Robert A. The Southern Baptist Convention and Its People, 1607-1972. Nashville: Broadman Press, 1974.

This is a solid, authorized history of the largest single denomination in the American evangelical mosaic.

466. Brackney, William Henry. The Baptists. Westport, CT: Greenwood Press, 1988.

This volume follows the format of the new history of denominations series, edited by Henry Warner Bowden, by providing a brief synopsis of Baptist history followed by an extensive biographical dictionary of major leaders in American Baptist history.

Eighmy, John L. Churches in Cultural Captivity: A History of the Social Attitudes of Southern Baptists. Rev. ed. Intro. and epilogue by Samuel S. Hill, Jr. Knoxville: University of Tennessee Press, 1987; orig., 1972.

(See 1078)

467. Garrett, James Leo, Jr., E. Glenn Hinson and James E. Tull. Are Southern Baptists "Evangelicals"? Macon, GA: Mercer University Press, 1983.

Hinson says "no"; Garrett, with qualifications, "yes"; Tull provides context. Of course it all depends on how you define "evangelical." In larger meanings of the term, the vote must go against Hinson. But this is still a stimulating discussion.

468. Leonard, Bill J. "Southern Baptists and Southern Culture." American Baptist Quarterly 4 (June 1985): 200-212.

Leonard, a historian at Louisville's Southern Baptist Seminary, charts recent controversies in the Southern Baptist Convention by their relationship to changes in the denomination and in the southern culture that has been the traditional home of the denomination.

469. McBeth, H. Leon. The Baptist Heritage: Four Centuries of Baptist Witness. Nashville: Broadman, 1987.

A large and authoritative book, this volume has much to say about Southern Baptists, but it also provides much useful information on other groups of Baptists in America, as well as on Baptist origins in the sixteenth and seventeenth centuries and on Baptists in other regions of the world.

470. Rosenberg, Ellen M. The Southern Baptists: A Subculture in Transition. Knoxville: University of Tennessee Press, 1989.

Rosenberg's is one of the recent studies trying to figure out the consequences when a previously regional and sectarian church goes national and public. As an anthropologist, she pays particular attention to the structures of Southern Baptist institutions and to the denomination's ritual life.

471. Shelley, Bruce L. Conservative Baptists: A Story of Twentieth-Century Dissent. 3rd ed. Wheaton, IL: Conservative Baptist Press, 1981.

The Conservative Baptist Foreign Mission Society came into existence in 1943 as a protest against liberalizing trends in the Northern Baptist Convention. That movement evolved into a larger fellowship of Baptist churches, which came to sponsor the Conservative Baptist Home Mission Society and a Conservative Baptist Association. The early history of those groups is well told here by a sympathetic insider.

472. Shurdan, Walter B. Not a Silent People: Controversies that Have Shaped Southern Baptists. Nashville: Broadman, 1972.

Shurdan's concerns are primarily twentieth-century battles over evolution, biblical criticism, and related questions. As such, his book was an inadvertent curtain-raiser to the internal battles that have divided Southern

Baptists into groups which to an outsider, may be labeled "moderate conservative" and "more conservative."

473. Shurdan, Walter B. "The Problem of Authority in the Southern Baptist Convention." Review and Expositor 75 (Spring 1978): 219-35.

Shurdan breaks the issue into three sub-questions: the infallibility of the Bible, the traditions of Baptist ecclesiology, and the place of creeds among Baptists. Shurdan observed a rise in creedal thinking among Southern Baptists since the early 1960s and stated the obvious, but also extremely important, truth that all who hold to the infallibility of the Bible do not interpret its teachings in the same way.

474. Spain, Rufus B. At Ease in Zion: Social History of Southern Baptists, 1865-1900. Nashville: Vanderbilt University Press, 1967.

This book traces the Southern Baptist resistance to social change in the antebellum South, with particular attention to the estrangement that developed between the Convention and the freedmen liberated as a consequence of the Civil War.

(C) Blacks

For blacks in America, the sound of the gospel was muffled by the crack of a whip. Given the slave conditions under which blacks received religious instruction in America, it is remarkable that any turned to Christianity. Yet the Christian faith turned out for blacks to be something more than whites had anticipated, for it provided slave and free blacks with an internal stability that nerved them for the founding of autonomous churches and the creation of a distinct Christian ethos. Blacks have worshipped in woods, tiny rural churches, store-fronts, and stately urban sanctuaries. They have been organized into large denominations (mostly Baptist, Methodist, and Pentecostal) and countless independent congregations. The beliefs of black Christians are almost always evangelical to some degree, but persistent racial tension and the heritage of slavery have made it difficult for strong bridges to be built between blacks and other evangelicals.

475. Bentley, William H. "Bible Believers in the Black Community." In The Evangelicals: What they Believe, Who They Are, Where They Are Changing, eds. David F. Wells and John D. Woodbridge, 108-121. Rev. ed. Grand Rapids: Baker, 1977.

Bentley's essay helpfully defines black "Bible-Believers" as Christians sharing much with white evangelicals. He notes they are found in both traditional and independent denominational arrangements. But he adds that they are separated from white evangelicals by important facts of history and social vision.

476. Epstein, Dena J. Sinful Tunes and Spirituals: Black Folk Music to the Civil War. Urbana: University of Illinois Press, 1977.

Epstein's solid work catalogues varieties of black folk music arising primarily from the slave experience, and so charts the wider dimensions of the origin of the spiritual, an immensely vital force in the history of black Christianity.

477. Evans, James H., Jr., ed. Black Theology: A Critical Assessment and Annotated Bibliography. Westport, CT: Greenwood Press, 1987.

An extensive introduction and 461 annotated bibliographical entries chart the rise and development of black theology, including its debt to the American slave experience and the recent de-colonization of Africa.

478. Frazier, E. Franklin. The Negro Church in America. Rev. ed., published together with C. Eric Lincoln, The Black Church Since Frazier. New York: Schocken, 1973.

This book has long been the standard introduction to the history of black Christianity in America. Frazier argues that black Christianity retained little of the African past, a view that has been much disputed since this work was first published in 1964.

479. Genovese, Eugene D. Roll, Jordan Roll: The World the Slaves Made. New York: Pantheon Books, 1974.

Genovese's account of slave culture is written from a Marxist perspective, but it nonetheless contains an extraordinarily sensitive account of the inner spirituality constructed by slaves from evangelical resources.

480. Hamilton, Charles V. The Black Preacher in America. New York: William Morrow, 1972.

Hamilton's survey reconstructs the high points of his subject, with special emphasis on the meaning of the sermon (as a central unifying event) and the nature of connection (speech and response) between preacher and congregation in black worship.

481. Jacobs, Sylvia M., ed. Black Americans and the Missionary Movement in Africa. Westport, CT: Greenwood Press, 1982.

Separate essays treat Afro-American missions in the Congo, the role of black women missionaries to South Africa, and black American missionaries in Portuguese areas. A helpful bibliography concludes the volume.

482. Levine, Lawrence W. Black Culture and Black Consciousness: Afro-American Folk Thought From Slavery to Freedom. New York: Oxford University Press, 1977.

Roughly the first third of this book expounds upon the importance of evangelical religion for the formation of black culture. An added bonus is the very funny section on the humor of blacks, some of which arises out of religious situations.

483. Paris, Arthur E. Black Pentecostalism: Southern Religion in an Urban World. Amherst: University of Massachusetts Press, 1982.

This is an intensive study of the three congregations of the Mount Calvary Holy Church of America, Inc., in Boston, written from research done in the early 1970s. Although these Boston blacks were active in social outreach (home for unwed mothers, orphanage), they did not see themselves as active agents of social change. The church had been founded in the 1960s by Bishop Bromfield Johnson from North Carolina.

484. Potter, Ronald C. "The New Black Evangelicals." In Black Theology: A Documentary History, 1966-1979, eds. Gayraud S. Wilmore and James H. Cone. Maryknoll, NY: Orbis, 1979.

Potter sees an emerging coalition between "left" evangelicals of the Sojourners type and representatives of a biblically-rooted black theology. This coalition is thought to offer a means of liberating black believers from the artificial constraints and the limiting hermeneutics of more conservative white evangelicals.

485. Raboteau, Albert F. "The Black Experience in American Evangelicalism: The Meaning of Slavery." In The Evangelical Tradition in America, ed. Leonard I. Sweet. Macon, GA: Mercer University Press, 1984.

486. Raboteau, Albert F. Slave Religion: The "Invisible Institution" in the Antebellum South. New York: Oxford University Press, 1978.

Raboteau is the premier interpreter of slave Christianity. His essay in the Sweet volume carries further the themes that were developed magisterially in Slave Religion. According to Raboteau, blacks increasingly accepted evangelical forms of Christianity from the Revolutionary period onwards, but usually by modifying its teachings and practices through the influence of traditional African perspectives and to fit the extraordinary circumstances of slavery.

487. Richardson, Joe M. Christian Reconstruction: The American Missionary Association and Southern Blacks, 1861-1890. Athens: University of Georgia Press, 1986.

After the Civil War, the American Missionary Association, inspired mostly by northern Congregationalists, sought to provide freed slaves with the capacities to fend honorably for themselves. Despite considerable paternalism and often violent hostility from white southerners, the mission did achieve a measure of success, particularly in the founding of black colleges, which until after the Civil Rights Movement of the 1960s provided the main source of higher education for blacks in the South.

488. Sernett, Milton C. Black Religion and American Evangelicalism: White Protestants, Plantation Missions and the Flowering of Negro Christianity, 1787-1865. Metuchen, NJ: Scarecrow Press, 1975.

Sernett tells the story of valiant efforts by black slaves to appropriate a form of Christianity for their own by selective filtration of the message preached by white slave owners and by intense meditation on the Christian meaning of their own bondage.

489. Sernett, Milton C., ed. Afro-American Religious History: A Documentary Witness. Durham, NC: Duke University Press, 1985.

This book is the best documentary collection of its kind. Its over fifty excerpts provide compelling justification for perceiving the Christianity of American blacks as part of the evangelical stream, but also ample reasons (with slavery itself at the fount) for why blacks are often so uncomfortable with that identification.

490. Smith, Timothy L. "Slavery and Theology: The Emergence of Black Christian Consciousness in Nineteenth-Century America." Church History 41 (Dec. 1972): 497-512.

This essay argues powerfully that the evangelical beliefs which slaves adopted in the antebellum period provided them with "endurance without acquiescence" in the face of their bondage.

491. Sobel, Mechel. Trabelin' On: The Slave Journey to an Afro-Baptist Faith. Princeton: Princeton University Press, 1989; orig. 1979.

Sobel's story of black Baptists in the colonial and antebellum period shows well how influences from whites drew blacks toward Baptist polity, but also how blacks appropriated Baptist themes to construct churches different from what whites expected.

492. Washington, James Melvin. Frustrated Fellowship: The Black Baptist Quest for Social Power. Macon, GA: Mercer University Press, 1986.

This is a history of the early years of the large and important National Baptist Convention, U.S.A., Inc. The "frustration" of the title is the drag on efforts at unification exerted by the Baptist propensity for local and voluntary organization. The book offers a solid analysis of how white patterns of church organization have influenced black groups and how churches have carried the burden for blacks' religious and social organization.

493. Williams, Walter L. Black Americans and the Evangelization of Africa, 1877-1900. Madison: University of Wisconsin Press, 1982.

Williams has studied the 116 black missionaries sent from the United States to Africa during his period, as well as the 80 Africans dispatched to the U.S. on mission-related tasks in the same era. His important conclusion is that these kinds of missionary efforts provided the first important impetus for black Americans to recover their own African past.

494. Wills, David W. "The Central Themes of American Religious History: Pluralism, Puritanism, and the Encounter of Black and White." Religion and Intellectual Life 5:1 (Fall 1987): 30-41.

Wills makes a forceful case for the thesis that black-white tensions, exemplified first in the South, should be a controlling theme in writing the history of American Christianity every bit as much as the more standard attention to New England Puritanism and middle colony denominational pluralism.

(D) Fundamentalists

Fundamentalism is a distinctly American phenomenon. When at the end of the nineteenth century the nation's prevailing evangelical consensus broke down, the group that protested most militantly against change in the churches and against secularization in society became known as fundamentalists. More a mood than a movement before World War I, fundamentalists, moderates, and liberals joined in a three-way struggle for control of several denominations during the 1920s (especially the Northern Baptist Convention, the northern Presbyterian church, and the Disciples of Christ). The spectacle of the Scopes trial in 1925 and the condescending dismissal by cultural elites led many supposedly knowledgeable pundits to write the obituary for the movement. Fundamentalism, however, was not dead but merely gathering its energies. After World War II, a more progressive wing of the fundamentalists began calling themselves "new evangelicals," but many others continued to be content with the name. Since the 1970s, the fundamentalists have been the most visible element in the evangelical coalition, in part because of their expertise in modern means of communication like television, in part because of increased political involvement, and in part because of an innate identification with populist themes and needs of the American population at large. As one might expect with the recent public presence of fundamentalists, the literature on them has expanded exponentially. Some of the more general studies appear below.

495. Beale, David O. In Pursuit of Purity: American Fundamentalism Since 1850. Greenville, SC: Unusual Publications, 1986.

This comprehensive study offers a multitude of facts and a standpoint shaped by the author's identification with Bob Jones University, an institution that has repudiated alliances with evangelicals, neo-evangelicals, pentecostals, and other deviants from strict fundamentalist norms. The book may be considered an update of George Dollar's History of Fundamentalism (Bob Jones University Press, 1973) which remains useful especially for its extensive biographical sketches of early fundamentalist leaders. See also Louis Gaspar's The Fundamentalist Movement (Mouton de Gruyter, 1963) which highlights the different strategies pursued since the 1930s by the American Council of Christian Churches (militant, under the leadership of

Carl McIntire) and the National Association of Evangelicals (moderating, under the unofficial guidance of Billy Graham).

496. Carpenter, Joel A., ed. Fundamentalism in American Religion, 1880-1950: A 45-Volume Facsimile Series. New York: Garland, 1988.

Many of the volumes in this series are mentioned at the appropriate chronological junctures below. With Donald Dayton's comparable series, "The Higher Christian Life", it offers the fullest possible introduction to the development of evangelicalism in the twentieth century.

497. Marsden, George M. "Defining Fundamentalism." Christian Scholar's Review 1 (Winter, 1971): 141-151.

498. Sandeen, Ernest R. "Defining Fundamentalism: A Reply to Professor Marsden." Christian Scholar's Review 1 (Spring 1971): 227-233.

Marsden and Sandeen are the authors of the two best books on the origin of fundamentalism (see Chapter 10). This spirited exchange, which took place after Sandeen had published his volume and while Marsden was mid-way in the research and writing of his, offers an excellent capsule summary of their positions. Sandeen felt the movement was defined by premillennialism and biblical inerrancy, two relatively recent doctrinal innovations. Marsden did not discount these factors, but held that fundamentalism arose more organically out of the nineteenth-century matrix of revivalistic American Protestantism.

(E) Holiness

The holiness churches are a branch of Methodism that holds firmly to John Wesley's position on sanctification. Wesley had considered his teaching about the possibility of Christian perfection to be the special reason for his ministry, and Holiness groups have continued that emphasis. Denominations like the Free Methodists, the Wesleyan Methodists, and the Nazarenes came into being in the nineteenth century to embody the Wesleyan concern for sanctification. Similar teachings had by that time grown up elsewhere, for example, with Charles G. Finney (who stressed the possibility for Christians going on to a higher, more refined plane of spirituality), in the Salvation Army, with certain branches among the Quakers, and in the Keswick Movement (imported from England) with its stress on the higher Christian life. Holiness groups, who define themselves more by inward piety than outward doctrinal conformity, have not been as visible in the historiography of American evangelicalism as Presbyterian, Baptist, and other Reformed groups (although holiness emphases of a general sort have also been important among these bodies). That situation, however, has begun to change with the publication of materials like those described below and works on similar themes in the historical sections that follow.

499. Bassett, Paul M. "Fundamentalist Leavening of the Holiness Movement, 1914-1940; The Church of the Nazarene: A Case Study." Wesley Theological Journal 13 (Spring 1978): 65-91.

Under fundamentalist influence, Nazarenes earlier in the century began to use the language of biblical inerrancy to describe their own allegiance to Scripture. Bassett argues that this language represented a distinct shift in Nazarene traditions, which had tended to speak of the Bible's inspiration as plenary rather than verbal.

500. Dayton, Donald W., ed. "The Higher Christian Life": Sources for the Study of the Holiness, Pentecostal and Keswick Movements. New York: Garland, 1984.

The forty-eight volumes of this series are a treasure trove for the general study of holiness emphases in American religious life, but also for a fuller understanding of how holiness themes shaped both the fundamentalist movement and modern evangelicalism. Dayton's series along with Joel Carpenter's collection, Fundamentalism in American Religion, offers a library of essential evangelical history.

501. Dieter, Melvin E. The Holiness Revival of the Nineteenth Century. Metcuhen, NJ: Scarecrow Press, 1980.

When the commitment of American Methodists to the new birth, to fervent holiness of life, and to the camp meeting began to waver in the mid-nineteenth century, a series of protests arose. Dieter's volume is an expert summary of those protests and the new denominations (e.g., Church of the Nazarene) that arose as a result.

502. Jones, Charles Edwin. Perfectionist Persuasion, the Holiness Movement and American Methodism, 1867-1936. Metuchen, NJ: Scarecrow Press, 1974.

Jones's work anticipated some of the insights of Dieter's Holiness Revival, but focused more directly on the debates within Methodism over the shape and direction of the holiness impulse.

503. McKinley, Edward H. Marching to Glory: The History of the Salvation Army in the United States. San Francisco: Harper & Row, 1980.

The Salvation Army, established by William Booth and his family in England during the 1860s, was imported to the United States shortly thereafter. Its doctrines have been a fairly standard expression of holiness teachings, but its activity in social outreach has made it a notable exemplar for other American evangelicals. The story is told here very well.

504. Roberts, Arthur O. The Association of Evangelical Friends: A Story of Quaker Renewal in the Twentieth Century. Newberg, OR: Barclay Press, 1975.

Roberts' history is a sturdy account of the sub-grouping of the Quakers who have cooperated most closely with other holiness and evangelical groups.

505. Smith, Timothy L. Called Unto Holiness. Kansas City, MO: Beacon Hill, 1962.

This is the first volume of the officially sponsored history of the Church of the Nazarenes. Written by a historian whose work opened the door to much more careful examination of evangelicalism in America, it is one of the finest histories of an evangelical denomination.

(F) Lutherans and American Groups with European Lutheran Heritage

Lutherans are the first "evangelicals." To this day, *evangelisch* in German means "Lutheran" or more simply, "Protestant." Several strands of Lutheranism also have prominent characteristics in common with the johnny-come-lately "evangelicals" in America. Lutheran Orthodoxy has stressed the infallibility of the Bible much like fundamentalist and conservative American evangelicals. Lutheran Pietism has emphasized the new birth, holiness of life, and missionary service in forms very similar to emphases of American evangelicals. Yet, with a few exceptions, connections between Lutherans and American evangelicals have been slight. Linguistic and cultural barriers have stood in the way (Lutherans have been primarily German and Scandinavian, earlier American evangelicals came primarily from British stock). So has the faithfulness of Lutherans to the Augsburg Confession and other doctrinal standards from the Reformation, for confessionalism does not go down well with American evangelicals who appeal to "no creed but the Bible." Only among Lutheran pietists who had already begun to break from the European state churches before immigration has a rapprochement occurred with American-style evangelicals.

506. Arden, G. Everett. Augustana Heritage: A History of the Augustana Lutheran Church. Rock Island, IL: Augustana Press, 1963.

The Swedish Lutherans who made up the Augustana Synod (now part of the Evangelical Lutheran Church in America) included many pietists whose Christian faith bore uncanny formal resemblance to the piety practiced by the immigrants' evangelical neighbors.

507. Graebner, Alan. Uncertain Saints: The Laity in the Lutheran Church--Missouri Synod, 1900-1970. Wesport, CT: Greenwood, 1975.

The Missouri Synod has always been conscious of its traditions, and these traditions have included a prominent role for the clergy. This study of lay activity, which rose and then declined over the course of the century, is a solid contribution to what "life on the ground" has meant in a large, important denomination.

508. Jordahl, Leigh D. "The Theology of Franz Pieper: A Resource for Fundamentalistic Thought Modes Among American Lutherans." Lutheran Quarterly 23 (May 1971): 118-137.

Pieper's Christian Dogmatics was the summation of Missouri Synod systematic theology when it was published around 1920. Jordahl here examines the ways it may have been drawn toward American expressions of dogma, including the doctrine of Scripture, and away from traditional Lutheran formulation of such matters.

509. Lueking, F. Dean. Mission in the Making: The Missionary Enterprise Among Missouri Synod Lutherans, 1846-1963. St. Louis: Concordia Publishing House, 1964.

The Missouri Synod has sustained an active missionary outreach in other lands since its earliest days in the United States. This study shows how that missionary effort came close to paralleling similar efforts by American evangelicals, but also how Missouri Synod cooperation with other evangelicals on the mission field led to fears at home of compromised purity.

510. Marquart, Karl E. Anatomy of an Explosion: Missouri in Lutheran Perspective. Fort Wayne, IN: Concordia Theological Seminary Press, 1977.

During the early 1970s, disputes within the Missouri Synod between those who wanted to retain the letter of European confessions and those who wished to draw the denomination closer to modern understandings of Scripture, led eventually to a schism, in which a small faction broke off to form the Evangelical Lutheran Church in Mission (which later joined the new Evangelical Lutheran Church in America). This account of the battle is by a partisan of the conservative confessionalists.

511. Nelson, Clifford E. Lutheranism in North America, 1914-1970. Minneapolis: Augsburg, 1972.

The recent history of Lutherans is a nearly classic tale of Americanization. This account provides an excellent overview of how the German and Scandinavian immigrant bodies became, often through processes of merger, the American Lutheran churches of the late twentieth century.

512. Noll, Mark A. "Children of the Reformation in a Brave New World: Why 'American Evangelicals' Differ from 'Lutheran Evangelicals'." dialog: A Journal of Theology 24 (Summer 1985): 176-180.

The argument here is that the Lutheran and Reformed theologies of the Reformation era are not as different as their defenders often suppose. Rather, the author suggests that the nearly complete isolation of Lutheran "evangelicals" from American "evangelicals" has come about because of the cultural and theological histories experienced by the two streams since the sixteenth century.

513. Olson, Arnold T., ed. Heritage Series: I. Olson, ed., The Search for Identity (1980); II. Olson, The Significance of Silence (1981); III. Olson, Stumbling Toward Maturity (1981); IV. Roy A Thompson, The Dynamics of The Printed Page in Evangelical Free Church History (1981). Minneapolis: Free Church Publications.

The Free Church movement began in nineteenth-century Scandinavia as a pietistic sub-grouping within the state Lutheran churches. Migration to the new world and growing involvement with American evangelicals moved the Scandinavian Free Churches further away from their Old World roots. Among their other themes, these books tell the story of the mergers that created the Evangelical Free Church of America from several of these immigrant bodies.

514. Olsson, Karl A. By One Spirit: A History of the Evangelical Covenant Church of America. Chicago: Covenant Press, 1962.

The Evangelical Covenant Church, like the Evangelical Free Church, began as a movement within Scandinavian (mostly Swedish) state-church Lutheranism. As compared to the Free Church, the Covenant has retained a bit more of the heritage of European pietism. Yet like the history of the Evangelical Free Church, its story also shows how pietistic European Protestants have been brought closer to common patterns of American evangelicalism.

515. Rudnick, Milton L. Fundamentalism and the Missouri Synod. St. Louis: Concordia Publishing House, 1966.

The Lutheran Church-Missouri Synod, as a denomination ardent in its fidelity to historic Protestant orthodoxy and (especially in recent years) determined in its defense of biblical inerrancy, is often linked with American fundamentalists. This book shows, however, why Missouri's confessional fidelity to the Augsburg Confession, its preservation of European styles of life (that did not conform to fundamentalist ideals of the "separated life"), and its possession of an immigrant mentality kept connections between fundamentalists and Missouri Synod Lutherans to a minimum.

516. Valleskey, David. "Evangelical Lutheranism and Today's Evangelicals and Fundamentalists." Wisconsin Lutheran Quarterly 80 (Summer 1983).

In shorter compass than Rudnick's Fundamentalism and the Missouri Synod, Valleskey offers the same sort of analysis. Certain features of American evangelicalism are pleasing to Wisconsin Synod Lutherans (a body of several hundred thousand members which keeps itself even more isolated than the Missouri Synod), but not the Americans' disdain for confessions and slighting of justification by faith as interpreted authoritatively by Martin Luther.

(G) Mennonites, Brethren

The Mennonites are the most prominent body in America that descended from the Anabaptists of the Reformation. For centuries they were the "Stille im Lande," the quiet ones in the countryside who sought isolation wherever they could find it (Switzerland, Holland, Germany, Russia, Pennsylvania, Kansas, Manitoba) in order to practice their Christian pacifism and their more communal approach to life. Several waves of Mennonite migration to the United States in the nineteenth and twentieth centuries has resulted in the presence of several small, but consequential, denominations. Mennonite faithfulness to the New Testament and Mennonite seriousness about the separated life (along with the inevitable process of Americanization) have brought Mennonites ever closer to more general currents of evangelicalism. Mennonites have divided over how much of this evangelicalism to adopt (the Amish accept the least, groups like the Mennonite Brethren a great deal, and other Mennonites bodies are somewhere in between). For several generations, the Mennonites have been blessed with outstanding historians, some of whose work is mentioned below.

The Brethren groups from Germany (to be distinguished from the Plymouth Brethren who arose in England and Ireland) were off-shoots of the German pietist movements of the seventeenth and eighteenth centuries. Their bent toward pacifism and a reluctant participation in the larger enterprises of American evangelicals have led to fairly close ties between themselves and the Mennonites.

517. Boyer, Paul. Mission on Taylor Street: The Founding and Early Years of the Dayton Brethren in Christ Mission. Grantham, PA: Brethren in Christ Historical Society, 1987.

This book, by a distinguished historian from the University of Wisconsin, illustrates how Brethren social service could resemble that of many other evangelical denominations, even while the Church of the Brethren remained somewhat isolated within the American evangelical mosaic.

518. Hershberger, Guy F. War, Peace and Nonresistance. Rev. ed. Scottdale, PA: Herald Press, 1969.

Anabaptist pacifism is a sharp rock of offense that prevents closer fellowship between Mennonites, with related groups, and American evangelicals. This book is a comprehensive introduction to the biblical and historical roots of that view.

519. Kraus, Norman C., ed. Evangelicals and Anabaptism. Scottdale, PA: Herald Press, 1979.

This is probably the best recent book by representatives of an evangelical sub-group seeking to define how their own particular traditions do or do not conform to the more general patterns of American evangelicalism. The book's nine essays note general parallels and cooperation between Anabaptists, especially Mennonites, and the broad stream of evangelicals in America, but also specify areas (e.g., the stress on premillennialism, the fervor for biblical inerrancy, the practice of war, the meaning of discipleship) where Anabaptist traditions diverge in subtle or dramatic ways from more common evangelical patterns.

520. The Mennonite Experience in America. Vol.I: Land, Piety and Peoplehood, by Richard K. MacMaster; Vol.II: Peace, Faith, Nation: Mennonites and Amish in Nineteenth-Century America, by Theron F. Schlabach; Vol.III: Vision, Doctrine, War: Mennonite Identity and Organization in America, 1890-1930, by James C. Juhnke. Scottdale, PA: Herald Press, 1984, 1988, 1989.

These three volumes in a new series are outstanding denominational history. They trace faithfully the way in which different Mennonite communities brought traditional Anabaptist convictions to the New World, but also how the process of integration into American society began very early on as well, though that process would not bring about extensive contact between Mennonites and other evangelicals until after the First World War.

521. Toews, John A. A History of the Mennonite Brethren Church: Pilgrims and Pioneers. Hillsboro, KS: Kindred Press, 1975.

The Mennonite Brethren have come closest of Mennonite denominations to the norms and standards of American evangelicals.

522. Trever, John C. "A Closer Look At the Meaning of 'Evangelical Christianity.'" Brethren Life 32 (Summer 1987): 148-153.

This essay explains what a modern Brethren likes and does not like in popular evangelical life.

(H) Methodists

Methodists were an insignificant presence in the American colonies at the time of the Revolution. Seventy-five years later they were the largest denomination in the country. In a word, Methodism--with its combination of discipline (exemplified by an episcopal church order), theology (with a stress on free will), and holiness (leading to active involvement in the faith)--was made for America. The impact of Methodism upon American evangelicalism has been great in every way. And Methodists continue to contribute great energy and significant personnel to the evangelical mosaic in the late twentieth century. At the same time, however, the Methodist identification with American culture took its toll. Methodists became so closely wedded to American norms that its leaders more easily accepted the liberalization of theology that became fashionable in some circles at the end of the nineteenth century. The result has been a heritage that enshrines much of what it means to be evangelical, along with significant departures from evangelical norms of belief. Methodist history remains relatively unexplored (at least by comparison with the Methodists' importance in America), but significant works like those mentioned below are at hand to assess the Methodist contribution to the evangelical experience in America.

523. Bucke, Emory Stevens, ed. The History of American Methodism. 3 Vols. Nashville: Abingdon, 1964.

The several authors of this large history treat fully the originally evangelical character of Methodists in America and the full range of changes in Methodism since its earliest days.

524. Byrne, Donald E., Jr. No Foot of Land: Folklore of American Methodist Itinerants. Metuchen, NJ: Scarecrow Press, 1975.

This is a compendium of off-beat information about the Methodist circuit riders who tamed the American frontier while in the process making their denomination the largest Protestant body in the new world. Chapters cover the circuit riders' dreams, providential deliverances, clairvoyant experiences, humor, preaching, and personalities.

525. Chiles, Robert E. Theological Transition in American Methodism, 1790-1935. New York: Abingdon, 1965.

This fine book traces the evolution of John Wesley's theology in the American Methodist church through a close examination of works by the Englishman, Richard Watson (1781-1833) and the Americans, John Miley (1813-1895) and Albert Knudson (1873-1953). Chiles finds it inevitable that this theology would move from Wesley's evangelical emphases to a liberalism reflecting the currents of later periods, but also manages to sound consistently wistful about the loss of Wesley's convictions on revelation, sin, and grace.

526. Holifield, E. Brooks. Health and Medicine in the Methodist Tradition. New York: Crossroad, 1986.

Of several recent books in Crossroad's series on health and medicine in various denominations, this is the best. Holifield excels both because he grasps so thoroughly the implications of John Wesley's Methodism for these concerns and because he traces so competently the changes in Methodist attitudes over time.

527. Richey, Russell E. and Kenneth E. Rowe. Rethinking Methodist History: A Bicentennial Historical Consultation. Nashville: Kingswood Books, 1985.

To mark the 200th anniversary of the organization of the Methodist church in America, twenty-three essays describe aspects of that history. Several studies of important individuals and specific turning points are joined by more general treatment. Of the latter, Donald G. Mathews, "Evangelical America--The Methodist Ideology," is most relevant for understanding why Methodism flourished as it did in the early United States.

(I) Pentecostals

The modern pentecostal movement began in the United States, but has spread in the last eighty years literally around the world. Pentecostals believe that the special dispensations of God's presence (including healing and glossolalia) predicted for "the last days" have now begun to appear. As in many such dynamic Christian movements, the early years of pentecostalism were chaotic, but soon more customary denominational structures emerged. A prominent feature of early pentecostalism was the participation of blacks and whites in the movement together, a situation which led eventually to the founding of several large black pentecostal denominations. Pentecostal energies were also soon turned to active missionary endeavors. In its early decades, most other evangelical groups looked upon pentecostals with suspicion. But for a number of reasons pentecostals since World War II have exerted a much larger presence in general evangelical concerns. Pentecostals participated in the National Association of Evangelicals from the start, they have taken part increasingly in cooperative, intra-denominational activities, and the growth of the charismatic movement in older denominations has provided many forms of contact. Not the least sign of the growing presence of pentecostalism in American religion life is the emergence of first-class historians of the movement, some of whose works are highlighted below.

528. Anderson, Robert Mapes. Vision of the Disinherited: The Making of American Pentecostalism. New York: Oxford, 1979.

This is the most authoritative study of American pentecostal origins. Approaching the subject from a naturalistic perspective, it is thoroughly researched and methodologically sophisticated, drawing heavily on the social sciences.

529. Blumhofer, Edith L. Restoring the Faith: The Assemblies of God, Pentecostalism and American Culture. Urbana: University of Illinois Press, 1991.

This study, a condensation and adaptation of the author's previously published book, The Assemblies of God: A Chapter in the Story of American Pentecostalism, examines the social and cultural context in which the denomination emerged and traces the significance of the restorationist impulse in shaping its identity.

530. Conn, Charles. Like a Mighty Army Moves the Church of God. Rev. ed. Cleveland, TN: Pathway Press, 1977.

The Church of God (Cleveland, TN) is among the oldest pentecostal denominations. This substantial sympathetic account first published in 1955 traces its story from its origins as a small restorationist movement through its identification with pentecostalism and turbulent years of leadership transition to its emergence as a stable, growing denomination.

531. de Leon, Victor. The Silent Pentecostals. Taylors, SC: Faith Printing Co., 1979.

Scholarly resources for the study of socially or culturally marginal American pentecostals are sparse. This book offers a starting point for further studies. It surveys Assemblies of God Latin American outreaches.

532. Hollenweger, Walter J. The Pentecostals: The Charismatic Movement in the Churches. Peabody, MA: Hendrickson, 1988. (reprint, 1972 ed.)

A detailed guide to global pentecostalism, this serviceable one-volume survey was first published in German. Despite factual errors and its lack of a coherent thesis, it offers a helpful introduction and bibliography.

533. Poloma, Margaret M. The Assemblies of God at the Crossroads: Charisma and Institutional Dilemmas. Knoxville: University of Tennessee Press, 1989.

This fine book examines the ethos and structure of the Assemblies of God. Poloma notes especially both the significance of local clergy in shaping the spirituality of adherents and the place of women in local churches and in leadership.

534. Richardson, James C., Jr. With Water and Spirit: A History of the Black Apostolic Denominations in the United States. Washington, DC: Spirit Press, 1980.

No comprehensive treatment of black pentecostalism in the United States has been written, but several monographs have probed aspects of the black pentecostal experience. Richardson tells the story of black apostolic churches, which are numerous.

535. Robeck, Cecil M., Jr. "Pentecostals and the Apostolic Faith: Implications for Ecumenism." Pneuma 9 (1987): 61-84.

This essay documents the stated ecumenical intentions of early pentecostals who perceived themselves as participants in the restoration of the apostolic faith to the end times church. The apostolic faith belongs to the entire church, Robeck reminds us. The exclusivism of American pentecostal denominations denies a fundamental component in their heritage.

536. Synan, Vinson. The Holiness-Pentecostal Movement in the United States. Grand Rapids: Eerdmans, 1971.

In this sympathetic relating of the story of American pentecostalism, Synan maintains that the Wesleyan Holiness movement was the source of pentecostalism as a whole.

537. Synan, Vinson. The Old-Time Power: A History of the Pentecostal Holiness Church. Circleville, OH: Advocate, 1973.

A non-critical participant's account of this holiness pentecostal denomination.

538. Synan, Vinson. The Twentieth-Century Pentecostal Explosion: The Exciting Growth of Pentecostal Churches and Charismatic Renewal Movements. Altamonte Springs, FL: Strang Comms. Co., 1987.

A popular overview of the global extent of the pentecostal and charismatic movements. Brief and readable, this book emphasizes the movements' recent expansion in the third world.

539. Wacker, Grant. "The Functions of Faith in Primitive Pentecostalism." Harvard Theological Review 77:3-4 (July-Oct.1984): 353-375.

An examination of the factors that sustained the pentecostal movement as it began to emerge from the throes of revival fervor.

Warner, Wayne E. The Woman Evangelist: The Life and Times of Charismatic Evangelist Maria B. Woodworth-Etter. Metuchen, NJ: Scarecrow Press, 1986.
(See 1572)

(J) Presbyterian and Reformed

Representatives of Presbyterian and Reformed churches have never been numerically dominant among American evangelicals, but they have taken the leadership in cultural activities and doctrinal definition. During the Revolutionary era, Presbyterians pointed the way in support of the new nation. During the nineteenth century, Presbyterian theologians were among the most articulate evangelical spokesmen on doctrinal questions (including the champion of free will, Charles G. Finney, who began his career as a Presbyterian; the popular Bible expositor, Albert Barnes, who represented the New School, or Americanist position; and the leading theologian at Princeton Seminary, Charles Hodge, an Old School leader who defended Calvinistic notions of evangelical orthodoxy). In the twentieth century, the large northern and southern Presbyterian denominations (which in the early 1980s merged as the Presbyterian Church in the United States of America) have contained a large number of evangelicals, and the evangelical presence is represented also in most of the smaller, more confessional Presbyterian churches. In recent decades fresh Reformed insights have also been provided for the American context by the second and third generation descendents of Dutch immigrants.

540. Bratt, James D. Dutch Calvinism in Modern America: A History of a Conservative Subculture. Grand Rapids: Eerdmans, 1984.

This is a gem of a book that tells the story of how immigrant Dutch Reformed communities (primarily in western Michigan, Iowa, and New Jersey) negotiated the transit from tightly enclosed ethnic enclaves to broader, but still restricted, connections with the world of "Methodistic" evangelicals that once had seemed so very strange.

541. DeKlerk, Peter and Richard R. DeRidder, eds. Perspectives on the Christian Reformed Church: Studies in Its History, Theology, and Ecumenicity. Grand Rapids: Baker, 1983.

The studies here fill out details that Bratt treated as a narrative in his Dutch Calvinism. The Christian Reformed Church, though small in numbers as American denominations go, has had a large impact on recent evangelical efforts to articulate a self-conscious Christian stance within modern American culture.

542. Dennison, Charles G. and Richard C. Gamble, eds. Pressing Toward the Mark: Essay Commemorating Fifty Years of the Orthodox Presbyterian Church. Philadelphia: Committee for the Historian of the Orthodox Presbyterian Church, 1986.

The Orthodox Presbyterian Church began in 1936 as a protest against liberal, or "inclusivist," trends in the northern Presbyterian church. This volume presents a potpourri of essays on doctrinal concerns that have exercised its members, as well as several historical pieces touching on the denomination's connections with broader currents in American evangelical life.

543. Hutchinson, George P. The History Behind the Reformed Presbyterian Church Evangelical Synod. Cherry Hill, NJ: Mack Publishing, 1974.

The Reformed Presbyterian Church Evangelical Synod (now folded into the Presbyterian Church in America) resulted from the post-World War II merger of a splinter from the Orthodox Presbyterian Church and the immigrant descendents of a Scottish seceder church. Hutchinson's narrative provides an excellent summary and interpretation of the many complicated developments in the American sojourn of the smaller, dissenting Presbyterian denominations.

544. Loetscher, Lefferts A. The Broadening Church: A Study of Theological Issues in the Presbyterian Church Since 1869. Philadelphia: University of Pennsylvania Press, 1954.

This book, by a long-time historian at Princeton Theological Seminary, describes expertly the process that saw the evolution of Presbyterians from a comprehensively evangelical denomination to one in which evangelical impulses (of several varieties, including the neo-orthodox) came to coexist with more liberal theological opinions.

545. Thompson, Ernest Trice. Presbyterians in the South. 3 vols. Richmond: John Knox, 1963-1972.

Southern Presbyterians, like Southern Baptists, long had a history of their own. The southern Presbyterian church arose as an official denomination early in the Civil War, but distinctive southern positions (especially a biblical sanction for slavery and the promotion of "the spirituality of the church") had developed before that time. This full history contains much on how evangelical currents among the southern Presbyterians both shaped and reflected the regional setting.

546. Van Hoeven, James W., ed. Piety and Patriotism: Bicentennial Studies on the Reformed Church in America, 1776-1976. Grand Rapids: Eerdmans, 1976.

The Reformed Church in America is the modern representative of the first major Dutch migrations to the New World (the Christian Reformed Church is made up mostly of Dutch who immigrated after the Civil War). Its history, which has always been colored by evangelical convictions and contact with other evangelical bodies, is a classic account of how an immigrant group adjusts to the American setting.

(K) Restorationists

Early in the nineteenth century a number of effective leaders began to call Christians out of the traditional denominations in the effort to restore the church to its New Testament character. Led especially by Barton W. Stone (1772-1844) and Alexander Campbell (1788-1866), the restorationist movement resulted in several church families, including the Disciples of Christ, Christian Churches, and the Churches of Christ. Concentrated in the upper South, Texas, and the West, these "Christians" sought strict congregational autonomy, disavowed all authorities except the Bible, and generally preserved themselves from other sorts of evangelicals. In the last several decades, however, a flourishing of historical interest and wider contacts in cooperative efforts of several sorts have made "Christians" more conscious of shared bonds with other evangelicals and vice versa.

547. Allen, C. Leonard and Richard T. Hughes. Discovering Our Roots: The Ancestors of Churches of Christ. Abilene, TX: ACU Press, 1988.

Allen and Hughes are among the leaders in recent years at restoring historical consciousness to the Churches of Christ. This book asks for members of this denominational family to recover insights from their own heritage, while also realizing more fully how much their tradition shares with other Christian groups.

548. Harrell, David Edwin, Jr. Quest for a Christian America: The Disciples of Christ and American Society to 1866. Nashville: Disciples of Christ Historical Society, 1966.

549. Harrell, David Edwin, Jr. The Social Sources of Division in the Disciples of Christ, 1865-1900. Atlanta and Athens, GA: Publishing Systems, 1983.

Along with Timothy Smith's Called Unto Holiness, Harrell's books on the Disciples set a new standard for sensitive denominational history of groups that had previously wandered in the borderlands of religious historiography. These volumes are especially adept at tracing the subtle web of influences sustained between the Disciples and American culture.

550. Hughes, Richard T. "Twenty-five Years of Restoration Scholarship: The Churches of Christ." Restoration Quarterly 25:4 (1982): 233-256; and 26:4 (1983): 39-62.

This full bibliography testifies to the maturity in historical scholarship that now exists for this family of churches.

551. Humble, Bill J. The Story of the Restoration. Austin, TX: Firm Foundation, 1969.

This history of the Churches of Christ is a good introduction for broader audiences with little knowledge about the background of this evangelical family.

(L) The South

There are several "Souths": the territory in which black chattel slavery survived the Revolutionary period; the political entity established by The Confederate States of America; the cultural unit defined by Emancipation, Reconstruction, and "the religion of the lost cause"; and since the mid-twentieth century a bewildering melange of economic boom, racial transformation, political competition, and social expansion. But over all of Southern history since the early nineteenth century has brooded an evangelical Protestant presence. That evangelicalism has taken many, many forms--from the tiny churches that sustained black sharecroppers to the magnificent urban tabernacles built to display golden-throated orators. The South, however defined, has always produced more than its fair share of story-tellers and historians. No less is that the case for religious history. Since World War II, works by masters like John Boles, David Edwin Harrell, Samuel Hill, Donald Mathews, Bertram Wyatt-Brown, along with many other volumes by distinguished historians, have brought new light to the religion of a distinctive American region and new insight into the evangelical faith that has played such a central role there.

552. Bailey, Kenneth K. Southern White Protestantism in the Twentieth Century. New York: Harper & Row, 1964.

This study was one of the first of recent efforts to write the history of southern evangelicalism against the backdrop of the South's distinctive regional culture. Informative chapters treat the crusade against Darwinism in the 1920s, the anti-Catholic reaction to Alfred Smith in 1928, and the impact of the Depression and the Second World War.

553. Boles, John B. "Religion in the South: A Tradition Recovered." Maryland Historical Magazine 77 (Winter 1982): 388-401.

Boles is himself one of those who recovered the tradition of southern Christian experience, especially in the early nineteenth century. This article represents a state of the art discussion after nearly two decades of mature publications on the theme.

554. Clarke, Erskine. Wrestlin' Jacob: A Portrait of Religion in the Old South. Atlanta: John Knox Press, 1979.

Clarke here tells the story of efforts by whites, Charles Colcock Jones in rural Georgia and a larger group in Charleston, South Carolina, to evangelize black slaves. That a measure of success attended their efforts, within a slave society itself, is a testimony to their dedication, even more to the religious sensitivity of the black converts, and most of all to the power of the gospel.

555. Harrell, David Edwin, Jr., ed. Varieties of Southern Evangelicalism. Macon, GA: Mercer University Press, 1981.

Something of the dynamism now present in writing about religion in the South can be sensed by the solid essays in this book: Martin E. Marty on the roll of evangelicalism in the nation-wide revival of Southern religion; Wayne Flynt on the wide diversity among southern evangelicals; the editor on the impulse to sectarianism long characteristic of southern religion; James Washington on black folk religion; and William Martin on Billy Graham.

556. Hill, Samuel S., ed. Religion in the Southern States: A Historical Survey. Macon, GA: Mercer University Press, 1983.

The editor's perceptive introduction as well as many of the individual essays in this book contain much fruitful reflection on the evangelicalism of Southern religion. The chapters--with a different author writing on Alabama, Arkansas, Florida, Georgia, Kentucky, Louisiana, Maryland, Mississippi, Missouri, North Carolina, Oklahoma, South Carolina, Tennessee, Texas, Virginia, and West Virginia--appeared first in the Encyclopedia of Southern Religion.

557. Hill, Samuel S. The South and the North in American Religion. Athens, GA: University of Georgia Press, 1980.

This masterful set of lectures by a leading interpreter of southern religion traces the early associations, intense engagements (and disagreements), and the progressive separation of northern and southern religion throughout the nineteenth century. A telling epilogue suggests that, although regional barriers are rapidly falling in modern America, it stills means something in the 1980s for the South to have had its own religious tradition since the Civil War and before.

558. Mathews, Donald G. Religion in the Old South. Chicago: University of Chicago Press, 1977.

This volume is one of the best short books ever written on a subject in American religious history. Its sensitive insights into the internal character of evangelical faith (a stern message of humility that yet brought dignity to the downcast) show how evangelicalism could effect both social conformity and social upheaval and how it could serve equally well, if also in different ways, enslaving masters and enslaved blacks.

559. Smith, H. Shelton. In His Image, But...Racism in Southern Religion. Durham, NC: Duke University Press, 1972.

Smith, a long-time teacher at the Duke Divinity School, here charts the ambiguities, hypocrisies, and griefs of southern Christian whites in their attitudes toward blacks. The book is a powerful cautionary tale in large part because of how thoroughly it shows how such attitudes were a product of Christian, as well as social, experience.

560. Wilson, Charles Reagan, ed. Religion in the South. Jackson, MS: University Press of Mississippi, 1986.

Another outstanding collection illustrating the maturity of southern religious historiography, this one includes essays by John Boles (the antebellum movement of evangelicals from dissent to establishment), C. Eric Lincoln (blacks), David Edwin Harrell (Southern pluralism with Catholics, Jews, and sectarians), J. Wayne Flynt (on the social outreach of Southern Presbyterians), Samuel Hill (religion and politics), and Edwin Gaustad (regionalism in American religion).

561. Wyatt-Brown, Bertram. Southern Honor: Ethics and Behavior in the Old South. New York: Oxford University Press, 1982.

Evangelicalism is an important sub-theme in this book since the attitudes stimulated by revivalism usually worked at cross purposes against the code of honor that otherwise had such a deep impact on life in the South before the Civil War.

CHAPTER 9
REVIVAL MATRIX, 1730-1865

American evangelicalism arose as the product of several developments. The religious heritage of the Protestant Reformation, and more specifically the influence of English Puritanism, laid a theological foundation. But events and circumstances in this country also had a profound influence as well. Among the most important of these were the colonial Great Awakening of the 1740s (which turned to itinerant preaching and more democratic styles of communication), the overwhelming religious support for the American Revolution (which wedded Christian and republican aspirations together), and the series of early nineteenth-century revivals known as the Second Great Awakening (which saw the rise of the Methodists, the Baptists, voluntaristic organizations, and democratic theology). Since the 1930s, the "revival matrix" of these years has been the subject of superlative historical study. Only a small portion of the books and articles pertinent to these early days of American evangelicalism can be mentioned in what follows below, but even this sample can suggest the richness of analysis that is now available to study this formative period.

562. Allen, C. Leonard and Richard T. Hughes. Illusions of Innocence: Protestant Primitivism in America, 1630-1875. Chicago: University of Chicago Press, 1988.

A prominent theme in the early history of the English colonies and also in the early decades of the United States was the desire to return to unsullied Christian origins (especially the norms of the New Testament church). This book, by two leading historians from and of the Restorationist Movement, is the definitive study of that impulse and its connections with other intellectual and cultural trends in early America.

563. Baker, Frank. From Wesley to Asbury: Studies in Early American Methodism. Durham, NC: Duke University Press, 1975.

These essays illuminate important subjects in what might be called the pre-history of American Methodism, before it burgeoned after the Revolution into the largest American denomination.

564. Banner, Lois. "Religious Benevolence As Social Control: A Critique of an Interpretation." Journal of American History 60 (June 1973): 23-41.

Older studies suggested that threatened New England elites had promoted the revivals of the early nineteenth century in order to preserve their own status in a rapidly changing culture. Banner's essay is a nearly definitive refutation of that thesis; she shows, rather, that personal, religious, and cultural motives were more important than the search for power.

565. Boles, John B. The Great Revival, 1787-1805: The Origins of the Southern Evangelical Mind. Lexington: University of Kentucky Press, 1972.

Boles has been a pioneer in reconstructing the development of religion in the antebellum South. This book, which traces the series of revivals in the first decade of the nineteenth century in Kentucky, Tennessee, Virginia, North Carolina, and South Carolina, along with their immense impact on the region's culture, is an outstanding example of his work.

566. Bowden, Henry Warner. American Indians and Christian Missions: Studies in Cultural Conflict. Chicago: University of Chicago Press, 1981.

This well-researched book filled a long-standing need for a comprehensive synthesis of relationships between missionaries and native Americans. Bowden is scrupulously fair in treating the Franciscan, Jesuit, Puritan, Moravian, and later missionaries, pointing out both their noble motives but also the nearly complete failure to present the gospel as something other than a European ideology.

567. Bozeman, Theodore Dwight. Protestants in an Age of Science: The Baconian Ideal and Antebellum Religious Thought. Chapel Hill: University of North Carolina Press, 1977.

This book is a masterful explanation of how and why Protestant intellectuals between the Revolution and the Civil War turned to ideals of inductive science (symbolized in the person of Francis Bacon) as norms for theological method and building blocks of popular apologetics. Without necessarily intending it for that purpose, Bozeman provides essential background for comprehending why devotees of this "early modern" science have found "recent modern" science (e.g., Darwin) such a problem.

568. Bumsted, J. M. and John E. Van de Wetering. What Must I Do to Be Saved? The Great Awakening in Colonial America. Hinsdale, IL: Dryden Press, 1976.

This is a good survey of the revivals in colonial America that had such an important shaping effect on evangelicalism. It is distinguished by an effort to bring together events in all three major colonial regions.

569. Butler, Jon. Power, Authority, and the Origins of American Denominational Order: The English Churches in the Delaware Valley, 1680-1730. Philadelphia: The American Philosophical Society, 1978.

New England Puritans provided the intellectual foundation for later evangelicalism, but, as near theocrats believing in the practical union of church and state, they did not provide the model for the religious pluralism and the separation of church and state that have characterized the United States. This pioneering study of middle colony religious life describes the origin of those later norms of American religious life.

570. Calhoon, Robert M. Evangelicals and Conservatives in the Early South, 1740-1861. Columbia: University of South Carolina Press, 1988.

Before roughly 1820, evangelicalism was a dissenting, disruptive force in the South. Afterwards it became a prop of the slave-holding establishment. Where Donald Mathew's Religion in the Old South explains the history of that turn-around, Robert Calhoon offers a sensitive meditation on the achievements and ironies that these developments entailed.

571. Carwardine, Richard. Transatlantic Revivalism: Popular Evangelicalism in Britain and America, 1790-1865. Westport, CT: Greenwood Press, 1978.

British models were important for the voluntary organizations through which American evangelicals came to channel their greatest energies. But soon influences began to flow eastward across the Atlantic as well. This is the best book for its period on these transatlantic evangelical connections.

572. Caskey, Marie. Chariot of Fire: Religion and the Beecher Family. New Haven, CT: Yale University Press, 1978.

In many ways the Beechers (patriarch Lyman and a whole host of influential children, including Harriet Beecher Stowe and Henry Ward Beecher) simply were nineteenth-century American evangelicalism. This satisfying study takes seriously both the religious faith of the family members and the effects of their capable, energetic, and (sometimes) excessive personalities.

573. Cremin, Lawrence A. American Education: The Colonial Experience, 1607-1783. New York: Harper & Row, 1970.

574. Cremin, Lawrence A. American Education: The National Experience, 1788-1876. New York: Harper & Row, 1980.

These volumes give full scope to the way that evangelical impulses were at the heart of American concern for education. The third volume in this magisterial series (American Education: The Metropolitan Experience, 1876-1980, 1988) reflects the general secularization of recent American life, but still considers fully the intimate ties between religion and education in America.

575. Cross, Whitney R. The Burned-Over District: The Social and Intellectual History of Enthusiastic Religion in Western New York, 1800-1850. Ithaca, NY: Cornell University Press, 1950.

Many others have studied aspects of "the burned-over district" since Cross's book first appeared, but it remains one of the most satisfying accounts of the fervent revivalism that flourished in this region and that come to have such a powerful effect on American evangelicalism.

576. Essig, James D. The Bonds of Wickedness: American Evangelicals Against Slavery, 1770 1808. Philadelphia: Temple University Press, 1982.

Under the twin impulses of revivalistic religion and Revolutionary republicanism, evangelicals spoke out vociferously against slavery in the 1770s and 1780s, but gradually muted their protest in the early decades of the new nation. This fine book, by a historian sadly taken from us prematurely by cancer, is the authoritative account of that reversal.

577. Fiering, Norman. Jonathan Edwards's Moral Thought and Its British Context. Chapel Hill: University of North Carolina Press, 1981.

Jonathan Edwards's revivalism and the form of his piety had an immense impact on later evangelicals (especially through the diary of David Brainerd which he edited). But later evangelicals repudiated Edwards's philosophical position (a stance against the "moral sense" ethics of the eighteenth-century) and his theology (high Calvinism). This difficult, but outstanding book traces Edwards's reasons for opposing the dominant trends of the moral philosophy of his day, trends that Edwards's evangelical heirs would adopt by the end of the eighteenth century.

578. Finney, Charles G. Lectures on Revivals of Religion, ed. William C. McLoughlin. Cambridge, MA: Harvard University Press, 1960.

Finney was the most representative figure of American evangelicalism from the Revolution to the Civil War, and his book on revival, expertly introduced and edited by McLoughlin, was the most widely influential of his many works.

579. Foster, Frank Hugh. A Genetic History of the New England Theology. Chicago: University of Chicago Press, 1907.

To some extent superseded by Kuklick's Churchmen and Philosophers (see 596), Foster's detailed study still provides a good survey (with commentary shaped by the author's moderate liberalism) of main theological developments from Jonathan Edwards in the eighteenth century through Nathaniel W. Taylor and Horace Bushnell, the most creative American theologians of the antebellum period.

580. Gaustad, Edwin Scott. The Great Awakening in New England. New York: Harper & Bros., 1957.

Gaustad's solid book remains the best survey of the immensely influential events inspired by the preaching of George Whitefield, assessed by the theology of Jonathan Edwards, and questioned by the opposition of Charles Chauncy.

581. Goen, C. C. Broken Churches, Broken Nation: Denominational Schism and the Coming of the American Civil War. Macon, GA: Mercer University Press, 1985.

Goen's argument is that in the first half of the nineteenth century denominations were among the few truly national institutions binding the United States together. When the Presbyterians divided in 1837 and both Methodists and Baptists in 1844, Civil War was that much more likely. Goen's history is solid and his moral indignation at what happened provocative.

582. Goen, C. C. Revivalism and Separatism in New England, 1740-1800: Strict Congregationalists and Separate Baptists in the Great Awakening. New Haven, CT: Yale University Press, 1962.

Hard on the heels of George Whitefield's revival preaching came the formation of independent congregations "separate" from the New England Congregational establishments. Goen's carefully researched book well describes these efforts that inspired an increasingly common pattern for church formation among American evangelicals.

583. Gravely, Will B. "African Methodists and the Rise of Black Denominationalism." In Rethinking Methodist History, eds. Russell E. Richey and Kenneth E. Rowe. Nashville: Kingswood Books, 1985.

Gravely makes a good case for the argument that the ideology of the American Revolution and the ecclesiology of Methodist connectionalism inspired the rise of Black Methodist associations. Only when the bonds they shared with similar movements among whites gave way did the black Methodists form racially separate denominations.

584. Hardesty, Nancy A. Women Called to Witness: Evangelical Feminism in the Nineteenth Century. Nashville: Abingdon, 1984.

In the liberating atmosphere of nineteenth-century America, Christian women took a much more active public role than heretofore in promoting evangelism and social reform. Hardesty's book is a well constructed description of that phenomenon.

585. Hardman, Keith J. Charles Grandison Finney, 1792-1875: Revivalist and Reformer. Syracuse, NY: Syracuse University Press, 1987.

As the best biography to date of Finney, this book is essential reading for understanding the character, strengths, and weaknesses of nineteenth-century American evangelicalism.

586. Haroutunian, Joseph. Piety Versus Moralism: The Passing of the New England Theology. New York: Henry Holt, 1932.

Haroutunian, an early American advocate of neo-orthodox theology, thought it was a tragedy for the theological descendents of Jonathan Edwards to exchange his God-centered perspective for one focusing more on the rights and capabilities of humans.

587. Hatch, Nathan O. The Democratization of American Christianity. New Haven, CT: Yale University Press, 1989.

Denominational historians are subject to the nearly irresistible temptation of prettying up their churches' pasts. The result is to picture the various American denominations as progressive supporters of civilization, decorum, and strong institutions. In this prize winning book, on the other hand, Hatch argues that the real story was much more aggressive, individualistic, competitive, and anti-institutional. Religion in the early United States among Baptists, Methodists, Disciples, "Christians," and Mormons was much more a rough-and-ready struggle than a steady glide to respectability.

588. Hatch, Nathan O. The Sacred Cause of Liberty: Republican Thought and the Millennium in Revolutionary New England. New Haven, CT: Yale University Press, 1977.

Details of Hatch's interpretation in this book have been questioned since its publication, but his main contention about the tight bond between the ideology of the Revolution and the self-identity of the New England churches continues to be immensely helpful for understanding why American evangelicals have so thoroughly accepted the conventions of American political and social ideology.

589. Hatch, Nathan O. and Harry S. Stout, eds. Jonathan Edwards and the American Experience. New York: Oxford University Press, 1988.

Edwards' reputation continues to grow, as philosopher, theologian, and revivalist. This book's fifteen essays focus on the contexts (cultural and philosophical) and legacies (intellectual, literary, and theological) of Edwards' massive work.

590. Heimert, Alan. Religion and the American Mind: From the Great Awakening to the American Revolution. Cambridge, MA: Harvard University Press, 1966.

This influential revisionist study argued that a direct line tied the revivalism of George Whitefield, Gilbert Tennent, and similar colonial revivalists to the popular democracy of Andrew Jackson. Perhaps overstated, Heimert's book was nonetheless one of the most significant influences of recent decades in pushing evangelicals from the margins close to the center of American historical study.

591. Henry, Stuart Clark. George Whitefield: Wayfaring Witness. Nashville: Abingdon, 1957.

Whitefield (1714-1770) was the key public figure in the creation of American revivalism, and as such a very important, though understudied, figure in the history of evangelicalism.

592. Holifield, E. Brooks. The Gentlemen Theologians: American Theology in Southern Culture, 1795-1860. Durham, NC: Duke University Press, 1978.

Southern clerical intellectuals, it turns out, shared most of the same intellectual concerns as those described in Bozeman's Protestants in an Age of Science. They applauded Baconian method, exploited the Scottish philosophy of common sense, and expected intellectual life to aid in civilizing barbarism. Holifield's model study of one hundred publishing ministers shows how easily evangelical themes could be adapted to urban as well as frontier environments.

593. Hood, Fred J. Reformed America: The Middle and Southern States, 1783-1837. University: University of Alabama Press, 1980.

Hood suggests persuasively that the work of learned Presbyterians like John Witherspoon (1723-1794) and Samuel Stanhope Smith (1751-1819), successive presidents of Princeton College, by combining Enlightenment thought, Reformed traditions, and American patriotism, bequeathed a distinct ethos to southern Christian thought. Revivalism popularized, but did not displace, that combination.

594. Isaac, Rhys. The Transformation of Virginia, 1740-1790. Chapel Hill: University of North Carolina Press, 1982.

Isaac's signal contribution in this ethnography is to show how early evangelical Baptists challenged the values of deference, honor, and personal esteem that had made the elite South so different from Puritan New England.

595. Johnson, Paul E. A Shopkeeper's Millennium: Society and Revivals in Rochester, New York, 1815-1837. New York: Hill and Wang, 1978.

Johnson studied evangelical religion in Rochester, especially Charles Finney's influential tours in the 1830s, with an eye to connections between the uses of religion and the values of consumer capitalism. Whether or not he gave religious motives their full due, he nonetheless showed clearly that Rochester's religious, commercial, and social spheres were always intertwined.

596. Kuklick, Bruce. Churchmen and Philosophers from Jonathan Edwards to John Dewey. New Haven, CT: Yale University Press, 1985.

Kuklick's altogether persuasive argument is that a tradition of trinitarian theology stretching from Jonathan Edwards to the teachers (and even early sentiments) of John Dewey was (a) the United States's most important philosophical tradition of the eighteenth and nineteenth century, and (b) a system of thought unexpectedly respectable in its intellectual rigor if not (for Kuklick) in its theological convictions.

597. Lovelace, Richard F. The American Piety of Cotton Mather: Origins of American Evangelicalism. Grand Rapids: Eerdmans, 1979.

Boston's Cotton Mather (1663-1728), author of over 400 separate publications, was the last polymath in the history of American religion. He was also, in Lovelace's convincing portrait, a very important bridge between Puritanism and evangelicalism, especially with his practice of activistic pietism.

598. Loveland, Anne C. Southern Evangelicals and the Social Order, 1800-1860. Baton Rouge: Louisiana State University Press, 1980.

This book complements nicely Holifield's intellectual history (Gentlemen Theologians) and Mathews' social history (Religion in the Old South) to describe the continuing fixation of Southern religious leaders on the questions of order inspired by both the inner impulses of evangelical Christianity and the external constraints of chattel bondage.

599. Marini, Stephen A. Radical Sects of Revolutionary New England. Cambridge, MA: Harvard University Press, 1982.

Marini anticipated some of the arguments in Nathan Hatch's Democratization of American Christianity in this study of Shakers, Free Will Baptists, and Universalists. Their antiestablishmentarianism, individualism, and apocalypticism was a harbinger of what was in store more generally for American religion.

600. Marsden, George M. The Evangelical Mind and the New School Presbyterian Experience: A Case Study of Thought and Theology in the Nineteenth-Century Mind. New Haven, CT: Yale University Press, 1970.

New School Presbyterians mediated between the earthy American faiths promoted by the leaders described in Allen & Hughes's Illusions of Innocence, Hatch's Democratization of American Christianity, and Marini's Radical Sects on the one hand, and the traditionalist Old School confessionalism of the Princeton Theologians and their allies on the others. As described in this persuasive book they incorporated nineteenth-century values wholesale into their convictions, thus making their opinions immensely influential in their own day but problematic for later evangelical generations.

601. Mathews, Donald G. "The Second Great Awakening As an Organizing Process, 1780-1830." American Quarterly 21 (1969): 23-43.

With Lois Banner's essay, "Religious Benevolence as Social Control: A Critique," (see 564) Mathews's influential paper helped put to rest the notion of the Second Great Awakening as a manipulative struggle for power.

Rather, the revivals represented cultural and social, as well as religious, efforts to reduce to manageable proportions the near chaos of life in the early United States.

602. May, Henry F. The Enlightenment in America. New York: Oxford University Press, 1976.

This great book proposes that the Enlightenment in America always reflected the dialogue between traditional religion (mostly evangelical Calvinism) and the forces of secularizing modernity (best exemplified by Thomas Jefferson). Americans perceived the Enlightenment in four forms: Moderate (of Newton and Locke) which they admired; Skeptical (of Voltaire and Hume) which they repudiated; Revolutionary (of Rousseau and Paine) which they abominated; and Didactic (of Scotland's Francis Hutcheson and Thomas Reid) which they embraced as their own. The history of evangelical thought since the 1770s is largely made up of variations on that embrace.

603. McLoughlin, William G. Isaac Backus and the American Pietistic Tradition. Boston: Little, Brown, 1967.

604. McLoughlin, William G. New England Dissent, 1630-1833: The Baptists and the Separation of Church and State. 2 vols. Cambridge, MA: Harvard University Press, 1971.

McLoughlin's path-breaking studies of New England Baptists in the colonial and Revolutionary periods led him to the conclusion that the religious style of these evangelical pietists was more directly influential on later evangelical religion than the better known Puritans. His comprehensive study of dissent in New England and his helpful biography of Backus, leading figure of the New England Baptists, go far to support that conviction.

605. Miller, Perry. The Life of the Mind in America: From the Revolution to the Civil War. New York: Harcourt Brace and World, 1965.

Miller, the most influential American historian of his generation, did not live to complete the book projected under this title, but he did finish the first section of the volume, "The Evangelical Basis." That essay provides a captivating summary of how evangelicalism drew into itself colonial religious traditions, Revolutionary conventions, and frontier resourcefulness.

606. Moorhead, James H. American Apocalypse: Yankee Protestants and the Civil War, 1860-1869. New Haven, CT: Yale University Press, 1978.

With this book Moorehead did for the North in the Civil War what several historians have done for the Revolution, which is to describe in careful detail how the trauma of armed conflict drove Northern ministers to interpret their national struggle as part of the universal drama of salvation.

607. Nichols, James Hastings. Romanticism in American Theology: Nevin and Schaff at Mercersburg. Chicago: University of Chicago Press, 1961.

The Mercersburg Theologians were odd men out in antebellum American history, for they were evangelicals who took their philosophical cues from Germany instead of Scotland, and their theological guidance from church history instead of the needs of the moment. The result was a theology that has drawn increasing attention from twentieth-century Christians weary of Scottish philosophy and American presentism, but which (for better or for worse) had very little influence in its own day.

608. Noll, Mark A. Christians in the American Revolution. Grand Rapids: Eerdmans, 1977.

Noll describes the reactions of four Christian groups to the American Revolution: Loyalists, who stuck with England (in some measure for religious reasons); Pacifists, who repudiated all wars, including that one; Patriots, who uncritically linked the values of the Kingdom of God to the ideology of the new United States; and Reformers, who were patriots who nonetheless exploited the times to argue against slavery and for the disestablishment of the colonial churches.

609. Noll, Mark A. Princeton and the Republic, 1768-1822: The Search for a Christian Enlightenment in the Era of Samuel Stanhope Smith. Princeton, NJ: Princeton University Press, 1989.

Under three successive presidents--John Witherspoon (1768-1794), Samuel Stanhope Smith (1795-1812), and Ashbel Green (1812-1822)-- Princeton College, its trustees, and students struggled to be at once republican, patriotic, Reformed, enlightened, and scientific. The synthesis, which had been molded by Witherspoon, exploded into student rebellion and ecclesiastical suspicion under Smith and was pulled back toward confessional and revivalistic norms under Green. The complicated intellectual connections of this period lived on at Princeton College until the 1890s, at Princeton Theological Seminary (founded in 1812 by this same Princeton circle) until 1929, and in American evangelicalism more broadly to the present day.

610. Orr, J. Edwin. The Fervent Prayer: The Worldwide Impact of the Great Awakening of 1858. Chicago: Moody Press, 1974.

The "business men's revival" of 1858 was one of the least politicized of the major national (or at least Northern) awakenings. Although it may have had something to do with the tensions that eventuated in the Civil War, its determinedly evangelical surge was felt in many other countries and in the revivals described by Gardiner Shattuck (see 614) during the War Between the States.

611. Pointer, Richard. Protestant Pluralism and the New York Experience: A Study of Eighteenth-Century Religious Diversity. Bloomington: Indiana University Press, 1988.

Pointer joins the growing chorus (with, for example, Jon Butler's study of colonial churches in the Delaware Valley) to argue for the centrality of the middle colonies in American religious history. New York's relatively easy acceptance of different denominations and the relative prosperity of its churches after the War may indeed have been more influential in setting the standards for later evangelical patterns than the more thoroughly studied events of New England.

612. Rosenberg, Carroll Smith. Religion and the Rise of the American City: The New York City Mission Movement, 1812-1870. Ithaca, NY: Cornell University Press, 1971.

This accomplished social history shows how revivalism of the type sponsored by Charles Finney helped create many of New York's most active aid and reform societies, but also how the energy behind these societies passed from evangelical piety to secular moralism over the course of the century.

613. Scherer, Lester B. Slavery and the Churches in Early America, 1619-1819. Grand Rapids: Eerdmans, 1975.

This is a solid survey but a dreary tale. With very few exceptions (at first Mennonites and Quakers, later a few theological heirs of Jonathan Edwards), churches in early America sanctioned slavery and stood by silently while it developed. In so doing they bequeathed a legacy of wormwood and gall to evangelicals and all other Christians in the history of the United States.

614. Shattuck, Gardiner H., Jr. A Shield and Hiding Place: The Religious Life of the Civil War Armies. Macon, GA: Mercer University Press, 1987.

Shattuck's succinct, lucid account of the chaplains, the voluntary agencies for evangelism and social welfare, and the revivals in the Civil War armies points to an important revisionist conclusion: neither leaders nor followers, especially in the South, were as guilty of reflexive religious-nationalism as early studies have suggested.

615. Shipps, Jan. Mormonism: The Story of a New Religious Tradition. Urbana, IL: University of Illinois Press, 1985.

The Mormons distanced themselves first theologically and then geographically from their contemporaries. But Shipps's innovative study, which makes full use of methods from the History of Religions, suggests that Joseph Smith intended the "new" of Mormon tradition to build upon the "old" of evangelical Protestantism as it had developed in America.

616. Smith, Timothy L. Revivalism and Social Reform: American Protestantism on the Eve of the Civil War. New introduction. Baltimore: John Hopkins University Press, 1980; orig., 1957.

617. Smith, Timothy L. "Righteousness and Hope: Christian Holiness and the Millennial Vision in America, 1800-1900." American Quarterly 31 (Spring 1979): 21-45.

Timothy Smith has been a pioneer in two senses: first as a sensitive interpreter of nineteenth-century evangelicals, second as himself an evangelical writing the history of his own religious tradition. The influential book and summative article here both propound forcefully the thesis that generally evangelical and specifically Wesleyan themes (holiness, millennialism, social activism) exerted a determinative influence on the shape of nineteenth-century American society.

618. Stoeffler, F. Ernest, ed. Continental Pietism and Early American Christianity. Grand Rapids: Eerdmans, 1976.

Religious life in colonial America meant more than New England Puritanism and Southern Anglicanism, for the colonial period also witnessed the introduction of European Protestantism into the New World. This collection contains outstanding essays on Lutherans, Reformed Dutch and Germans, Mennonites, Moravians, Methodists, and Brethren, all of whom add a subtle counterpoint to the more dominant English themes in American evangelical history.

619. Stout, Harry S. The New England Soul: Preaching and Religious Culture in Colonial New England. New York: Oxford University Press, 1986.

Stout's magisterial book argues several influential theses: that the preaching of God's law and grace was the heart of New England public speech from the earliest days through the Revolution, that a shift in communication strategies with George Whitefield and the Great Awakening resulted in a significant democratization of New England life, and that preaching was the life-blood of New England's special sense of divine mission (which ministers defended against perceived British aggression in the Revolution). Stout is altogether successful in demonstrating how important it is to research unpublished manuscript sermons, along with the published variety, to gain a full sense of New England life.

620. Sweet, Leonard I. The Minister's Wife: Her Role in Nineteenth-Century American Evangelicalism. Philadelphia: Temple University Press, 1983.

In the early United States, ministers' wives measurably enhanced not only their husbands' ministries but also the general spread of evangelical influence. Sweet's account of four styles--Companion, Sacrificer, Assistant, and Partner--shows how and why the role of these "ministers without portfolio" became as important as it did.

621. Walters, Ronald G. American Reformers. New York: Hill and Wang, 1978.

Almost all significant reforms in the nineteenth century (abolition, women's rights, prison reform, temperance) were either dominated or substantially influenced by evangelicals. This good survey puts those various movements into their larger cultural perspectives.

622. Weddle, David L. The Law as Gospel: Revival and Reform in the Theology of Charles G. Finney. Metuchen, NJ: Scarecrow Press, 1985.

Weddle suggests that Finney's early training as a lawyer, and the general search by Americans in the early republic for manageable guidelines for life, had a great influence on Finney's theology and revival practice. The book is a welcome stimulus to further study of these types of vital, but understudied connections.

623. Welter, Barbara. "The Feminization of American Religion: 1800-1860." In Dimity Convictions: The American Woman in the Nineteenth Century. Athens: Ohio University Press, 1976.

Welter's oft-reprinted essay argues that in the antebellum period public evangelical Christianity became more and more the preserve of women and that women became more and more the cutting edge of religious activity. What such a circumstance might mean and how it relates to previous American patterns (where virtually all churches with records show more women members than men) is not as clear as the fact that it did indeed take place.

624. Wolf, William J. The Almost Chosen People: A Study of the Religion of Abraham Lincoln. Garden City, NY: Doubleday, 1959.

In the face of persistent historical legerdemain suggesting the contrary, the fact remains that Lincoln was never an evangelical Protestant. What Wolf's careful book shows, however, is that Lincoln had a deep faith in divine providence (understood almost in fatalistic terms), an encyclopedic knowledge of the Scriptures (especially the Old Testament), and an abiding respect for the morality of the universe.

625. Wood, Gordon S. "Evangelical America and Early Mormonism." New York History 61 (Oct.1980): 359-386.

This is a very important essay because of its stated subject, for Wood shows clearly how many formal similarities existed between general evangelical currents and the new religion of Joseph Smith. But it is also important because of its wider assertions about the way the American Revolution and the social crisis following in its wake transformed American religion into democratic evangelicalism.

626. Wyatt-Brown, Bertram. Lewis Tappan and the Evangelical War Against Slavery. Cleveland: Press of Case Western University, 1969.

Tappan and his brother, Arthur, were well-to-do New York merchants who funded many of the evangelical ventures of the antebellum period. Wyatt-Brown's insightful study clarifies especially the central role of lay people in establishing the evangelical culture of the nineteenth century.

CHAPTER 10
THE CHALLENGES OF MODERNITY, 1865-1915

Evangelicals had earlier set the norms for Protestantism in the United States. In religious history after the Civil War they gradually became only one among several varieties of Protestants. The emergence of a more liberal variety was of course a major preoccupation of some evangelicals, but the presence of increasing numbers of immigrants, for example, German and Scandinavian Lutherans as well as Dutch Reformed, meant that the earlier American evangelicals now had more competition than once was the case. And this is not even to mention the rapid growth of the Roman Catholic Church, which had made it by the end of the century the largest Christian body in the country. Cultural change dominated the agenda for Protestants between the Civil War and the 1920s: with the growth of industry and cities, the influx of immigrants, and the reorganization of the American university. All these cultural challenges had the effect of pushing evangelicals off the central place they had long enjoyed in American culture. A militant opposition to theological liberalism and cultural dislocation, which came to be known as fundamentalism, was one of the products of the era. But other important evangelical developments occurred as well, some of them only tangentially related to fundamentalism. Of these the most important were the rise of holiness motifs in several locations on the American church landscape and the emergence after the turn of the century of pentecostalism. In the listing that follows, considerable attention is paid to writings produced by evangelical leaders themselves. Several of the volumes have been published as a part of two outstanding reprint series: Joel A. Carpenter, ed. Fundamentalism in American Religion, 1880-1950 (Garland, 1988) and Donald W. Dayton, ed. "The Higher Christian Life": Sources for the Study of the Holiness, Pentecostal and Keswick Movements (Garland, 1984).

527. Bartleman, Frank. Witness to Pentecost: The Life of Frank Bartleman, ed. Cecil M. Robeck, Jr. New York: Garland, 1984. (Dayton 5)

The several autobiographical writings collected in this well introduced edition are especially important, because they include Bartleman's recollections of the 1906 Azusa Street revival in Los Angeles that became the fount of world wide pentecostalism.

628. Bass, Clarence B. Backgrounds to Dispensationalism: Historical Genesis and Ecclesiastical Implications. Grand Rapids: Eerdmans, 1960.

This book presents a good overview of the main tenets of dispensational theology, a primary influence among fundamentalists and many other varieties of evangelicals. The author writes from the perspective of one who grew up a dispensationalist, but then became a mild critic of the position.

629. Boardman, W. E. The Higher Christian Life. Boston: Henry Hoyt, 1858. (Dayton 6)

Broadman's book, a product of the widespread urban revivals of 1857-1858, spread in America and Britain the teaching that a higher form of sanctification was possible for the believers who sought it with their whole hearts. It had particular appeal among non-Methodists who were perturbed by the language of "Christian perfection" through which the teaching was often spread.

630. Bode, Frederick A. Protestantism and the New South: North Carolina Baptists and Methodists in Political Crisis, 1894-1903. Charlottesville: University Press of Virginia, 1975.

Bode's account of controversies over the University of North Carolina, over public education, and over race shows how traditional evangelical attitudes survived (despite considerable opposition from some progressive thinkers) in the move toward a more metropolitan and more capitalistic society.

631. Bordin, Ruth. Frances Willard: A Biography. Chapel Hill: University of North Carolina Press, 1986.

632. Bordin, Ruth. Woman and Temperance: The Quest for Power and Liberty, 1873-1900. Philadelphia: Temple University Press, 1981.

Bordin is one of the leading interpreters of the nineteenth-century temperance movement and Frances Willard, one of its guiding spirits. These books show that while the assault on drink was never less than it appeared to be, it was also often a vehicle for women raised in Protestant (usually evangelical) traditions to exert a widespread public impact.

633. Boyer, Paul. Urban Masses and Moral Order in America, 1820-1920. Cambridge, MA: Harvard University Press, 1978.

Boyer's thorough study includes much about evangelical aspirations for, and efforts in, the new American cities of the nineteenth century. The structural movement he traces is from voluntary organization to reliance on professionals. The movement in expectation is from a focus on individuals to a focus on environment. In the course of the book's century, the struggle for order in the cities passed from an evangelical enterprise to one engineered by moral reformers more generally.

634. Bryan, William Jennings. William Jennings Bryan on Orthodoxy, Modernism, and Evolution. New York: Garland, 1988. (Carpenter 27)

This reprint edition includes two of the works through which Bryan defended the Bible, opposed evolution, and communicated his fears about the fate of Christian civilization: Seven Questions in Dispute: Shall Christianity Remain Christian (1924), and The Last Message of William Jennings Bryan (1925).

635. Carpenter, Joel A., ed. The Premillennial Second Coming: Two Early Champions. New York: Garland, 1988. (Carpenter 2)

The belief that Christ would return to earth to establish a thousand-year reign of peace and justice had become a central tenet of fundamentalist teaching by 1900. Two of the most persuasive works arguing for that interpretation of the Bible are presented in this volume, A. J. Gordon's Ecce Venit: Behold He Cometh (1889) and William E. Blackstone's Jesus Is Coming (see 1403).

636. Carter, Paul A. The Spiritual Crisis of the Gilded Age. DeKalb: Northern Illinois University Press, 1971.

This path-breaking study had the effrontery to take seriously the thoughts and aspirations of an age that other historians regularly passed over as beneath contempt. The pay-off is a book rich with insight into the way that modern views of science and modern demands of technology disrupted the (mostly evangelical) forms of faith inherited from before the Civil War.

637. Clark, Norman H. Deliver Us From Evil: An Interpretation of American Prohibition. New York: W. W. Norton, 1976.

Prohibition has been a butt of many jokes, but it was no laughing matter to its promoters. Clark's unusually perceptive book set a new standard for taking the crusade and its impact with the deadly seriousness that it deserves.

638. Clifford, N. Keith. The Resistance to Church Union in Canada, 1904-1939. Vancouver: University of British Columbia Press, 1985.

Canadian church life never saw the violent extremes of the United States's fundamentalist-modernist controversies. But when Methodist, Congregationalist, and some Presbyterian churches merged into a United Church in 1925, protesters against that move, which are well described in this book, were able to borrow some of the arguments of conservatives south of the border for their cause.

639. Coletta, Paolo E. William Jennings Bryan, Volume 3: Political Puritan, 1915-1925. Lincoln: University of Nebraska Press, 1969.

This last volume of Coletta's thorough, judicious biography expertly traces the transition in Bryan's career from populist champion of Democratic causes to popular spokesmen for fundamentalist concerns.

640. Dayton, Donald W., ed. Late Nineteenth Century Revivalist Teachings on the Holy Spirit. New York: Garland, 1984. (Dayton 12)

This collection shows well how emphasis on the special work of the Holy Spirit had become a major part of the nation's central revival tradition by the end of the nineteenth century. Included here are works by the leading revivalist, D. L. Moody (Secret Power: Or, the Secret of Success in Christian Life and Work, 1881), Moody's successor, R.A. Torrey (The Baptism with the Holy Spirit, 1895), and J. Wilbur Champman, another popular revivalist of the same era (Received Ye the Holy Ghost?, 1894).

641. Dayton, Donald W. Theological Roots of Pentecostalism. Grand Rapids: Zondervan, 1987.

Dayton's major study makes a strong case for the thesis that pentecostalism emerged from the Wesleyan, holiness, victorious life, and Keswick traditions. As Dayton sees it, these experience-oriented movements, rather than dogmatic notions concerning biblical inerrancy or the second coming of Christ, had become the heart of American evangelical experience in the nineteenth century.

642. Dayton, Donald W., ed. Three Early Pentecostal Tracts. New York: Garland, 1984. (Dayton 14)

The three are all accounts of the early years of pentecostalism, which combine description with advocacy: D. Wesley Myland, The Latter Rain Covenant and Pentecostal Power (see 1425); G. F. Taylor, The Spirit and the Bride (1907); and B. F. Lawrence, The Apostolic Faith (1961, with reminiscences of events fifty years before).

643. Dixon, Amzi C., Louis Meyer and Reuben A. Torrey, eds. The Fundamentals: A Testimony to the Truth. 12 vols. Chicago: Testimony Publishing, 1910-1915. (Carpenter 14-17, with intro by George M. Marsden)

Although The Fundamentals (1910-1915) predate "fundamentalism" (identifiable as a movement only after World War I), these booklets present a good precis of the doctrines and practices (including the infallibility of the Bible, the deity and Virgin Birth of Christ, the need for discrimination in ecclesiastical fellowship) later "fundamentalists" would defend even more militantly. Over 3,000,000 copies of these pamphlets, sponsored by Lyman Stewart of the Sun Oil Company, were sent out to pastors and Christian workers.

644. Ellis, Walter E. "Gilboa to Ichabod: Social and Religious Factors in the Fundamentalist-Modernist Schisms among Canadian Baptists, 1895-1934." Foundations 20 (1977): 109-26.

Baptists in Ontario came as close to experiencing the sort of Fundamentalist-Modernist struggles taking place in the United States as any Canadian denomination. Ellis, who has also written on T. T. Shields, the focal point of much Ontario Baptist controversy, here insightfully describes the lay of the land for those Canadian disputes.

645. Ellis, William E. A Man of Books and a Man of the People: E. Y. Mullins and the Crisis of Moderate Southern Baptist Leadership. Macon, GA: Mercer University Press, 1985.

E. Y. Mullins (1860-1928), the most influential Southern Baptist of his generation, contributed articles to The Fundamentals and engineered the acceptance of a conservative creed by his denomination, but he was more irenic and more concerned about the nature of religious experience than most of the self-proclaimed fundamentalist leaders. This book makes a good start on studying an influential evangelical leader.

646. Findlay, James F. Dwight L. Moody: American Evangelist, 1837-1899. Chicago: University of Chicago Press, 1969.

Moody was the Billy Graham of his day, known and beloved by more Christians in Britain and America than any of his contemporaries. Findlay's is with justice the standard biography, as essential for understanding Moody's turn from social activism to private pietism as for grasping Moody's mediation of doctrinal conservatism and Higher Life experientialism.

647. Frank, Douglas. Less Than Conquerors: How Evangelicals Entered the Twentieth Century. Grand Rapids: Eerdmans, 1986.

This is the most challenging book yet written about the origins of twentieth-century evangelicalism. There is too much preaching (of grace against self-righteousness), too much exhortation (toward self-sacrifice and away from spiritual escapism), and too much ideological self-confidence (in the irredeemable character of consumerist capitalism) to keep this from being a widely accepted historical interpretation. But Frank's insights (especially concerning Billy Sunday's ministry) into the meaning of modern evangelicalism makes this book required reading, most of all for those who in the end must disagree with its message.

648. God Hath Spoken: Twenty-Five Addresses Delivered at the World Conference on Christian Fundamentals, May 25-June 1, 1919. Philadelphia: Bible Conference Committee, 1919. (Carpenter 22)

At this meeting in 1919 was founded the World Christian Fundamentals Association. Its concern to defend supernatural, biblical, and premillennial Christianity did much to define the public image of fundamentalism.

649. Gordon, Ernest B. Adoniram Judson Gordon. New York: Fleming H. Revell, 1896. (Dayton 20)

Boston's A. J. Gordon (1836-1895) emphasized the work of the Holy Spirit throughout his long and influential career and so contributed an essential element to the emergence of twentieth-century evangelicalism. This biography by his son includes consideration of the Boston Training Institute that years later evolved into two institutions, Gordon College and Gordon-Conwell Theological Seminary.

650. Gray, James M. The Bible in Faith and Life, as Taught by James M. Gray. New York: Garland, 1988. (Carpenter 18)

Gray was a Reformed Episcopalian who became the president of Moody Bible Institute in 1904. From that strategic post his quiet, but effective teaching of premillennial and dispensational themes had a major impact on fundamentalism in the Midwest and far beyond. This volume includes Gray's Christian Worker's Commentary on the Old and New Testaments (1915) and Bible Problems Explained (1913).

Hill, Patricia R. The World Their Household: The American Women's Foreign Mission Movement and Cultural Transformation, 1870-1920. Ann Arbor: University of Michigan, 1985.
(see 1311)

651. Hopkins, C. Howard. John R. Mott, 1865-1955: A Biography. Grand Rapids: Eerdmans, 1979.

Mott was a leader of the ecumenical and missions movements at a time when they were substantially evangelical enterprises. This large, authoritative biography contains a full recital of the ways in which Mott's activities embodied an evangelical spirit, but also of the ways in which ecumenicism began to be suspect in the eyes of fundamentalists and some evangelicals.

Hunter, Jane. The Gospel of Gentility: American Women Missionaries in Turn-of-the-Century China. New Haven, CT: Yale University Press, 1984.
(see 1313)

652. Hutchison, William R. The Modernist Impulse in American Protestantism. Cambridge, MA: Harvard University Press, 1976.

This is an outstanding study of the movement within American Protestantism to accommodate Christianity to the spirit of the modern age. An idea of God adjusted to notions of immanence and evolution as well as a vision of humanity progressing in the nineteenth century beyond barbarism to maturity were principal components of the "modernist impulse." It was this modernism that fundamentalism arose to oppose and that has remained the central theological foe to most twentieth-century evangelicals.

653. Levine, Lawrence W. Defender of the Faith, William Jennings Bryan: The Last Decade, 1915-1925. New York: Oxford University Press, 1965.

Levine's portrait of Bryan in the years of his fundamentalist leadership complements nicely the fuller study by Coletta, noted above.

McLoughlin, William G. Billy Sunday Was His Real Name. Chicago: University of Chicago Press, 1955.
(see 1384)

654. McPherson, Aimee Semple. This is That: Personal Experiences, Sermons and Writings. Los Angeles: The Bridal Call Publishing House, 1919. (Dayton 27)

McPherson, a controversial pentecostal revivalist, was the founder of the International Church of the Foursquare Gospel. This book illustrates the message that she proclaimed from her spectacular Angeles Temple in Los Angeles and suggests the power that made her activities so important to the early spread of pentecostalism.

655. Magnuson, Norris. Salvation in the Slums: Evangelical Social Work, 1865-1920. Grand Rapids: Baker, 1990; orig. 1977.

The stereotype has a great divide opening within Protestantism at the end of the nineteenth century between advocates of liberalism and the Social Gospel on one side, and fundamentalists and social reactionaries on the other. Magnuson's book, which focuses on the Salvation Army and similar little noticed bodies, is a most useful reminder that many evangelicals continued to be very active in city social work long after the doctrinal breach had supposedly removed all theological conservatives from such endeavors.

656. Marsden, George M. Fundamentalism and American Culture: The Shaping of Twentieth Century Evangelicalism, 1870-1925. New York: Oxford University Press, 1980.

Marsden's magisterial study emphasizes the continuities between fundamentalism and major trends of nineteenth-century evangelical life, including especially the heritage of revivalism. While an increased concern for eschatology and a heightened sense of biblical inerrancy gradually became more important in that revivalistic tradition, it was the sharpened sense of cultural conflict and decay, occasioned especially by the trauma of World War I, that Marsden sees as marking the emergence of an identifiable fundamentalist movement. A luminous "Afterword" to this book offers a path-breaking statement about the possibility of studying a religious phenomenon like fundamentalism as an objective historical concern as well as a partisan theological matter.

657. Marsden, George. "Fundamentalism As an American Phenomenon: A Comparison With English Evangelicalism." Church History 46 (June 1977): 215-232.

British evangelicals did not experience as severe a fundamentalist-modernist crisis as Americans, Marsden says, because the considerable number of British evangelicals in the established Church of England continued to enjoy a place of relative security in that nation's church life, because British educational institutions remained somewhat more open to traditional patterns of belief, and because the British had a more relaxed attitude toward evolution.

658. Marty, Martin E. Modern American Religion, Volume I: The Irony of It All, 1893-1919. Chicago: University of Chicago Press, 1986.

Marty here describes several ways in which American religious groups responded to the growing sense at the turn of the century that the nation had entered a changed, "modern" situation. He describes fundamentalists as "anti-moderns" who in their zeal to roll back contemporary assumptions themselves became innovators doctrinally (with dispensational eschatology) and organizationally (with a move to extreme independency). A number of evangelical groups are also featured in Marty's section on ethnic communities, which he labels people of "the cocoon."

659. May, Henry F. Protestant Churches and Industrial America. New York: Harper and Brothers, 1949.

Social crisis, especially "large-scale, violent labor conflicts," was, according to May, more important for dislodging the monolith of evangelical Protestantism from its dominance in American culture at the end of the nineteenth century than specific issues of theology or the general drift of the climate of opinion. If the thesis is overstated, it nonetheless draws very helpful attention to the manifold (but under-appreciated) connections between evangelical religion and the full spectrum of American experience.

660. Palmer, Phoebe. The Devotional Writings of Phoebe Palmer, ed. Donald W. Dayton. New York: Garland, 1984. (Dayton 30)

As a most important promoter of holiness teachings in the mid-nineteenth century, Phoebe Palmer (1807-1884) exerted tremendous influence on her own generation and had an even greater impact on the later history of evangelicalism. This volume contains two of her works, The Way of Holiness, which went through more than fifty editions in the 1850s and 1860s, and Faith and Its Effects, which was circulated nearly as widely. Together they expound themes of total surrender, laying all on the altar, and complete dedication that would become standard in the evangelical movement by the end of the century.

661. Parham, Charles F. The Sermons of Charles F. Parham, ed. Donald W. Dayton. New York: Garland, 1984. (Dayton 36)

Parham was one of the leaders whose teachings sparked the 1906 pentecostal revival at Azusa Street in Los Angeles, which was the beginning of the world-wide pentecostal movement. The two books published together in this modern edition contain what would become standard pentecostal emphases on the baptism of the Holy Spirit, healing, and speaking in tongues.

662. Pierson, Arthur Tappan. Forward Movements of the Last Half Century. New York: Funk and Wagnalls, 1905. (Dayton 37)

Evangelical missionary work flourished at the end of the nineteenth century, and A. T. Pierson was one of its prime movers. Pierson was a particularly effective representative of Keswick or "Higher Life" emphases, which in this book he tied to the various missionary and moral reform movements that had flourished in and from America during the second half of the nineteenth century.

663. Piper, John F., Jr. American Churches in World War I. Athens: Ohio University Press, 1985.

Piper sets out to revise the contention of Ray Abrams' Preachers Present Arms (1933), that during the First World War Protestants consistently (and shamefully) redefined the faith to fit the needs of military propaganda. Not so, or at least not entirely so, is Piper's verdict, for he finds much evidence of spokespersons who agonized over the role of the churches in the war and who sought constructive means to preserve authentic Christian witness amid the tumult of the times.

664. Rausch, David A. Zionism Within Early American Fundamentalism, 1878-1918: A Convergence of Two Traditions. New York: Edwin Mellen Press, 1979.

Fundamentalist support for the state of Israel is a well-known feature of modern evangelical life. But so is the lingering suspicion that fundamentalists are anti-Semitic. Rausch, the premier expositor on the subject, shows here that efforts both to evangelize Jews (hence the image of anti-Semitism) and to promote Zionism (hence the support for Israel) were part and parcel of early fundamentalists' premillennial eschatology.

665. Robert, Dana Lee. "Arthur Tappan and the Forward Movements of Late-Nineteenth Century Evangelicalism." Ph.D. dissertation, Yale University, 1984.

Pierson was one of the most important promoters of missionary work at the end of the nineteenth century. This fine dissertation shows how his premillennialism bequeathed great energy to his missiology and how his Moody-like concerns helped shape the emerging fundamentalist movement.

666. Ruffin, Bernard. Fanny Crosby. Philadelphia: United Church Press, 1976.

This is a serious book on a woman who probably has had more general influence on American evangelicalism than all but one or two men. Fanny Crosby (1823-1915) overcame blindness to write more than 2,000 hymns (including such standards as "Safe in the Arms of Jesus," "To God be the Glory," "Saved by Grace," "Blessed Assurance, Jesus is Mine"). Ruffin expertly situates her and the themes of her verse in the evangelical America that she helped to define.

667. Sandeen, Ernest R. The Roots of Fundamentalism: British and American Millenarianism, 1800-1930. Chicago: University of Chicago Press, 1970.

Sandeen's pioneering study stressed the role of doctrine in creating modern fundamentalism. The "roots" for Sandeen were a new view of biblical inerrancy derived from the work of theologians at Princeton Seminary and the new picture of the End Times proposed by dispensational premillennialists. Subsequent studies have questioned how absolutely new Princeton views of inerrancy were and also whether premillennialism acted apart from more general cultural attitudes, but Sandeen's volume undoubtedly captured much of the intellectual dynamic of the emerging fundamentalist movement. For that reason, it remains, with Marsden's Fundamentalism and American Culture, the essential starting place for serious study of the movement.

668. Shelley, Bruce. "Sources of Pietistic Fundamentalism." Fides et Historia 5 (Fall/Spring 1972): 68-78.

Shelley provides a useful account of the pietistic strand that along with rationalistic and militant impulses created fundamentalism. That pietism was seen most obviously in the fundamentalist institutions (like the Christian and Missionary Alliance denomination, Nyack College, and Columbia Bible College, and the American Keswick) which adapted the teachings on higher life and victorious living.

669. Singleton, Gregory H. "Fundamentalism and Urbanization: A Quantitative Critique of Impressionist Interpretations." In The New Urban History: Quantitative Explorations by American Historians, ed. Leo F. Schnore. Princeton, NJ: Princeton University Press, 1975.

Singleton uses census data of church preferences for 1916, 1926, and 1936, as well as his own research into church membership patterns in Los Angeles, to argue for the need to study fundamentalism as a social rather than an intellectual phenomenon.

670. Singleton, Gregory H. Religion in the City of the Angels. Ann Arbor, MI: UMI Research, 1979.

The subject of this social-demographic study is the shift in Los Angeles' public leadership during the period 1880-1930 from old-line Protestants to secular, pluralistic, and sectarian (including evangelical) forces.

671. Sizer, Sandra S. Gospel Hymns and Social Religion: The Rhetoric of Nineteenth-Century Revivalism. Philadelphia: Temple University Press, 1978.

This landmark book studies seriously the hymns of Protestants and so has much to say about the sort of subjects--motivation, vision, mood, stance over against the wider world--for which hymns are a wonderful barometer. Among other findings, Sizer traces an important movement from outward, social concern to inward, spiritual concentration as the nineteenth century moved towards its close.

672. Smith, Gary Scott. The Seeds of Secularization: Calvinism, Culture, and Pluralism in America, 1870-1915. Grand Rapids: Eerdmans, 1985.

Smith's study of Presbyterian and Reformed church leaders shows the importance within Protestantism of this numerically modest but intellectually formidable denominational family. The major contribution of these leaders was to continue the theological assessment of American culture; the main drawback of their effort was an inability to disentangle the principles of Reformed theology from conventions of the American middle class.

Smith, Robert Pearsall and Hannah Whitall Smith. The Devotional Writings of Robert Pearsall Smith and Hannah Whitall Smith, ed. Donald W. Dayton. New York: Garland, 1984. (Dayton 43)
(see 1467)

673. Szasz, Ferenc Morton. The Divided Mind of Protestant America, 1880-1930. University: University of Alabama Press, 1982.

Szasz's excellent study sensitively charts the divisions that separated Protestants from each other in his period. Included are standard issues in the rise of fundamentalism, but also regional and class differences that are often neglected.

674. Tomlinson, A. J. The Last Great Conflict. Cleveland, TN: Walter Rodgers, 1913. (Dayton 46)

Tomlinson was a moving figure in the Church of God wing of pentecostalism, which has divided into several distinct denominations since early in the century. This early history communicates Tomlinson's convictions about what was at stake in the emergence of the charismatic gifts and also his thoughts on the institutional future for what was in his day still a movement with only loose organizational structure.

675. Torrey, R. A. The Moody Bible Institute Correspondence Department: First Course--Bible Doctrines. Chicago: The Moody Bible Institute, 1901. (Carpenter 11)

Torrey (1856-1925) was the first dean of Moody Bible Institute and then of the Bible Institute of Los Angeles. As a successor of D. L. Moody, he stressed revival themes similar to those of his mentor, but as a defender of the faith, he spoke more militantly than did Moody against what he perceived as error in the churches. This correspondence course is a study edition of Torrey's What the Bible Teaches (1898), a large volume illustrating the fundamentalists' belief that the texts of the Bible could be arranged and collated with scientific precision.

676. The Victorious Life: Messages from the Summer Conferences. Philadelphia: Board of Managers of Victorious Life Conference, 1918. (Carpenter 20)

Charles G. Trumbull, long time editor of the Sunday School Times, founded the Victorious Life Conferences in 1913. They became important centers of a different sort of higher life teaching than that which led to pentecostalism. The emphasis at these meetings followed closely the themes of the English Keswick movement by emphasizing the gradual conquering of sin through the indwelling work of the Holy Spirit.

677. Wacker, Grant. Augustus H. Strong and the Dilemma of Historical Consciousness. Macon, GA: Mercer University Press, 1985.

Strong was a key Northern Baptist theologian who embodied a resolute defense of traditional Christian teaching (e.g., Strong was much distressed late in his life at deviations from traditional faith among Baptist missionaries) along with a cautious openness to new trends in theology and intellectual life (e.g., he had little difficulty incorporating evolutionary notions into his theology). This sensitive study focuses on the way Strong straddled issues of historical consciousness, at times confidently appropriating what could be learned from the past, at others seeming to partake of the modern skepticism about the deliverances of historical knowledge.

678. Wacker, Grant. "The Decline of Biblical Civilization." In The Bible in America, eds. Nathan O. Hatch and Mark A. Noll. New York: Oxford University Press, 1982.

This essay traces the painful process which saw a large segment of Protestant America turn away, under the influence of new evolutionary assumptions and the Higher Criticism of Scripture, from a reflexive reliance on traditional understandings of biblical infallibility.

679. Wacker, Grant. "The Holy Spirit and the Spirit of the Age in American Protestantism, 1880-1910." Journal of American History 72 (June 1985): 45-62.

What would it look like to study American Protestantism at the turn of the century if one was not aware of the fundamentalist-modernist divisions that followed? Wacker answers that question by recording the substantial commonality, especially in using language about the Holy Spirit, that prevailed among the originators of what later commentators would record as the division between fundamentalists and modernists.

680. Wacker, Grant. "Marching to Zion: Religion in a Modern Theocracy." Church History 54 (Dec. 1985): 496-511.

John Alexander Dowie (1847-1907), the subject of this article, was an itinerant healer who founded the Christian Catholic Apostolic Church in Zion and the theocratic community of Zion, Illinois. His career was an unusual, but also revealing episode in the rise of newer religious consciousness associated with the pentecostal movement.

681. Waldvogel, Edith L. "The 'Overcoming Life': A Study in the Reformed Evangelical Origins of Pentecostalism." Ph.D. dissertation, Harvard University, 1977.

In response to the claim that pentecostalism emerged exclusively from the ranks of the Wesleyan holiness movement, this dissertation examines late-nineteenth-century non-Wesleyan proto-pentecostal settings. It traces the significance of the Keswick movement and such North American advocates of the baptism with the Holy Spirit and healing as R. A. Torrey and A. B. Simpson for segments of American pentecostalism.

682. Warner, Wayne, ed. Touched By the Fire: Patriarchs of Pentecost: Eyewitness Accounts of the Early Twentieth-Century Pentecostal Revival. Plainfield, NJ: Logos, 1978.

Warner's collection of forty first-person accounts comes mainly from reminiscences of the 1960s and 1970s as elderly men and women looked back to recount their introduction to pentecostalism in the 1910s and 1920s. Although the normal cautions must apply to the use of such evidence (e.g., those who abandoned earlier pentecostal convictions would not, of course, be included), these testimonies are a treasure recorded not a moment too soon.

683. White, Charles E. The Beauty of Holiness: Phoebe Palmer as Theologian, Revivalist, Feminist, and Humanitarian. Grand Rapids: Zondervan, 1976.

Only recently has the importance of Phoebe Palmer (1807-1884) for American evangelicalism become a focus of serious historical study. She was an urban evangelist, a popular public speaker, and an author whose books were read around the world. The holiness themes of her message, especially her proclamation of total consecration in the power of the Spirit, have materially shaped evangelicalism since the 1840s when she began her public ministry in New York. White's study is the most satisfying of several recent efforts to take the measure of her work.

684. White, Ronald C., Jr. and C. Howard Hopkins. The Social Gospel: Religion and Reform in Changing America. Philadelphia: Temple University Press, 1976.

The social gospel became a whipping boy for fundamentalists and some conservative evangelicals. This definitive study shows, however, that a number of important themes from the evangelicalism of the early nineteenth century contributed substantially to the origins and development of the Protestant effort to save the cities and reform American civilization.

685. Wilson, Charles Reagan. Baptized in Blood: The Religion of the Lost Cause, 1865-1920. Athens: University of Georgia Press, 1980.

Meanwhile, back in the South, a distinctive ethos was developing that shared doctrinal convictions with northern evangelicals and fundamentalists, but that differed markedly in attitudes toward the church, toward divisions between the races, and toward expectations for religion itself. Wilson's account is a good survey that helps explain why northern and southern evangelicals in the twentieth century so often give the impression of talking past each other.

CHAPTER 11
CONFLICT, ALIENATION AND REGROUPING, 1920-1945

After the bad publicity generated for fundamentalists by the Scopes Trial in 1925, and after northern fundamentalists lost struggles to control Baptist and Presbyterian denominations in roughly the same period, evangelical Protestantism largely dropped from the consciousness of national media and intellectual elites. Evangelicalism in its many and varied forms was, however, far from dead. In the North, fundamentalists worked diligently beyond the public sphere to reassure constituencies, to launch new ventures, to begin a cautious re-examination of the fundamentalist heritage, and to steel forces for a future day of national revival. In the South, regionally distinctive forms of evangelicalism continued to exert a comprehensive influence on public life. And in this period several families of evangelical churches, which previously had been content to carry out their work in isolation, began to move more toward public involvement with other bodies of similar disposition. The truer historical view, in other words, is one that regards this period as an understudied, but no less dynamic period in the history of evangelicals. The works below are some of those describing that dynamism, as well as others concerned with the controversies of the 1920s.

686. Carpenter, Joel A. "From Fundamentalism to the New Evangelical Coalition." In Evangelicalism and Modern America, ed. George Marsden. Grand Rapids: Eerdmans, 1984.

687. Carpenter, Joel A. "Fundamentalist Institutions and the Rise of Evangelical Protestantism, 1929-1942." Church History 49 (March 1980): 62-75.

688. Carpenter, Joel A. "Revive Us Again: Alienation, Hope, and the Resurgence of Fundamentalism, 1930-1950." In Transforming Faith: The Sacred and the Secular in Modern American History, eds. James Gilbert and Miles Bradbury, 105-125. Westport, CT: Greenwood, 1989.

689. Carpenter, Joel A. Revive Us Again: The Recovery of American Fundamentalism, 1930-1950. New York: Oxford University Press, 1991.

Carpenter's work is now the most important body of writing re-interpreting the place of northern fundamentalism in the quiet years of the

1930s and 1940s. What he has shown definitively is that fundamentalist churches, publishing houses, youth organizations, campgrounds, radio programs, itinerant evangelists, and educational institutions were all buzzing with activity during this supposedly quiescent time. Carpenter also demonstrates that the perception of dislocation made fundamentalists yearn all the more for a recovery of both the gospel and their dominant role in American life. It also led to different strategies among fundamentalists about how best to achieve those goals. The fundamentalists who remained content with defensive strategies and who continued to be preoccupied with the malefactions of Protestant liberals remained "fundamentalists." On the other hand, a somewhat younger cohort, which began to express doubts about the jots and tittles of fundamentalist convictions and which looked to a selective re-engagement with the worlds of culture and learning, began to call themselves "new evangelicals" or simply "evangelicals." The internal dynamics of fundamentalist spirituality, the external outworking of public strategies, and heightening intramural differences figure large in the previously neglected story of these eventful decades.

690. Carpenter, Joel A., ed. Fighting Fundamentalism: Polemical Thrusts of the 1930s and 1940s. New York: Garland, 1988. (Carpenter 32)

Fundamentalists may have been discredited in the eyes of learned east coast liberals, but opinions from such quarters were never more than temporary distractions. The works gathered into this reprint volume illustrate the wide range of works that continued to upbraid American Protestants for harkening to the sirens of modernity: Robert T. Ketcham, Facts for Baptists to Face (1936); Judson E. Conant, The Growing Menace of the Social Gospel (1937); William Bell Riley, The Conflict of Christianity with Its Counterfeits (1940); and Chester E. Tulga, The Case Against Modernism (1949).

691. Carpenter, Joel A., ed. The Fundamentalist-Modernist Conflict: Opposing Views on Three Major Issues. New York: Garland, 1988. (Carpenter 23)

This work collects twelve combative essays and tracts illustrating the debates generated by fundamentalists over (1) the premillennial return of Christ, (2) the Interchurch World Movement sponsored by John D. Rockefeller, Jr., and (3) Harry Emerson Fosdick (1878-1969) whose 1922 sermon "Shall the Fundamentalists Win?" (included here) created a storm of controversy.

692. Carpenter, Joel A., ed. Fundamentalist Versus Modernist: The Debates Between John Roach Straton and Charles Francis Potter. New York: Garland, 1988. (Carpenter 26)

Straton (minister of the Calvary Baptist Church in New York City) and Potter (a New York Unitarian pastor) debated publicly in 1923 and 1924 to wide public interest (including radio audiences) issues like the Virgin Birth of Christ and evolution. These volume contains the booklets that resulted.

693. Carpenter, Joel A., ed. Modernism and Foreign Missions: Two Fundamentalist Protests. New York: Garland, 1988. (Carpenter 24)

A long-standing fear of fundamentalists was that missionary funds and energies would slide from evangelism to merely social welfare. This reprint edition contains pieces by two Protestant conservatives decrying that trend, a lengthy article by William Henry Griffith Thomas from 1921 and a substantial pamphlet by J. Gresham Machen from 1933.

694. Carpenter, Joel A., ed. Sacrificial Lives: Young Martyrs and Fundamentalist Idealism. New York: Garland, 1988. (Carpenter 37)

Hagiography has been a staple of fundamentalist literature as of most religious groups. In the 1930s and 1940s the most revered fundamentalist "saints" were those who dedicated themselves to full-time Christian service, usually on the mission field. The two books gathered into this volume are examples of the genre: Lillie F. Oliver, Richard Weber Oliver, A Challenge to American Youth: A Biography by His Mother (1932); and Mrs. Howard Taylor, The Triumph of John and Betty Stam (1935). The lives of the Stams, missionaries with the China Inland Mission who were assassinated by communist guerillas in 1934, had a particularly enduring impact on ideals of self-sacrifice among fundamentalists and later evangelicals.

695. Carter, Paul A. "The Fundamentalist Defense of the Faith." In Change and Continuity in Twentieth Century America: The 1920's, ed. John Braeman. Columbus: Ohio State University Press, 1968.

Carter is one of the shrewdest observers of the strains that have arisen since the Civil War between traditional evangelicalism and modern forms of life and thought. This revisionist essay was an early sign of more insightful treatment of fundamentalism. Fundamentalists of the 1920s, Carter suggests, maybe, just maybe, should be taken at their word: rather than trying to defend Americanism, *laissez faire* capitalism, the countryside, or ignorance, as many elite commentators suggested, they were primarily seeking to preserve "the faith once delivered to the saints."

696. Cauthen, W. Kenneth. The Impact of American Religious Liberalism. New York: Harper & Row, 1962.

Before the appearance of Hutchison's Modernist Impulse, this was the best study of Protestant Liberalism in America. Its chapters--on William Adams Brown, Harry Emerson Fosdick, Walter Rauschenbusch, A.C. Knudson, Eugene W. Lyman, Shailer Mathews, D.C. Macintosh, and Henry Nelson Wieman--are still worth reading by those interested in the villains whom fundamentalists and many of their evangelical descendents opposed.

697. Cole, Stewart G. The History of Fundamentalism. New York: Richard Smith, 1931.

This early account of the fundamentalist movement focuses on conflicts among Northern Baptists, northern Presbyterians, Disciples, Methodists, and

Episcopalians. It interprets the controversy as a sign of strain between laudably loyal (but benighted) evangelicals and laudably enlightened (but weak-willed) liberals.

698. Elliott, David R. and Iris Miller. Bible Bill: A Biography of William Aberhart. Edmonton, Alberta: Reidmore Books, 1987.

Aberhart (1878-1943) was a premillennialist, lay Baptist preacher, and radio evangelist who attracted a wide following in Alberta and western Saskatchewan in the 1920s and 1930s. His essentially fundamentalist convictions turned in an unusual direction, however, when in response to the Depression he adopted the convictions of "social credit," created a political party to promote those convictions, and rode them to victory in 1935 in Saskatchewan provincial elections. Unlike the United States, where fundamentalist convictions usually remained politically latent, Aberhart's career, as told in this solid biography, illustrates again the ways in which fundamentalism in Canada advanced on paths unknown in the United States.

Fuller, Daniel P. Give the Winds a Mighty Voice: The Story of Charles E. Fuller. Waco, TX: Word, 1972.
(see 1221)

699. Furniss, Norman F. The Fundamentalist Controversy, 1918-1931. New Haven, CT: Yale University Press, 1954.

Furniss's book, which began as a doctoral dissertation at Yale, looked upon fundamentalism as a passing excitement of the 1920s. Fundamentalism expired, he claimed, due to the deaths of leaders like William Jennings Bryan and the spread of enlightenment throughout the land ("just as ignorance was one cause for the rise of the dispute, so comprehension of the new theological and biological concepts on the part of the people did much to end the controversy"). Ho-ho.

700. Gatewood, Willard B. Controversy in the Twenties: Fundamentalism, Modernism, and Evolution. Nashville: Vanderbilt University Press, 1969.

Although somewhat dated by its treatment of fundamentalism as an antiquity, Gatewood's documents are still the best single-volume collection illustrating the strife of the 1920s. In the book's pages we hear from such proponents as William Bell Riley, James M. Gray of Moody Bible Institute, and J. Gresham Machen; opponents like Harry Emerson Fosdick and the University of Chicago's Shailer Mathews; and many more.

701. Gatewood, Willard B. Preachers, Pedagogues, and Politicians: The Evolution Controversy in North Carolina, 1920-1927. Chapel Hill: University of North Carolina Press, 1966.

The Scopes Trial in Tennessee was more famous than other disputes over evolution in the South in the 1920s. Gatewood's well researched study probes the equally strong animus against new theories of evolution that stimulated conservatives, many of them fundamentalists or evangelicals, in North Carolina during the same period.

702. Johnson, R. K. Builder of Bridges: The Biography of Bob Jones, Sr. Murfreesboro, TN: Sword of the Lord, 1969.

Jones (1883-1963) was a Methodist itinerant who became disenchanted with the drift toward liberal forms of Christianity that he perceived in his denomination and the nation. In response, he preached undeviating doctrinal conservatism (including dispensational premillennialism), defended the traditional social conservativism of the South (including the separation of the races), and founded a university bearing his name that remains a center of aggressive fundamentalism to this day.

Kuhn, Isobel. By Searching. London: China Inland Mission, 1957. (see 1318)

703. Machen, J. Gresham. Christianity and Liberalism. New York: Macmillan Co., 1923.

Machen, the one time professor at Princeton Theological Seminary who founded both Westminster Theological Seminary and the Orthodox Presbyterian Church, was the most learned of the conservative Protestants who in the 1920s became known as fundamentalists. Machen may have been mislabeled with that name, for he rejected dispensationalism, held firmly to Presbyterian confessions, was not particularly troubled by scientific evolution, and opposed prohibition. Yet as in this book, the period's most impressive defense of historic orthodoxy over against the doctrinal changes promoted by Protestant modernists, Machen shared fully the alarm of the fundamentalists at the modernist alteration of the faith and the corresponding threat posed by secularism to the future of western civilization.

704. Meyer, Donald B. The Protestant Search for Political Realism, 1919-1941. Berkeley: University of California Press, 1960.

This sound study, focused on Reinhold Niebuhr and his critics, charts the uncertain path of liberal Protestantism in an age of punctured confidence. That story, while not directly involving evangelicals, speaks of a changed national landscape in which liberal certainties were becoming less secure and fundamentalist orthodoxies less obviously irrelevant.

705. National Association of Evangelicals. A New Evangelical Coalition: Early Documents of the National Association of Evangelicals. New York: Garland, 1988. (Carpenter 41)

The NAE was founded in 1942 as an effort to draw together moderate fundamentalists eager for a broader, more positive role in American life. The choice of its name and of a strategy aimed at unification rather than division marked it as an important herald (and continuing influence in) the evangelical movement of the post-war period. This volume includes official statements from the associations' earliest years.

706. Rausch, David A. Arno C. Gaebelein, 1861-1945: Irenic Fundamentalist and Scholar. Lewiston, NY: Edwin Mellen, 1983.

Gaebelein was a Bible student, premillennial stalwart, and concerned educationist who had a particular concern for the place of the Jews. Rausch, the leading scholar of fundamentalist-Jewish connections, sets Gaebelein's life within the broader contexts of the fundamentalist movement and Jewish-Protestant relations.

707. Rawlyk, G. A. "Fundamentalism, Modernism and the Maritime Baptists in the 1920s and 1930s." Acadiensis: Journal of the History of the Atlantic Region 17 (Autumn 1987): 3-33.

Despite the presence in Canada of many religious circumstances similar to those in the United States, only in scattered locations did anything like fundamentalist-modernist struggles explode north of the border. In this perceptive essay Rawlyk describes one such scene, where a small band of Maritime Baptists attempted to purge its provincial association in the American fashion, but also explains why the effort had much less impact than similar efforts in the states.

708. Rian, Edwin H. The Presbyterian Conflict. Grand Rapids: Eerdmans, 1940. (Carpenter 28)

Rian was an ally of J. Gresham Machen, who led a small group of conservatives out of the northern Presbyterian denomination to create the Orthodox Presbyterian Church. This is a vivid account of the strife that led to this division and of the splinter's early years. Rian himself later repudiated the separation and returned to the larger Presbyterian communion.

709. Ribuffo, Leo P. The Old Christian Right: The Protestant Far Right from the Great Depression to the Cold War. Philadelphia: Temple University Press, 1983.

Ribuffo's book deals objectively with three hard-core militants about whom it is difficult to be objective: William Dudley Pelley, Gerald B. Winrod, and Gerald L. K. Smith. This is an exemplary study of highly partisan figures which includes a persuasive argument for treating such people in terms of their own history and background instead of as irrational social deviants.

710. Russell, C. Allyn. "Adoniram Judson Gordon: Nineteenth-Century Fundamentalist." American Baptist Quarterly 4 (March 1985): 61-89.

711. Russell, C. Allyn. "Donald Grey Barnhouse: Fundamentalist Who Changed." Journal of Presbyterian History 59 (Spring 1981): 33-57.

712. Russell, C. Allyn. "Thomas Todhunter Shields: Canadian Fundamentalist." Foundations 24 (January-March 1981): 15-31.

713. Russell, C. Allyn. Voices of American Fundamentalism: Seven Biographical Studies. Philadelphia: Westminster, 1976.

714. Russell, C. Allyn. "W. A. Criswell: A Case Study in Fundamentalism." Review and Expositor 81 (Winter 1984): 107-113.

Russell is the Boswell of American fundamentalism. His illuminating biographical sketches add great insight to other studies of well-known figures like J. Gresham Machen and William Jennings Bryan, and also present path-breaking work on many of the second rank of fundamentalist leaders. His reach extends from Gordon, a proto-fundamentalist with greater influence in the 1870s and 1880s, to Barnhouse, who held forth as a conservative Presbyterian in Philadelphia until the 1950s, and Criswell, a leader of contemporary conservatives in the Southern Baptist Convention. Besides Machen and Bryan, the figures treated in Voices are J. Frank Norris, John Roach Straton, William Bell Riley, J. C. Massee, and Clarence E. Macartney.

715. Shelley, Bruce. "The Rise of Evangelical Youth Movements." Fides et Historia 18 (January 1986): 45-63.

Youth groups have been the life-blood of modern evangelicalism. This useful article spotlights the work of Methodist layman and Chicago businessman Herbert J. Taylor (1893-1978) who played a strategic role in founding many of the mainstream evangelical youth organizations of the post-war period, including InterVarsity Christian Fellowship, Young Life Campaign, Youth for Christ, Christian Service Brigade, Pioneer Girls, and Child Evangelism Fellowship.

716. Stonehouse, Ned B. J. Gresham Machen: A Biographical Memoir. Grand Rapids: Eerdmans, 1954.

Machen (1881-1937) was a scholarly Presbyterian who published academic defenses of the essential harmony between the teaching of Paul and Jesus (1927) and of the Virgin Birth (1930). But he is best known as a polemicist for confessional traditionalism and conservative theology within his denomination, polemics that were associated with the founding of Westminster Theological Seminary in 1929, with the establishment of an independent board to support Presbyterian foreign missionaries, and with the creation of a new denomination in 1936 that eventually came to be known as the Orthodox Presbyterian Church. Stonehouse was Machen's successor in the chair of New Testament at Westminster Seminary. His book is one of the most valuable early studies of conservative leaders from the fundamentalist era.

717. Tarr, Leslie K. Shields of Canada. Grand Rapids: Baker, 1967.

Thomas Todhunter Shields (1873-1955) was (by American standards) the most fully authentic fundamentalist in Canada. From his pulpit in the Jarvis Street Baptist Church in Toronto, and as the organizer of the Ontario-Quebec Association of Regular Baptist Churches and the Baptist

Bible Union of North America, Shields propounded standard fundamentalist teachings as well as standard denunciations against modernism. His criticisms accelerated the movement of Ontario's Baptist McMaster University in a secular direction. Tarr's is a useful preliminary study.

718. Thompson, James J., Jr. Tried as by Fire: The Southern Baptists and the Religious Controversies of the 1920s. Macon, GA: Mercer University Press, 1982.

This study shows well how Southern Baptists responded to fundamentalist-modernist issues. They were almost uniformly conservative, but also entertained considerable suspicions for independent fundamentalist leaders like J. Frank Norris of Ft. Worth.

719. Trollinger, William. God's Empire: William Bell Riley and Midwestern Fundamentalism. Madison: University of Wisconsin Press, 1990.

This perceptive biography concentrates on the leading regional role Riley (1861-1947) played as a proponent of fundamentalist doctrines and social attitudes during a nearly fifty-year tenure as pastor of the First Baptist Church of Minneapolis.

720. Wright, J. Elwin. "The Federal Council." United Evangelical Action (December 1942): 1,2,4; (January 1943) 1,4; (February 1943): 1-4.

Wright was the leader of the New England Evangelical Association which led in turn to the founding of the National Association of Evangelicals. This series of articles is an example of the evangelicals' view of their Liberal opponents and the emerging style and tone that differentiated the "new evangelicals" from their fundamentalist brethren.

CHAPTER 12
RESURGENCE, 1945-1988

Since World War II, dramatic events in the world of evangelicals and fundamentalists have become far too numerous to record. Despite predictions of demise, evangelicals and fundamentalists once again intruded into American public life. Some like Billy Graham did so with widely-respected public speaking; others like Oral Roberts, Pat Robertson, and Jimmy Swaggart exploited new possibilities in radio and television to make their presences felt; still others like Jerry Falwell were galvanized into action by political circumstances. More than ever, the last half century has witnessed ample justification for perceiving evangelicalism, in Timothy Smith's terms, as a mosaic or a kaleidoscope. Pentecostals both black and white have burgeoned; charismatics, who share convictions but not institutions with pentecostals, have become a major presence across the denominations, including Catholicism; the Southern Baptist Convention has grown by leaps and bounds, but also has experienced a wrenching internal debate over the nature of biblical authority; a reinvigorated historiography has gained wider attention for Wesleyan and holiness groups; the "new evangelical" descendants of northern fundamentalists enjoyed a brief moment in the sun as a kind of designated mouthpiece for the mosaic and still continue to exert considerable influence through publications and educational institutions; immigrant bodies as diverse as the Mennonite General conference and the (Dutch) Christian Reformed Church have interacted much more than in the past with other evangelical groups; some leaders of previously isolated groups like the Churches of Christ and the Seventh-day Adventists have sought out closer contact with other evangelicals; and those who are quite content to retain the name fundamentalist have mobilized millions of adherents in rural and urban settings alike. Who can make sense of it all? A whole army of scholars and journalists is at work on the project, but only a fraction of their work can be mentioned below.

721. Ammerman, Nancy Tatom. Bible Believers: Fundamentalists in the Modern World. New Brunswick, NJ: Rutgers University Press, 1987.

This report resulted from the time that Ammerman spent as a participant-observer in a Connecticut fundamentalist church. It is a sensitive, empathetic portrait of fundamentalist activities, but even more of the aspirations, hopes, and fears that defined northern fundamentalism in the 1980s.

722. Balmer, Randall. Mine Eyes Have Seen the Glory: A Journey into the Evangelical Subculture in America. New York: Oxford University Press, 1989.

In the manner of William Least Heat Moon's Blue Highways, Balmer visited a dozen evangelical and fundamentalist locales. What he saw at a Bible camp in the Adirondacks, a movie set in Des Moines, a pentecostal mega-church in California, a counter cultural logging campus in Oregon, and several places in between forms the subject matter of this readable, winsome book.

723. Bloesch, Donald. The Evangelical Renaissance. Grand Rapids: Eerdmans, 1973.

724. Bloesch, Donald. The Future of Evangelical Christianity: A Call for Unity Amid Diversity. Garden City, NY: Doubleday, 1983.

Bloesch is an immensely learned Congregationalist clergyman who has taught for decades in a Presbyterian seminary. Besides a substantial theological contribution (cited below) he has been an active observer of the vicissitudes and the potential of an evangelical movement inspired by the most compelling features of its heritage.

Boyer, Paul. "Minister's Wife, Widow, Reluctant Feminist: Catherine Marshall in the 1950's." In Women in American Religion, ed. Janet W. James. Philadelphia: University of Pennsylvania Press, 1980.
(see 1541)

725. Branch, Taylor. Parting the Waters: America in the King Years, 1954-63. New York: Simon and Schuster, 1988.

Some accounts of Martin Luther King, Jr., play down his religious heritage. This one, with especially compelling accounts of his preaching (partially evangelical in content, entirely evangelical in form), does not.

726. Bruce, Steve. Firm in the Faith. Brookfield, VT: Gower, 1984.

727. Bruce, Steve. The Rise and Fall of the New Christian Right: Conservative Protestant Politics in America, 1978-1988. Oxford: Clarendon, 1988.

Bruce, a sociologist at the Queen's University of Belfast, has become one of the shrewdest foreign observers of American evangelical life. The earlier volume offers illuminating contrasts between politically conservative fundamentalists in Northern Ireland, Scotland, and the U.S. The latter is a persuasive account of why the religious strengths lying behind the New Christian Right make it next to impossible for the movement ever to become the nation's moral majority.

728. Caplow, Theodore, et al. All Faithful People: Change and Continuity in Middletown's Religion. Minneapolis: University of Minnesota Press, 1983.

Caplow and a team of fellow-sociologists visited Muncie, Indiana, to replicate the famous studies down there by Robert and Helen Lynd in earlier decades. What they found was a high rate of religious involvement and remarkable rates of adherence to traditional beliefs about the existence of God, but also increasing competition from the affluent life with traditional involvements in church.

729. Carpenter, Joel A., ed. The Early Billy Graham: Sermons and Revival Accounts. New York: Garland, 1988. (Carpenter 44)

Graham got his public start as the first full-time worker for Youth for Christ. What that early career looked like is the subject of the two books gathered into this one reprint volume: Billy Graham, Calling Youth To Christ (1947), and Revival in Our Time: The Story of the Billy Graham Evangelistic Campaigns, Including Six of His Sermons.

730. Carpenter, Joel A., ed. Two Reformers of Fundamentalism: Harold John Ockenga and Carl F. H. Henry. New York: Garland, 1988. (Carpenter 45)

The two books making up this volume are Harold Lindsell's biography of Ockenga, Park Street Prophet: A Life of Harold John Ockenga (1951), which chronicles Ockenga's leadership of the "new evangelical" movement from his Boston pulpit and as absentee president of Fuller Theological Seminary in California; and Carl F. H. Henry, The Uneasy Conscience of Modern Fundamentalism (1947), a brief but compelling argument for the need to go beyond fundamentalism and engage the struggles and perplexities of modern society.

731. Carpenter, Joel A. "Youth for Christ and the New Evangelicals' Place in the Life of the Nation." In Religion and the Life of the Nation: American Recoveries, ed. Rowland A. Sherrill. Urbana: University of Illinois Press, 1990.

732. Carpenter, Joel A., ed. The Youth for Christ Movement and Its Pioneers. New York: Garland, 1988. (Carpenter, 43)

This essay and the book of documents highlights the work of Youth for Christ, a post-war movement of Saturday-night rallies and high-school young people's clubs. As the early employer of Billy Graham, as a mobilizer of energies stimulated by the overseas experience of GIs, and as a more "with-it" voice among fundamentalism, Youth for Christ greatly stimulated the movement whereby reactionary fundamentalists became evangelicals more open to engagement with contemporary society.

733. Catherwood, Christopher. Five Evangelical Leaders. Carol Stream, IL: Harold Shaw, 1985.

This book contains biographical sketches of John Stott, Martin Lloyd-Jones, J. I. Packer, Francis Schaeffer, and Billy Graham. The first three are British evangelicals who have offered visions of more profound preaching and more thoughtful scholarship to their American cousins. The last two were unusually influential Americans whose contributions are detailed in other volumes in this bibliography.

734. Coleman, Richard J. Issues of Theological Conflict: Evangelicals and Liberals. Rev. ed. Grand Rapids: Eerdmans, 1980.

Coleman, a Presbyterian minister, was concerned already in the early 1970s about the widening gap within Protestantism. This book is an effort to get a conversation started between evangelicals and liberals on issues like the nature of God and the Scriptures, the meaning of providence, and the role of the church in society.

735. Dayton, Donald W. "Yet Another Layer of the Onion: Or Opening the Ecumenical Door to Let the Riffraff In." Ecumenical Review 40 (Jan. 1988): 87-110.

Dayton has long contended that the historiography of evangelicals is dominated by Reformed and Presbyterian types at the expense of those with a Wesleyan, holiness, or pentecostal perspective. In this essay, he asks what it would mean for an ecumenical audience if the balance were redressed.

736. Dennis, Lane, ed. Francis A. Schaeffer: Portraits of the Man and His Work. Westchester, IL: Crossway, 1986.

Schaeffer (1912-1984) operated from a base in Switzerland to call evangelicals to dedicated involvement with culture, both mass and high. Toward the end of his life he also became an influential proponent of the anti-abortion movement and of other activities to recall the nation to what he perceived as a threatened Christian heritage. The essays in this commemorative volume are more celebratory and less critical than those in Ruegsegger's Reflection on Francis Schaeffer.

737. Dobson, Edward. Fundamentalism Today. Chicago: Moody Press, 1984.

738. Dobson, Edward. In Search of Unity: An Appeal to Fundamentalists and Evangelicals. Nashville: Thomas Nelson, 1985.

Dobson was an engaging associate of Jerry Falwell when he wrote these books. They both pull off what would have seemed unimaginable only short years before by being books as thoroughly committed to fundamentalist convictions as they are to cordial dialogue, humanity, and even self-deprecating humor.

Elliot, Elisabeth. Shadow of the Almighty: The Life and Testament of Jim Elliot. New York: Harper, 1958.
(See 1305)

Elliot, Elisabeth. Through Gates of Splendor. New York: Harper, 1957.
(See 1306)

739. Ellwood, Robert S., Jr. One Way: The Jesus Movement and Its Meaning. Englewood Cliffs, NJ: Prentice-Hall, 1973.

Ellwood, a religionist, provides a sympathetic reading of the unconventional, extra-institutional "Jesus Movement" of the late 1960s. The book situates the movement with the history of nineteenth-century evangelicalism and twentieth-century fundamentalism, and suggests (as it turned out, correctly) that the movement's combination of "evangelicalism, pentecostalism, and apocalypticism" would continue to exert an influence in America.

Enroth, Ronald M., Edward E. Ericson, Jr. and C. Breckenridge Peters. The Jesus People: Old-Time Religion in the Age of Aquarius. Grand Rapids: Eerdmans, 1972.
(see 1374)

740. Fairclough, Adam. To Redeem the Soul of America: The Southern Christian Leadership Conference and Martin Luther King, Jr. Athens, GA: University of Georgia Press, 1987.

This account of the ways in which the SCLC drew on black religious traditions as the material for both its triumphs and internal disputes illustrates graphically the ways in which black evangelicalism has paralleled, and also differed from, white varieties.

Falwell, Jerry, ed., with Ed Dobson and Ed Hindson. The Fundamentalist Phenomenon: The Resurgence of Conservative Christianity. Garden City, NY: Doubleday, 1981.
(see 1086)

741. Falwell, Jerry. Strength for the Journey: An Autobiography. New York: Simon and Schuster, 1987.

The life of Falwell, the leading figure in the fundamentalist resurgence of the 1970s and 1980s, is an intriguing tale. Much will remain for later historians to figure out, but this book will help with Falwell's own account of his conversion, his training by militant fundamentalists, his gradual move to political activism, and his increasing savvy in the struggle to achieve a political coalition of moral conservatives (not all of whom are fundamentalists).

742. Fitzgerald, Frances. "Liberty Baptist." In Cities on a Hill: A Journey Through Contemporary American Culture. New York: Simon and Schuster, 1986.

It is not quite clear what Fitzgerald expected to find when she brought her sharp pen and skeptical New Yorker's eye to Jerry Falwell's Lynchburg, Virginia. What she found confirmed some of the suspicions about what her circle is wont to describe as new barbarians, but also elicited a measure of grudging respect for Falwell's genius at keeping alive old religious ideas through modern means in contemporary America.

743. Flake, Carol. Redemptorama: Culture, Politics, and the New Evangelicalism. New York: Doubleday, 1984.

This book is better than its title might suggest. Flake, who grew up in a Texas fundamentalist household, does not like what modern evangelicalism has become, but her reports are insightful and often fair on important subjects like evangelical attitudes toward women, the evangelical sports fixation, the evangelical embrace of consumer capitalism, and the complicated pilgrimage of Billy Graham.

Flowers, Ronald B. Religion in Strange Times: The 1960's and 1970's. Macon, GA: Mercer University Press, 1984.
(see 1084)

744. Frady, Marshall. Billy Graham: A Parable of American Righteousness. Boston: Little, Brown, 1979.

Frady, unfortunately, does not get too far in his goal of explaining the "Billy Graham phenomenon," and it is not quite clear that his luxuriant, good-ol'-southern-boy style of writing is up to the complexities of Graham's career, but this book nonetheless remains the most impressive attempt by a non-evangelical to grasp the immense significance of Billy Graham for post-war evangelicalism.

Hamilton, Michael Pollock, ed. The Charismatic Movement. Grand Rapids: Eerdmans, 1975.
(see 1377)

745. Harrell, David Edwin, Jr. All Things Are Possible: The Healing and Charismatic Revivals in Modern America. Bloomington: Indiana University Press, 1976.

746. Harrell, David Edwin, Jr. Oral Roberts: An American Life. Bloomington: Indiana University Press, 1985; San Francisco: Harper & Row, 1987.

747. Harrell, David Edwin, Jr. Pat Robertson: A Personal, Political and Religious Portrait. San Francisco: Harper & Row, 1987.

748. Harrell, David Edwin, Jr. White Sects and Black Men in the Recent South. Nashville: Vanderbilt University Press, 1971.

With George Marsden, David Edwin Harrell is the premier interpreter of modern American evangelicalism. Unlike Marsden, who tends to look north and west, Harrell's focus is on the South. His biographies of Oral Roberts (one of the finest such works ever written about a living religious figure) and Pat Robertson (a book that will have to be revised according to the future career of its subject) grew naturally from his earlier attention to the charismatic revival, of which both Roberts and Robertson were a part. Even earlier work on black-white relations in the South captured securely the ambiguities at work in a culture where major social groupings share evangelical or fundamentalist religious convictions but are divided by persistent racial stand-offs.

749. Henry, Carl F. H. Confessions of a Theologian: An Autobiography. Waco, TX: Word, 1986.

Henry was the major-domo of much that put "new evangelicals" on the map of modern America. A founding professor at Fuller Theological Seminary, inaugural editor of Christianity Today, friend and fellow-organizer with Billy Graham, lecturer world-wide, and imminent theologian, Henry's autobiography is an essential resource for studying this strand of modern evangelicalism.

750. Henry, Carl F. H. Evangelicals in Search of Identity. Waco, TX: Word, 1976.

751. Henry, Carl F. H. Remaking the Modern Mind. Grand Rapids: Eerdmans, 1946.

752. Henry, Carl F. H. The Uneasy Conscience of Modern Fundamentalism. Grand Rapids: Eerdmans, 1946.

Early and late, Carl Henry called his fellow-evangelicals to mobilize all internal strength possible for challenging ungodly conventions of modern thought. His first works with such themes were oriented outward to the weaknesses of contemporary intellectual assumptions; later ones took on an elegiac tone by observing that the rising evangelical movement of the 1950s had largely squandered its opportunities to reshape modern thinking on a large scale.

753. Hill, Samuel S., Jr. Southern Churches in Crisis. New York: Holt, Rinehart and Winston, 1967.

At a time of hesitation in the Civil Rights Movement, Samuel Hill offered this probing history of the distinctive features of religion in the South. Solid history leads to an interpretation of "the confrontation between traditional religious patterns and the region's new social-cultural ethos" that calls for a rejection of "churchly" and "priestly" roles in favor of "sectarian" and "prophetic" Christian witness.

754. Hinson, E. Glenn. "Neo-Fundamentalism: An Interpretation and Critique." Baptist History and Heritage 16 (April 1981): 33-42.

From Hinson's perspective, the fundamentalism of the early twentieth century was superior to the variety surfacing among Southern Baptists in the 1980s for three reasons: earlier fundamentalists had more room for scholarship, they were less dogmatic on matters of science and faith, and they were broader theologically.

755. Hollinger, Dennis. Individualism and Social Ethics: An Evangelical Syncretism. Lanham, MD: University Press of America, 1983.

This study of the early Christianity Today argues convincingly that standard "new evangelical" ethics of the 1950s and 1960s represented the not entirely easy coalition of two different ideological strands: a conventional American reliance upon individual effort and a biblically rooted notion of social responsibility.

756. Jones, Lawrence N. "The InterVarsity Christian Fellowship in the United States." Ph.D. dissertation, Yale University, 1961.

InterVarsity (imported from England by way of Canada) was established in the 1930s and may be considered the actual start of the "new evangelicalism" that later produced Fuller Seminary, Christianity Today, and the Billy Graham network. Jones' early history of this important student work makes a good start on a subject that desperately needs a modern, definitive study.

Jorstad, Erling. Evangelicals in the White House: The Cultural Maturation of Born Again Christianity, 1960-1981. New York: Edwin Mellen Press, 1981.
(see 1118)

757. Kelley, Dean. Why Conservative Churches Are Growing. New York: Harper & Row, 1972.

They grow, said Kelly of the National Council of Churches, because they place real demands on their members. Most of Kelly's "conservative churches" fit somewhere in the evangelical mosaic, so this study by a knowledgeable outsiders has offered evangelical groups much to ponder.

758. Knapp, Steve. "Radical Evangelicals: Who Are They and Where in the World Are They Headed?" Other Side 88 (January 1979): 34-39.

The Other Side and Sojourners are the major periodical voices for radical forms of evangelicalism that began, in concert with counter-cultural impulses more generally, during the 1960s. This mid-course assessment offers useful perspective on a movement that has grown closer to the groups with which it shares political views and further from the evangelical communities in which it began.

Koop, Allen V. American Evangelical Missionaries in France, 1945-1975. Lanham, MD: University Press of America, 1986.
(see 1317)

759. Lightner, Robert P. Neoevangelicalism Today. Rev. ed. Schaumburg, IL: Regular Baptist Press, 1979.

Lightner speaks for fundamentalists and conservative evangelicals nervous, but not altogether disillusioned, with the trends marking the "new evangelical" re-engagement with modern scholarship and social issues.

760. Marsden, George M. "Preachers of Paradox: The Religious Right in Historical Perspective." In Religion and America: Spiritual Life in a Secular Age, eds. Mary Douglas and Steven Tipton. Boston: Beacon, 1982.

Marsden offers an elementary account of how the Falwells, Roberts, and Robertsons of the 1980s resemble the Finneys, Welds, and Moodys of the nineteenth century for a collection that first appeared in Daedelus without his contribution. It is a credit to the editors to recognize, even late in the day, that their title would have hidden a yawning gap if an article like Marsden's had not been solicited for the book.

761. Marsden, George. Reforming Fundamentalism: Fuller Seminary and the New Evangelicalism. Grand Rapids: Eerdmans, 1987.

Fuller was founded as a "new evangelical" institution in 1947, but what exactly that meant for the traditions of fundamentalism was not entirely clear. Marsden shows that Fuller's founding generation became troubled when its own students took seriously the founders' claims to be moving beyond the blind spots and inwardness of fundamentalism. This compelling narrative provides ample reason for continuing to look upon Fuller as a key player in the ongoing efforts at defining the essence and limits of the post-fundamentalist "new evangelicalism" which brought it into existence.

762. Morris, Andrew Michael. Southern Civil Religions in Conflict: Black and White Baptists and Civil Rights, 1947-1957. Athens: University of Georgia Press, 1987.

Morris describes the tensions when two versions of the American dream, both significantly evangelical, collided. He also notes how official leadership in the Southern Baptist Convention made cautious moves pointing toward acceptance of the later civil rights movement.

763. Nash, Ronald H. Evangelical Renewal in the Mainline Church. Westchester, IL: Good News, 1987.

This book introduces evangelical renewal movements that are currently active among Presbyterians, Methodists, Episcopalians, Congregationalists, and other "old Protestant" denominations.

764. Nelson, Rudolph. The Making and Unmaking of an Evangelical Mind: The Case of Edward Carnell. New York: Cambridge University Press, 1987.

Carnell was the leading theologian of the "new evangelical" movement responsible for the establishment of Fuller Theological Seminary. This is a fascinating study--partly for its insights into Carnell, the development of his thought from rationalism toward existentialism, his dreadful mistake in accepting the presidency of Fuller, and Nelson's debatable conclusions about the tensions he sees in Carnell's theology--but also partly for what we learn of Nelson's own pilgrimage in, out of, and part way back to the evangelicalism of his youth.

Orr, James Edwin. The Flaming Tongue: The Impact of Twentieth Century Revivals. Chicago: Moody Press, 1973.
(see 1389)

765. Patterson, Bob E. Carl F. H. Henry. Waco, TX: Word Books, 1983.

This valuable introductory study of Carl Henry helps set the stage for what will no doubt be future and more definitive works on a leading figure in the "new evangelical" movement.

766. Pierard, Richard V. "Billy Graham and the US Presidency." Journal of Church and State 22 (Winter 1980): 107-127.

767. Pierard, Richard V. "Billy Graham and Vietnam: From Cold Warrior to Peacemaker." Christian Scholar's Review 10:1 (1980): 37-51.

Pierard is a veteran Graham-watcher who is ever alert to Billy's relations with the political Right, but who also is able to chart a growing political maturity in this best-known of American evangelicals.

768. Pierard, Richard V. "Cacophony on Capital Hill: Evangelical Voices in Politics." In The Political Role of Religion, eds. S. Johnson and J. Tamney. Boulder, CO: Westview, 1986.

This essay charts the reemergence of specifically evangelical and fundamentalist political perspectives during the 1970s and the 1980s as they emerged from the non-sectarian prayer breakfast movement of the 1940s and 1950s.

769. Pierard, Richard V. "The Quest for Historical Evangelicalism: A Bibliographical Excursus." Fides et Historia 11 (Spring 1979): 60-72

Pierard, one of the founders of the Conference of Faith and History that publishes Fides et Historia, here offered sage comments on early efforts to write the history of recent evangelicalism. As such, it was a predecessor for later works of a similar sort by Donald Dayton, Douglas Sweeney and Leonard Sweet.

770. Pollock, John Charles. To All Nations: The Billy Graham Story. San Francisco: Harper & Row, 1985.

This study by a British historian is a reliable account of Graham's globe-trotting career. It is richer in detail than in interpretation, but that is a small price to pay for an authorized biography that at least gets the facts straight.

Quebedeaux, Richard. I Found It! The Story of Bill Bright and Campus Crusade. San Francisco: Harper & Row, 1979.
(see 1288)

771. Quebedeaux, Richard. The New Charismatics II. San Francisco: Harper & Row, 1983.

This book, a thorough revision of Quebedeaux's New Charismatics (1976), details the process by which the expression of charismatic gifts moved from the margins of American religion among pentecostals, then to an uncertain status impinging upon other Protestants, and finally to a place of centrality in the life of American Protestantism.

Quebedeaux, Richard. The Worldly Evangelicals. San Francisco: Harper & Row, 1978.
(see 1157)

Quebedeaux, Richard. The Young Evangelicals: Revolution in Orthodoxy. New York: Harper & Row, 1974.
(see 1158)

772. Ruegsegger, Ronald, ed. Reflections on Francis Schaeffer. Grand Rapids: Zondervan, 1986.

This volume contains a mixture of appreciation for, and criticism of, the influential intellectual work of Francis Schaeffer, about whom more is said under the book edited by Lane Dennis, Francis A. Schaeffer.

773. Silk, Mark. Spiritual Politics: Religion and America since World War II. New York: Simon and Schuster, 1988.

Silk, a reporter for the Atlanta Constitution who holds a history Ph.D. from Harvard, examines the many political circumstances in recent decades (including the civil rights movement, anti-Vietnam protests, the rise of conservative politics) that have involved religious (including evangelical) activity. The book documents the strains (conceptual, social, and political) experienced by the "Judeo-Christian" tradition in America, but also (despite massive assault) its enduring persistence.

774. Smith, Wilbur M. Before I Forget. Chicago: Moody Press, 1971.

Smith was involved in many of the most visible enterprises of northern, white evangelicals from the 1930s to the 1970s, including Moody Bible Institute, Peloubet's Notes for the International Sunday School lessons, Christianity Today, the revision of the Scofield Bible, Fuller Seminary, Trinity Evangelical Divinity School, and many more. This autobiography leaves out most controversies that touched institutions with which Smith was associated, but still offers considerable insight into the man who was the best known bibliophile of the "new evangelical" movement.

775. Stackhouse, John G., Jr. "Proclaiming the Word: Canadian Evangelicalism Since World War I." Ph.D. diss., University of Chicago, 1987.

Stackhouse charts the emergence of a self-conscious evangelical movement in Canada. That this development is so recent (dating from the 1960s) and that it emerged in other contexts than the sort of fundamentalist-modernist strife experienced in the United States helps to explain why Canadian evangelicalism shares what it does, and does not, with the American variety.

Streiker, Lowell D. and Gerald S. Strober. Religion and the New Majority: Billy Graham, Middle America, and the Politics of the 70's. New York: Association Press, 1972.
(see 1182)

776. Sweeney, Douglas. "The Neo-Evangelical Movement, 1941-1960: Toward a More Thorough Historiographical Approach." M.A. thesis, Trinity Evangelical Divinity School, 1989.

Sweeney finds the recent historiography of evangelicals broken into two factions, a Reformed group whose major representatives are George Marsden and Joel Carpenter, and a Holiness group shaped by the work of Timothy Smith and Donald Dayton. If Sweeney does not address many of the other groups that belong in the evangelical mosaic, grandly considered, he nonetheless offers shrewd commentary on how efforts to write the history of evangelicalism are related to the goals, convictions, and even embarrassments of evangelicals.

777. Sweet, Leonard I. "Wise as Serpents, Innocent as Doves: The New Evangelical Historiography." Journal of the American Academy of Religion 56 (Fall 1988): 397-416.

Sweet broadens a review of George Marsden's Reforming Fundamentalism: Fuller Seminary and the New Evangelicalism and Mark Noll's Between Faith and Criticism: Evangelicals, Scholarship, and the Bible in America into an examination of the growing number of historians who have begun writing about the movement from positions as participants as well as observers. The essay notes well the ambiguities involved in such activity and asks (with justification) for more attention to the Methodist and Wesleyan side of the story.

Voskuil, Dennis. Mountains Into Goldmines: Robert Schuller and the Gospel of Success. Grand Rapids: Eerdmans, 1983.
(see 1494)

778. Wacker, Grant. "Searching for Norman Rockwell: Popular Evangelicalism in Contemporary America." In The Evangelical Tradition in America, ed. Leonard I. Sweet. Macon, Georgia: Mercer University Press, 1984.

779. Wacker, Grant. "Uneasy in Zion: Evangelicals in Postmodern Society." In Evangelicalism and Modern America, ed. George M. Marsden. Grand Rapids: Eerdmans, 1984.

Wacker's gimlet eye allows him to see modern evangelicals and fundamentalists as sharing the values of modernity at the same time as they worry about them. These two essays offer especially shrewd assessment of the pentecostal and southern factors in the modern configuration of the movement.

780. Wallis, Jim. Agenda for Biblical People. New York: Harper & Row, 1976.

781. Wallis, Jim, ed. Waging Peace: A Handbook for the Struggle to Abolish Nuclear Weapons. San Francisco: Harper & Row, 1982.

Wallis is the motivator behind the Sojourners community in Washington, D. C., which has become a leading exponent of radical Christianity. The Sojourners magazine that he edits is the consistently best place to read about what could be called "Green Evangelicalism." It is expounded also in these two books.

782. Warner, R. Stephen. New Wine in Old Wineskins: Evangelicals and Liberals in a Small-Town Church. Berkeley: University of California, 1988.

Warner's narrative describes the recent history of a mainline Presbyterian church in Mendocino, California, which is led to new growth and outreach through the ministry of an evangelical pastor from Fuller Seminary. The book is compelling both for its personal stories, but also for Warner's sensitive work as a sociologist to differentiate between "nascent" and "establishment" forms of religious activity.

783. Wuthnow, Robert. The Restructuring of American Religion: Society and Faith Since World War II. Princeton, NJ: Princeton University Press, 1988.

784. Wuthnow, Robert. The Struggle for America's Soul: Evangelicals, Liberals, and Secularism. Grand Rapids: Eerdmans, 1989.

The first book is a major study of post-war religion. It argues that voluntary societies have become more important than traditional denominations, that increased levels of higher education and increased involvement by government in daily life have both acted as agents of secularization, and that a large and growing gap now divides religious conservatives and religious liberals from each other. Evangelicals, usually but not exclusively ranged on the conservative side of the equation, play a prominent role in the story, a role expanded upon in the more popular insights of the second volume.

785. Wuthnow, Robert with Robert C. Liebman, ed. The New Christian Right: Mobilization and Legitimation. Hawthorne, NY: Aldine, 1983.

The learned essays in this book are one of the best early assessments of political mobilization by fundamentalists and conservative evangelicals.

SECTION III: LIFE OF THE MIND

Mark A. Noll

CHAPTER 13
HIGHER EDUCATION

Evangelical higher education is a faithful reflection of the evangelical experience in America. It is divided into countless small institutions, much as the evangelical mosaic is so divided; it is strong in theological seminaries, for evangelicals have always stressed the place of biblical and related studies; its many Bible schools bespeak the pragmatic urgency that has long characterized the movement; and its lack of attention to doctoral level study reflects a long-standing evangelical ambiguity about research and the conventions of modern scholarship. Educational changes in the country as a whole after World War II have affected evangelicals, so that there is now a greater push for more and better quality academic training than in earlier periods. Yet many traits from those earlier periods are still to be found in the world of evangelical higher education.

786. Barnard, Jon. From Evangelicalism to Progressivism at Oberlin College, 1866-1917. Columbus: Ohio State University Press, 1969.

Oberlin (final home of Charles G. Finney) was once the flagship college of American evangelicalism. How it came to abandon that position during the academic revolution at the end of the nineteenth century is the subject of this sturdy work.

787. Bechtel, Paul M. Wheaton College: A Heritage Remembered, 1860-1984. Wheaton, IL: Harold Shaw, 1984.

This informative history traces the evolution of a typical small midwestern college to what became after the 1920s a central institution in the network of northern, white evangelicals.

788. Bond, Horace M. "The Origin and Development of the Negro Church-Related College." The Journal of Negro Education 29 (1960): 217-226.

This essay shows that since the first surge of college-founding immediately after the Civil War, black colleges have always had a greater concern for religious expression and religious training than the general run of American colleges and universities.

789. Brereton, Virginia L. "Protestant Fundamentalist Bible Schools, 1882-1920." Ph.D. dissertation, Columbia University, 1981.

Bible schools, of which Chicago's Moody Bible Institute has long been the standard, were a product of evangelical efforts to hand on a protected faith but also a result of more general pragmatic instincts to train students in immediately useful knowledge. This fine study is a pioneering look at a very important, but also much neglected, subject.

790. Calvin College: Curriculum Study Committee. Christian Liberal Arts Education. Grand Rapids: Calvin College, 1970.

This book came out of the effort by the Calvin faculty in the 1970s to define the principles and practicalities of a theologically responsible curriculum. It remains the most thorough and sophisticated effort of its kind.

791. Carpenter, Joel A.and Kenneth Shipps, eds. Making Higher Education Christian: The History and Mission of Evangelical Colleges in America. Grand Rapids: Eerdmans, 1987.

This volume contains the fullest account to date of the background and current shape of evangelical higher education. Its sections include papers on the history of Christian higher education (mostly in America), essays on the various tasks (intellectual, theological, practical) of evangelical education, and chapters on the current state of the colleges which call themselves evangelical.

792. Christian College Coalition. Consider a Christian College: 75 Colleges Combining Academic Excellence and Enduring Spiritual Values. Princeton, NJ: Peterson's Guides, 1988.

The Christian College Coalition represents most of the colleges in the United States that would wish to be known as "evangelical." This annual publication provides information for prospective students and a brief amount of historical material on the various institutions.

793. Findlay, James. F. "Agency, Denominations and the Western Colleges, 1830-1860: Some Connections Between Evangelicalism and American Higher Education." Church History 50 (Mar.1981): 64-80.

Findlay shows dramatically how important the promotion of Christian civilization, understood primarily in evangelical terms, was for most of the colleges founded in the nineteenth century.

794. Frey, Bradshaw, William Ingram, Thomas E. McWhertor and William David Romanowski. All of Life Redeemed: Biblical Insight for Daily Obedience. Jordan Station, Ontario: Paideia, 1983.

The authors make a persuasive case for the assertion that every facet of intellectual life as well as every question of day-to-day existence needs to be understood in terms of the salvation won through Jesus Christ. The book clearly articulates a goal to which many evangelical institutions of higher learning dedicate their existence.

795. Gangel, Kenneth O. Toward a Harmony of Faith and Learning: Essays on Bible College Curriculum. Farmington Hills, MI: William Tyndale College, 1985.

Gangel is a leading theoretician of Bible college education whose essays here reflect the effort by these institutions to impart both intellectual substance and evangelical spirituality.

796. Hamilton, Michael. "Wheaton College, Fundamentalism and Evangelicalism: The Role of Liberal Arts College in the Development of a Popular Religious Movement, 1919-1964." Ph.D. dissertation, University of Notre Dame, 1990.

This is the best analysis of Wheaton in relation to the wider religious movements for which it has served as both a place of education and a meeting point for far-flung voluntary networks.

797. Hatch, Nathan O. "Evangelical Colleges and the Challenge of Christian Thinking." Reformed Journal (September 1985): 10-18.

Hatch explains why the activistic, democratic, and personality- centered character of American evangelicalism has left the movement ill equipped to mount and sustain meaningful ventures in higher learning as it has come to be defined since the academic revolution at the end of the nineteenth century.

798. Heie, Harold and David L. Wolfe, eds. The Reality of Christian Learning. Grand Rapids: Eerdmans, 1987.

The editors, who concluded that talk about "the integration of faith and learning" was pretty cheap, set out to provide examples of such efforts in several disciplines. Stimulating forays in political science (can there be such a thing as a Christian political science?), biology (what is the relation of the brain to the person?), philosophy (are divine rewards required for morality?), and several other disciplines was the result. One of the best, but least likely pieces, is Heie's "Mathematics: Freedom within Bounds."

799. Holmes, Arthur F. All Truth is God's Truth. Grand Rapids: Eerdmans, 1977.

800. Holmes, Arthur F. The Idea of a Christian College. Rev.ed. Grand Rapids: Eerdmans, 1987.

801. Holmes, Arthur F., ed. The Making of a Christian Mind: A Christian World View and the Academic Enterprise. Downers Grove, IL: InterVarsity Press, 1984.

Holmes, a philosopher at Wheaton College in Illinois, has been a leader since the 1950s in articulating a rationale for higher education from a Christian standpoint. His All Truth is God's Truth uses traditional evangelical categories of sin, revelation, and Christology to defend the academic enterprise against anti-intellectualism. The Idea of a Christian College presents a confessional evangelical setting as an ideal place to study the liberal arts. In The Making of a Christian Mind, Holmes is joined by four of his Wheaton colleagues to suggest how "Christian thinking" can take place within the disciplines and as an influence upon them.

802. Malik, Charles. A Christian Critique of the University. Downers Grove, IL: InterVarsity Press, 1982.

Malik, a former leader of the United Nations who was an Orthodox Christian from Lebanon, here describes the power of universities in western civilization and their role in promoting modern conventions of secularity. The point of his book is to ask what a Christian stance toward the university education should be, in light of the fact that the most important critic of the western universities "in the final analysis is Jesus Christ himself."

803. Marsden, George. "The Collapse of American Evangelical Academia." In Faith and Rationality: Reason and Belief in God, eds. Alvin Plantinga and Nicholas Wolterstorff. Notre Dame, IN: University of Notre Dame Press, 1983.

Marsden charts expertly how the evangelical commitment to a form of "early modern" science associated with Francis Bacon and Isaac Newton led to a clash of paradigms with the "more recent modern science" of Darwin, Huxley, Spencer, and the new American university. This is the best essay to date on how American evangelical life moved overnight, as it were, from an hereditary evangelical orbit to the more secular precincts of the modern university.

804. Noll, Mark A. "The Founding of Princeton Seminary." Westminster Theological Journal 42 (Fall 1979): 72-110.

The founders of Princeton in 1812 exhibited diligent concern for academic thoroughness, aspirations to be scientific according to the best lights of the early nineteenth century, and pragmatic concern for the cultivation of piety with learning. These goals, as well as the central place of Princeton in evangelical intellectual life and the unusually large number of college presidents who studied there, make the circumstances of the seminary's founding broadly significant of much that would come later in evangelical educational ventures.

805. Rawlyk, G.A., ed. Canadian Baptists and Christian Higher Education. Kingston and Montreal, Canada: McGill-Queen's University Press, 1988.

The four essays in this volume treat different chapters in Canadian Baptist educational experiments in the Maritimes, Ontario, and the West. Most interesting is the editor's essay on changes at McMaster University in the 1920s and 1930s, when a new language of consumerism gradually came to replace the evangelical conceptions that had prevailed since the founding of the institution.

806. Riesman, David. "The Evangelical Colleges: Untouched by the Academic Revolution." Change (January/February, 1981): 13-20.

This brief, appreciative report alerted the wider academic world to the continuing existence of colleges that hoped to survive the academic changes of the 1960s and 1970s with purposes relatively unchanged.

807. Ringenberg, William. The Christian College: A History of Protestant Higher Education in America. Grand Rapids: Eerdmans, 1984.

Ringenberg provides a comprehensive institutional history of evangelical higher education from the Puritans' Harvard College to Jerry Falwell's Liberty University. The scope is vast, but the work successfully paves the way for later, more analytical studies of the multifaceted enterprises of evangelical higher education.

808. Smith, Timothy L. Uncommon Schools: Christian Colleges and School Idealism in Midwestern America, 1820-1950. Indianapolis: Indiana Historical Society, 1978.

Smith's lengthy essay shows how important Christian concerns were to the founding of most midwestern colleges and universities, and also in turn how important these institutions were in fulfilling the social and intellectual aspirations of the communities in which they were located.

809. Stevenson, Louise L. Scholarly Means to Evangelical Ends: The New Haven Scholars and the Transformation of Higher Learning in America, 1830-1890. Baltimore: Johns Hopkins University Press, 1986.

Yale was a staunchly evangelical institution that throughout the nineteenth century evolved slowly in the direction of more secular academic conventions. This authoritative book nicely captures the ethos of a transitional generation that looked with kindly eye on its evangelical past, but that had already turned its face to the more scientific and secular scholarship that would come to dominate the American educational landscape.

810. Timmerman, John J. Promises to Keep: A Centennial History of Calvin College. Grand Rapids: Calvin College and Seminary, 1975.

Timmerman's winsome history helps explain why Calvin faculty, though situated by their Dutchness at the margin of American religious life, have contributed so significantly to the recent intellectual life of American evangelicals.

811. Walsh, Brian J. and J. Richard Middleton. The Transforming Vision: Shaping a Christian World View. Downers Grove, IL: InterVarsity Press, 1984.

In the manner of Frey, et al.'s All of Life Redeemed the authors, who are Canadians, call for a comprehensive intellectual strategy shaped at every point by a Christian worldview. An extensive bibliography of works in the various academic disciplines complements the exposition of the book.

812. Yandell, Keith E., ed. "A New Agenda for Evangelical Thought." Christian Scholar's Review 17 (June 1988): 341-488.

This special issue published summary essays on evangelical scholarly participation in the academic disciplines. Besides essays mentioned elsewhere in this bibliography, the issue included papers by Mary Stewart Van Leeuwen on psychology, Patricia Ward and David Jeffrey on literature, Nicholas Wolterstorff on the arts, Carl F. H. Henry on Christian scholarship in a fallen world, and George Marsden on the general state of evangelical Christian scholarship.

CHAPTER 14
BIBLE, THEOLOGY, PHILOSOPHY

(A) Bible

Evangelicals read the Bible, memorize biblical passages, fight over divergent understandings of Scripture, and write book after book on the Bible's nature, interpretation, application, authority, and character. Only a few titles in the vast evangelical library on Scripture can be presented here. The works below are recent statements from representative individuals or groups, as well as a few second-order studies looking directly at the subject of how evangelicals have put the Bible to use.

813. Abraham, William J. The Divine Inspiration of Holy Scripture. New York: Oxford University Press, 1981.

814. Abraham, William J. Divine Revelation and the Insights of Historical Criticism. New York: Oxford University Press, 1982.

Abraham, an Irish Methodist teaching in the United States, criticizes common evangelical notions of inerrancy as not taking seriously enough the human character of Scripture. As an alternative, he proposes to treat the inspiration of the Bible as a higher order of the way that pupils are inspired by their best teachers.

815. Armerding, Carl. The Old Testament and Criticism. Grand Rapids: Eerdmans, 1983.

As opposed to approaches he labels "traditional conservative" and "rational critical," Armerding feels that "evangelical criticism" is able to affirm both special revelation from God and the proper role of historical and literary studies of the meaning of the Bible.

816. Bush, Russ and Tom Nettles. Baptists and the Bible. Chicago: Moody Press, 1980.

Issues of biblical criticism came late in the day to Southern Baptists, but their arrival in the 1960s and 1970s has been the occasion for much discussion. Bush and Nettles argue here that traditional, if not always articulated, views of the Bible held by Baptists conform quite well to the more articulate notions of inerrancy that have featured centrally in northern evangelical and fundamentalist concern since the late nineteenth century.

817. Cameron, Nigel M. de S. Biblical Higher Criticism and the Defense of Infallibilism in 19th Century Britain. Lewiston, NY: Edwin Mellen, 1987.

Cameron's study focuses on Britain, but is nonetheless probably the fullest discussion of the theological challenges posed when hereditary confidence in the inspiration of Scripture was challenged by the nineteenth century's new notions of history, religion, and literary composition.

818. Carson, D. A. and John D. Woodbridge, eds. Hermeneutics, Authority, and Canon. Grand Rapids: Zondervan, 1986.

819. Carson, D. A. and John D. Woodbridge, eds. Scripture and Truth. Grand Rapids: Zondervan, 1983.

These two volumes offer the last decade's fullest and most nuanced defense of biblical inerrancy. Especially noteworthy are essays in Scripture and Truth by Carson on unity and diversity in the New Testament and by Paul Helm on faith and/or evidence as the basis for confidence in the Bible; and in Hermeneutics, Authority, and Canon by Kevin Vanhoozer on the Bible's diverse literary forms and by Moses Silva on efforts to reconstruct the historical occurrences of the New Testament.

820. France, R. T. "Evangelical Disagreements About the Bible." Churchman 96 (1982): 226-40.

France writes about his fellow Britons, but with words equally applicable to the American scene. His concern is to differentiate between controversies over what the Bible means (which should be taken in stride) and debates over what it is (where innovative ideas require more careful scrutiny).

821. Glover, Willis B. Evangelical Nonconformists and Higher Criticism in the Nineteenth Century. London: Independent Press, 1954.

With Cameron's Biblical Higher Criticism, this volume offers a full account of the way British evangelicals debated issues that have been the center of American controversy for over a century.

822. Gundry, Robert H. Matthew: A Commentary on His Literary and Theological Art. Grand Rapids: Eerdmans, 1982.

Gundry's proposal that part of Matthew's gospel was *midrash* (an intentionally fictional embellishment of the historical narrative) posed especially delicate questions for evangelicals, since Gundry defended his approach as falling within the borders of traditional inerrancy.

823. International Council on Biblical Inerrancy. "Chicago Statement on Biblical Inerrancy." Journal of the Evangelical Theological Society 21 (December 1978): 289-296.

The ICBI was founded to shore up views of scriptural authority that seemed to its leaders to be slipping. Its pronouncements set out a fresh statement of traditional understandings, but its organization illustrated once again the tendency of evangelicals to solve intellectual issues through the creation of populist organizations.

824. Jacobsen, Douglas. "From Truth to Authority to Responsibility: The Shifting Focus of Evangelical Hermeneutics, 1915-1986." TSF Bulletin 10 (March/April 1987): 8-15; (May/June 1989): 10-14.

825. Jacobsen, Douglas. "The Rise of Evangelical Hermeneutical Pluralism." Christian School Review 16 (July 1987): 325-335.

Jacobsen well describes the shifting nuances within the evangelical community as more representatives from more of the evangelical families enter the professional worlds of Bible scholarship.

826. Johnston, Robert K., ed. The Use of the Bible in Theology: Evangelical Options. Atlanta: John Knox, 1985.

Johnston enlisted ten authors (Clark Pinnock, J. I. Packer, Russell Spittler, Donald Bloesch, John Howard Yoder, Donald Dayton, Robert Webber, William Dyrness, David Wells, and Gabriel Fackre) to show how they used the Bible in theology. The similarities are strong enough to reassure skeptics about the potential for traditional confidence in Scripture to unify otherwise disparate evangelicals. But contrasts are strong enough to worry evangelicals who insist blithely that unity will flow simply from trusting "the Bible alone."

827. Ladd, George E. The New Testament and Criticism. Grand Rapids: Eerdmans, 1967.

Ladd was one of the first scholars after World War II to attempt an evangelical use of modern biblical criticism. This is his landmark report on the effort, with its declaration that with a growing number of evangelicals he wished to abandon fundamentalist withdrawal and take his stand "within the contemporary stream of philosophical, theological, and critical thought."

828. Lindsell, Harold. The Battle for the Bible. Grand Rapids: Zondervan, 1976.

Lindsell, who taught at Fuller before becoming editor of Christianity Today, felt that evangelical interaction with modern scholarship was leading to too much sacrifice of traditional positions. This book is a spirited, popular account of why he thought that was the case.

829. Longman, Tremper, III. "Form Criticism, Recent Developments in Genre Theory, and the Evangelical." Westminster Theological Journal 47 (Spring 1985): 46-67.

Longman is among those evangelical Bible scholars who believes in, as Augustine put it, "plundering the Egyptians." This essay shows how it is possible to use refined notions of literary genre in order to practice form criticism (one of the contemporary fashions in biblical scholarship) in such a way as to conform to, rather than undercut, traditional evangelical views of Scripture.

830. Maring, Norman H. "Baptists and Changing Views of the Bible, 1865-1918." Foundations 1 (July 1958): 52-75; (October 1958): 30-61.

Maring's careful historical work shows how Northern Baptists came to moderate traditional views of the Bible without becoming captives to the latest critical fashions.

831. Marsden, George M. "Everyone's Own Interpreter?: The Bible, Science, and Authority in Mid-Nineteenth-Century America." In The Bible in America, eds. Nathan O. Hatch and Mark A. Noll. New York: Oxford University Press, 1982.

The legacy of early nineteenth-century evangelical scienticism is Marsden's theme in this seminal essay. If evangelicals rest their claims to the Bible's truthfulness on chains of reasoning modeled on the best science of the day, what happens when the best science of the day begins to counteract traditional interpretations of the Bible? The situation as described here helps to explain the peculiar evangelical mix of faiths, in science and Scripture, that continue to show up in movements like "creation science."

832. McKim, Donald K., ed. The Authoritative Word: Essays on the Nature of Scripture. Grand Rapids: Eerdmans, 1983.

"McKim's Anthologies" have become as frequent as they are helpful. This one draws together moderately conservative views of scriptural authority from Continental, Anglo-American evangelical, mainline, and Catholic scholars (e.g., respectively, G. C. Berkouwer and Herman Ridderbos, F. F. Bruce and Donald Bloesch, Paul Achtemeier and Robert Grant, Avery Dulles) on the meaning of biblical authority. The verdict: too conservative and evangelical for liberals, too liberal for conservative evangelicals.

833. McKim, Donald K., ed. A Guide to Contemporary Hermeneutics: Major Trends in Biblical Interpretation. Grand Rapids: Eerdmans, 1986.

The twenty contributions to this book include several that outline evangelical approaches to the interpretation of the Bible. Especially useful for charting the intense debates of evangelicals on these questions are essays on hermeneutics from the International Council on Biblical Inerrancy, David Steinmetz (Duke Divinity School), William Sanford LaSor (Fuller

Theological Seminary), Anthony Thiselton (St. Johns College, Nottingham), Walter Kaiser (Trinity Evangelical Divinity School), Thomas Gillespie (Princeton Theological Seminary), C. Rene Padilla (Buenos Aires), and Charles Kraft (Fuller Theological Seminary).

834. McKim, Donald K. What Christians Believe About the Bible. Nashville: Thomas Nelson, 1985.

This book is by McKim himself, but it continues the pattern of the anthologies by providing succinct, objective accounts of several approaches to Scripture: viz., Roman Catholic, sixteenth-century Protestant, liberal, fundamentalist, scholastic Protestant, neo-orthodox, neo-evangelical, existentialist, process, narrative, liberation, and feminist.

835. Noll, Mark A. Between Faith and Criticism: Evangelicals, Scholarship, and the Bible in America. San Francisco: Harper & Row, 1986.

This is an account of early evangelical responses to higher criticism late in the nineteenth century, of evangelical withdrawal from the academic study of Scripture between the wars, and of evangelical re-engagement with professional Bible study from the 1960s. Its concern is to view Bible study as part of cultural and intellectual history as well as theological development.

836. Osborne, Grant R. "Evangelical Interpretation of Scripture." In The Bible in the Churches with Kenneth Hagen and Daniel J. Harrington, S.J. and Joseph A. Burgess. Mahwah, NJ: Paulist, 1985.

A Lutheran historian (Hagen) invited three biblical scholars--a Catholic (Harrington), a Lutheran (Burgess), and an evangelical (Osborne)--to explain how each of their groups interpreted the Bible. Osborne stresses the usual evangelical commitment to inerrancy and the grammatical-historical interpretation, while at the same time recognizing that responsible evangelicals try to take full consideration of the contexts in which the Bible was written and is read.

837. Pinnock, Clark H. The Scripture Principle. San Francisco: Harper & Row, 1984.

Over the course of his career, Pinnock has moved from a strict inerrantist to a modified inerrantist position. This book represents an appeal to secularists to recognize the divine character of the Bible and to conservative evangelicals to acknowledge the human dimensions of scriptural writings.

838. Price, Robert M. "Neo-Evangelicals and Scripture: A Forgotten Period of Ferment." Christian Scholar's Review 15:4 (1986): 315-330.

Debates among evangelicals over the exact character of Scripture occasioned much public debate in the 1970s, but Price here suggests that the "neo-evangelical" effort in the 1950s and 1960s to break loose from fundamentalist constraints carried with it a less-well-publicized debate on whether the inspiration of the Bible was verbal or conceptual.

839. The Proceedings of the Conference on Biblical Inerrancy 1987. Nashville: Broadman, 1987.

These papers are from a conference held at Ridgecrest, North Carolina, at which Southern Baptists and a crew of Yankee evangelicals from the North discussed the meaning of inerrancy and the history of Southern Baptist engagement with the topic. The volume illuminates especially the way that Southern Baptists are dealing with an issue that had earlier engaged most of the nation's major Protestant denominations.

840. Radmacher, Earl D. and Robert D. Preus, eds. Hermeneutics, Inerrancy, and the Bible. Grand Rapids: Zondervan, 1984.

The chapters in this volume came from a meeting sponsored by the Biblical Inerrancy Council. It proposed conservative guidelines for the interpretation of Scripture as a way of responding to recent innovations in genre and literary study of the Bible.

841. Rogers, Jack B. and Donald K. McKim. The Authority and Interpretation of the Bible. San Francisco: Harper & Row, 1979.

The authors suggest that biblical inerrancy is a relatively recent concept that detracts from the church's historic concentration on the authority of Scripture in matters of faith and practice.

842. Silva, Moses. Has the Church Misread the Bible? The History of Interpretation in the Light of Contemporary Issues. Grand Rapids: Zondervan, 1987. (Foundations of Contemporary Interpretations Series)

Silva shows how it is possible to exploit modern understandings of ancient written texts to restate traditional understandings of biblical inspiration and authority.

843. Thiselton, Anthony C. The Two Horizons: New Testament Hermeneutics and Philosophical Description. Grand Rapids: Eerdmans, 1980.

This work by a British evangelical offers pioneering reflection on the stance of the reader in the process of biblical interpretation. Its fruitful use of modern philosophers, especially Wittgenstein, made it an important instance of renewed evangelical efforts to employ modern forms of thought for the appropriation of traditional evangelical convictions.

844. Trembath, Kern Robert. Evangelical Theories of Biblical Inspiration: A Review and Proposal. New York: Oxford University Press, 1987.

Trembath feels that evangelical views of inspiration would be improved by adding selective insights from Roman Catholic perspectives, especially

Karl Rahner's emphasis on the functional character of inspiration in communities of believers.

845. Vander Stelt, John. Philosophy and Scripture: A Study in Old Princeton and Westminster Theology. Marlton, NJ: Mack Publishing Co., 1978.

Vander Stelt argues that the Old Princeton tradition (Charles Hodge, B. B. Warfield) was overly dependent upon the use of Scottish common sense philosophy. He finds a proper antidote in the continental Reformed theology associated with G. C. Berkouwer.

846. Warfield, Benjamin Breckinridge. The Inspiration and Authority of the Bible. Philadelphia: Presbyterian and Reformed, 1948.

As an anti-millennialist, pro-evolution scholar, Warfield should have been an oddity in fundamentalist and conservative evangelicals circles. Yet his careful defense of biblical inerrancy in the face of the earliest critical modifications of traditional dogmas made him a very influential figure in the evangelical understanding of Scripture. This volume contains some of his most perceptive essays on the subject.

847. Weber, Timothy P. "The Two-Edged Sword: The Fundamentalist Use of the Bible." In The Bible in America, eds. Nathan O. Hatch and Mark A. Noll. New York: Oxford University Press, 1982.

Weber rings the changes on the irony that saw fundamentalists attack liberal theology for violating historic Protestant commitments to the ordinary person's access to Scripture, while at the same time they followed without question the dogmatic utterances of their own teachers on the nature and meaning of the Bible.

848. Woodbridge, John D. Biblical Authority: A Critique of the Rogers/McKim Proposal. Grand Rapids: Zondervan, 1982.

Against Rogers and McKim, Woodbridge argues that biblical inerrancy is the historic position of the church and that it alone undergirds a proper understanding of the Bible's authority.

849. Youngblood, Ronald, ed. Journal of the Evangelical Theological Society 26 (March 1983): 3-121.

A special issue on evangelicalism, inerrancy, and R.H. Gundry's Matthew commentary. The publication of Gundry's commentary on Matthew led to many attempts by evangelicals to explain why Gundry's position, though still inerrantist, was nonetheless erroneous. Some of the most persuasive rebuttals are gathered together in this publication.

(B) Theology

Evangelicals probably write even more on theology, broadly considered, than on Scripture. Again, great selectivity has been necessary in gathering the works that follow. Included are some of the most important statements by recent theological leaders as well as a few systematic theologies that are standard for one or another sub-group of evangelicals.

850. Bentley, William H. National Black Evangelical Association: Evolution of a Concept of Ministry. Chicago: By the author, 1979.

The National Black Evangelical Association was founded in Los Angeles in 1963. Bentley, its moving figure, here wrestles with what its relation should be to the influential black theology of James H. Cone. Bentley has reservations about Cone's project, but also is not satisfied with white evangelical tendencies to separate the "social" and the "sacred."

851. Bloesch, Donald G. Essentials of Evangelical Theology. 2 vols. San Francisco: Harper & Row, 1978, 1979.

Bloesch is the contemporary evangelical who comes closest to a harmonious melding of themes from Reformation orthodoxy, the pietistic movements of Britain and the Continent, and the work of Karl Barth.

852. Bolich, Gregory C. Karl Barth and Evangelicalism. Downers Grove, IL: InterVarsity Press, 1980.

Evangelical attitudes toward Barth, as chronicled here, have moved over time from stern opposition to cautious and discriminating acceptance.

853. Bruce, Calvin E. "Black Evangelical Christianity and Black Theology." In Black Theology II: Essays on the Formation and Outreach of Contemporary Black Theology. Lewisburg, PA: Bucknell University Press, 1978.

The ways in which traditional black emphases, which share religious if not cultural features with those of white evangelicals, anticipated and diverge from the black theology of the 1960s and following is the subject of this essay.

854. Bruner, Dale. A Theology of the Holy Spirit: The Pentecostal Experience and the New Testament Witness. Grand Rapids: Eerdmans, 1970.

Bruner, a missionary educator, offers a painstaking comparison between the work of the Holy Spirit as described in the New Testament and the work of the Spirit as claimed by modern pentecostalism. His conclusion is that the latter does not in fact replicate the former, even though the former provides a warrant for looking for experience of the Holy Spirit today.

855. Buswell, J. Oliver. A Systematic Theology of the Christian Religion. 2 vols. Grand Rapids: Zondervan, 1962.

Buswell's Calvinistic, rational, moderately dispensational theology is a summary of beliefs held by many evangelical Presbyterians, northern Baptists, and similar individuals.

856. Carnell, Edward John. The Case for Orthodox Theology. Philadelphia: Westminster, 1959.

857. Carnell, Edward John. Christian Commitment: An Apologetic. New York: Macmillan, 1957.

858. Carnell, Edward John. An Introduction to Christian Apologetics: A Philosophic Defense of the Trinitarian-Theistic Faith. Grand Rapids: Eerdmans, 1948.

859. Carnell, Edward John. A Philosophy of the Christian Religion. Grand Rapids: Eerdmans, 1952.

Carnell was the theological star among the "new evangelicals." His quest for a conservative theology satisfying to both the mind and the heart led him away from the more rationalistic note to be found in his earlier works to a more existential note in the later. Also in the later books he made sharper criticisms of fundamentalism as a cultic and dessicated form of orthodox belief. In the end, Carnell was a transitional figure, someone who showed others the way beyond fundamentalism but who himself was not able to leave an entirely compelling body of writing to indicate what a more thoroughly evangelical synthesis should look like.

860. Carter, Charles W., ed. A Contemporary Wesleyan Theology: Biblical, Systematic, and Practical. 2 vols. Grand Rapids: Zondervan, 1983.

This full summary includes welcome chapters on hymnody, worship, and the practical religious life as well as standard themes on God, salvation, and authority. The team of writers responsible for these volumes have their differences with the modified Calvinistic themes frequently heard among contemporary evangelicals, but also present their constructive work more as modifications than alternatives to those positions.

861. Chafer, Lewis Sperry. Systematic Theology. 8 vols. Dallas: Dallas Seminary Press, 1947.

Chafer was the Dallas Theological Seminary's systematician whose work presented a thoroughly dispensational understanding of the Bible.

862. Erickson, Millard. Christian Theology. 3 vols. Grand Rapids: Baker, 1983.

Erickson's volumes offer a solid summary of mainstream, northern, white evangelical thinking from the 1970s and 1980s. The general tone is moderate (for example, on issues that regularly divide Calvinists from Arminians), as are the positions taken.

863. Fackre, Gabriel. The Christian Story: A Pastoral Systematics. 2 vols. to date. Grand Rapids: Eerdmans, 1984.

Fackre puts a narrative approach to use in presenting a more dynamic account of traditional evangelical belief.

864. Geehan, E. R. Jerusalem and Athens: Critical Discussions on the Theology and Apologetics of Cornelius Van Til. Philadelphia: Presbyterian and Reformed, 1971.

The spirited exchanges in this volume focus on Van Til's presuppositional apologetics, a stance dependent upon Dutch Calvinist thinking that denies the objectivity of participants in the quest for God and religious truth.

865. Hamilton, James E. "Epistemology and Theology in American Methodism." Wesleyan Theological Journal 10 (Spring 1975): 70-79.

Hamilton is especially able at showing the influence among Methodists of Scottish forms of common sense philosophy.

866. Henry, Carl F. H. Christian Personal Ethics. Grand Rapids: Eerdmans, 1957.

Against what he called naturalistic, idealistic, and existentialist ethical systems, Henry posited the revelation of Scripture as a secure and always-relevant source of ethical norms. When it was published, this was the fullest statement by a "new evangelical" on such matters.

867. Henry, Carl F. H., ed. Contemporary Evangelical Thought series: Contemporary Evangelical Thought (Great Neck, NY: Channel, 1957); Revelation and the Bible (Grand Rapids: Baker, 1958); Basic Christian Doctrines (New York: Holt, Rinehart and Winston, 1962); Christian Faith and Modern Theology (New York: Channel, 1964); Jesus of Nazareth: Saviour and Lord (Grand Rapids: Eerdmans, 1966); Fundamentals of the Faith (Grand Rapids: Zondervan, 1969).

The fifty-nine authors that Henry enlisted for these symposia included twenty-six scholars from outside the United States; these came primarily from Baptist, Presbyterian, and Episcopalian/ Anglican circles, with a few Lutherans and Methodists as well. For the patient reader, these essays provide the fullest account of general evangelical views for the 1950s and 1960s and a good indication of the background out of which many contemporary discussions among evangelicals arise.

868. Henry, Carl F. H. God, Revelation, and Authority. 6 vols. Waco, TX: Word, 1976-1983.

Henry's own master work is a learned defense of the rational character of Christianity and of God's ability to reveal himself and his will propositionally to the human race.

869. Kraus, C. Norman. Dispensationalism in America: Its Rise and Development. Richmond, VA: John Knox Press, 1958.

The account by Kraus, who is not himself a dispensationalist, attempts to convey the force and attractiveness of the theological system that is basic for most American fundamentalists and many conservative evangelicals.

870. Ladd, George E. Jesus and the Kingdom: The Eschatology of Biblical Realism. New York: Harper & Row, 1964.

871. Ladd, George E. A Theology of the New Testament. Grand Rapids: Eerdmans, 1974.

Ladd was the leading biblical theologian among the first wave of "new evangelicals" who returned to the universities in the 1940s. His works carried on an often tense effort simultaneously to convince the skeptical of basic evangelical positions and to disabuse especially dispensationalists of the errors of their way.

872. Langford, Thomas A. Practical Divinity: Theology in the Wesleyan Tradition. Nashville: Abingdon, 1983.

Langford's account includes substantial discussion of Wesley's legacy and the ways that legacy has been adjusted in both British and American environments.

873. McKim, Donald K., ed. How Karl Barth Changed My Mind. Grand Rapids: Eerdmans, 1986.

In proper evangelical fashion, McKim collects testimonies concerning the influence of Karl Barth in the more progressive evangelical circles. The volume is in effect an update of Bolich's Karl Barth and Evangelicalism.

874. Morris, Thomas V. Francis Schaeffer's Apologetics: A Critique. Chicago: Moody Press, 1976.

Morris, who subsequently blossomed as a forceful philosopher of religion, devoted this early work to charting the theoretical strengths and weaknesses of a popular theologian and apologist.

875. Mouw, Richard. Political Evangelism. Grand Rapids: Eerdmans, 1974.

876. Mouw, Richard. Politics and the Biblical Drama. Grand Rapids: Eerdmans, 1976.

Mouw is a leader in describing the potential of a traditional evangelical faith for social reformation and the pursuit of justice. In terms that may stretch matters a little, he is trying to show how an evangelical theology mediating between Dutch Reformed and American evangelical emphases can embody a holistic approach to life more typical among black evangelicals.

877. Noll, Mark A. "Common Sense Traditions and American Evangelical Thought." American Quarterly 37 (Summer 1985): 216-238.

Common sense philosophy has been an important part of evangelical theology since the Revolutionary period, but evangelicals have turned more easily to the epistemological aspects of that philosophy (in efforts to defend the faith scientifically) than to the ethical (which assumes a natural capacity for virtuous action that most evangelicals deny).

878. Noll, Mark A., ed. The Princeton Theology: 1812 - 1921. Grand Rapids: Baker, 1983.

The Princeton emphasis on rational and confessional Reformed orthodoxy was a central feature of nineteenth-century evangelical thought, and remains a prominent influence throughout the twentieth century. The selections in this anthology present the views of Archibald Alexander, Charles Hodge, A. A. Hodge, and B. B. Warfield on Scripture, science, and theological method.

879. Noll, Mark A. and David F. Wells, eds. Christian Faith and Practice in the Modern World: Theology From an Evangelical Point of View. Grand Rapids: Eerdmans, 1988.

For this book, evangelical academics concerned about the theological contexts of their disciplines join professional theologians to ponder three general subjects: the image of God, the self-disclosure of God, creation and its restoration. Essays include up-to-date evangelical reflections on the Trinity, the human person, revelation and its reception, work, poverty, science, secularism, and the future.

880. Packer, James I. Evangelism and the Sovereignty of God. Chicago: InterVarsity Press, 1961.

881. Packer, James I. "Fundamentalism" and the Word of God: Some Evangelical Principles. Grand Rapids: Eerdmans, 1958.

Packer, a Briton now teaching in Canada, has had an altogether salutary effect on American evangelicals through these and related works. The first argues that there is no oddity in combining notions of evangelistic urgency and divine control of the world, the second that confidence in Scripture need not lead to mindless religious enthusiasm.

882. Pinnock, Clark H., ed. Grace Unlimited. Minneapolis, MN: Bethany Fellowship, 1975.

This symposium features arguments against the Calvinistic notion that God's grace comes only, or primarily, to those who will be redeemed, as well as several different defenses for the belief that the divine grace is given to all in equal measure. It is a book that well illustrates the continuing divide among American evangelicals on historic matters at issue between Calvinists and Arminians. But it is also a volume that implicitly raises the question why the calm tone characterizing this debate cannot be carried over into more heated exchanges on the nature of the Bible.

883. Pinnock, Clark H. Reason Enough: A Case for the Christian Faith. Downers Grove, IL: InterVarsity Press, 1980.

This winsome apologetics suggests that there are reasons for Christian faith that all should acknowledge, while withholding the judgment that those reasons are equally compelling on all people in all circumstances.

884. Ramm, Bernard. After Fundamentalism: The Future of Evangelical Theology. San Francisco: Harper & Row, 1983.

Ramm, a major theological voice in the generation of contemporary Carl Henry, here vents some spleen at what he considers to be obscurantist theological method among his fellow-evangelicals. Karl Barth, according to Ramm, showed the way to better methods of theological construction.

885. Schaeffer, Francis. The Complete Works of Francis A. Schaeffer. 5 vols. Westchester, IL: Crossway Books, 1982.

Schaeffer exerted a powerful influence in drawing evangelicals back to engagement with modern culture and the arts, and also at the end of his career to forceful advocacy of political causes (anti-abortion, anti-big government). The books, tracts, and biblical expositions of his mature career, after he himself had turned from an earlier sectarian period, are collected in this well-edited edition.

Sider, Ronald J. Rich Christians in an Age of Hunger: A Biblical Study. Rev. ed. Downers Grove, IL: InterVarsity Press, 1984.
(see 1503)

886. Sproul, R. C., John Gerstner and Arthur Lindsley. Classical Apologetics: A Rational Defense of the Christian Faith and a Critique of Presuppositional Apologetics. Grand Rapids: Zondervan, 1984.

This is the fullest recent argument (against the presuppositionalism promoted by Cornelius Van Til and his disciples) for evidentialist apologetics, or an approach that assumes that all are able to rightly evaluate the evidence for God, the Scriptures, and the deity of Christ. The fact that the authors' opponents are, like themselves, confessional Calvinists, suggests the range of issues in which American Calvinists have influenced general evangelical thought in America.

887. Wells, David F. "An American Evangelical Theology: The Painful Transition From Theoria to Praxis." In Evangelicalism and Modern America, ed. George M. Marsden. Grand Rapids: Eerdmans, 1984.

Wells ponders why American evangelicals, who regularly speak of theology's timeless character, nonetheless often practice a kind of "cultural-Protestantism" themselves. Self-conscious contextualization is the path Wells outlines for preserving both the integrity of the Christian message and its relevance to the modern world.

888. Wells, David F. and Clark H. Pinnock, eds. Toward a Theology for the Future. Carol Stream, IL: Creation House, 1971.

This symposium brought together well established evangelical theologians and Bible scholars (e.g., R.K. Harrison, Everett Harrison, Bernard Ramm, Harold Ockenga, Geoffrey Bromiley) and younger voices (e.g., the editors) to provide a statement of evangelical theological norms against the background of contemporary circumstances.

889. Wells, David F., ed. Reformed Theology in America. Grand Rapids: Eerdmans, 1985.

The essays in this book explored one of the families that has exerted the most impact on American evangelical theology in general. Separate sections are devoted to the Princeton Theologians, theology at Westminster Seminary, Dutch-Americans, Southern Presbyterians, and the Niebuhrs. A noteworthy introductory essay by George Marsden describes Doctrinal, Cultural, and Pietist varieties of Reformed experience in America.

890. Wiley, H. Orton. Christian Theology. 3 vols. Kansas City, MO: Nazarene Publishing House, 1947.

Wiley's volumes provide a full theology for Nazarenes, with the emphases on "Christian perfection" that defined the theological position of this evangelical denomination.

891. Wynkoop, Mildred Bangs. A Theology of Love: The Dynamic of Wesleyanism. Kansas City, MO: Beacon Hill, 1972.

Wynkoop, sometime president of Japan Nazarene Theological Seminary and professor of theology at Trevecca Nazarene College, has been one of the most influential expounders of holiness theology in the post-War period. This book sets out a full theology of sanctification by stressing the centrality of love in Scripture and by frequent reference to the emphases of John Wesley's work.

892. Yoder, John Howard. The Politics of Jesus: Vicit Agnus Noster. Grand Rapids: Eerdmans, 1972.

Yoder finds in the words of Jesus and works of the Apostle Paul a well defined rationale for Christian pacifism and for radical discipleship in the contemporary world. This book measurably enhanced the impact of Mennonite biblical ethics on the more general evangelical community.

(C) Faith and Philosophy

Philosophy has never been a preoccupation of evangelicals, primarily because they tend much more readily to action than contemplation, move much more easily to explicit theological debate than to background conceptual thinking. Exceptions to this rule have included Jonathan Edwards, whose brilliance as a philosopher cum theologian has not been equalled in the evangelical tradition, and authors of sturdy texts in the nineteenth century like Francis Wayland of Brown and James McCosh of Princeton. In the twentieth century, the fundamentalist movement warned off several evangelical generations from philosophy under the impression that formal philosophical study was too much contaminated by modern intellectual fashions. The same effect, without necessarily the same animus, was achieved in sectarian evangelical communities that saw little reason for engaging in the debates of the philosophers. During the years between the wars, however, philosophy began once again to stir among evangelical groups. The Reformed Presbyterian Gordon Clark convinced some students at Wheaton College of the value of philosophical inquiry; Harry Jellema and O. K. Bouwsma, with roots in a Dutch Reformed tradition that had always enjoyed an active philosophical side, did the same for members of their communion. In part because of the work of these pioneers, in part because of rumblings undercutting the once confident secularism of the philosophical establishment, and in part because of the appearance of outstanding philosophical minds, evangelicals have exerted growing influence in this field throughout the 1970s and 1980s. The works below suggest the outlines of a resurgence that the history of neither American evangelicals nor the academic study of philosophy would have led us to expect.

893. Evans, C. Stephen. Philosophy of Religion: Thinking About Faith. Downers Grove, IL: InterVarsity Press, 1985.

Evans' study of Kierkegaard as well as his efforts to integrate philosophical and psychological understanding contribute to the effectiveness of this basic text.

894. Geisler, Norman L. and Paul D. Feinberg. Introduction to Philosophy: A Christian Perspective. Grand Rapids: Baker, 1980.

Geisler, a leading proponent of rational evidentialist approaches to philosophical and theological questions, here sets out comprehensively one evangelical approach to the subject.

895. Holmes, Arthur F. Christian Philosophy in the Twentieth Century: An Essay in Philosophical Methodology. Nutley, NJ: Craig Press, 1969.

Holmes' survey is a compendious account of how major philosophers in the western tradition have dealt with the Christian faith. Its underlying appeal for a philosophy as technically proficient as it is faithfully Christian represented the brief that Holmes has presented to countless students and philosophical colleagues since the 1950s.

896. Holmes, Arthur F. Contours of a World View. Grand Rapids: Eerdmans, 1983.

This book describes the way in which large-scale intellectual gestalts, or worldviews, express and influence human thinking, and then turns to a description of how a traditional Christian faith sustains a satisfying worldview for all of life's dimensions.

897. Mavrodes, George. Belief in God: A Study in the Epistemology of Religion. Washington, DC: University Press of America, 1981.

Mavrodes, who exhibits both Dutch Reformed and American evangelical sensibilities, here presents a lucid account of what is involved in arguing for the existence of God and related beliefs.

898. Morris, Thomas V. The Logic of God Incarnate. Ithaca, NY: Cornell University Press, 1986.

Morris is a leader of the second generation of evangelical philosophers. This work argues learnedly that the doctrine of Christ's Incarnation does not violate any accepted canon of human rationality.

899. Morris, Thomas V., ed. Divine and Human Action: Essays in the Metaphysics of Theism. Ithaca, NY: Cornell University Press, 1988.

900. Morris, Thomas V., ed. Philosophy and the Christian Faith. Notre Dame, IN: Notre Dame University Press, 1988.

Like the quarterly numbers of Faith and Philosophy, these symposia, which draw together essays by theists of traditional Christian persuasions, testify to the contemporary vigor of Christian philosophical reflection. The philosophers contributing to this enterprise share the assumption, as Morris put it in Divine and Human Action, that "religion, in particular the Judeo-Christian religious tradition, is not just a domain of poetry, imagery, mystical transport, moral directive, and noncognitive, existential self-understanding." Rather, they believe Christian faith provides "key insights into, and resources for, the construction of comprehensive metaphysics."

901. Mouw, Richard J. "Evangelicalism and Philosophy." Theology Today 44 (October 1987): 329-337.

Mouw's essay is a state-of-the-art report on the recent emergence of a network of philosophers (Anglo-American evangelical, Dutch Calvinist, and Roman Catholic) attempting to work from explicit Christian bases. The essay includes discussion of how philosophical perspectives might assist seminary training to be both more pastoral and more practical.

902. Plantinga, Alvin, ed. Faith and Philosophy: Philosophical Studies in Religion and Ethics: Essays Published in Honor of W. Harry Jellema. Grand Rapids: Eerdmans, 1964.

This festschrift honored a significant philosophical intelligence, but even more a great teacher who inspired a generation of American-born Dutch

Calvinists to extraordinary philosophical exertions. The book contains early essays by several of the contemporary pace-setters, including Nicholas Wolterstorff, William Frankena, and the editor.

903. Plantinga, Alvin and Nicholas Wolterstorff, eds. Faith and Rationality: Reason and Belief in God. Notre Dame, IN: University of Notre Dame Press, 1983.

In the philosophical section of this work, the editors are joined by George Mavrodes and William Alston in propounding a "Reformed epistemology" that questions the epistemological foundationalism usually assumed to be necessary for proper arguments concerning the existence and nature of God.

904. Tomberlin, James E. and Peter Van Inwagen. Alvin Plantinga. Boston: D. Reidel, 1985.

Plantinga's path-breaking work on the nature of being, the problem of evil, the ontological argument, and the status of epistemological axioms has placed him in the front rank of contemporary theistic philosophers. This biographical retrospective of his work summarizes his major intellectual contributions to date against the backdrop of his ongoing participation in the life of the Christian Reformed Church.

905. Wolterstorff, Nicholas. Reason Within the Bounds of Religion. Rev. ed. Grand Rapids: Eerdmans, 1984.

Wolterstorff reverses Kant's intention to confine religion within the bounds of reason with an argument about how pre-rational "control beliefs" shape all of thought and action.

906. Wolterstorff, Nicholas, Hendrik Hart and Johan van der Hoeven, eds. Rationality in the Calvinian Tradition. Lanham, MD: University Press of America, 1987.

This volumes testifies to at least two recent developments: the growing technical competence of Christian (largely Protestant evangelical) philosophers, and the leadership in such philosophical enterprises by Calvinists of Dutch-immigrant background. The essayists here include British and American Anglos as well as representatives of Dutch immigrant communities in Canada and the United States. Topics include the relation of rationality to historical communities, to the Bible, and to God.

907. Yandell, Keith E. Christianity and Philosophy. Grand Rapids: Eerdmans, 1984.

Yandell's book is the second volume (after Holmes's Contours) in the "Studies in a Christian World View" sponsored by the Institute for Advanced Christian Studies. It argues that it is possible rationally to assess claims for the existence of God, and that those claims are persuasive.

CHAPTER 15
NATURAL AND SOCIAL SCIENCES

Popular conceptions of "evangelical science" are dominated by battles over evolution. This is an understandable, but regrettable state of affairs. Beginning with Jonathan Edwards and John Wesley, evangelicals have displayed a continual fascination with scientific questions. The reason for this fascination concerns primarily the character of evangelicalism as a popular movement and the status of science (whether technical or popular) as one of the few remaining authorities for modern societies that have foresworn the authority of history, tradition, or deference. For a popular movement like evangelicalism, therefore, it has been important (at least when debating intellectual questions in the general marketplace) to possess scientific credibility for cherished beliefs as an important way of buttressing the authority of scriptural revelation and personal religious experience. In these terms, the fundamentalist episode, with its strident denunciations of the secular intellectual world, was a controversy over the use of science. Fundamentalists saw no reason for abandoning their forms of "early modern" (and, it seemed, religion defending) science in favor of the widely heralded "late modern" (and, so it appeared, religion denying) science of the modern academy. Since the 1930s, an increasing number of evangelicals have reconsidered their allegiance to at least some aspects of "early modern" science and begun to promote or practice (often through conscious dialogue with the university world) various forms of "late modern" science. This process has proceeded at different rates for the various disciplines in the natural and social sciences. And especially for the question of human origins, much uncertainty remains in the evangelical and fundamentalist worlds over the relative merits of "early modern" and "late modern" science. Yet for most of the natural and social sciences, it is possible to find renewed determination among evangelicals either to define theoretical Christian justification for selective participation in "late modern" science or to study evangelicals themselves through the techniques of "late modern" science. Work of these two kinds is represented in the very selective lists that follow. First are general works and those in the natural sciences, followed by examples from the various social sciences.

(A) General

908. Anderson, D. Elving. "Evangelicals and Science: Fifty Years After the Scopes Trial (1925-1975)." In The Evangelicals, eds. David F. Wells and John D. Woodbridge. Rev. ed. Grand Rapids: Baker, 1977.

Anderson, a geneticist, provides a mid-course survey of efforts by evangelicals to regain competence and standing in the scientific community.

909. Bube, Richard H. The Human Quest. Waco, TX: Word, 1971.

Bube, a professor of materials science and electrical engineering at Stanford, has been a leading figure in the American Scientific Affiliation, the professional society of evangelicals who are committed to fruitful interchange, rather than strife, between the domains of theology and science. This book is a popular statement in defense of that stance.

910. Henry, Carl F. H., ed. Horizons of Science: Christian Scholars Speak Out. San Francisco: Harper & Row, 1978.

Twelve papers on a wide variety of subjects, from the environment to brain research, reveal evangelicals responding (usually with considerable finesse) to recent scientific problems.

911. Houston, James M. I Believe in the Creator. Grand Rapids: Eerdmans, 1980.

The author is a geographer who argues here that traditional belief in God's creating power is fully compatible with dedicated work as a modern scientist.

912. Hummel, Charles E. The Galileo Connection: Resolving Conflicts Between Science and the Bible. Downers Grove, IL: InterVarsity Press, 1986.

Hummel joins a swelling chorus of evangelicals who contend that past battles over issues like evolution were regrettable examples of misplaced concreteness. While chiding ideological use of science by secularists, he nonetheless holds out high hope for rapprochement between religion and science in the modern world.

913. Kraft, Charles H. Christianity and Culture: A Study in Dynamic Biblical Theologizing in Cross-Cultural Perspective. Maryknoll, NY: Orbis, 1979.

Kraft is an anthropologist whose wide-ranging book explores the importance of culture for the Christian message, especially its proclamations in non-Western areas of the world. The book's argument, to which some of his evangelical peers have objected, intends to jar fellow-evangelicals loose from overly static conceptions of the way Christian faith is embodied in culture.

914. Livingstone, David N. "Farewell to Arms: Reflections on the Encounter Between Science and Faith." In Christian Faith and Practice in the Modern World: Theology From an Evangelical Point of View, eds. Mark A. Noll and David F. Wells. Grand Rapids: Eerdmans, 1988.

This learned summary of a vast literature (on Christianity and science as well as the history of science) shows convincingly how unnecessary the antagonistic stance between the practice of science and the exercise of faith has become.

915. Maloney, H. Newton and A. Adams Lovekin. Glossolalia: Behavioral Science Perspectives on Speaking in Tongues. New York: Oxford University Press, 1985.

With the rapid spread of pentecostalism and related movements, social scientific investigation of charismatic phenomena has become inevitable. This collection is one of the most wide-ranging and objective examples of such study.

916. Marshall, Paul A., Sander Griffioen and Richard J. Mouw. Stained Glass: Worldviews and Social Science. Lanham, MD: University of Press of America, 1989.

Drawing upon the legacies of Dutch Reformed thinkers (especially Abraham Kuyper and Herman Dooyeweerd), the contributors to this collection offer the most comprehensive discussions to date of American evangelical consideration of the theory of the social sciences.

917. Owens, Virginia Stem. And the Trees Clap Their Hands: Faith, Perception, and the New Physics. Grand Rapids: Eerdmans, 1983.

This lyrical meditation explores serendipitous points of intersection between Christian faith and the newest conceptions of science.

918. Ramm, Bernard. The Christian View of Science and Scriptures. Grand Rapids: Eerdmans, 1954.

This landmark volume repudiated the notion of a standoff between evangelical or fundamentalist faith and the practice of modern science. It called especially for a new sensitivity in interpreting the cosmological sections of the Bible.

919. Ratzsch, Del. Philosophy of Science: The Natural Sciences in Christian Perspective. Downers Grove, IL: InterVarsity Press, 1986.

Ratzsch draws lessons for evangelicals from modern discussions concerning seminal works like Thomas Kuhn's The Structure of Scientific Revolutions, but also wonders if more general principles may be found in Scripture for orienting the scientific enterprise than what evangelicals commentators on the subject now think are possible.

(B) Natural Science/Evolution

A significant faultline within evangelicalism divides those who have in general made peace with evolution and those who have not. The first group is marked by a desire to address evolution as an empirical subject relevant for consideration of secondary causes, the other is convinced it remains a question of biblical faithfulness relevant for final causes. The titles below, which reflect only a tiny portion of an immense literature, concentrate on historical studies offering perspective for the debate.

920. American Scientific Affiliation. Teaching Science in a Climate of Controversy. Ipswich, MA: American Scientific Affiliation, 1986.

This attractive teaching aid sets out a moderate stance that has come to prevail widely among evangelicals. It does not balk at evolutionary conclusions about life forms, but also rebuts secular cosmology based on evolutionary reasoning.

921. Larson, Edward J. Trial and Error: The American Controversy over Creation and Evolution. New York: Oxford, 1985.

Larson's informative account of legal controversies surrounding the teaching of evolution and "creation science" in public schools has much more appreciation than is usually found among writers-at-large for the rights of creationists.

922. Lindberg, David and Ronald Numbers, eds. God and Nature: Historical Essays on the Encounter Between Christian and Science. Berkeley: University of California Press, 1986.

Several of the splendid essays in this book treat subjects relevant to American evangelicals and science, including papers (e.g., on geology, evolution, creationism, modern physics) by J. S. Rudwick, James R. Moore, A. Hunter Dupree, Frederick Gregory, Ronald L. Numbers, and Keith Yandell.

923. Livingstone, David N. Darwin's Forgotten Defenders: The Encounter Between Evangelical Theology and Evolutionary Thought. Grand Rapids: Eerdmans, 1987.

Livingstone, a historian of science from Belfast, offers an especially full account of the large number of evangelical intellectuals in the late nineteenth and early twentieth centuries who found it possible to adopt some form of evolution as compatible with their evangelical faith.

924. Livingstone, David N. "Evangelicals and the Darwinian Controversies: A Bibliographical Introduction." Evangelical Studies Bulletin 4:2 (Nov. 1987): 1-6.

This essays offers a valuable introduction to the proliferating literature on its subject.

925. Marsden, George M. "A Case of the Excluded Middle: Creation Versus Evolution in America." In Uncivil Religion: Interreligious Hostility in America, eds. Robert N. Bellah and Frederick E. Greenspahn. New York: Crossroad, 1987.

Marsden shows how escalating strife over the question of evolution has hardened both secularists and fundamentalists in their positions, thus drawing attention away from the plethora of mediating options that find it neither anti-Christian to contemplate evolution nor anti-scientific to defend Christianity.

926. Mixter, Russell L., ed. Evolution and Christian Thought Today. Grand Rapids: Eerdmans, 1959.

Consternation in some fundamentalist circles was the result when this volume by thirteen members of the American Scientific Affiliation was published to mark the centennial of Darwin's Origin of Species. Its message--that once implacable opposition to evolutionary theory may have been overstated--seems modest today, but when it appeared, it gave a material stimulus to fresh evangelical thought on empirical and theological questions respecting the origins of humanity.

927. Moore, James R. The Post-Darwinian Controversies: A Study of the Protestant Struggle to Come to Terms with Darwin in Great Britain and America, 1870-1900. New York: Cambridge, 1979.

Moore's lengthy introduction on the historical inaccuracy of the "warfare metaphor" for the relation of science and Christianity precedes a learned account of the many different reactions that British and American Protestants explored in response to Darwin's work.

928. Morris, Henry M. The Biblical Basis for Modern Science. Grand Rapids: Baker, 1984.

Morris sets down broad principles for scriptural authority and for interpreting the Bible in order to justify his contention that "creation science" rightfully belongs in the mainstream of genuine scientific thinking.

929. Numbers, Ronald L. "The Dilemma of Evangelical Scientists." In Evangelicalism and Modern America, ed. George Marsden. Grand Rapids: Eerdmans, 1984.

930. Numbers, Ronald L. "George Frederick Wright: From Christian Darwinist to Fundamentalist." ISIS 79 (1988): 624-645.

Numbers is the premier student of the twentieth-century "creation science" movement. These are carefully researched papers on subjects related to his central concern. The first traces the strain within evangelicalism since World War II on questions related to evolution. The second treats the career of a geologist-theologian who long argued that Darwinism, properly understood, supported orthodox Calvinism, but who had begun to move away from a Christian evolutionist stance by the end of his life.

931. Rimmer, Harry R. Modern Science and the Genesis Record. Grand Rapids: Eerdmans, 1937.

This book was an early and influential effort to derive guidelines from Scripture for interpreting natural history as an alternative to evolutionary theories.

932. Roberts, Jon H. Darwinism and the Divine in America: Protestant Intellectuals and Organic Evolution, 1859-1900. Madison: University of Wisconsin Press, 1988.

Roberts provides a scrupulously objective account of the stages by which American Protestants moved in the 1860s and early 1870s from confidently dismissing Darwin's theories (because scientists were not all that convinced either) to dividing in the 1880s and 1890s over whether and how it was possible to incorporate evolutionary insights into either liberal or conservative versions of the faith.

933. Van Til, Howard L. The Fourth Day: What the Bible and the Heavens Are Telling Us About Creation. Grand Rapids: Eerdmans, 1986.

Van Til suggests that a proper understanding of the primarily theological intentions of Genesis would leave scientists free to pursue conclusions from their research, wherever those results might lead.

934. Van Til, Howard L., Davis A. Young and Clarence Menninga. Science Held Hostage: What's Wrong with Creation Science and Evolutionism?. Downers Grove, IL: InterVarsity Press, 1988.

The authors of this orienting study are professors at Calvin College who feel that the cosmologies of secular, atheistic evolution and fundamentalistic "creation science" both do grave disservice to understanding the Bible and pursuing the scientific enterprise.

935. Whitcomb, John C. and Henry M. Morris. The Genesis Flood: The Biblical Record and Its Scientific Application. Philadelphia: Presbyterian and Reformed, 1961.

This book presents a comprehensive case for the idea that the physical effects of the Noahic flood are entirely capable of explaining the geological phenomena that lead others to posit an extremely old age for the earth.

936. Wright, Richard T. Biology Through the Eyes of Faith. San Francisco: Harper & Row, 1989.

Wright offers his text as a way of employing Christian insights for a full range of biological issues, not merely matters relating to the origin of humans and the earth.

937. Young, Davis A. Christianity and the Age of the Earth. Grand Rapids: Zondervan, 1982.

Young makes the case that efforts by evangelicals to demonstrate that the earth appeared quite recently are faulty for both geological and theological reasons.

938. Young, Davis A. "Scripture in the Hands of Geologists." Westminster Theological Journal 49 (Spring 1987): 1-34; (Fall 1987): 357-304.

Young, who has battled questions concerning the age of the earth, here mounts an extensive argument to the effect that strategies to harmonize the research of scientists and the supposed cosmological implications of early Genesis are bankrupt.

(C) Psychology

Evangelical interaction with modern psychology is comparatively well established, perhaps because of the long-standing formal parallels between pastoral counseling and psychological therapy. Whether this is the reason or not, a lively literature by evangelicals on psychological themes has been growing for the last quarter century. Only a tiny sampling of that literature is mentioned below.

939. Adams, Jay. Competent to Counsel. Nutley, NJ: Presbyterian and Reformed, 1970.

Adams has achieved a wide hearing among some evangelical groups by down-playing the need for most psychological therapy while promoting a form of counseling embodying principles from Scripture.

940. Benner, David G., ed. Baker Encyclopedia of Psychology. Grand Rapids: Baker, 1985.

This comprehensive reference work, with its full roster of well-trained authors, testifies to the breadth of evangelical involvement in psychological theory and practice.

941. Benner, David G. Psychotherapy and the Spiritual Quest. Grand Rapids: Baker, 1988.

This is a particularly engaging book for its suggestion that, if psychotherapy is not considered a replacement for religion, the insights it offers about the integration of personality may actually clarify spiritual understanding.

942. Evans, C. Stephen. Preserving the Person: A Look at the Human Sciences. Downers Grove, IL: InterVarsity Press, 1977.

Evans helpfully describes different approaches Christians have taken to the study of the person, including positions assuming the compatibility of psychology and theology, as well as those stressing one at the expense of the other.

943. Jones, Stanton L., ed. Psychology and the Christian Faith: An Introductory Reader. Grand Rapids: Baker, 1986.

The representative essays in this collection discuss the various sub-disciplines of psychology, with special concentration on personality and psychotherapy.

944. Myers, David G. and Malcolm A. Jeeves. Psychology Through the Eyes of Faith. San Francisco: Harper & Row, 1987.

This text examines main themes of psychological study (e.g., intelligence, mental disorders, social psychology) from an evangelical perspective. The position of the authors is that psychology offers valid, but limited understanding of the human condition that complements biblical and theological teachings.

945. Van Leeuwen, Mary Stewart. The Person in Psychology: A Contemporary Christian Appraisal. Grand Rapids: Eerdmans, 1985.

946. Van Leeuwen, Mary Stewart. The Sorcerer's Apprentice: A Christian Looks at the Changing Face of Psychology. Downers Grove, IL: InterVarsity Press, 1987.

Van Leeuwen criticizes scientistic as well as anti-Christian aspects of modern psychology, while providing an analysis of what a Christian orientation to the discipline might look like. Her work represents some of the most trenchant efforts by contemporary evangelicals to critique the assumptions of "normal science" as it has come to be practiced by social scientists in North American academe.

947. Vandekemp, Hendrika. Psychology and Theology in Western Thought (1672-1965): A Historical and Annotated Bibliography. Millwood, NY: Kraus, 1984.

Among the many significant works annotated here are most of the early efforts made within the evangelical traditions to appropriate and exploit the developing categories of psychology for Christian purposes.

948. Vitz, Paul C. Psychology as Religion: The Cult of Self-Worship. Grand Rapids: Eerdmans, 1977.

949. Vitz, Paul C. Sigmund Freud's Christian Unconscious. New York: Guilford, 1988.

In the first book, Vitz, a Roman Catholic widely read in evangelical circles, attacks the humanistic psychology of Erich Fromm, Carl Rogers,

Abraham Maslow, and Rollo May as a fatally flawed form of ultimate concern. The second argues that Freud had a life-long ambivalent relationship to Christianity, caused in large part by a traumatic separation from a beloved Roman Catholic nanny at the age of three.

(D) Sociology

Evangelical sociologists have only recently begun to take an active part in the larger academic community, and have also only recently begun to write popularly for evangelicals. Nonetheless, significant work has gone on, of which the following are examples.

950. Balswick, Jack O. The Inexpressive Male. Lexington, MA: Lexington Books, 1989.

Balswick, who now teaches at Fuller Theological Seminary, has been a pioneer in evangelical efforts to use modern sociological theory. This book applies religious and social reasoning to a recently isolated difficulty, by no means unknown in evangelical churches.

951. Gaede, S. D. Where Gods May Dwell: On Understanding the Human Condition. Grand Rapids: Zondervan, 1985.

This well-written guide is perhaps the best introduction by an American evangelical to Christian approaches to the social study of humans.

952. Guinness, Os. The Grave-Digger File: Papers on the Subversion of the Modern Church. Downers Grove, IL: InterVarsity Press, 1983.

Guinness is a British lecturer and writer, now residing in the U.S., who studied the sociology of religion at Oxford with Bryan Wilson. This thought-provoking popular study employs insights on "modernization" and religion from Wilson, Peter Berger, Malcolm Muggeridge, and David Martin to warn contemporary Christians against the danger of being coopted by the individualism, indifferentism, and secularism that characterizes modern society.

953. Hunter, James Davison. American Evangelicalism: Conservative Religion and the Quandary of Modernity. New Brunswick, NJ: Rutgers University Press, 1983.

954. Hunter, James Davison. Evangelicalism: The Coming Generation. Chicago: University of Chicago Press, 1987.

Hunter is a leader in using research data to make large-scale assessments of evangelical values and future prospects. As a student of Peter Berger, he assesses evangelical communities by the degree to which they have progressed in the direction of "modernization" (characterized by less concern for ideological boundary maintenance and more interest in self-expression than had once been customary among evangelicals). Both of these major books see at least some groups of evangelicals sliding gradually and almost inevitably to the norms of the larger culture.

955. Hunter, James Davison. "Operationalizing Evangelicalism: A Review, Critique and Proposal." Sociological Analysis 42 (Winter 1981): 363-372.

This methodological essay focuses on the value of belief measures as a way of surveying large groups within the evangelical community.

956. Mathisen, Gerald S. and James A. Mathisen. "The New Fundamentalism: A Sociorhetorical Approach to Understanding Theological Change." Review of Religious Research 30 (Sept. 1988): 18-32.

The authors use Jerry Falwell's Fundamentalist Journal as a source for understanding the process by which Falwell's type of fundamentalists began once again to take part in public dialogue concerning the contemporary political situation.

957. Moberg, David O. The Church as a Social Institution: The Sociology of American Religion. 2nd ed. Grand Rapids: Baker, 1984.

Moberg, long-time professor at Marquette University, was one of the first evangelicals seriously to study the church in its social setting. The revised edition of this large-scale effort carries further the author's conviction that sociological method makes possible better, rather than reduced, spiritual understanding of the church.

958. Poloma, Margaret M. "Toward a Christian Sociological Perspective: Religious Values, Theory and Methodology." Sociological Analysis 43 (1982): 95-108.

Poloma, a Catholic charismatic, offers here a series of sane proposals on the values of objective social scientific research on religious questions, provided that the religious components of experience do not get reduced to other, supposedly more basic aspects of experience. She asks especially that sociologists would exert the same care against expressing anti-religious bias as they have in reducing prejudices of gender, race, and class.

959. Warner, R. Stephen. "Theoretical Barriers to the Understanding of Evangelical Christianity." Sociological Analysis 40 (Spring 1979): 1-9.

This was one of the earliest, and best, methodological essays on the study of fundamentalists and evangelicals. It rang the changes on how difficult it is for a secular academy to take seriously the basic religiosity of the conservative Protestant community, but also pointed out how tricky simple creedal measures could be in identifying the members of that community.

960. Wuthnow, Robert. Meaning and Moral Order: Explorations in Cultural Analysis. Berkeley: University of California Press, 1987.

Princeton's Wuthnow, whose work is an inspiration to evangelical sociologists, explores in this book the possibility of studying "religion" and "ideology" in ways that respect the essential integrity of what it is that people say they believe.

(E) Political Science

Evangelical work in professional political science is also fairly recent. But the quantity and quality of such work are both rising rapidly, partly because of greater involvement in graduate education, partly through increased concern by churches to understand the moral dimensions of local and international crises, and partly from the rise of Protestant conservatives as a force in domestic politics. The works mentioned below illustrate evangelical explorations in normative political science as well as writings (often by evangelicals) on the political behavior of theological conservative Protestants.

961. Amstutz, Mark R. Christian Ethics and United States Foreign Policy. Grand Rapids: Zondervan, 1987.

Amstutz borrows insights from political realists and from Reinhold Niebuhr to suggest that Christian ventures into international politics need to exhibit, along with the innocence of doves, the wisdom of serpents (though not necessarily hawks).

Fowler, Robert Booth. A New Engagement: Evangelical Political Thought, 1966-1976. Grand Rapids: Eerdmans, 1982.
(see 1091)

962. Guth, James, Ted Jelen, Lyman Kellstedt, Corwin Smidt and Kenneth Wald. "The Politics of Religion in America." American Politics Quarterly 16 (1988): 357-397.

This comprehensive essay shows both how much good work has been done and how much vitally necessary study remains in the effort to trace the effect of religious convictions on modern electoral behavior.

963. Guth, James and John Green. "Robertson's Republicans: Christian Activists in the GOP." Election Results 4 (Fall 1987): 9-14.

Guth has been a leader in describing new political trends among Southern Baptists. Here he is joined by John Green in showing the effects of New Right evangelicals and fundamentalists on the internal operations of the GOP.

964. Kellstedt, Lyman A. "The Meaning and Measurement of Evangelicalism: Problems and Prospects." In Religion and American Political Behavior, ed. Ted G. Jelen. New York: Praeger, 1989.

Kellstedt, who teaches at Wheaton College, calls for more precision in defining who evangelicals are and what they are now contributing to recent political life. The essay shows well that the sharper the definition, the more obvious the religious impact on political life.

965. McCarthy, M. Rockne, James W. Skillen and William A. Harper. Disestablishment A Second Time: Genuine Pluralism for American Schools. Grand Rapids: Eerdmans, 1983.

The authors, who are influenced by the example of Dutch Protestant politics in the nineteenth and twentieth centuries, make a plea for parent-organized schools as a means of redressing injustices promoted by a state monopoly on supposedly "public education."

966. Marshall, Paul. Thine is the Kingdom: A Biblical Perspective on the Notion of Government and Politics Today. Grand Rapids: Eerdmans, 1984.

Marshall, a Briton who teaches at Toronto's Institute of Christian Studies, sets out a notion of politics, not as a necessary evil, but as a sphere of life in which Christian action may be devoted to positive goals of enhancing justice and clarifying rights.

967. Rothenberg, Stuart and Frank Newport. The Evangelical Voter: Religion and Politics in America. Washington: The Institute for Government and Politics of the Free Congress Research and Education Foundation, 1984.

This is the most thorough study to date of the political behavior of those who might loosely be called evangelical. Despite some problems with defining "evangelical," the study does attest to a gradual shift of evangelical allegiance from the Democratic Party to the Republican.

968. Smidt, Corwin. "'Praise the Lord' Politics: A Comparative Analysis of the Social Characteristics and Political Views of American Evangelical and Charismatic Christians." Sociological Analysis 50 (Spring 1989): 52-72.

969. Smidt, Corwin. "Evangelicals Within Contemporary American Politics: Differentiating Between Fundamentalist and Non-Fundamentalist Evangelicals." Western Political Quarterly 41 (1988): 601-620.

970. Smidt, Corwin and Lyman Kellstedt. "Evangelicalism and Survey Research: Interpretive Problems and Substantive Findings." In The Bible, Politics, and Democracy, ed. Richard John Neuhaus (Encounter Series). Grand Rapids: Eerdmans, 1987.

971. Smidt, Corwin, ed. Contemporary Evangelical Political Involvement. Lanham, MD: University Press of America, 1989.

Smidt of Calvin College has been--with Kellstedt, Guth, and a few others--a leader in studying the political behavior of evangelicals and fundamentalists. These works all make significant contributions, the first as the only effort to date at sorting out political styles between charismatics and other conservative believers, the second by attempting the same for evangelical and fundamentalist variations, the third by gathering (with Kellstedt) a great deal of useful data on evangelical political allegiance, and the fourth by joining what political scientists like to call "impressionistic" responses to numerical analyses of recent political situations.

972. Wald, Kenneth, Dennis Owen and Samuel Hill. "Churches as Political Communities." American Political Science Review 82 (June 1988): 531-548.

This is a model study of how to assess the importance of religion in a particular areas (in this case a Florida community in which evangelical churches happened to figure prominently).

(F) Economics

Evangelical tradition has often made room for attempts to analyze economic questions from a Christian frame of reference. Such efforts proliferated before the Civil War and during the depressions of the 1890s and 1930s. They have also been a major presence in recent evangelical history. To date, however, only the first steps have been taken to professionalize these debates by methods of analysis practiced among university economists. Most evangelical writing on economic questions remains simply moral and biblical, and all too often simplistically so. The list that follows includes examples of works that follow more that older tradition, but also a few illustrations of professional economic analysis undertaken for Christian purposes.

973. Clouse, Robert G., ed. Wealth and Poverty: Four Christian Views of Economics. Downers Grove, IL: InterVarsity Press, 1984.

This book is a valuable presentation, with opportunity provided for formal rebuttal, among evangelicals holding to what are styled "free market capitalism" (Gary North), "the guided-market" (William E. Diehl), decentralized economics (Art Gish), and centralist economics (John Gladwin).

974. Elzinga, Kenneth G. "A Christian View of the Economic Order." Reformed Journal 31 (Oct. 1981): 13-16.

The author, who teaches at the University of Virginia, thinks that general principles from Scripture can delimit the range of acceptable options on economic questions, but also confesses that the notion of "Christian economics" is capable of an unusually wide variety of interpretations.

975. Gay, Craig M. "Recent Evangelical Appraisals of Capitalism and American Class Culture." Ph.D. dissertation, Boston University, 1989.

This dissertation is an outstanding survey of recent evangelical opinions on matters economic, views that range from a libertarian extreme to the moderate left, with not a few positions present that do not fall readily into recognizable slots on the conventional spectrum.

976. Goudzward, Bob. Capitalism and Progress: A Diagnosis of Western Society. Grand Rapids: Eerdmans, 1979.

Goudzward, a Dutch economist with considerable influence in American Reformed communities, argues that the historic link between capitalism and visions of progress has lead to the moral impoverishment of modern society.

977. Griffiths, Brian. The Creation of Wealth: A Christian Case for Capitalism. Downers Grove, IL: InterVarsity Press, 1972.

978. Griffiths, Brian. Morality and the Market Place: Christian Alternatives to Capitalism and Socialism. London: Hodder and Stoughton, 1982.

Griffiths is a British economist who has held various governmental positions in his native land. This book admits that capitalism has been practiced immorally and unjustly, but suggests that the exercise of Christian principles could purify and ennoble the system.

979. Halteman, James. Market Capitalism and Christianity. Grand Rapids: Baker, 1988.

Halteman, an economics professor and a Mennonite, offers a balanced perspective on the workings of western economies, but also calls for the church to dare to function as an economic community with rules drawn from the Christian faith instead of what have become contemporary Western conventions.

980. Nash, Ronald H. Poverty and Wealth: The Christian Debate Over Capitalism. Westchester, IL: Crossway Books, 1986.

Nash resolutely defends capitalism, which he feels should be restrained by internal religious impulses rather than external governmental checks.

981. Nichols, Alan. An Evangelical Commitment to Simple Life-Style: Exposition and Commentary. Wheaton, IL: Lausanne Committee for World Evangelization, 1980.

The author fleshes out the succinct call by the Lausanne Congress in 1974 for a life-style de-emphasizing consumption and stressing the use of goods in an altruistic, stewardly way.

982. North, Gary. An Introduction to Biblical Blueprints. Fort Worth, TX: Dominion Press, 1987.

North, who is associated with the Christian Reconstruction movement, finds principles in the Old Testament for organizing economic life in the twentieth century.

983. Richardson, J. David. "Frontiers in Economics and Christian Scholarship." Christian Scholar's Review 17 (June 1988): 381-400.

The author, an economist at the University of Wisconsin, calls on fellow evangelicals to eschew broad (and pretentious) economic theorizing in favor of detailed analyses of specific problems and issues.

(G) History

Like their professional colleagues more generally, evangelical historians would rather research than reflect. The result is that while evangelicals have made sterling contributions to the explosion of historical knowledge on their own traditions they have not devoted as much energy to theoretical discussion of history-writing itself. The works below (along with reflective sections in monographs by Timothy Smith, Richard Lovelace, and George Marsden cited elsewhere) suggest steps that have been taken toward that goal.

984. Bebbington, David W. Patterns in History: A Christian View. Downers Grove, IL: InterVarsity Press, 1979.

This study is the most satisfying general assessment by an evangelical of main trends in the writing of recent and classical history. Its author, a British historian of evangelicalism in his own country, concentrates on the way Christian approaches to history complement, but also sometimes contradict, cyclical, progressive, Marxist, and historicist views of the past.

985. Brown, Colin, ed. History, Criticism and Faith: Four Exploratory Studies. Downers Grove, IL: InterVarsity Press, 1976.

The four authors of essays in this book are British evangelicals who have taught or lectured in the United States. Its particular attraction is to link a general study of historical understanding and Christian faith (by the editor) with three papers (by Gordon Wenham, F.F. Bruce, and, R.T. France) on the historical character of the Old Testament and the New Testament.

986. Butterfield, Herbert. Writings on Christianity and History, ed. C. T. McIntire. New York: Oxford University Press, 1979.

987. Coll, Alberto R. The Wisdom of Statecraft: Sir Herbert Butterfield and the Philosophy of International Politics. Durham, NC: Duke University Press, 1985.

Butterfield, a British Methodist and a historian with nearly universal interests, has been an inspiration to fellow-believers on this side of the Atlantic. McIntire ably edits and introduces the main themes of Butterfield's occasional writings on the subject (these are in addition to Butterfield's own, Christianity and History [1949]). Coll's study, though directed at Butterfield's writings on problems in national relationships, is filled with insight on more general concerns of history-writing and Christian faith.

988. Holmes, Arthur F. Faith Seeks Understanding: A Christian Approach to Knowledge. Grand Rapids: Eerdmans, 1971.

Holmes is one of the few evangelical philosophers who have examined the question of historical knowledge. His chapter on that subject in this book is a good defense of what he calls "interpretive realism," a stance confident in the reality of historical knowledge but not simplistically or positivistically so.

989. McIntire, C. T. God, History, and Historians: Modern Christian Views of History. New York: Oxford University Press, 1977.

This outstanding anthology includes excerpts from the writings of theologians, cultural critics, and working historians. Especially interesting for Americans are selections from Protestants of an earlier generation, Kenneth Scott Latourette and E. Harris Harbison, who anticipated many of the themes currently promoted by members of the Conference on Faith and History.

990. McIntire, C. T. and Ronald A. Wells, eds. History and Historical Understanding. Grand Rapids: Eerdmans, 1984.

"Closet evangelicals" Robert Handy and Martin Marty join several of the card-carrying variety (e.g., George Marsden) with an assist from Dutch Reformed allies (Howard Rienstra, Robert Swierenga, Dale Van Kley) in this stimulating collection organized around the title of Marty's chapter, "The Difference in Being a Christian and the Difference it Makes--for History."

991. Marsden, George and Frank Roberts. A Christian View of History? Grand Rapids: Eerdmans, 1975.

"Yes" is the answer that the nine authors of this effort give to the question of their title. The book, a product of the Calvin College history department plus a few friends, is highlighted by George Marsden's general reflections on "A Christian Perspective for the Teaching of History," and Edwin J. Van Kley's bracing defense of traditional forms of history-writing in "History as a Social Science: A Christian's Response."

992. Noll, Mark A. "'And the Lion Shall Lie Down with the Lamb': The Social Sciences and Religious History." Fides et Historia 20:3 (Oct. 1988): 5-30.

Noll argues that, while theoreticians and practitioners of social scientific history have both been less than friendly to religion, there is nothing intrinsically alien in Christianity to a social scientific approach. In fact, there may be principles in the major Christian traditions to justify the use of the social sciences (when properly limited) to writing the history even of the church.

993. Nash, Ronald H. Christian Faith and Historical Understanding. Grand Rapids: Zondervan, 1984.

This well informed survey of modern problems of historical knowledge, especially as applied to biblical writings, concludes with a lengthy discussion of the resurrection of Christ. In particular, Nash argues for the relevance, rather than the irrelevance, of faith in assessing events like the resurrection.

994. Wells, Ronald A. History Through the Eyes of Faith. San Francisco: Harper & Row, 1989.

This thought-provoking textbook is designed to accompany surveys in the history of western civilization. It calls upon students to think as Christians about the course of that history without implying that there is automatically one set of stock Christian conclusions about the meaning of important historical events and transitions.

CHAPTER 16
ARTS AND LETTERS

Evangelicals, for better and for worse, are not aesthetes. While story-telling and a vigorous hymnody are indigenous to the movement, "high art" of the kind studied for the past century in colleges of arts and letters is not. The period of cultural alienation corresponding to the fundamentalist-modernist conflict saw most forms of artistic expression ignored or avoided. But the evangelical re-engagement with the wider intellectual culture has led to a flurry of creative and artistic efforts as well. The works cited below, which represent recent efforts to encourage a more vigorous aesthetic sensibility, often make extensive use of Anglicans, Catholics, or authorities in other Christian traditions with longer traditions of artistic expression.

(A) General

995. Gambone, Robert L. Art and Popular Religion in Evangelical America, 1915-1940. Knoxville: University of Tennessee Press, 1989.

Gambone offers a promising survey of a much neglected subject. His treatment of the pre-television years presents essential background for understanding the aesthetics of modern use of television by pentecostals, fundamentalists, and other evangelicals.

996. Huttar, Charles, ed. Imagination and the Spirit: Essays in Literature and the Christian Faith Presented to Clyde S. Kilby. Grand Rapids: Eerdmans, 1971.

Most of the contributors to this volume studied under Kilby at Wheaton College, where he held forth gently for over forty years with an appealing blend of high romanticism and warm-hearted evangelical piety. Essays, mostly written from a Kilbeyesque point of view, treat philosophical, critical, and contemporary aspects of literary endeavor.

997. Reynolds, David S. Faith in Fiction: The Emergence of Religious Literature in America. Cambridge, MA: Harvard University Press, 1981.

Reynolds highlights the novels and stories by (mostly) women authors that began to appear in the first half-century of the republic and shows how the main features of that fiction fit (generally) into the evangelical cultural ethos of the new nation.

998. Ryken, Leland, ed. The Christian Imagination: Essays on Literature and the Arts. Grand Rapids: Baker, 1981.

This book's nearly forty well-integrated essays explore Christian perspectives on aesthetics, literature, the Christian writer, the visual arts, and music. Notable among the largely evangelical authors is the central influence of C. S. Lewis and his British friends.

999. Timmerman, John J. Markings on a Long Journey, eds. Rodney J. Mulder and John H. Timmerman. Grand Rapids: Baker, 1982.

1000. Timmerman, John J. Through a Glass Lightly. Foreword by Frederick Manfred. Grand Rapids: Eerdmans, 1987.

The occasional essay is almost a lost cause among evangelicals for whom most things are obviously serious, obviously useful, or obviously joyful. Timmerman is a marvelous exception with his ability to add whimsy to edification in reflection on life in the Christian Reformed communities of rural Iowa, suburban New Jersey, and Grand Rapids, Michigan. Somehow he makes baseball, reluctant readers of Shakespeare, and lapsed Calvinist authors seem as important as the weightiest moral imperative.

(B) Textbooks

1001. Lundin, Roger, and Susan V. Gallagher. Literature Through the Eyes of Faith. San Francisco: Harper & Row, 1989.

This text, designed to accompany introductory courses, admirably displays ways of studying literature as a function of culture and theological commitments, on the one hand, but also as a product of personal creativity in response to social injustices, on the other.

1002. Ryken, Leland. The Liberated Imagination: Thinking Christianly About the Arts. Wheaton, IL: Harold Shaw, 1990.

Ryken here mounts a comprehensive argument for the necessity of Christian aesthetic expression as well as for the joy and goodness to be found in such efforts.

1003. Timmerman, John H. and Donald R. Hettinga. In the World: Reading and Writing as a Christian. Grand Rapids: Baker, 1987.

The authors combine basic guidelines for writing clear prose with extensive examples, often with Christian or moral themes, of the kind of essays they wish their students would write.

(C) Criticism and Aesthetics

1004. Howard, Thomas. The Novels of Charles Williams. New York: Oxford University Press, 1983.

The author's personal pilgrimage has taken him from the sectarian Plymouth Brethren through a period as a high Episcopalian into the Roman Catholic Church. The attractions of Episcopalianism and Catholicism to those of literary turn are explicit subjects of other writings by Howard. In this book he provides a critical introduction to one of the Anglicans whose works have exerted considerable influence on the aesthetic sensibilities of American evangelicals.

1005. Lundin, Roger. "Offspring of an Odd Union: Evangelical Attitudes Toward the Arts." In Evangelicalism and Modern America, ed. George Marsden. Grand Rapids: Eerdmans, 1984.

Lundin wonders if evangelical enthusiasm for romantic fashions in literature and theory do not amount to an ironic repudiation of principles implicit in orthodox doctrines of creation, the fall, and redemption.

1006. Lundin, Roger, Anthony C. Thiselton and Clarence Walhout. The Responsibility of Hermeneutics. Grand Rapids: Eerdmans, 1985.

The authors advocate what they call a hermeneutics of action and responsibility, in which sensitivity to modern hermeneutical theory is combined with fidelity to Christian understandings of language and reality.

1007. Ryken, Leland. Windows to the World: Literature in Christian Perspective. Downers Grove, IL: InterVarsity Press, 1979.

This volume offers general reasons for Christians to read literature and guidelines by which to make moral and aesthetic judgments on what is read.

1008. Sayers, Dorothy L. The Mind of the Maker. New York: Harcourt, Brace, 1941.

Sayers, an "Oxford Christian" best known for her detective stories, is also an eager Christian controversialist whose analogy between the divine creation of the world and the human creation of a literary work (as spelled out in this book) has had a telling influence among American evangelicals starved for reasons to justify the creative impulses that fundamentalist and sectarian Protestantism so regularly deny.

1009. Wolterstorff, Nicholas. Art in Action: Toward a Christian Aesthetic. Grand Rapids: Eerdmans, 1980.

In opposition to the romantic theories more widely in vogue among American evangelicals, Wolterstorff proposes that a proper Christian perspective points more to regarding artistic creation as a craft, exercised in and with a community of faith, rather than as an expression of individualistic, self justifying genius.

1010. Zylstra, Henry. Testament of Vision. Grand Rapids: Eerdmans, 1958.

This pioneering work was one of the first apologies for aesthetic sophistication to receive a hearing in American evangelicalism after World War II.

(D) Fiction

1011. Bayly, Joseph. The Gospel Blimp. Elgin, IL: David C. Cook Publishing, 1960.

Although transparently didactic in its attempt to get evangelicals to exercise more judicious behavior in evangelizing others, this humorous novelette was important in its day because it uncharacteristically used fiction to make its point to its audience.

1012. DeVries, Peter. The Blood of the Lamb. New York: Penguin, 1987.

DeVries, an accomplished writer and sometime editor of The New Yorker, is an alumnus of both Calvin College and the Dutch Calvinist branch of Christianity. This novel about the anguish of a father who witnesses the suffering of his dying daughter, is a profound treatment of modern doubts of God's goodness--or existence--in the face of evil.

1013. Elliot, Elisabeth. No Graven Image. New York: Harper & Row, 1966.

Realistic novels by evangelicals about the missionary experience are almost nonexistent. This one, which draws on the author's own service in South America, is a significant exception.

1014. Fickett, Harold. The Holy Fool. Westchester, IL: Crossway, 1983.

Fickett's protagonist is a failing evangelical preacher whose trials receive a treatment more expert and more sympathetic than is the norm for fiction of this sort.

1015. Fickett, Harold, Richard J. Foster, Emilie Griffin, et al. Carnage at Christhaven. San Francisco: Harper & Row, 1989.

A collection of contemporary evangelical writers join forces in this offbeat, but delightful, murder mystery set at a Christian retreat center.

The authors, who obviously enjoy the interaction with likeminded souls, take some playful swipes at evangelicals--and each other--along the way.

1016. Frederic, Harold. The Damnation of Theron Ware. Chicago: Stone and Kimball, 1896.

The portrait of a young Methodist minister's personal confrontations with modernity at the end of the 19th century and his gradual move towards the secular life.

1017. Gardner, Martin. The Flight of Peter Froom. Los Altos, CA: W. Kaufmann, 1973.

Gardner's novel about an Okie fundamentalist who in the midst of the Great Depression comes north to convert the modernists at the University of Chicago Divinity School is short on action and very long on talk. It is also written from the perspective of a lapsed evangelical. These circumstances notwithstanding, it remains a significant attempt to capture the gist of what was, at least at one time, a common set of evangelical attitudes.

1018. Holmes, Marjorie. Two From Galilee: A Love Story. Old Tappan, NJ: Fleming H. Revell, 1972.

A briskly-selling novel in evangelical bookstores in the mid-1970s, Two From Galilee retells the story of Joseph and Mary in the form of a pious historical romance. Representative of the growing body of historical fiction based on the lives of Biblical characters. For other characteristic examples see the works of Ellen Gunderson Taylor, author of such novels as Song of Abraham (Tyndale House, 1973), and Lois T. Henderson, author of a series of novels based on women of the Bible (as in her Hagar [Harper & Row, 1978]).

1019. Hutchens, Paul. The Indian Cemetery. The Sugar Creek Gang. Chicago: Moody Press, 1947. (Originally published as Adventures in an Indian Cemetery.)

For a generation of children in evangelical homes, the adventures of Bill Collins and his friends, Dragonfly, Big Jim, Little Jim, Poetry and Circus, have been standard reading and storytime fare. This book, with its combination of mystery, morality, and evangelism is representative of the series.

1020. Johnson, James L. The Last Train From Canton. Grand Rapids: Zondervan, 1981.

A semi-new thing under the sun. Johnson's Code Name Sebastian series represent the development of a different literary genre, the Christian Spy Novel. This book is representative of his work. For another look at this developing category of "baptized" fiction, see Jerry Jenkins, The Operative (Harper & Row, 1987).

1021. Keillor, Garrison. Leaving Home. New York: Viking Penguin Inc., 1987.

Raised in a Plymouth Brethren family, the former radio host of *The Prairie Home Companion* has much to say (most of it wry and not unsympathetic) regarding fundamentalism and religion in general in his essays and fictional explorations of Lake Wobegon, Minnesota. Leaving Home contains probably the greatest amount of this material of any of his books to date, however his other books Happy to be Here (1982), Lake Wobegon Days (1985), and We Are Still Married (1989) are all helpful in understanding the mores, sensibilities, and mindset of the fundamentalist community.

1022. L'Engle, Madeliene. A Wrinkle in Time. New York: Farrar, Strauss, and Giroux, Inc., 1962.

L'Engle is a masterful writer for both children and adults, although it is her work for the former that has achieved the most recognition. A Wrinkle in Time, winner of the 1962 Newberry Award, tells of the adventures of the Murry children after a mysterious stranger informs them that, indeed, there is such a thing as a *tesseract*, a wrinkle in time.

1023. Lewis, C. S. The Narnia Tales. 7 vols. New York: Macmillan, 1950-1956.

Lewis (1898-1963) was neither an American nor, strictly considered by American criteria, an evangelical, but his apologetic and imaginative works have exerted an incalculably large influence on almost all varieties of American evangelicalism. The Narnia Tales have been especially important as an example of how to use literary creation to re-create the traditional Christian story, a service performed also by an essay often reprinted in America, "On Fairy Stories," by Lewis's Roman Catholic friend and fellow "Inkling," J.R.R. Tolkien.

1024. Lewis, C. S. The Screwtape Letters. New York: The Macmillan Company, 1942.

Lewis' fiction has become a template for evangelical authors in their attempts to combine creativity with a sacramental raison d'etre. In The Screwtape Letters, he uses a series of letters from senior demon Screwtape to his nephew, a junior tempter named Wormwood, to wittily examine both the modern secular worldview and the pitfalls of the Christian life.

1025. Lewis, C. S. The Space Trilogy. London: Bodley Head, 1938-1945.

In a series of well-done science fiction novels, Out of the Silent Planet, Perelanda, and That Hideous Strength, Lewis explores the potential for evil in the combination of human pride, modern science, and secular philosophy.

1026. MacDonald, George. Phantastes (1858); reprint, ed., Grand Rapids: Eerdmans, 1981.

A Scottish pastor and novelist of the Victorian era, MacDonald was oft-cited by C.S. Lewis as the biggest influence on his own fiction. In recent years, MacDonald's romantic fiction and fantasy novels have found a growing audience among American evangelicals. Phantastes is a typical example of his fantasy work.

1027. Marshall, Catherine. Christy. New York: McGraw Hill, 1967.

One of the better examples of evangelical fiction of the romantic historical stripe. Based on her mother's early life, Marshall's novel tells the story of a young missionary-schoolteacher in the mountains of western North Carolina at the turn of the century. For other representative examples of this genre see the works of Grace Livingstone Hill (author of such novels as Where Two Ways Met [Harper & Row, 1946, reprint ed. Tyndale House, 1989]), Michael Phillips and Judith Pella (authors of the Stonewycke Trilogy and the Stonewycke Legacy series, [Bethany House, 1985-1988]) and Eugenia Price (see her Savannah [Doubleday and Company, 1983]).

1028. Miller, Calvin. The Singer Trilogy. Downers Grove, IL: InterVarsity Press, 1975-1979.

An anomaly in today's publishing world, The Singer (1975), The Song (1977), and The Finale (1979) are a best-selling, free-verse poetic allegory based on the Gospels, the Acts of the Apostles, and Revelation. Written by a Baptist pastor.

1029. Nelson, Shirley. The Last Year of the War. San Francisco: Harper & Row, 1978.

This semi-autobiographical story of a young New Englander who finds herself at Moody Bible Institute in 1944 is the best novel yet written on the internal dynamics of modern evangelicalism.

1030. O'Connor, Flannery. A Good Man is Hard to Find. New York: Harcourt Brace Jovanovich, Inc., 1953.

While O'Connor was herself an outsider as a Catholic in pre-Sun Belt Georgia, her dark, discomfiting stories about life in the South display a mixture of fascination, repulsion, and grudging admiration for the fundamentalist beliefs of her Protestant neighbors. The strong moral and Christian thrust of her writing has made her an important figure to aspiring evangelical writers.

1031. Palmer, Bernard. Danny Orlis Makes the Team. Chicago: Moody Press, 1946; rev. ed., The Final Touchdown. Wheaton, IL: Tyndale House, 1989.

These short novels are part of a juvenile fiction series, formulaic tales of athletic trials and exploits or mysteries. They have been a widely-read evangelical equivalent of the Hardy Boys for adolescent boys since the mid-1940s. For a more recent series along these same lines, see Jerry Jenkins' Dallas O' Neill series (Moody Press).

1032. Peretti, Frank. This Present Darkness. Westchester, IL: Crossway, 1986.

This unusually successful novel combines several elements that have been staples in recent evangelical fiction: fantasy along the lines pioneered by C. S. Lewis and Charles Williams, struggle between powers of evil and good, and a preoccupation with stark moral choices. See also Peretti's sequel, Piercing the Darkness (Westchester, IL: Crossway, 1989).

1033. Rader, Paul. Big Bug. New York: Fleming H. Revell, 1932.

Paul Rader (1879-1938), a prominent Chicago evangelist and radio pioneer, wrote this romance/mystery novel to promote his vision for lay evangelism and missionary expansion. Interesting for the strategies it advocates and its feel for popular culture, Big Bug is also notable as a rare example of a major fundamentalist figure's use of fiction during this era.

1034. Richardson, Arleta. In Grandma's Attic. Elgin, IL: David C. Cook Publishing, 1974.

The author shares sentimental tales of her grandmother's life on the farm and coming of age at the turn of the century in this popular series aimed at young girls. Other popular series for young women include Jane Sorenson's Katie Hooper series (Standard Publishing) for the middle school set, and Hilda Stahl's Elizabeth Gail series (Tyndale House), combining mystery and romance for young teens.

1035. Tolkien, J. R. R. The Lord of the Rings. London: Allen & Unwin, 1954-1955.

Achieving cult status in America and the United Kingdom during the 1960s, The Lord of the Rings provided inspiration for everything from an outbreak of "renaissance faires," to Dungeons & Dragons, to a slew of fantasy novelist imitators. In the evangelical community his trilogy, while not as openly spiritual as that of fellow "Inkling" C. S. Lewis, were important examples for aspiring Christian saga-spinners such as Stephen R. Lawhead (see his Pendragon Cycle, Crossway Books).

1036. Wangerin, Walter. The Book of the Dun Cow. New York: Harper & Row, 1978.

Wangerin, a former Lutheran pastor in Evansville, Indiana, has emerged as an important figure in the evangelical literary revival. This allegorical fantasy centers around the barnyard kingdom of Chauntecleer the Rooster in the days when animals could speak.

1037. Williams, Charles. The Place of the Lion London: Gollancz, 1931, reprint, Grand Rapids: Eerdmans, 1976.

Yet another "Inkling." Williams' novels are a strange amalgamation of fantasy, science fiction, and mystical imagery set in his contemporary Post-WWI England. While not widely read in the evangelical community, they have had a significant impact on evangelical artists: literary, graphic, and musical. The Place of the Lion, representative of his work, is perhaps more accessible than some of his other novels.

1038. Woiwode, Larry. Born Brothers. New York: Farrar, Straus, and Giroux, 1988.

The closely observed family drama that sustains this sequel to Beyond the Bedroom Wall (1975) reflects the author's powerful conversion during the 1970s to a conservative Presbyterian form of evangelical faith.

(E) Poetry

1039. Meeter, Merle, ed. The Country of the Risen King: An Anthology of Christian Poetry. Grand Rapids: Baker, 1978.

This illuminating volume adds samples of contemporary poems reflecting Christian (often evangelical) sensibility to what might be termed the classical canon of Christian verse (e.g., Herbert, Milton, Hopkins, Eliot).

1040. Mollenkott, Virginia R., ed. Adam Among the Television Trees: An Anthology of Verse by Contemporary Christian Poets. Waco, TX: Word, 1971.

1041. Shaw, Luci, ed. A Widening Light: Poems of the Incarnation. Wheaton, IL: Harold Shaw, 1984.

No Shakespeares or Audens, or even William Cowpers, have yet appeared among modern American evangelicals, though if the Massachusetts Puritan Edward Taylor counts as an evangelical, he certainly belongs in that exalted company. At the same time, however, the quality of poems from the evangelical/Episcopalian artists presented in these anthologies is remarkably good--e.g., these lines from "Like Every Newborn" by Madeliene L'Engle: "Girded for war, humility his mighty dress, / He moves into battle wholly weaponless."

F) The Visual Arts

042. Rookmaaker, H. R. Modern Art and the Death of a Culture. Downers Grove, IL: InterVarsity Press, 1970.

Rookmaaker, a co-worker for several years with the apologist Francis Schaeffer, expresses in this book two convictions nurtured by his Dutch Calvinist experience--that the visual arts may be pursued with all good conscience by Christian believers, but also that dominant modern forms of artistic expression have degenerated into degenerate representations of human meaning and dignity.

1043. Veith, Gene Edward, Jr. The Gift of Art: The Place of the Arts in Scripture. Downers Grove, IL: InterVarsity Press, 1983.

To audiences drawn to the Scriptures much more for the purposes of conversion and moral guidance, Veith shows how the implicit (and even sometimes explicit) witness of the Bible justifies a full-blown embrace of the arts.

(G) The Bible as Literature

1044. Ryken, Leland. How to Read the Bible as Literature. Grand Rapids: Zondervan, 1984.

1045. Ryken, Leland. Words of Delight: A Literary Introduction to the Bible. Grand Rapids: Baker, 1987.

Ryken is a leader in using literary techniques for studying and appreciating the Bible while not (as is sometimes the case with other students of the Bible as literature) implying that the literary character of the Bible exhausts its potential meaning for modern men and women.

(H) Hymnody and Worship

1046. Adams, Doug. Meeting House to Camp Meeting: Toward a History of American Free Church Worship From 1620 to 1835. Saratoga, NY: Modern Liturgy-Resource Publications, 1981.

This overview explains some of the historical background behind the populist, word-centered, non-liturgical worship that characterizes most of the evangelical traditions.

1047. DeJong, Mary G. "'I Want to Be Like Jesus': The Self-Defining Power of Evangelical Hymnody." Journal of the American Academy of Religion 54 (Fall 1986): 461-93.

Scholars like Donald Davie and Lionel Adey have shown how fruitful it is to study seriously the hymns of British evangelicals. DeJong joins Sandra Sizer (whose Gospel Hymns and Social Religion is cited elsewhere) with some of the same discriminating attention to the hymns of American evangelicals.

1048. Hustad, Donald P. Jubilate: Church Music in the Evangelical Tradition. Carol Stream, IL: Hope, 1981.

This popular work conveys a great deal of useful information about the sources and nature of evangelical hymns, along with sensible reflections on the purposes of congregational and choral singing in worship.

SECTION IV: THE PUBLIC ARENA

17. Social Change and Political Evangelism--Randall Balmer
18. Media and Entertainment--Randall Balmer & Larry K. Eskridge

CHAPTER 17
SOCIAL CHANGE AND POLITICAL EVANGELISM

The literature on evangelicals and American public life belies a persistent myth about twentieth-century evangelicalism: that evangelicalism is a monolithic movement with a unified political agenda.

Political consensus has eluded evangelicals for all of the twentieth century, and certainly since the resurgence of fundamentalists into the political arena in the mid-seventies. Although the majority of evangelicals are politically conservative and have mobilized in opposition to such standard conservative targets as abortion, homosexuality, and communism, there is also an articulate minority of evangelicals who match the vigor of their right-wing counterparts in defense of generally liberal concerns like nuclear disarmament, feminism, and advocacy for the poor.

1049. Alcorn, Randy C. *Christians in the Wake of the Sexual Revolution*. Portland, OR: Multnomah Press, 1985.

States that the sexual revolution has unleashed a Pandora's box of sexual perversions on our society. Outlines the extent of the scourge, and closes with a detailed proposal for action by Christians against sources of sin within the church and in society.

1050. Anderson, John B. *Between Two Worlds: A Congressman's Choice*. Grand Rapids: Zondervan, 1970.

Culling concrete examples from his experiences as a politician, Congressman Anderson attempts to reconcile spiritual ideals with harsher realities. He believes that Christianity offers solutions to the economic, social and moral crises of our times, and that it is the duty of all Christians to attempt to resolve these difficulties by heeding the precepts of their faith.

1051. Anderson, John B. *Vision and Betrayal in America*. Waco, TX: Word Books, 1975.

A "collapse of moral values" in America has resulted in the corruption of our leadership and institutions. Anderson outlines the extent of these inequities, focusing especially upon Watergate. In order to right the course of their government, Americans first must reaffirm their faith in the ideals expressed in the Constitution.

1052. Bailey, Kenneth K. Southern White Protestantism. New York: Harper & Row, 1964.

Notes that the fundamentalist faith to which many southerners subscribe is imbued with a tradition of fervent concern over certain social issues, including school prayer, creationism, and evolution.

1053. Bajema, Clifford A. Abortion and the Meaning of Personhood. Grand Rapids: Baker, 1974.

Argues that abortion, except in cases in which pregnancy endangers the mother's life, is murder. A concluding chapter calls for increased support for pregnant women by churches.

1054. Baker, William H. On Capital Punishment. Chicago: Moody Press, 1985.

Provides historical and biblical bases to support the contention that the death penalty is still an "unpleasant necessity." Intended for the popular audience.

1055. Bellah, Robert N. and Frederick E. Greenspahn, eds. Uncivil Religion. New York: Crossroad, 1987.

While this volume focuses on inter- and intra-religious conflicts among Protestants, Catholics, and Jews, it does suggest the incredible variety of political visions espoused by religious groups in the United States. See especially for George M. Marsden's analysis of the polarization of groups espousing and denying evolution: "A Case of the Excluded Middle: Creation Versus Evolution in America."

Bendroth, Margaret L. "The Search for 'Women's Role' in American Evangelicalism, 1930-1980." In Evangelicalism and Modern America, ed. George Marsden. Grand Rapids: Eerdmans, 1984. (see 1535)

1056. Blamires, Harry. Where Do We Stand? Ann Arbor: Servant Books, 1980.

Contends that secular thought has infected Christian thinking, twisting interpretations of the Gospel to suit modern ideologies. Examines a few "border areas"--social issues--in which Christian thinking is most susceptible to dilution. Blamires calls for renewed service to the Word rather than the world.

1057. Bockelman, Wilfred. Gothard: the Man and His Ministry. Santa Barbara, CA: Quill Publications, 1976.

Evaluates Bill Gothard's Institute in Basic Youth Conflicts Ministry. Extremely popular in the mid-seventies, Gothard directed seminars which promoted a traditional Christian approach to family, emphasizing the internal hierarchy of parents of child, husband over wife, and God over all.

1058. "Born Again Politics." Newsweek 96 (September 15, 1980): 28-36.

Related the ambitious plans held by the New Christian Right in the 1980 election year. Accompanied by a separate profile on Jerry Falwell, the most outspoken fundamentalist leader.

1059. Bromley, David G. and Anson Shupe, eds. New Christian Politics. Macon, GA: Mercer University Press, 1984.

Important collecton of twenty scholarly articles on the New Christian Right's constituency, historical roots, relationship with the media, and political impact. Includes case studies as well as more comprehensive essays.

1060. Brown, Harold O. J. Death Before Birth. Nashville: Thomas Nelson, 1977.

Brown decries the loss of respect for human life that attends wholesale abortion and the depraved conscience of a nation that tolerates it. He implores Christians to campaign at every level of society against the scourge.

1061. Brunkow, Robert de V., ed. Religion and Society in North America: An Annontated Bibliography. Santa Barbara: American Bibliographical Center-Clio Press, 1983.

1062. Buzzard, Lynn, and Paula Campbell. Holy Disobedience--When Christians Must Resist the State. Ann Arbor: Servant Books, 1984.

Calls for more vigorous resistance by Christians against immoral practices committed by the government, especially the legalization of abortion and the propagation of the arms race. Proposes biblically based guidelines for action, ranging from reluctant compliance to obstructive disobedience.

063. Campolo, Anthony Jr. The Power Delusion. Wheaton, IL: Victor Books, 1983.

This readily comprehensible book examines the pursuit of power within the family and in government. The author holds that Christians must reject the desire for domination, replacing it with an ideal of egalitarianism just as Jesus did.

064. Campolo, Anthony Jr. Who Switched the Price Tags? Waco, TX: Word Books, 1986.

Christian sociologist Campolo decries the warped values of the materialistic 1980s. He calls for a return to true Christian ideals through conversion, public service, tithing, and love.

1065. Cannon, Lou. Reagan. New York: Putnam's, 1982.

Excellent analysis of Reagan's acting and political career explores his complex relationship with the New Christian Right. Shows that despite the NCR's sponsorship of the President, it was not always rewarded with active executive support for its conservative social policies.

1066. Carper, James C. "The Christian Day School." In Religious Schooling in America., eds. James C. Carper and Thomas C. Hunt. Birmingham, AL: Religious Education Press, 1984.

Dissatisfaction with public schools and the resurgence of evangelical revivalism have contributed to the fantastic growth of private Christian day schools. These schools, which vary widely in both size and quality, now represent a viable alternative for most Christian students. The author acknowledges a few problems, however. For example: Will the proliferation of these institutions slacken evangelical involvement in the public schools?

1067. Carter, Jimmy. Why Not the Best? Nashville: Broadman Press, 1975.

Written in order to introduce himself to the nation during his first bid for the presidency, Carter portrays himself as a reborn Christian with a penchant for honest, decent, and compassionate government. In order to achieve this goal, ethical and spiritual leadership must be integrated into politics.

1068. Cizik, Richard, ed. The High Cost of Indifference--Can Christians Afford Not to Act? Ventura, CA: Regal Books, 1984.

Compendium of evangelical commentaries on such pressing social issues as poverty, abortion, religious liberty, crime, pornography, and the nuclear arms race. The editor includes a "Plan for Action" for Christian lay people which emphasizes the role of individual involvement in easing social problems.

1069. Clabaugh, Gary K. Thunder on the Right. Chicago: Nelson-Hall, 1974.

Alarmist assessment of the extreme right of Christian activism which equates the ideology of men like Billy James Hargis and Carl McIntire with totalitarianism. Encourages more moderate citizens to fight against the threat.

1070. Cleaver, Eldridge. Soul on Fire. Waco, TX: Word Books, 1978.

One of the most surprising celebrity conversions of the 1970s was that of Eldridge Cleaver, former Black Panther. This autobiography covers his childhood, political activities, imprisonment, exile, conversion and subsequent return to the United States, where he worked for a time in Eldridge Cleaver Crusades, a ministry to the prison population.

1071. Clouse, Robert G., Robert D. Linder and Richard V. Pierard, eds. The Cross and the Flag. Carol Stream, IL: Creation House, 1972.

An early attempt by evangelical scholars to make sense of the variety of political attitudes tendered by Christians in the United States. Twelve essays, preface by Mark O. Hatfield.

1072. Conway, Flo and Jim Siegelman. Holy Terror. Garden City, NY: Doubleday, 1982.

Sensationalistic report on the power and political agenda held by fundamentalists and conservative evangelists. An example of the fear that right-wing Christian groups and politicized televangelists inspired in certain liberal circles in the early 80s.

1073. Cotham, Perry C. Politics, Americanism and Christianity. Grand Rapids: Baker, 1976.

Examines the theological and ethical roots of a wide range of Christian attitudes towards politics, from disavowal to activism. Concludes with a call for Christian action to provide the nation with moral backbone.

1074. Dahms, John V. "The Social Interest and Concern of A. B. Simpson." In The Birth of a Vision, ed. David E. Hartzfeld and Charles Nienkirchen, 49-74. Beaverlodge, Alberta: Buena Book Services, 1986.

Contends that although Simpson's rhetoric was overwhelmingly pietistic and evangelistic in tone, his Christian and Missionary Alliance nonetheless was involved in a number of social welfare programs.

1075. Dayton, Donald W. "Social and Political Conservatism and Modern American Evangelicalism: A Preliminary Search for the Reasons." Union Seminary Quarterly Review 32 (1977): 71-80.

Dayton's contributions to a special symposium on evangelicals, draws upon his unique knowledge of nineteenth century holiness sources and the growing social conservatism of 20th century evangelicals. The themes sketched here are developed in greater detail in his study Discovering an Evangelical Heritage (see 430).

076. DeKoster, Lester. Communism and Christian Faith. Grand Rapids: Eerdmans, 1956.

Marxist ideology is explained and contrasted with Christian doctrine in this unusually comprehensive McCarthy era tract. Communism is portrayed as a terrible threat, but the need for a Christian social program to counteract its attractiveness is also pointed out.

1077. Dobson, James. Dr. Dobson Answers Your Questions. Wheaton, IL: Tyndale House, 1982.

The Dr. Spock of the evangelical world addresses a number of questions about children and families. Ever sensitive to the rapidly changing mores of secular society, Dobson discusses everything from heroin to homosexuality.

1078. Eighmy, John L. Churches in Cultural Captivity: A History of the Social Attitudes of Southern Baptists. Knoxville: University of Tennessee Press, 1972.

Refutes the notion that Southern Baptists have either historically lacked a social conscience or regularly endorsed reactionary programs. Eighmy maintains in a solid piece of scholarship that Southern Baptists have always had a sense of social responsibility. The books reveals much about southern culture as well as about Southern Baptists. It contains an extensive bibliography.

1079. Eller, Vernard. Christian Anarchy: Jesus' Primacy over the Powers. Grand Rapids: Eerdmans, 1987.

Eller rejects the partisan politicking of both right-wing and left-wing evangelicals in favor of what he calls "Christian Anarchy." This entails primal allegiance to the lordship of Jesus Christ, and resistance to civil authority only when it infringes on one's personal ethics. The philosophies of Karl Barth, Dietrich Bonhoeffer, and Jacques Ellul, among others, are examined.

Ellisen, Stanley A. Divorce and Remarriage in the Church. Grand Rapids: Zondervan, 1977.
(see 1513)

1080. Ellul, Jacques. The Meaning of the City. Grand Rapids: Eerdmans, 1970.

This radical analysis of modern cities by a French Protestant theologian identifies them as today's Babylons--confused, immoral places where man concentrates his efforts on temporal matters rather than spiritual quests. Ellul, who was eagerly studied by American evangelical intellectuals in the 1960s and 1970s, foresees the decline of the city as God exercises his wrath and the subsequent rise of the "New City," whose inhabitants will be in close communion with the Lord.

1081. Ellul, Jacques. Violence: Reflections from a Christian Perspective. New York: Seabury, 1969.

Prominent French social critic and theologian Ellul asserts that violence is the usual instrument of human discourse. Thus it is incumbent upon the Christian to combat this failing through non-violent resistance and dogged identification with the victims.

Enroth, Ronald M., Edward E. Ericson Jr. and C. Breckinridge Peters. The Jesus People: Old Time Religion in the Age of Aquarius. Grand Rapids: Eerdmans, 1972.
(see 1513)

1082. Ericson, Edward L. American Freedom and the Radical Right. New York: Frederick Ungar Publishing, 1982.

Notes that the Radical Christian Right has rejected the traditional evangelical respect for the separation of church and state. Ericson warns that this dangerous movement seeks to slowly dismantle the Bill of Rights through censorship, government enforces school prayer, creationism, anti-abortionism and rabid nationalism.

1083. "The Evangelicals--New Empire of Faith." TIME 110 (December 26, 1977): 52-58.

This cover story reports on the massive resurgence of evangelical activity during the mid-seventies. While noting the rapid growth of the conservative 'superchurch,' and the corresponding decline of the liberal Protestant flock, it asserts that this traditionally fractious movement may prove not to be a formidable political force. Recent converts in the public eye, including athletes, entertainers, businessmen, and politicians, are listed.

1084. Fackre, Gabriel. The Religious Right and Christian Faith. Grand Rapids: Eerdmans, 1982.

Theological critiques of the Christian Right's political agenda. Fackre lauds biblically grounded actions, but decries the use of moralistic attacks to create the impression of having an exclusive divine mandate.

1085. Falwell, Jerry. Listen, America! New York: Bantam Books, 1980.

The jeremiad of the fundamentalist television preacher from Virginia who founded the Moral Majority. Falwell warns that if the American people do not return to traditional moral values, strengthen their nation's role as the world's defender against communist aggression, and unequivocally support the nation of Israel, God will bring judgment. Calls Christians to actively promote this agenda in American public life.

1086. Falwell, Jerry, ed. [with Ed Dobson and Ed Hindson]. The Fundamentalist Phenomenon: The Resurgence of Conservative Christianity. Garden City, NY: Doubleday, 1981.

Traces the development of fundamentalism from Puritan times and describes its current ideological and cultural manifestations and internal tensions. Includes Falwell's "Agenda for the Eighties," a list of moral, social, religious and political issues that are to be priorities in the coming decade.

1087. Finke, Roger and Rodney Stark. "Religious Economies and Sacred Canopies: Religious Mobilization in American Cities, 1906." American Sociological Review 53 (1989): 41-49.

Two prominent sociologists reexamine statistics and refute the common wisdom that urban America was less religious than its rural counterpart.

1088. Flowers, Ronald B. "President Jimmy Carter, Evangelicalism, Church-State Relations, and Civil Religion." Journal of Church and State 25 (Winter 1983): 113-132.

Demonstrates that although Carter's heartfelt Christianity influenced his politics, he was constantly aware that the legal vehicles which separate the church and state protect both of them. Flowers does not view his 1980 defeat as a wholesale rejection of these values by the voters, but rather as the result of Carter's image as an ineffective administrator.

1089. Flowers, Ronald B. Religion in Strange Times: The 1960s and 70s. Macon, GA: Mercer University Press, 1984.

Argues that the trauma caused by the unsettling political events of the last two decades resulted in the development of several new trends in American Christianity, including Black Theology, Feminist Theology, Born-Againism, and televangelism. Explores the cultural roots of these movements and new church/state issues.

1090. Ford, Leighton. One Way to Change the World. New York: Harper & Row, 1970.

Canadian-reared evangelist Ford claims that the world can be saved only through Christian love (conversions) and justice (good works). He offers an activist social agenda and a new vision of the church structured as a family, but, like his renowned brother-in-law, Billy Graham, his emphasis is placed squarely on the development of personal Christian virtues.

1091. Fowler, Robert Booth. A New Engagement: Evangelical Political Thought 1966-1976. Grand Rapids: Eerdmans, 1982.

Reviews a wide range of the social and political ideologies of evangelicals, from liberals such as Jim Wallis and Mark Hatfield to conservatives like Francis and Edith Schaeffer. Points out the error in stereotyping this highly diverse community.

1092. Fowler, Robert Booth. Religion and Politics in America. Metuchen, NJ: Scarecrow Press, 1985.

Argues that the diversity of religious traditions in America combined with their reluctance to get involved with politics contribute to the surprisingly negligible influence religion has on American life. Furthermore, the author suggests, religious institutions have provided a refuge from the turmoil of our society, rather than an altar from which to alter it.

Frady, Marshall. Billy Graham: A Parable of American Righteousness. Boston: Little, Brown & Co., 1979.
(see 744)

1093. Frye, Roland Mushat, ed. Is God a Creationist? New York: Scribner's, 1983.

Excellent compilation of essays which point out the essential scriptural, scientific, and historical features of the recent creationism/evolution debate. In his summation, Frye accounts for the re-emergence of this issue as a result of the populism and revivalism that thrive far from educational centers.

1094. Furguson, Ernest B. Hard Right: The Rise of Jesse Helms. New York: W. W. Norton, 1986.

Charts the personal and political career of Helms, Republican senator from North Carolina, and the concomitant rise of the New Right. Demonstrates that "Senator No!" is supported by millions of citizens who feel that they are ignored by other politicians.

1095. Gallivan, C. E., ed. A Nation Under God? Waco, TX: Word Books, 1976.

An important element of American evangelical thought is the contention that the United States was established by Christians for the purpose of protecting and fostering Christianity. The essays in this book stress the religious roots of our country and exhort Christians to experience the true faith in this God-given land.

1096. Geisler, Norman L. Ethics: Alternatives and Issues. Grand Rapids: Zondervan, 1971.

The influential conservative theologian and philosopher surveys a variety of ethical approaches (including situationism, generalism, absolutism, etc.) and explores the biblical response to such sensitive issues as sex, abortion, suicide and capital punishment. Each topic is accompanied by a brief but informative bibliography for additional reading.

1097. Gilkey, Langdon. Creationism on Trial: Evolution and God at Little Rock. San Francisco: Harper & Row, 1985.

Absorbing personal account of the author's experience as a witness, on behalf of the American Civil Liberties Union, at the 1981 creationist trial in Arkansas. Though hardly sympathetic to the goals of the anti-evolutionists, Gilkey offers an interesting sociological perspective on the interaction of the scientific ideas and religious symbolism in modern society. A transcript of the trial is included.

1098. Gish, Arthur G. The New Left and Christian Radicalism. Grand Rapids: Eerdmans, 1970.

Compares the New Left and the emergence of Christian radicalism in the late 1960s to the Anabaptist movement of the 16th century. Gish also calls for a new theology of radical pacifism to challenge the unjust system.

1099. Granberg-Michaelson, Wesley. A Worldly Spirituality: The Call to Redeem Life on Earth. San Francisco: Harper & Row, 1984.

Radical Christian Granberg-Michaelson deplores the fact that man has usurped divine powers through his manipulation of new technologies. Calls for a Christian agenda of ecological awareness and the restraint of those innovations, such as genetic engineering and nuclear technology, which stretch the capacity for moral judgment.

1100. Greenwalt, Kent. Religious Convictions and Political Choice. New York: Oxford University Press, 1988.

While this work does not specifically address evangelical issues, it will prove essential to anyone seeking to understand the interaction of law and religion in our society. The author holds that laws based entirely on an abstract sense of sin cannot be justified under our constitution, but that lawmakers may rely on religious convictions when secular morality is inclusive. Examines a number of areas in which the public discourse has been heavily charged with religious arguments.

1101. Grounds, Vernon. Revolution and the Christian Faith. Philadelphia: Lippincott, 1971.

Part of the Evangelical Perspectives series edited by John Warwick Montgomery, this book offers an evangelical critique of liberation theologians and other Christian advocates of radical change by violence. Relies heavily on the work of French sociologist Jacques Ellul.

1102. Hadden, Jeffrey K. and Charles E. Swann. "Responding to the Christian Right." Theology Today 39 (January 1983): 377-84.

While a plethora of secular organizations arose to combat the political activities of the New Christian Right, mainline churches have been notably absent from the fray. The authors discuss reasons for this reticence and call for renewed efforts on the part of mainline leaders to work against the Moral Majority and similar groups.

1103. Halsell, Grace. Prophecy and Politics: Militant Evangelists on the Road to Nuclear War. Westport, CT: Lawrence Hill & Company, 1986.

Many fundamentalists have focused their millennialist activities on enforcing the prophecy that Israel will be ruled by Jews. In Halsell's view, the resulting Israeli/fundamentalist alliance is a dangerous one, based on expansionist policies by the Israeli government and an expectation of Armageddon by its fundamentalist supporters in the United States.

1104. Hargis, Billy James. Communist America . . . Must It Be? Tulsa, OK: Christian Crusade, 1960.

The founder of the Christian Crusade and American Christian University (Tulsa), Billy James Hargis wrote and published many ultra-right wing attacks on a variety of liberal and moderate policies. In this volume he fires at many targets: the United Nations, labor unions, the National Council of Churches, the Supreme Court, and other institutions that supposedly thrive under the protective cloak of the international communist conspiracy.

Hatch, Nathan O. "Evangelicalism as a Democratic Movement." In Evangelicalism and Modern America, ed. by George Marsden. Grand Rapids: Eerdmans, 1984.
(see 437)

1105. Hatfield, Mark. Between a Rock and a Hard Place. Waco, TX: Word Books, 1976.

The senator from Oregon describes the agenda of the Christian politician, whose faith naturally allies him with the "poor and oppressed" against "structures of injustice," such as Americans' blind and uncritical nationalism. Hatfield uses theological and sociological analyses to explain his left-of-center politics, including his well-known anti-war activities in the Vietnam era.

1106. Hatfield, Mark. Conflict and Conscience. Waco, TX: Word Books, 1971.

Hatfield laments the era's difficulties, especially the Vietnam War, racial enmity, and the growing gap between the wealthy and the poor. He argues that Christians must not abandon politics, but rather transform them, for our leadership reflects our moral condition. Orthodox Christianity automatically has supported conservative political programs for too long. In fact, revolution, when it overturns injustice and inequity, can be a Christian imperative.

Hefley, James C. Textbooks on Trial. Wheaton, IL: Victor Books, 1976.
(see 1346)

1107. Hefley, James C. and Edward E. Plowman. Washington: Christians in the Corridors of Power. Wheaton, IL: Tyndale House, 1975.

Cites evidence of a Christian resurgence in the capitol. Lists hundreds of evangelicals in the House, Senate, and elsewhere, and discusses the impact of their faith upon their politics.

1108. Helms, Jesse. When Free Men Shall Stand. Grand Rapids: Zondervan, 1976.

Baptist deacon and U.S. Senator Helms shares his extremely conservative views on social and political issues.

1109. Henry, Carl F. H., ed. Baker's Dictionary of Christian Ethics. Grand Rapids: Baker, 1973.

This comprehensive reference work includes articles on hundreds of social and theological issues written by over 140 contributors. Consult for moderately conservative Christian positions on issues such as abortion, capitalism, church and state, artificial insemination, race relations and so forth.

1110. Henry, Carl F. H. The Christian Mindset in a Secular Society: Promoting Evangelical Renewal and National Righteousness. Portland, OR: Multnomah Press, 1984.

Prominent evangelical theologian Henry combines ominous predictions with moral outrage to create a compelling case for Christian activism. A moderate conservative politically, the author believes that Christian ethical imperatives can be developed within the existing political structure. This is one of several manifestos by Henry on a similar theme.

1111. Henry, Paul B. Politics for Evangelicals. Valley Forge, PA: Judson Press, 1974.

Prods Christians to enter the political arena where they can temper greed with justice. Discusses the philosophic and theological bases for this mandate, as well as describing practical avenues for its achievement. The author, who is the son of Carl F. H. Henry the theologian, later became a U.S. congressman.

1112. Hilgers, Thomas W., David J. Horan and David Mall, eds. New Perspectives on Human Abortion. Frederick, MD: University Publications, 1981.

Collection of 31 essays, written by physicians, professors of law, and theologians, espousing extremely conservative anti-abortion views. Titles include "Mongolism," "Sexual Assault and Pregnancy," "The Experience of Pain by the Unborn," and "Abortion and Jewish Law," among others.

1113. Hill, Samuel S. and Dennis E. Owen. The New Religious Political Right in America. Nashville: Abingdon, 1982.

Analyzes the rise of what the authors call the "new religious/political right" in American politics in 1980. Discusses the movement's origins, goals, tactics, and reception, concluding that although this movement is a dynamic element of American political life, it is limited by a relatively small and factious popular base. The authors anticipate that it will continue to influence, but not transform, the political system.

1114. Hofman, Brenda D. "Political Theology: The Role of Organized Religion in the Anti-Abortion Movement." Journal of Church and State 28 (Spring 1986): 225-248.

Shows that the Catholic Church and evangelicals have joined forces with the common goal of eliminating abortion. Their effort is a politically sophisticated one that seeks to promote the influence of religion in political decision making.

1115. Hoffmeier, James K., ed. Abortion: A Christian Understanding and Response. Grand Rapids: Baker, 1987.

Includes 15 scholarly articles on the nature and ethics of abortion. Surveys scientific issues, pro-abortion arguments, and political avenues for anti-abortion activism. A good source for evangelical views on this volatile issue.

Hollinger, Dennis. Individual and Social Ethics: An Evangelical Syncretism. Lanham, MD: University Press of America, 1984.
(see 755)

Hull, Gretchen Gaebelein. Equal to Serve. Old Tappan, NJ: Fleming H. Revell, 1987.
(see 1553)

Hunter, James Davison. American Evangelicalism: Conservative Religion and the Quandary of Modernity. New Brunswick, NJ: Rutgers University Press, 1983.
(see 953)

Hunter, James Davison. Evangelicalism: The Coming Generation. Chicago: University of Chicago, 1987.
(see 954)

1116. Jenkinson, Edward B. Censors in the Classrooms. Carbondale: Southern Illinois University Press, 1979.

Exposes the widespread practice of censorship in public schools by both left-wing and right-wing groups. Evangelicals, like Mel and Norma Gabler, are involved in a large part of this activity. Jenkinson lists the goals and methods of the censors.

1117. Johnston, Jon. Will Evangelicalism Survive Its Own Popularity? Grand Rapids: Zondervan, 1980.

Johnston's enthusiasm over the resurgence of evangelicalism is tempered by worry that its popularization could lead to the slow dilution of its moral agenda. His discussion of American society and modern evangelicalism's new methods explains his conviction that Christians must stand apart from culture and refuse to compromise principles.

1118. Jorstad, Erling. Evangelicals in the White House: The Cultural Maturation of Born Again Christianity, 1960-1981. New York: The Edwin Mellen Press, 1981.

Jorstad explains the transformation of the resurgence of religious feeling of the 1960s and early 1970s into the politically active evangelical movement in the late seventies and early eighties as indicative of the "cultural maturation of revivalism". A variety of personalities and issues are discussed within this context, including Marabell Morgan, Bill Gothard, Jimmy Carter, Ronald Reagan, the Christian school boom, Biblical inerrancy, and evangelical thought on sex roles.

1119. Jorstad, Erling. The New Christian Right 1981-1988: Prospects for the Post-Reagan Decade. New York: The Edwin Mellen Press, 1987.

Reviews the activities of the New Christian Right during the Reagan presidency, noting the tendency of many of its leaders to work closely with the President. Jorstad shows that despite this relationship, the movement has not successfully implemented its social agenda, and failed to elect many favored candidates to office in 1986.

1120. Jorstad, Erling. The Politics of Doomsday. Nashville: Abingdon, 1970.

Describes the careers, policies, and backers of extremely right-wing, politically active, fundamentalists such as Carl McIntire, Billy James Hargis, Edgar C. Bundy and Verne P. Kaub. Suggests that while "ultrafundamentalism" may remain an active force on the American scene in the foreseeable future, it is unlikely to prove a cohesive, powerful movement.

1121. Jorstad, Erling. The Politics of Moralism: The New Christian Right in American Life. Minneapolis: Ausburg Publishing House, 1981.

Explains the spectacular success of the New Christian Right in the 1980 campaign as the inevitable result of the combination of sophisticated media manipulation by evangelists and the increasing tensions within American political and cultural life. Argues that the "politics of moralism" has replaced the "politics of doomsday" of the 1960s.

1122. Kater, John L., Jr. Christians on the Right. New York: Seabury, 1982.

Theologian and historian Kater views the New Right as a natural outgrowth of American history and culture. He commends it for bringing a voice to those who have felt abandoned by society, but condemns it for being a servant to the middle class culture from which it sprang.

1123. Keysor, Charles W., ed. What You Should Know about Homosexuality. Grand Rapids: Zondervan, 1979.

The social, psychological and theological aspects of homosexuality are explored in this volume. The sinful nature of the gay lifestyle is stressed, but God's forgiveness and His ability to change people are also promised.

1124. Kucharsky, David. The Man from Plains: The Mind and Spirit of Jimmy Carter. New York: Harper & Row, 1976.

Explores Carter's evangelical faith and describes its generally favorable impact on Christian voters. Written from a Christian viewpoint, the book does not fail to comment on the anxiety expressed by some evangelicals over Carter's liberal positions on many economic and social issues.

1125. Kurtz, Paul. In Defense of Secular Humanism. Buffalo, NY: Prometheus Books, 1983.

Kurtz, the primary draftsman of the Humanist Manifesto II (1973), defends his human-centered, atheistic philosophy against what he feels are misinformed attempts by fundamentalists to label it a religion, and blame it for the collapse of ethics and morals in America. The text of the Humanist Manifesto II, and update of the 1933 original, is printed in full.

LaHaye, Beverly. I Am a Woman by God's Design. Old Tappan, NJ: Fleming H. Revell, 1980.
(see 1558)

LaHaye, Tim. The Battle for Public Schools. Old Tappan, NJ: Fleming H. Revell, 1983.
(see 1351)

1126. LaHaye, Tim. The Battle for the Family. Old Tappan, NJ: Fleming H. Revell, 1982.

Expanding on the ideas expressed in the weekly television program, "LaHayes on Family Life," Tim LaHaye rails against humanism, and other perceived threats to traditional family structure: the liberal values espoused by the media and public schools, television sex and violence, feminism, materialism, divorce, pornography, drug abuse, rock music, and homosexuality. Christians must fight these evils on the individual level and through legislation.

1127. LaHaye, Tim. The Battle for the Mind. Old Tappan, NJ: Fleming H. Revell, 1980.

The most influential of LaHaye's books, this volume outlines the author's argument that humanists seek to promote atheism and immorality through the media and legal and political avenues. Lists the humanist organizations LaHaye considers most dangerous as well as many of the wakening body of conservative Christian pressure groups. Intended to spur outraged Christians to action.

1128. Lender, Mark Edward. Dictionary of American Temperance Biography: From Temperance Reform to Alcohol Research, the 1600's to the 1980's. Westport, CT: Greenwood Press, 1984.

1129. Liebman, Robert C. and Robert Wuthnow, eds. The New Christian Right: Mobilization and Legitimation. New York: Aldine Publishing Co., 1983.

Sociologists investigate the organizational constructs and ideological imperatives of the New Christian Right. Based on original research.

1130. Linder, Robert D. "The Resurgence of Evangelical Social Concern (1925-75)." In The Evangelicals: What They Believe, Who They Are, Where They Are Changing, eds. David F. Wells and John D. Woodbridge. Nashville: Abingdon Press, 1975.

Traces the ups and downs of evangelicals' social conscience since the First World War. Argues that the recent evidence of social concern is really a return to normality after a thirty year downturn, not a major innovation or reversal of evangelical attitudes.

1131. Lindsell, Harold. The World, the Flesh, and the Devil. Minneapolis: Canon Press, 1973.

Lindsell, one time editor of Christianity Today, offers a practical guide to a variety of Christian ethical responses to an array of individual and social issues.

Lindsey, Hal [with C. C. Carlson]. The Late Great Planet Earth. Grand Rapids: Zondervan, 1970.
(see 1419)

1132. Lockard, David. The Unheard Billy Graham. Waco, TX: Word Books, 1971.

Graham's ethical system is discussed in this very warm review of his message. Concludes that Graham has been unjustly accused of being insensitive to issues of social injustice.

1133. Longenecker, Richard N. New Testament Social Ethics for Today. Grand Rapids: Eerdmans, 1984.

Provides a guide to help resolve modern ethical problems by contrasting historical practice with biblical principle. Major topics addressed include ethnic conflict, slavery, and the role of women.

1134. Luker, Kristin. Abortion and the Politics of Motherhood. Berkeley, CA: University of California Press, 1984.

Examines the development of abortion into a moral and political issue. Well-written and objective, this sociological and historical study concludes that the polarization between anti- and pro-abortion forces is unlikely to dissolve, although the fury of the debate may wane.

Magnuson, Norris. Salvation in the Slums: Evangelical Social Work 1865-1920. Metuchen, NJ: Scarecrow Press, 1977.
(see 655)

1135. McIntire, Carl. Twentieth Century Reformation. Collingswood, NJ: Christian Beacon Press, 1944.

For years Carl McIntire, head of the American Council of Churches, founder of the Bible Presbyterian Church and editor of The Christian Beacon was America's most prominent symbol of the mix of fundamentalist separatism and political conservatism. This is perhaps his best-known book and ably details his feelings about liberals, the NAE, Catholics, pacifists and communists. For a later glimpse of his views on all the above and such evangelical personalities as Billy Graham and Oral Roberts see his Outside the Gate (Christian Beacon Press, 1967).

1136. McIntyre, Thomas J. with John C. Obert. The Fear Brokers: Peddling the Hate Politics of the New Right. Boston: Beacon, 1981.

Extremely detailed description of the rise of the New Christian Right, especially as it happened in New Hampshire, where the author lost a senatorial election to one of its candidates. McIntyre believes that the New Right differs essentially from the old right because its adherents are driven by a quest for status, rather than a desire for economic self-protection. Their disregard for traditional political avenues and structures makes the New Right a threatening entity in a society that takes certain ideas--such as the separation of church and state--for granted.

1137. McLean, Gordon R. and Haskell Bowen. High on the Campus. Wheaton, IL: Tyndale House, 1970.

One of a spate of drug-abuse exposes printed by evangelicals in the early and middle seventies. The authors, who were active in Youth for Christ/Campus Life crusades, rely on anecdotes and newspaper accounts to establish the devastation drugs can bring. Christian faith, they assert, can fill the void young people feel and steer them away from dangerous vices.

McLoughlin, William G. Billy Graham: Revivalist in a Secular Age. New York: Ronald Press, 1960.
(see 1383)

McMillan, Richard C. Religion in the Public Schools: An Introduction. Macon, GA: Mercer University Press, 1984.
(see 1354)

Marsden, George M. Fundamentalism and American Culture: The Shaping of Twentieth Century Evangelicalism, 1870-1925. New York: Oxford University Press, 1980.
(see 656)

1138. Marty, Martin E. "Fundamentalism as a Social Phenomenon." In Evangelicalism and Modern America, ed. George Marsden. Grand Rapids: Eerdmans, 1984.

Lists those qualities that define fundamentalism as a social phenomenon with inherent political aspirations. Attributes the development of the political aspect of the movement to several worldwide trends, including the "retreat from modernity." Marty predicts that fundamentalists will be unable to significantly expand their base of support, even though they will remain in the public eye through the effective manipulation of the media and modern technologies.

1139. Marty, Martin E. The Public Church: Mainline, Evangelical, Catholic. New York: Crossroad, 1981.

Marty terms the religious center of America--mainline Protestant churches, the Catholic Church, and many evangelical churches--the "public church". These institutions respect each other's beliefs and seek to help society without imposing sectarian beliefs on others. Most fundamentalist churches do not belong to the public church because they do seek to force their social and religious code upon others.

1140. Maston, T. B. Segregation and Desegregation: A Christian Approach. New York: Macmillan, 1959.

Explores the twin issues of segregation in society and in the church, concluding that neither situation is acceptable to the Lord. Enjoins Christians to immediately and unreluctantly help blacks achieve equality in all phases of American life.

1141. Menendez, Albert J. Religion at the Polls. Philadelphia: Westminster Press, 1977.

Analyzes voting behavior by religious affiliation and examines the religious factors influencing elections in the twentieth century. Concludes with a chapter on Jimmy Carter's faith and the effect it had on his campaign. This volume can serve as an excellent introduction to understanding the complex relationship of religion and voting behaviors.

Moberg, David O. The Great Reversal: Evangelicalism and Social Concern Rev. ed. Philadelphia: Lippincott, 1977.
(See 444)

1142. Monsma, Stephen V. Pursuing Justice in a Sinful World. Grand Rapids: Eerdmans, 1984.

The author, a former Michigan state legislator, argues that political involvement ought not be neglected by Christians; indeed, activist Christianity is a crucial element in the pursuit of justice. The exigencies of the political world often demand imperfect compromises; it is the duty of the Christian to minimize these.

1143. Monsma, Stephen V. The Unraveling of America. Downers Grove, IL: InterVarsity Press, 1974.

Reformed evangelical Monsma calls for an interventionist government which would intercede to protect the powerless and inject a forceful morality into the international political scene. No specific agenda is outlined; instead, in the wake of Watergate, Monsma attempts to redefine the ideal relationship of government and people from a Christian perspective.

1144. Mooneyham, W. Stanley. What Do You Say to a Hungry World? Waco, TX: Word, 1975.

The president of World Vision International contrasts the wealth of the West with the deprivation of the Third World. His analysis of the cycle of starvation is accompanied by a call for Christian action on behalf of the hungry.

Morgan, Marabel. The Total Woman. Old Tappan, NJ: Fleming H. Revell, 1973.
(see 1522)

1145. Mouw, Richard. Called to Holy Wordliness. Philadelphia: Fortress Press, 1980.

Deals with issues faced by lay people seeking to minister in society by implementing a fully Christian lifestyle. Addressed to an ecumenical audience, the book encourages all Christians to view business, politics, homes, schools, theaters and hospitals--in short, all spheres of life--as settings in which to bear Christian witness.

Mouw, Richard. Political Evangelism. Grand Rapids: Eerdmans, 1974.
(see 875-876)

1146. Nathanson, Bernard N. Aborting America. Garden City, NY: Doubleday, 1979.

The former abortion-performing physician and pro-choice activist explains his complete change of heart. Now a leading spokesman for the pro-life movement (and producer of the controversial film, "The Silent

Scream"), Dr. Nathanson provides an alternately emotional and intellectual appeal for the abolition of abortion.

1147. Nelson, Leonard J., ed. The Death Decision. Ann Arbor: Servant Books, 1984.

Eight Roman Catholics and evangelical Protestants examine the controversial ethics surrounding the "new biology"--abortion, amniocentesis, and euthanasia. Politically and socially conservative.

1148. Neuhaus, Richard John. The Naked Public Square: Religion and Democracy in America. Grand Rapids: Eerdmans, 1984.

Decries the disappearance of religious values from the public sectors of American life, citing this absence for the rise of the New Religious Right as well as a general moral malaise.

1149. Neuhaus, Richard John, ed. Unsecular America. Grand Rapids: Eerdmans, 1986.

Essays by Paul Johnson, Everett Carl Ladd, George Marsden, and the editor examine the interelationship of the secular and religious spheres in America. Followed by a discussion on the same topic by evangelicals, Jews, atheists and mainline Protestants.

1150. Neuhaus, Richard John and Michael Cromartie. Piety and Politics. Washington, DC: Ethics and Public Policy Center, 1987.

Twenty-six essays both by and about evangelicals and fundamentalists. A variety of issues are addressed, including the historical roots of the movement, the conservative agenda, radical liberation theology, and televangelism. Contributors include George Marsden, Carl F.H. Henry, Jerry Falwell, Jim Wallis, William F. Buckley Jr., and Martin E. Marty, among others. An excellent starting point for exploration in this area.

Noll, Mark A., Nathan O. Hatch and George M. Marsden. The Search for Christian America. Westchester, IL: Crossway Books, 1983. (see 450)

1151. Paris, Peter J. The Social Teaching of the Black Churches. Philadelphia: Fortress Press, 1985.

1152. Perkins, John. With Justice for All. Ventura, CA: Regal Books, 1982.

Black evangelical Perkins describes the growth of his Voice of Calvary Ministries, which is helping poor blacks in Jackson, Mississippi transform their lives. Perkins advocates "redistribution," a plan under which wealthy Christians would voluntarily simplify their lifestyles in order to share with the less fortunate.

1153. Pfeffer, Leo. "The 'Religion' of Secular Humanism." Journal of Church and State 29 (Autumn 1987): 495-507.

Fundamentalists often attack public school curricula by asserting that secular humanism is a religion, and thus may not be promoted in the schools. The author reviews recent Supreme Court decisions on public school/religion issues, and notes that until it addresses the question of whether or not secular humanism is indeed a religion, fundamentalists will continue to employ that line of argument.

Pierard, Richard V. "Billy Graham and the U.S. Presidency." Journal of Church and State 22 (Winter 1980): 107-127.
(see 766-767)

1154. Pierard, Richard V. "Religion and the New Right in Contemporary American Politics." In Religion and Politics, ed. James E. Wood, Jr. Waco, TX: Baylor University Press, 1983.

The marriage of conservative politics and the evangelical movement in the 1970s created a potent and creative political force. Contrary to popular belief, however, it is hardly a united entity.

1155. Pierard, Richard V. The Unequal Yoke--Evangelical Christianity and Political Conservatism. Philadelphia: Lippincott, 1970.

Influential denunciation of the alliance of political conservatism and evangelical Christianity. Argues that "selfish interest groups that throttle the Christian witness" must be abandoned in favor of an agenda that addresses the social and economic inequities in American life.

1156. Pippert, Wesley G., ed. The Spiritual Journey of Jimmy Carter--In His Own Words. New York: MacMillan, 1978.

Compilation of Carter's biblically based views on everything from personal sin to governmental principles. Pippert's comments introduce major themes of Carter's thought, especially his reliance on Bible-based ethical behavior.

1157. Quebedeaux, Richard. The Worldly Evangelicals. San Francisco: Harper & Row, 1978.

Sequel to The Young Evangelicals examines the cultural transformations and diverse attitudes found within the evangelical community in the 1970s. Though Quebedeaux treats right-wing evangelicalism in detail, his sympathies clearly lie to the left.

1158. Quebedeaux, Richard. The Young Evangelicals: Revolution in Orthodoxy. New York: Harper & Row, 1974.

Reviews the historical and intellectual roots of contemporary evangelicalism, dividing the movement into four basic groups: Separatist

Fundamentalism, Open Fundamentalism, Establishment Evangelicals, and New Evangelicalism. Quebedeaux, who labels himself an evangelical, predicts that the latter group, with its emphasis on social concern and its rejection of conservative class values, will lead the movement in coming years.

1159. Reagan, Ronald. Abortion and the Conscience of the Nation. Nashville, TN: Thomas Nelson, 1984.

President Reagan affirms his commitment to halt abortion in this unusual essay published while he was in office. His occasionally emotional appeal insists that abortion must be banned not only to save babies, but also to rescue the conscience of the nation. Afterwords by British Christian sage Malcolm Muggeridge and C. Everett Koop, U.S. Surgeon General.

1160. Reichley, A. James. Religion in American Public Life. Washington, DC: The Brookings Institute, 1985.

Stresses the continuing impact that religious beliefs have on political decisions and discusses the legal structures which limit their influence. Shows that the interaction of religion and politics leads to a vigorous and creative public discourse.

1161. Rekers, George A. Growing Up Straight. Chicago: Moody Press, 1982.

Written for parents, this book asserts that homosexuality is the result of choice, not chance, and emphasizes the parental role in the sexual development of children. Dr. Rekers believes that a just, understanding, and kind Christian home will encourage the natural heterosexuality of youngsters.

Ribuffo, Leo P. The Old Christian Right: The Protestant Far Right from the Great Depression to the Cold War. Philadelphia: Temple University Press, 1983.
(see 709)

1162. Ribuffo, Leo P. "God and Jimmy Carter." In Transforming Faith: The Sacred and Secular in Modern American History, ed. M. L. Bradbury and James B. Gilbert. Westport, CT: Greenwood Press, 1989.

Examines Carter's personal beliefs, his relationships with other sectors of the American religious mosaic and the impact of his religious convictions on his policies and popularity with the electorate. Argues that Carter's Southern, born-again beliefs and style made him culturally alien to many Catholic and Jewish Democrats, costing him crucial support in the 1980 election.

1163. Rifkin, Jeremy. The Emerging Order: God in the Age of Scarcity. New York: Putnam's, 1979.

Argues that the erosion of the U.S. economy, government and environment has been caused by the bankrupt liberal ideology and signals the end of its predominance. Charismatics, with their firm belief in the supernatural, and evangelicals, with their intellectual and political commitments, will remodel the old order and bring another Protestant reformation, probably by the year 2000.

1164. Salley, Columbus and Ronald Behm. What Color Is Your God? Downers Grove, IL: InterVarsity Press, 1981.

The authors chart the historic indifference to the black plight by the white churches in America. They suggest that Christianity can redeem itself only if its adherents divorce themselves from racist predilections. Revised edition of the powerful Your God is Too White (1970).

1165. Sandeen, Ernest R., ed. The Bible and Social Reform. Philadelphia: Fortress Press, 1982.

A collection of essays assessing the Bible's role in determining American social attitudes affecting such issues as women's place in the church, peace movements and black churches.

1166. Scanzoni, Letha and Virginia Ramey Mollenkott. Is the Homosexual My Neighbor? San Francisco: Harper & Row, 1978.

Notes that evangelical churches have usually rejected homosexual activity and too often homosexual people as well. This intolerance is contrasted with Jesus' message of love and acceptance of the oppressed. The final chapter offers various ethical systems for gays based on Christian teachings, including one which admits the possibility of a covenantal, monogamous, homosexual relationship.

1167. Schaeffer, Francis A. A Christian Manifesto. Westchester, IL: Crossway Books, 1984.

Prolific evangelical apologist Schaeffer charges that humanism has wrenched American government and society from their Judeo-Christian roots and turned it into the champion of amorality and decadence. He concludes that it is the Christian's duty to resist the state when it flouts God's authority. This jeremiad has radical sound but supports conservative causes.

1168. Schaeffer, Francis A. The Great Evangelical Disaster. Westchester, IL: Crossway Books, 1984.

Schaeffer decries the moral relativism that has infected the evangelical church in the guise of tolerance, homosexuality and other nontraditional lifestyles. Such practices and beliefs are judged to be incompatible with the Bible's norms. Calls for a restoration of the true faith.

1169. Schaeffer, Franky. Bad News for Modern Man: An Agenda for Christian Action. Westchester, IL: Crossway Books, 1984.

Author decries lack of moral leadership by evangelicals, especially those on the left such as Jim Wallis, Ron Sider, and Letha Scanzoni. Calls for a reaffirmation of the absolute truths of Christianity and an unceasing battle against legalized abortion, the amoral media, radical feminism, and related foes.

1170. Shriver, Peggy L. The Bible Vote: Religion and the New Right. New York: The Pilgrim Press, 1981.

Defined the agenda of the New Christian Right of the late 1970s. Lists its representatives and presents comments by both proponents and detractors within and outside the evangelical community.

1171. Shriver, Peggy L. "Religion's Very Public Presence." Annals of the American Academy of Poilitical and Social Science 480 (July 1985): 142-153.

The 1984 presidential campaign underscored the importance of religion and religious themes in both political parties. It also emphasized the difference between those whose religious beliefs lead them to espouse nationalism and individualism and those who nurture a communal faith.

1172. Sider, Ronald J., ed. The Chicago Declaration. Carol Stream, IL: Creation House, 1973.

The Chicago Declaration is an admission that evangelicals have not actively pursued social justice and an avowal to get started. Signed by 53 prominent and not-so-prominent evangelicals, it is reprinted here along with reflections by several of the participants, including Sider, John Howard Yoder, Nancy Hardesty, Jim Wallis, and Carl F. H. Henry.

1173. Sider, Ronald J. Christ and Violence. Scottdale, PA: Herald Press, 1979.

Calls for a reappraisal of Christian teaching on violence, arguing that Christians should have something better to offer than affirmations of the arms race endorsed by capitalism and communism.

1174. Sider, Ronald J. Cry Justice. Mahwah, NJ and Downers Grove, IL: Paulist Press and InterVaristy Press, 1980.

A collection of Bible readings pertaining to God's concern for the poor; economic relationships among God's people; property and possessions; and justice. Sider's passionate calls for socially responsible Christianity are evident in this and other biblically based writings like Rich Christians in an Age of Hunger (InterVarsity Press, 1979).

1175. Sider, Ronald J., ed. Evangelicals and Development: Toward A Theology of Social Change. Philadelphia: Westminster, 1981.

Examines the relationship between evangelism and social ministry abroad. Offers guidelines and critical insight into the problems that wealthy Westerners face when attempting to aid Third World people.

Sider, Ronald J. Rich Christians in an Age of Hunger. Downers Grove, IL: InterVarsity Press, 1977.
(see 1503)

1176. Sider, Ronald J. and Richard K. Taylor. Nuclear Holocaust and Christian Hope. Downers Grove, IL: InterVarsity Press, 1982.

Chilling inventory of the world's nuclear arms arsenal and its potential for destruction is followed by a plan of passive resistance and personal renouncement of violence for concerned Christian peacemakers.

Sine, Tom. The Mustard Seed Conspiracy. Waco, TX: Word Books, 1981.
(see 1504)

1177. Skinner, Tom. Black and Free. Grand Rapids: Zondervan, 1968.

Skinner recounts his transformation from Harlem Lords gang leader to prominent black evangelist. He also attempts to explain the origin of black rage and admonishes white Christians to confront the race issue rather than sidestepping it.

1178. Smarto, Donald. Justice and Mercy. Wheaton, IL: Tyndale House Publishers, Inc., 1987.

Examines reform of the penal system and various alternatives to imprisonment. Urges the Church to give greater attention to ministry among victims and offenders.

1179. Spain, Rufus. At Ease in Zion: A Social History of Southern Baptist, 1865-1900. Nashville: Vanderbilt University Press, 1967.

This analysis by a Southern Baptist of his denomination as a major contributor to the southern social fabric is an excellent introduction to related issues in the twentieth-century South. Southern Baptists, he argues, chose to resist social change rather than to confront the problems with which it confronted them. Includes a useful bibliographic essay.

1180. Sproul, R. C. Lifeviews: Understanding the Ideas that Shape Society Today. Old Tappan, NJ: Fleming H. Revell, 1986.

The author contends that American society is non-Christian and dominated by secularism, existentialism, humanism, pragmatism, positivism, relativism and hedonism. After chapters introducing readers to the sources and symptoms of these ideas, Sproul concludes with biblical perspectives on art, science, literature, economic and government, arguing that these are areas in which Christians need to be "salt" and "light".

1181. Stedman, Elaine. A Woman's Worth. Waco, TX: Word Books, 1975.

Encourages women to liberate themselves from societal pressures and accept God's plan--separate roles for men and women--as a blessing. Wholeness comes through this complementary fulfillment of biblically ordained duties.

1182. Streiker, Lowell D. and Gerald S. Strober. Religion and the New Majority: Billy Graham, Middle America, and the Politics of the 70's. New York: Association Press, 1972.

Asserts that Billy Graham's faith and politics represent those of a "New Majority" in America. Predicts that Graham's influence will increase as middle Americans recognize their political solidarity.

1183. Stringfellow, William. An Ethic for Christians and Other Aliens in a Strange Land. Waco, TX: Word Books, 1973.

Characterizes America as a "fallen nation" and decries the lack of morality as betrayed by the Vietnam War and the tremendous disparity of wealth. Holds that Christians must confront today's Babel with the Word, avoiding any compromise with evil.

1184. Thomas, Cal. Book Burning. Westchester, IL: Crossway, 1983.

Attacks liberal political forces and the media as being the censors of traditional American values in our schools and textbooks. Calls for the open expression of all ideas in the public arena, rather than just those approved of by the secular community. The author, a syndicated columnist, writes from a fundamentalist viewpoint.

1185. Valentine, Foy and Edwin S. Gaustad. A Historical Study of Southern Baptists and Race Relations, 1917-1947. The Baptist Tradition Series. Salem, NH: Ayer Co., 1980.

1186. Viguerie, Richard A. The New Right: We're Ready to Lead. Falls Church, VA: The Viguerie Co., 1980 [rev. ed. 1981].

This was one of the most influential manifestos of the extremely conservative religious right wing that surged in the 1980 elections. Includes statements of purpose, lists of active conservatives and conservative action groups, and smug predictions of the impending death of liberalism. Viguerie masterminded the New Right's very successful direct-mail fund-raising campaign.

Wacker, Grant. "Uneasy in Zion: Evangelicals in Postmodern Society." In Evangelicalism and Modern America, ed. George Marsden. Grand Rapids: Eerdmans, 1984.
(see 779)

1187. Wald, Kenneth D. Religion and Politics in the United States. New York: St. Martins Press, 1987.

Scholarly assessment of the interchange between the religious and political cultures in the United States. The chapter on evangelical Protestants concentrates on the recent re-emergence of their social concern, and their influence on political process. Wald asserts that the New Christian Right will continue to play an important, though not decisive, role in the public arena, and may become a power broker within the Republican party. Extensive bibliography.

Wallis, Jim. Agenda for Biblical People. New York: Harper & Row, 1976.
(see 780-781)

1188. Webber, Robert E. The Secular Saint. Grand Rapids: Zondervan, 1979.

Encouraged evangelicals to help better the lot of the less fortunate through social involvement, rather than withdrawal into pious communities. The seeds of such action were planted by 19th-century evangelists who believed that because Jesus lived among men, Christians must do the same.

1189. Wheeler, Richard S. Pagans in the Pulpit. New Rochelle, NY: Arlington House, 1974.

Wheeler derides the thesis that the church can, or should, be turned to as a guiding force in politics, especially left-wing politics. Several chapters ridicule well-known liberal figures such as Gloria Steinem and Martin Luther King, Jr.

1190. White, John. Eros Defiled: The Christian and Sexual Sin. Downers Grove, IL: InterVarsity, 1977.

Discusses a variety of sexual sins, defined as including--among others--masturbation, homosexuality and adultery. The author recommends vigorous church guidance and individual self-control.

1191. White, John. The Golden Cow--Materialism in the Twentieth Century Church. Downers Grove, IL: InterVarsity, 1977.

Offers primarily anecdotal evidence to support the claim that materialism has become the predominant value in American churches. Calls for a reevaluation of church fund-raising techniques and challenges the wasteful lifestyle led by many prosperous Christians.

1192. Wilder, John B. The Shadow of Rome. Grand Rapids: Zondervan, 1960.

Traces the history of Catholic oppression from the Inquisition through modern times. Typical of the alarmist anti-Catholic literature that thrived in the shadow of John F. Kennedy's candidacy for the presidency.

1193. Wirt, Sherwood Eliot. The Social Conscience of the Evangelical. New York: Harper and Row, 1968.

Contends that evangelical Christians are at last becoming sensitive to social issues after years of ignoring them. Examines several important problems, including racism, environmental destruction, and war, stressing the need for change within the established framework of our society.

Wood, James E. Jr. "The Battle Over the Public School." Journal of Church and State 28 (Winter 1986): 5-14.
(see 1366)

1194. "The Year of the Evangelicals." Newsweek 88 (October 25, 1976): 68-78.

Reports a surge of evangelical religion, and lists a host of political figures who espouse it. Predicts that as the movement grows larger, internal opposing forces will destroy its current cohesion.

Yoder, John Howard. The Politics of Jesus: Vicit Agnus Noster. Grand Rapids: Eerdmans, 1972.
(see 892)

1195. Young, Perry Deane. God's Bullies. New York: Holt Rinehart, 1982.

Extremely hostile assessment of the New Christian Right by a former fundamentalist. Young is particularly sensitive to what he sees as intolerance and ignorance on every level of the movement.

CHAPTER 18
MEDIA AND ENTERTAINMENT

Down through the years American evangelicals have been especially adept at communicating their gospel to the common man. In their efforts they have shown a penchant for utilizing any and all available venues, be they street corners, printing presses or rear bumpers. In no area has this been more true than in the realm of electronic media. Indeed, ever since the 1920s evangelicals have seized upon new communications technologies, from hand-cranked crystal sets to computerized satellite uplinks, with alacrity. The embracing of electronic media has been a major factor in evangelicalism's resurgence, making broadcasters as diverse as Charles E. Fuller, Oral Roberts, and Jerry Falwell into national figures. This phenomenon has been the object of much comment--and often, alarm--among reporters, scholars and societal pundits in recent years. Unfortunately, too much of the analysis has tended to dwell on an inflated estimate of the political implications of televangelism: evangelical use of the mass media is a much broader phenomenon. While it certainly serves as an evangelistic tool it is even more important in its role as a powerful catechizer and--increasingly, as old scruples against worldly entertainment fall by the wayside--as a "baptized" alternative source of radio and television programming, music and film. The books below are a mix of evangelical and non-evangelical, popular and scholarly works that provide a good overview of evangelicals' relationship with the world of media and entertainment.

1196. Abelman, Robert and Kimberly Neuendorf. "How Religious is Religious Television Programming?" Journal of Communication 35 (Winter 1985): 98-110.

Report on a 1983 analysis of religious television's programming content. Looks at the issues addressed on the broadcasts, the quantity and types of various appeals for money, and the political content of the programs.

1197. Allen, Tom. Rock 'N' Roll, the Bible and the Mind. Alberta, Canada: Horizon House, 1982.

Alerts parents and educators to the messages found in rock and roll music, such as the promotion of drug abuse, promiscuity, violence and moral decay. Includes practical suggestions for beleaguered parents.

1198. Allworthy, A. W. [Lorenzo Milan and Jeremy Lansman]. The Petition Against God: The Full Story of the Lansman-Milan Petition. Dallas: Christ the Light Works, 1975.

Milan and Lansman were a pair of eccentric California public broadcasters who in 1973 petitioned the FCC to dispute the right of religious broadcasters to obtain FM licenses on educational wavebands. This petition, RM-2493, was the germ of the infamous "Madalyn Murray O'Hair Rumor" that has motivated over 20,000,000 Americans to write the FCC. Their caustic book includes the full text of the original petition, responses from NRB members, sample letters from the public, and the FCC's final negative response.

1199. Armstrong, Ben. The Electric Church. Nashville: Thomas Nelson Publishers, 1979.

The former director of the National Religious Broadcasters, an evangelical organization, charts the spectacular growth of televangelism in this extremely comprehensive work. Though strongly biased in favor of religious broadcasting, this is an essential source for anyone investigating the topic.

1200. Armstrong, Ben, ed. 1990--The Directory of Religious Broadcasting. Morristown, NJ: National Religious Broadcasters, 1990.

Compendium of religious radio stations, publishers, schools, and programs. This is purely a reference source, and does not include any analysis.

1201. Bachman, John W. Media--Wasteland or Wonderland? Minneapolis, MN: Augsburg, 1984.

Encourages the establishment of federal regulations, consumer boycotts and other action to dilute television's corruptive influence and heighten the quality and diversity of its programs. Analyzes the messages spread by this media from a Christian perspective.

Baehr, Ted with Bruce W. Grimes and Lisa Ann Rice. The Movie and Video Guide for Christian Families. Nashville: Thomas Nelson, 1987.
(See 1508)

1202. Baker, Paul. Contemporary Christian Music: Where It Came From, What It Is, Where It's Going. Westchester, IL: Crossway Books, 1985.

Traces the rise of "CCM" from its beginnings in the Jesus Movement to the advent of "Christian Punk & Heavy Metal" in the early 80s. Part history, part apologetic, part fan notes, the book includes useful appendices and an interesting chart that compares Christian performers with comparable sounding secular artists.

1203. Bakker, Jim and Robert Lamb. Move That Mountain. Plainfield, NJ: Logos International, 1976.

Written for his viewers, this is an early look back at his years working for Pat Robertson at CBN and Paul Crouch at Trinity Broadcasting and the spiritual and financial trials involved in the creation and early expansion of PTL. Interesting look at how Bakker and his ghostwriter viewed both his past and his mission.

1204. Bakker, Jim. Survival: Unite to Live. Harrison, AK: New Leaf Press, 1980.

Televangelist Bakker warns that a host of recent catastrophes--from the eruption of Mt. St. Helens to the Iran hostage crisis--require Christians to unite under the protective cloak of evangelical faith.

1205. Barnhart, Joe E. Jim and Tammy: Charismatic Intrigue Inside PTL. Buffalo, NY: Prometheus Brooks, 1988.

Investigative report on the PTL debacle and other televangelist scandals that damaged the industry in 1987 and 1988. Barnhart emphasizes the packaging of materialism in the wrapping of spiritual values.

1206. Benson, Dennis C. Electric Evangelism. Nashville: Abingdon, 1973.

Intended for church groups and clergy, this book calls for the increased use of all mass media--television, radio, cable TV, etc.--by evangelists. Offers guidelines on how to start an electronic ministry.

1207. Billingsly, K. L. Film: The Seductive Image: A Christian Critique of the World of Film. The Turning Point Christian Worldview Series. Westchester, IL: Crossway Books, 1989.

A critical look at the milieu of film, the values it presents, and its presentation of moral and religious subject matter.

1208. Boone, Pat. A New Song. Altamonte Springs, FL: Creation House, 1970; revised, 1988.

Autobiography with specific focus on the trials and triumphs of the singer and family's spiritual journey. Although Boone's importance has waned, his Hollywood connections and white-bucked All-American boy image made him a highly visible figure on the evangelical scene during the Jesus movement and charismatic renewal of the late 60s and early 70s. Also see his book (co-authored with wife Shirley) The Honeymoon is Over (Creation House, 1977).

1209. Brown, Joan Winmill. No Longer Alone. Old Tappan, NJ: Fleming H. Revell Co., 1975.

Best-selling inspirational autobiography by a well-known British actress who was reborn at a Billy Graham rally. Typical of the genre.

1210. Bryant, Anita. The Anita Bryant Story: The Survival of Our Nation's Families and the Threat of the Militant Homosexuality. Old Tappan, NJ: Fleming H. Revell Co., 1977.

Entertainer Anita Bryant describes her successful campaign to repeal a Miami gay rights ordinance. The threat that legalized homosexuality ostensibly would pose to traditional families and innocent children is detailed, and Christian activists are encouraged to take steps to oppose the trend.

1211. Cardwell, Jerry D. Mass Media Christianity. Lanham, MD: University Press, 1984.

The careers and agendas of prominent televangelists are reviewed in this generally positive overview of religious television. Cardwell argues that televangelism is an efficacious and appropriate way to spread the Word in the modern age.

1212. Cash, Johnny. Man in Black. Grand Rapids: Zondervan, 1975.

Country music singer Cash recounts his childhood in a religious southern town, the backsliding that attended his rise to fame, and his ultimate rebirth into evangelical Christianity.

1213. Dabney, Dick. "God's Own Network." Harpers 261 (August 1980): 33-52.

Harshly critical description of the Christian Broadcasting Network that concentrates on the materialistic values and thin culture displayed by Pat Robertson's talk show and ministry. Dabney predicts that Robertson will thrive as secular culture continues to erode the traditional values of our society.

1214. Ellens, Harold J. Models of Religious Broadcasting. Grand Rapids: Eerdmans, 1974.

A brief history of televangelism is accompanied by an analysis that divides the broadcasts into four primary types according to their message and approach. Now somewhat dated, this book will prove useful only to those seeking a description of the electric church of the 1960s and early 70s.

1215. Elvy, Peter. Buying Time: The Foundations of the Electronic Church. Great Watering, Essex, UK: McCrimmon Publishing Co. Ltd., 1986; Mystic, CT: Twenty-Third Publications, 1987.

Written with an apprehensive eye toward the expansion of the Electronic Church into Europe and the UK. An outsider's sarcastic but probing look at the evolution of American religious broadcasting and the worldwide implications of its access to revolutionary technology.

1216. Eskridge, Larry K. "Evangelical Broadcasting: Its Meaning For Evangelicals." In Transforming Faith: The Sacred and Secular in Modern American History, ed. M. L. Bradbury and James B. Gilbert, 127-139. New York: Greenwood Press, 1989.

Contends that most of the study of evangelical broadcasting has centered on socio-political power questions such as political content, fundraising, and audience size, often ignoring its place within evangelicalism. Argues that within the sub-culture it serves as a symbol of power and status and as a hedge against modernity while fulfilling its primary tasks of promoting evangelism and piety.

1217. Evangelical Action! A Report of the Organization of the National Association of Evangelicals for United Action. By the Executive Committee. Boston: United Action Press, 1942.

Sets forth the agenda of the newly formed National Association of Evangelicals. Includes a report by the NAE's Special Committee on Religious Broadcasting outlining obstacles to evangelical broadcasting posed by the networks and the Institute for Education by Radio.

1218. Falwell, Jerry, ed. How You Can Help Clean Up America. Lynchburg, VA: Jerry Falwell, 1981.

Proposes a variety of strategies to help rid America of "moral pollutants" such as pornography, the Equal Rights Amendment, and the left-wing press. Advocates legal, economic, and religious action in the fight against policies promoted by homosexuals, feminists, secular humanists, and others.

Flake, Carol. Redemptorama: Culture, Politics, and the New Evangelicalism. New York: Penguin Books, 1984.
(see 743)

1219. Fore, William F. Television and Religion: The Shaping of Faith, Values, and Culture. Minneapolis, MN: Augsburg Publishing, 1987.

A good guide to mainline attitudes toward media and evangelical use thereof, written by the National Council of Churches' assistant general secretary for communications. Critical of TV violence, network hegemony, and FCC policies, Fore castigates the Electronic Church as being captive to the commercial broadcasting system. Proposes an alternative "democratic" media strategy for mainline churches and other interest groups.

1220. Frankl, Razelle. Televangelism: The Marketing of Popular Religion. Carbondale, IL: Southern Illinois University Press, 1987.

Exhaustive study traces the roots of televangelism back to the social and religious structures created by the major 19th and early 20th century revivalists. Concludes that televangelists have turned religion into business, and have taken it upon themselves to promote conservative social and economic policies among their vast viewing audience and beyond.

1221. Fuller, Daniel P. Give the Winds a Mighty Voice. Waco, TX: Word Books, 1972.

Written by his son, this loving biography of Charles E. Fuller, the famous radio evangelist and founder of the Fuller Theological Seminary, is a good source of facts on the heyday of radio evangelism.

1222. Gaither, Gloria. Because He Lives. Old Tappan, NJ: Fleming H. Revell Co., 1977.

This autobiographical-inspirational book tells the stories behind the success of the Bill Gaither Trio whose songs have become an important part of contemporary evangelical worship.

1223. Garay, Ronald. "Government Regulation and Religious Broadcast in the Matter of PTL/WJAN." Journal of Church and State 29 (Spring 1987): 269-283.

Explores the tricky church/state issues that were involved in the 1982 Federal Communications Commission's investigation of Jim and Tammy Bakker's PTL ministry. States that the FCC did not require that the ministry adhere to acceptable ethical standards because of its hesitancy to interfere with religious concerns.

1224. Gerbner, George, Larry Gross, Stewart Hoover, Michael Morgan, Nancy Signorielli, Harry E. Cotugno and Robert Wuthnow. Religion and Television: A Research Report by the Annenberg School of Communications. 2 vols. Philadelphia: University of Pennsylvania and the Gallup Organization, 1984.

Massive study of the impact of religious television commissioned by over 30 mainline and evangelical denominations and independent organizations. Examines such topics as its effect on local congregations, size and nature of its audience, program content, and social, political, and sexual attitudes. Presently the benchmark study of religious television.

1225. Green, Melody with David Hazard. No Compromise: The Life Story of Keith Green. Chatsworth, CA: Sparrow Press, 1989.

From the mid-70s until his tragic death in a plane crash in 1982, Keith Green was considered by many music industry insiders to be Contemporary Christian Music's first potential "crossover" star. However, Green resisted marketing and media pressures and committed himself to emphasizing various discipleship and lifestyle issues in his ministry. Written by his wife, this is an interesting look at a unique figure in evangelical popular culture.

1226. Hadden, Jeffrey K. "Religious Broadcasting and the Mobilization of the New Christian Right." Journal for the Scientific Study of Religion 26 (March 1987): 1-24.

Demonstrates that televangelism is an outgrowth of urban revivalism, and has spurred the emergence of the New Christian Right. The political agenda supported by these forces is less a reaction to the leftist victories of the 1960s and 70s than a response to an increasingly troubled America.

1227. Hadden, Jeffrey K. and Anson Shupe. Televangelism: Power and Politics on God's Frontier. New York: Holt & Co., 1988.

Written immediately after Jim and Tammy Bakker's PTL scandal, this book offers a critical assessment of televangelism without succumbing to easy generalizations. Sees religious television as a multifaceted entity with deep roots in American life and virtually limitless influence on the political convictions of millions.

1228. Hadden, Jeffrey K. and Charles E. Swann. Prime Time Preachers: The Rising Power of Televangelism. Reading, MA: Addison-Wesley, 1981.

Unsympathetic examination of the careers and political goals of major televangelists. The authors express concern about their shady financial practices and the enormous power they wield through the sophisticated manipulation of the media. For the popular audience.

Harrell, David Edwin, Jr. Oral Roberts: An American Life. Bloomington, IN: Indiana University Press, 1985.
(See 1379)

1229. Harrell, David Edwin, Jr. Pat Robertson: A Personal, Religious and Political Portrait. San Francisco: Harper & Row, 1987.

Neutral and insightful examination of Robertson's personal life and public image. Discusses his brilliant manipulation of the media and nascent political aspirations. Finds that Robertson is a non-compromiser who is likely to continue to play an important role in American political life for years to come.

1230. Humbard, Rex. To Tell The World. Nashville, TN: Thomas Nelson Publishers, 1980.

Autobiography of the televangelist who, along with Oral Roberts, was among the first generation "superstars" of the Electronic Church. Contains some interesting information on the expansion of his television ministry overseas.

1231. Jennings, Ralph M. "Policies and Practices of Selected National Religious Bodies as Related to Broadcasting in the Public Interest, 1920-1950." Ph.D. diss., New York University, 1968.

Exhaustive look at the beginnings of religious broadcasting, the relationship with Federal regulatory agencies and the networks, and broadcasting efforts of various denominations. Devotes considerable space to fundamentalist/evangelical attempts to gain access to the national airwaves.

1232. Jones, Clarence W. Radio: The New Missionary. Chicago: Moody Press, 1946.

An exhortation to American evangelicals to support new endeavors to spread the Gospel, written by the founder of the world's first missionary radio station, HCJB in Quito, Ecuador. Important for understanding the imperatives behind evangelicals' use of the broadcast media. See also the book by Paul Freed, founder of Transworld Radio, Let the Earth Hear (Thomas Nelson, 1980).

1233. Larson, Bob. The Day the Music Died. Carol Stream, IL: Creation House, 1972.

Renowned for his crusades against rock music, radio evangelist Larson claims that this music "represents a blatant form of idolatry for many teenagers" (p. 192), and can inspire a host of serious vices.

1234. Lawhead, Steve. Rock Reconsidered. Downers Grove, IL: InterVarsity Press, 1981.

Defends the genre by asserting that the Christian has a right and a duty to discriminate between good and sinful artists and songs by himself. Rejects old theories that posit rock music as a vehicle for atheism, immorality and Satanism; and rhythm as a source of violent and sexual feelings.

1235. Loveless, Wendell P. Manual of Gospel Broadcasting. Chicago: Moody Press, 1946.

A how-to book with advice on announcing, promotion, production, programming and spiritual preparation for religious broadcasting. Written by a long-time station manager of the Moody Bible Institute's WMBI. Contains sample scripts of various program types.

1236. Martin, William. "Perspectives on the Electric Church." In Varieties of Southern Religious Experience, ed. Samuel S. Hill. Baton Rouge, LA: Louisiana State University Press, 1988.

Evaluation of the size of religious television's audience concludes that this medium suffers from built-in liabilities that limit its growth and that many current estimates of its influence are grossly inflated.

1237. Myers, Kenneth A. All God's Children and Blue Suede Shoes: Christians and Popular Culture. The Turning Point Christian Worldview Series. Westchester, IL: Crossway Books, 1989.

Seeks to educate evangelicals about the origins, assumptions, and influence of popular culture in modern society. Calls for evangelicals to stand apart from the larger society in a more judicious use of popular culture and a renewed emphasis on more thoughtful forms of art and entertainment.

1238. Millard, Bob. Amy Grant: A Biography. Garden City, NJ: Doubleday and Company, 1986.

Written for her fans, this book charts the meteoric career of the first Gospel Music artist to sell a million copies of a single album and its first legitimate "crossover" star. Makes much of Grant as the symbol of a more confident, independent, and sexier "New Christian Woman."

1239. Muggeridge, Malcolm. Christ and the Media. Grand Rapids: Eerdmans, 1977.

Since his declaration of Christian faith in the 1960s, the former BBC personality and editor of Punch has been an oft-quoted commentator in certain American evangelical circles. Here, Muggeridge bites the hand that fed him and argues that television is a delusion-inducing monster with destructive tendencies.

1240. Nason, Donna and Michael Nason. Robert Schuller: The Inside Story. Waco, TX: Word Books, 1983.

An anecdotal biography by a former Schuller staffmember. While smacking of popular hagiography, it nonetheless provides insight into Schuller's career, personality, and philosophy.

1241. Olasky, Marvin. Prodigal Press: The Anti-Christian Bias of the American News Media. The Turning Point Christian Worldview Series. Westchester, IL: Crossway Books, 1989.

Olasky, a professor of journalism at the University of Texas, argues that the American media elite are characterized by a secular mindset and a sometimes blatant bias against religion (particularly Christianity) in its news coverage and content.

1242. Ostling, Richard N. "Evangelical Publishing and Broadcasting." In Evangelicalism and Modern America, ed. George Marsden. Grand Rapids: Eerdmans, 1984.

Chronicles the impressive expansion of communications industries sponsored by and for evangelicals, especially in publishing, journalism, radio and television. Notes that this growth complements the development of many separate institutions for the evangelical community in the last four decades.

1243. Owens, Virginia Stem. The Total Image. Grand Rapids: Eerdmans, 1980.

Deplores televangelism and calls for a return to the intimacy of traditional fellowship and the disavowal of secular technology to transmit spiritual messages.

1244. Parker, Everett C., David Barry and Dallas Smythe. The Television-Radio Audience and Religion. New York: Harper and Row, 1955.

Commissioned by the National Council of Churches, this early analysis concentrates primarily on the composition of the TV audience and the content of the broadcasts. Specifically evangelical concerns are not the main focus, though they are addressed tangentially.

1245. Rabey, Steve. The Heart of Rock and Roll. Old Tappan, NJ: Fleming H. Revell, 1986.

A glitzy, fan-oriented book that provides valuable information on ten major "Christian Rock" artists of the mid-1980s including Amy Grant, Stryper, Mylon Lefevre and Petra.

1246. Robertson, Pat [with Jamie Buckingham]. Shout It from the Housetops. Plainfield, NJ: Logos International, 1972.

Robertson's autobiography covers his youth, conversion, calling, and the development of his TV ministry, culminating in the establishment of the Christian Broadcasting Network. Informal and homey.

1247. Robison, James. America: Garden of the Gods. Atlanta: Cross Roads, 1976.

Televangelist Robison reminds Christians that they must worship God rather than succumb to the temptations of a sinful society.

1248. Roozen, David, guest editor. Review of Religious Research 29 (December 1987).

Special issue devoted entirely to analyses of religious television. A variety of topics are explored, including such essays as "The Religious Television Audience: A Matter of Significance or Size?" by Stewart M. Hoover, "The Social Significance of Religious Television" by Robert Wuthnow and "Why Do People Watch Religious Television" by Robert Abelman.

1249. Schuller, Robert H. I Am the American Flag. [pamphlet]. 1972.

Transcript of a sermon in which Schuller, speaking as if he were the American flag, exhorts citizens to be proud of their country and to renew their faith in God. Schuller is prominent televangelist and founder of the Garden Grove Community Church, the first drive-in church in the world.

1250. Schultze, Quentin J. Television: Manna From Hollywood? Grand Rapids: Zondervan, 1986.

Aimed at a popular evangelical audience, Manna is a generally critical analysis by a professor of communications at Calvin College that seeks to educate evangelicals about the hidden messages and agendas in various contemporary television genres.

1251. Schultze, Quentin J. "The Mythos of the Electronic Church." Critical Studies in Mass Communication 4 (1987): 245-261.

Probes the appeal of broadcast evangelism to conservative American Protestants by looking at the rhetoric of media evangelists and the National Religious Broadcasters. Defines a "mythos of the electronic church" based on a mixture of American technological utopianism, evangelical theology, and a Christian idea of progress.

1252. Schultze, Quentin J. "Evangelical Radio and the Rise of the Electronic Church, 1921-1948." Journal of Broadcasting & Electronic Media 32 (Summer 1988): 289-306.

An examination of the crucial, long-overlooked role of early fundamentalist radio pioneers such as Charles E. Fuller and Walter A. Maier in developing the programming, promotional, and fundraising techniques that paved the way for modern televangelism.

1253. Schultze, Quentin J., ed. Evangelicals, the Mass Media, and American Culture. Grand Rapids: Zondervan, 1990.

A collection of scholarly articles on the history and development of evangelicals' relationship with mass media in its many forms down through the years. Provides a good overview of evangelicals' traditional affinity for using the mass media.

1254. Shepard, Charles E. Forgiven: The Rise and Fall of Jim Bakker and the PTL Ministry. New York: Atlantic Monthly, 1989.

An excellent example of investigative journalism by the reporter who broke the Jessica Hahn story for The Charlotte Observer. Shepard, who won a 1988 Pulitzer Prize for his reporting, delves into Jim Bakker's past and the bizarre mix of piety, materialism and hypocrisy at PTL.

1255. Stewart, John. Holy War: An Inside Account of the Battle For PTL. Enid, OK: Fireside Publishing and Communications, 1987.

A chronology of the Bakker debacle written by a California lawyer/religious broadcaster involved in the early stages of the Jessica Hahn-PTL "settlement." Useful but thin and often repetitious.

1256. Straub, Gerard Thomas. Salvation for Sale. Buffalo, NY: Prometheus Books, 1986.

Anecdotal description of Pat Robertson and his ministry written by a former "700 Club" producer and ex-fundamentalist. Straub portrays Robertson as a demanding, rigid, intellectually simple man who imagines himself to be in direct communication with God. Warns that these characteristics could potentially have a disastrous effect if Robertson were to be elected president.

1257. Swindoll, Charles B. Strengthening Your Grip. Waco, TX: Word Books, 1982.

Internationally known evangelist and author of many best-selling Christian books, Swindoll takes aim at the spiritual apathy of the 1980s. Biblical reference, anecdotes and pep talks provide the reader with a guide to priorities in this "aimless" decade.

1258. Williams, Don. Bob Dylan: The Man, the Music, the Message. Old Tappan, NJ: Fleming H. Revell, 1985.

Written for fans, this book outlines the career and philosophy of the Jewish rock and roll star who announced his conversion to Christianity in 1979. Glossy photographs and analyses of his lyrics are included. Published before Dylan's subsequent disavowals and enigmatic statements.

1259. Wright, J. Elwin. The Old Fashioned Revival Hour and the Broadcasters. Boston: The Fellowship Press, 1940.

Written for the faithful, this book nonetheless provides an interesting glimpse of the life and early career of fundamentalist radio pioneer Charles E. Fuller. Contains numerous letters from listeners and a listing of stations carrying the "Old Fashioned Revival Hour."

SECTION V: EVANGELICAL IMPULSES

Edith L. Blumhofer

CHAPTER 19
EVANGELISM

Evangelism has played a central role in American evangelicalism, and it is an activity supported by a vast literature offering both motivation and practical advice. Evangelicals have exploited modern technology and exercised considerable creativity in devising techniques for evangelism and principles for church growth. "How-to" manuals offer instructions for addressing virtually any situation.

Several evangelical movements and programs have gained national prominence for such evangelistic efforts as "I Found It" and "Evangelism Explosion." Nationally-known evangelists like Charles Fuller and Billy Graham have given the evangelistic message wide visibility. The lives and writings of such people reveal much about evangelical attitudes toward American culture. An older stress on the proclamation of the gospel has been complemented during the past decade by an emphasis on lifestyle evangelism and the devising of new strategies for accomplishing world evangelization. The following books and articles address the questions evangelicals deem important and introduce the people and plans that have helped shape the way evangelicals approach the task of witnessing to their faith.

1260. Aldrich, Joseph. Life-Style Evangelism: Crossing Traditional Boundaries to Reach the Unbelieving World. Portland, OR: Multnomah, 1983.

A popular exhortation to develop a Christian lifestyle that attracts others to faith in Christ and therefore facilitates evangelism.

Bayly, Joseph. The Gospel Blimp. Elgin, IL: David C. Cook Publishing, 1960
(see 1021)

Benson, Dennis C. Electric Evangelism. Nashville: Abingdon, 1973.
(see 1206)

1261. Bright, Bill. A Movement of Miracles. San Bernardino, CA: Campus Crusade for Christ, 1977.

An account of the founding, message and method of Campus Crusade for Christ by its popular founder, Bill Bright, with emphasis on the ministry's highly visible "I Found It" evangelistic campaign/promotion during the 1970s. Bright's earlier Come Help Change the World chronicled Campus Crusade's early years. His Witnessing Without Fear describes personal evangelism as a way of life.

1262. Cailliet, Emile. Young Life. New York: Harper & Row, 1963.

A sympathetic, popular account of the Young Life movement's outreach to teenagers.

1263. Cho, Paul Y. More Than Numbers. Waco, TX: Word Books, 1984.

The pastor of the world's largest congregation shares basic principles of church growth. In Successful Home Cell Groups, he amplified this strategy which facilitated the rapid growth of his congregation.

1264. Coleman, Robert E. The Master Plan of Evangelism. Old Tappan, NJ: Fleming H. Revell, 1963.

This book by a prominent evangelical writer on evangelism introduced the message his later books amplified: evangelism is the product of a relationship with Christ, and its goal is to produce disciples. This book has become an evangelical classic on the subject and is an excellent introduction to the assumptions and goals that motivate evangelicals to the task of evangelism.

1265. Dayton, Edward R. and David Fraser. Planning Strategies for World Evangelization. Grand Rapids: Eerdmans, 1980.

Using management concepts, Dayton and Fraser develop a strategy for world evangelism. Their work represents both the strong contemporary evangelical focus on cross-cultural communication and the evangelical use of modern technology and method.

1266. Dorsett, Lyle. Billy Sunday and the Redemption of Urban America. Grand Rapids: Eerdmans, 1990.

This is the first biography of Billy Sunday to appear in thirty years. Because the author had access to Sunday family papers unavailable to previous biographers, he sheds new light on Sunday's personality and the dynamics of his relationship with his wife, children, and co-workers. The result is a portrait that neither cosmetizes Sunday's faults nor exaggerates his strengths.

1267. Douglas, J. D., ed. Let the Earth Hear His Voice. Minneapolis: World Wide Publications, 1975.

A study of the Lausanne Congress of 1974, this book indicates the strategies, message and theology of evangelism endorsed by many American evangelicals. It contains the plenary papers and special reports to the Lausanne Congress.

1268. Douglas, J. D., ed. The Calling of An Evangelist: The Second International Conference for the Itinerant Evangelists-1986. Minneapolis, MN: World Wide Publications, 1986.

The second of two books (the first was The Work of an Evangelist) recording the proceedings of two conferences for itinerant evangelists sponsored by the Billy Graham Association in Amsterdam. A compendium of worldwide evangelical theology and methodology on the subject.

1269. Ellison, Craig, ed. The Urban Mission. Grand Rapids: Eerdmans, 1974.

This collection of essays by such prominent evangelicals as Ron Sider and William Pannell offers insights into the evangelical sense of mission to urban America.

1270. Engel, James F. and Wilbert H. Norton. What's Gone Wrong with the Harvest? A Communications Strategy for the Church and World Evangelization. Grand Rapids: Zondervan, 1975.

Analyzing the frequent inability of evangelicals to communicate cross-culturally, these two educators urge the importance of assessing an audience's capacity for recognizing spiritual needs and understanding the gospel. This book is a succinct introduction to problems evangelicals perceive as they approach evangelism.

1271. Fish, Roy. Every Member Evangelism for Today. San Francisco: Harper & Row, 1976.

This updating of J. E. Connant's classic published in the 1920s, Every Member Evangelism, challenges all evangelicals to bear vocal witness to their faith.

1272. Ford, Leighton. Good News is for Sharing. Elgin, IL: Cook Publishing, 1977.

The convener of the Lausanne I and II analyzes common hesitations about personally sharing the Christian faith, clarifies biblical teaching and offers practical advice about evangelism.

Frady, Marshall. Billy Graham: A Parable of American Righteousness. Boston: Little, Brown & Co., 1979.
(see 744)

Fuller, Daniel P. Give the Winds a Mighty Voice. Waco, TX: Word Books, 1972.
(see 1221)

1273. Graham, Billy. How to be Born Again. Waco, TX: Word Books, 1977.

A succinct summary of Graham's essential message about the practical process of the new birth and Christian growth. See also Graham's Peace

With God and World Aflame, both of which present the gospel as the only hope of the world.

1274. Green, Michael. Evangelism in the Early Church. Grand Rapids: Eerdmans, 1970.

This important evangelical book traces the development of the church through its first 250 years. A critical analysis of evangelism strategy and method in the early church is supplemented by commentary on the church's strengths and weaknesses. Green's Evangelism Now and Then (InterVarsity, 1982) should also be consulted. Both offer well-researched information as well as indications of how evangelicals use the early church as a model.

Hadden, Jeffrey K. and Anson Shupe. Televangelism: Power and Politics on God's Frontier. New York: Holt & Co., 1988.
(see 1227)

Hadden, Jeffrey K. and Charles E. Swann. Prime Time Preachers: The Rising Power of Televangelism. Reading, MA: Addison-Wesley, 1981.
(see 1228)

1275. Henderson, Robert. Joy to the World: An Introduction to Kingdom Evangelism. Atlanta: John Knox Press, 1980.

This challenge to evangelicals to apprehend fully the present meaning of the kingdom of God includes a focus on congregational life and on the Sermon on the Mount as the essence of the Christian message.

1276. Hendricks, Howard. Say It With Love. Glendale, CA: Gospel Light, 1972.

A distinguished professor at Dallas Theological Seminary discusses personal witnessing.

1277. Hesselgrave, David J. Communicating Christ Cross-Culturally. Grand Rapids: Zondervan, 1978.

Acclaimed by evangelicals as the best treatment of the subject, this book has a popular companion volume, Planting Churches Cross-Culturally.

1278. Huston, Sterling W. Crusade Evangelism and the Local Church. Minneapolis: World Wide, 1984.

A guide to preparing for evangelistic crusades written by the director of Billy Graham's crusades.

1279. Hyles, Jack. Let's Build an Evangelistic Church. Murfreesboro, TN: Sword of the Lord, 1962.

A prolific pastor of one of America's largest churches describes an aggressive approach to evangelism. His pattern was widely accepted in independent fundamental Baptist churches.

Jones, Lawrence N. "The InterVarsity Christian Fellowship in the United States." Ph.D. diss., Yale University, 1961.
(see 756)

1280. Keith, Billy. W. A. Criswell: The Story of a Courageous and Uncompromising Christian Leader. Old Tappan, NJ: Fleming H. Revell, 1973.

Hagiography, but provides insights into Criswell's message and charisma.

1281. Kennedy, James. Evangelism Explosion. Rev. ed. Wheaton, IL: Tyndale House, 1983.

A practical and enormously popular "how to" manual for mobilizing laypersons to evangelize. Kennedy formulated the Evangelism Explosion program for his Coral Ridge Presbyterian Church in Ft. Lauderdale, and its dramatic success catapulted this book to prominence among evangelicals.

1282. Little, Paul. How to Give Away Your Faith. Lombard, IL: InterVarsity, 1966.

A practical primer on evangelism by an InterVarsity staff member.

1283. Mouw, Richard. Political Evangelism. Grand Rapids: Eerdmans, 1973.

Mouw urges evangelicals to accept the political consequences of a commitment to Christ. Evangelism, he argues, is the task of confronting sin with the gospel. Thus the church that bears witness in society will find itself at odds with cultural assumptions: evangelism has social and political as well as personal consequences.

1284. Newbigin, Lesslie. The Open Secret. Grand Rapids: Eerdmans, 1978.

This prominent ecumenical spokesman challenges the church to reconsider the nature, authority and goal of its world mission. He develops a trinitarian foundation for the church's mission--proclaiming the Father's kingdom; sharing the Son's life; bearing the Spirit's witness--and urges Christians to be prepared to state their faith in meaningful terms in a changing cultural context. See also Newbigin's Sign of the Kingdom (Eerdmans, 1980).

1285. Packer, J. I. Evangelism and the Sovereignty of God. Downers Grove, IL: InterVarsity Press, 1961.

These reflections on theological and biblical notions of evangelism and sovereignty by a prominent evangelical theologian are written in popular style and emphasize the Christian responsibility to bear effective witness.

1286. Pippert, Rebecca. Out of the Salt Shaker and Into the World. Downers Grove, IL: InterVarsity Press, 1979.

This popular book about lifestyle evangelism represents a growing evangelical concern about overemphasis on strategies and techniques. Pippert examines Christ's lifestyle and urges the evangelistic potential of Christ-centered living.

1287. Pollock, John. To All the Nations: The Billy Graham Story. San Francisco: Harper & Row, 1985.

A well-known evangelical biographer, Pollock examines major episodes from Graham's evangelistic career in a sympathetic, non-critical style.

1288. Quebedeaux, Richard. I Found It! The Story of Bill Bright and the Campus Crusade. San Francisco: Harper & Row, 1979.

A fascinating account of Bright's vision for taking evangelical Christianity to college campuses, this book offers a penetrating analysis of Bright's spirituality and identifies him as a central figure in the contemporary evangelical resurgence.

1289. Rice, John R. Soul-Winner's Fire. Chicago: Moody Press, 1941.

Eight chapters offering inspiration, encouragement and challenge to evangelism. Reveals the biblical basis for popular fundamentalist assumptions about "soul winning."

1290. Rudin, A. James and Marvin R. Wilson, eds. A Time to Speak: The Evangelical-Jewish Encounter. Grand Rapids: Eerdmans; Austin, TX: Center for Judaic-Christian Studies, 1987.

Essays and responses by prominent evangelicals and Jews. Part of an ongoing dialogue between representatives of the two groups, the essays deal with theology, lifestyles and mutual understanding. Includes a useful introductory bibliography.

1291. Trotman, Dawson. Born to Reproduce. Lincoln, NE: Back to the Bible, 1957.

The founder of the Navigators summarizes a philosophy and method of evangelism.

1292. Wagner, C. Peter. Church Growth and the Whole Gospel. New York: Harper and Row, 1981.

Wagner, a popularizer of Donald McGavran's principles of church growth and long-time faculty member at Fuller Theological Seminary, maintains that the church growth movement supports the whole gospel. Defending the movement from charges that it neglects social justice concerns and endorses materialism, he maintains that evangelism must be central to the church's mission and argues that some social issues are appropriate for congregational consideration whereas others are better addressed through other structures. Wagner's other influential books on the subject include Your Church Can Grow; Your Church Can Be Healthy; and Our Kind of People.

1293. Watson, David. I Believe in Evangelism. Grand Rapids: Eerdmans, 1976.

Watson urges evangelicals to pursue personal renewal so that their evangelism will flow from their own spiritual vitality. This is a well-written statement of a frequently urged evangelical viewpoint. Published as part of the "I Believe" series edited by Michael Green, this book examines biblical principles for evangelism in the local church with an emphasis on evangelism as the natural result of a vital relationship with God.

1294. Wilkerson, David with John and Elizabeth Sherill. The Cross and the Switchblade. New York: B. Geis Associates; distributed by Random House, 1963.

This powerful narrative of David Wilkerson's encounter with drug addicts in New York City documents the emergence of Teen Challenge, an Assemblies of God home missions outreach to substance-addicted youth. The book also helped trigger the emergence of the Catholic charismatic movement. It was made into a movie and offers insights into evangelical motivation and method for evangelism.

1295. Wimber, John with Kevin Springer. Power Evangelism. San Francisco: Harper & Row, 1986.

Wimber, a well-known advocate of healing and deliverance ministries, wrote this book that reached the top of the British religious bestseller lists within weeks of its publication, to extend his message about the power as well as the truth of the gospel. He argues that "signs and wonders" should be evangelistic tools to attract non-believers to the gospel.

1296. Woods, C. Stacey. The Growth of a Work of God. Downers Grove, IL: InterVarsity Press, 1978.

The story of InterVarsity Christian Fellowship, sympathetically told.

CHAPTER 20
FOREIGN MISSIONS

Twentieth-century evangelicals remain committed to world evangelization, and their efforts have met with dramatic success. While much of Christianity's recent growth as a world religion must be attributed to indigenous evangelization, the ranks of North American Protestant missionaries continue to grow, and missionaries play important roles in church extension in many lands.

The missionary impulse is reflected in many types of literature. Inspirational and motivational books, biographies and testimonies articulate the spirituality and eschatology that motivate evangelical missions. Strategies for church planting and church growth have become increasingly prominent since World War II. Traditional histories document the activities of specific agencies abroad. Despite the predominance of evangelicals in the American missionary force today, relatively little scholarly attention has been paid to evangelical missions since 1920. The works cited here are culled from many in an attempt to suggest the range of approaches and to introduce both key statements and key participants in the twentieth-century evangelical attempt to articulate an exportable Christianity.

1297. Anderson, Gerald H., comp. Bibliography of the Theology of Missions in the Twentieth Century. 2nd ed, revised and enlarged. New York: Missionary Research Library, 1960.

1298. Anderson, Gerald H., ed. The Theology of the Christian Mission. Nashville: Abingdon Press, 1961.

Twenty-five prominent scholars reflect on the biblical basis for mission, the history of missions, the relationship between Christianity and other faiths, and mission theory. Ranging in viewpoint from Paul Tillich to Harold Lindsell, they offer stimulating observations about the source and nature of the church's mission. An extensive (though dated) bibliography is included.

1299. Beaver, R. Pierce. American Protestant Women in Missions. 2nd ed. Grand Rapids: Eerdmans, 1980.

A well-known study of selected female missionaries, this was among the first studies to acknowledge the prominence and leadership of women in foreign missions. Beaver implied that women missionaries were motivated by and contributed to feminism. Recent studies challenge this, but this book remains significant.

1300. Boyd, Nancy. Emissaries: The Overseas Work of the American YWCA, 1895-1970. New York: The Woman's Press, 1986.

Boyd details the expansion of overseas YWCA efforts, noting how these differed from women's missionary societies' outreaches by early departing from sectarian goals and adopting broad social agendas. Boyd traces the evolution of the YWCA from its evangelical Protestant roots to an agency employing women of all faiths as emissaries of Christ, American womanhood and the global women's movement.

1301. Carmichael, Amy. God's Missionary. 12th reprint. Fort Washington, PA: Christian Literature Crusade, 1963.

British missionary to India Amy Carmichael achieved wide and enduring popularity in the United States through her writings. Like most of her books, this has a devotional thrust as it challenges missionaries to understand the full meaning of "separation to God for service."

Carpenter, Joel A. and Wilbert Shenk, eds. Earthen Vessels: American Evangelicals and Foreign Missions. Grand Rapids: Eerdmans, 1989. (see 429)

1302. Crawley, Winston. Global Mission–A Story to Tell. Nashville: Broadman Press, 1985.

A popular survey of Southern Baptist world missions.

1303. DeRidder, Richard. God Has Not Rejected His People. Grand Rapids: Baker, 1977.

An examination of evangelism among Jews. DeRidder has also written My Heart's Desire for Israel--Reflections on Jewish-Christian Relationships and Evangelism Today (1974).

1304. Dowdy, Homer Earl. The Bamboo Cross. Harrisburg, PA: Christian Publications, 1964.

The story of Christian and Missionary Alliance efforts in Viet Nam, detailing the implications of prolonged strife and encounter with communism for both the indigenous church and missionary personnel.

1305. Elliot, Elisabeth. Shadow of the Almighty: The Life and Testament of Jim Elliott. New York: Harper & Brothers, 1958.

1306. Elliot, Elisabeth. Through Gates of Splendor. New York: Harper & Brothers, 1957.

Elliot was the wife of Jim Elliot when he and four missionary companions were killed in the jungles of Ecuador by Auca Indians in 1956. These moving accounts of her husband's rigorously but also attractively pious life, and of the martyrdom itself, did much to convince insiders and outsiders alike of the genuine idealism remaining in the evangelical movement.

Fairbank, John K., ed. The Missionary Enterprise in China and America. Cambridge, MA: Harvard University Press, 1974.
(See 396)

1307. Glover, Robert Hall. The Progress of World-Wide Missions. New York: George H. Doran Co., 1924.

The best-known and most widely used evangelical survey of missions before 1945.

1308. Goff, James R., Jr. Fields White Unto Harvest: Charles F. Parham and the Missionary Origins of Pentecostalism. Fayetteville: The University of Arkansas Press, 1988.

The first scholarly look at a pivotal pentecostal leader, this book maintains that pentecostalism is to be understood primarily as a missionary movement. Well-written and insightful, it contains a valuable bibliography.

1309. Harder, Ben. "The Student Volunteer Movement for Foreign Mission and Its Contribution to Twentieth Century Missions." Missiology 8 (1980): 141-154.

A sympathetic and superficial overview of the growth and mission of the Student Volunteer Movement.

1310. Hesselgrave, David J. Planting Churches Cross-Culturally. Grand Rapids: Baker, 1980.

Influenced by Fuller Seminary's Institute for Church Growth. A "how-to" manual offering a master plan for church planting in non-Christian areas.

1311. Hill, Patricia R. The World Their Household: The American Woman's Foreign Mission Movement and Cultural Transformation, 1870-1920. Ann Arbor, MI: University of Michigan Press, 1985.

Missionary societies organized by women and sending out women as missionaries flourished at the end of the nineteenth century. Hill suggests that something like 3,000,000 American women were members of over forty such bodies. Their mission was to Christianize and civilize the world, a mission which was, however, undercut by 1920, when progress in removing some of the most scandalous marks of incivility around the world combined with more liberal notions of the faith to redirect the energies of what had once been a very important means for mobilizing womens' religious energies.

1312. Hodges, Melvin. The Indigenous Church. Springfield, MO: Gospel Publishing House, 1953.

A widely read statement of this time honored ideal in foreign missions by an Assemblies of God missionary.

1313. Hunter, Jane. The Gospel of Gentility: American Women Missionaries in Turn-of-the-Century China. New Haven, CT: Yale University Press, 1984.

Hunter's argument is that women found spheres of usefulness in China that were often closed to them in the United States. At the same time, the Victorian tinge characterizing the American evangelicalism of the period always left some ambiguity between what these women did almost naturally in China and what traditions kept them from doing in the States.

Hutchison, William R. Errand Into the World: American Protestant Thought and Foreign Missions. Chicago: University of Chicago Press, 1987.
(See 406)

1314. Jacobs, Sylvia. A Biographical Dictionary of Black American Missionaries in Africa, 1770-1970. New York: Garland Publishing, 1981.

Jacobs, Sylvia M., ed. Black Americans and the Missionary Movement in Africa. Westport, CT: Greenwood Press, 1982.
(see 481)

Jones, E. Stanley. Abundant Living. Nashville: Abingdon, 1942.
(see 1452)

1315. Kane, J. Herbert. A Global View of Christian Missions from Pentecost to the Present. Grand Rapids: Baker, 1971.

This comprehensive look at Christian missions by the foremost evangelical missionary scholar of the post-1945 era traces the history of missions from the time of Christ through 1800. The bulk of the remaining text is devoted to a global survey, country by country, summarizing the history, peoples, religions and Christian missions in each. His 20-page bibliography is a valuable guide to the literature. Among Kane's other writings are the widely used Christian Missions in Biblical Perspectives (Baker, 1976), Understandably Christin Missions (Baker, 1974) and A Concise History of Christian World Mission (Baker, 1978).

1316. King, Paul L. "Early Alliance Missions in China." In The Birth of a Vision, eds. David F. Hartzfeld and Charles Nienkirchen. Beaver Lodge, Alberta: Buena Book Services, 1986.

The Christian and Missionary Alliance supported an ambitious missionary program in China, and Paul King recounts the story of this part of the network of faith missions that have augmented the ranks of Americans abroad for the past century.

1317. Koop, Allen V. American Evangelical Missionaries in France, 1945-1975. Lanham, MD: University Press of America, 1986.

This study chronicles the dynamic surge of evangelical missionary effort that flowed from experiences during World War II, but also the difficulties evangelicals experienced in adapting American enthusiasm to French culture.

1318. Kuhn, Isobel. By Searching. London: Overseas Missionary Fellowship, 1957.

A China Inland Mission missionary, Kuhn intertwined devotional thoughts and autobiographical details in popular evangelical books. This one is largely autobiographical, but it is also a typical story of the struggle to internalize the ideals of the "higher Christian life" and then to translate them into a practical spirituality.

Lueking, F. Dean. Mission in the Making: The Missionary Enterprise Among Missouri Synod Lutherans, 1846-1963. St. Louis, MO: Concordia Publishing House, 1964.
(see 509)

1319. McGavran, Donald A. The Bridges of God: A Study in the Strategy of Missions. London: World Dominion Press; New York: Friendship Press, 1955.

Contrasts different approaches to missions, focusing especially on a people-oriented approach and a mission-station emphasis. This was followed by How Churches Grow (Friendship Press, 1959) and McGavran's most comprehensive treatment of church growth theory Understanding Church Growth (Eerdmans, 1970).

1320. McGee, Gary B. This Gospel Shall be Preached: A History and Theology of Assemblies of God Foreign Missions. 2 vols. Springfield, MO: Gospel Publishing House, 1986, 1989.

An institutional history focusing on Assemblies of God structure and missions personnel.

1321. Niklaus, Robert, et. al. All for Jesus: God at Work in the Christian and Missionary Alliance Over One Hundred Years. Camp Hill, PA: Christian Publications, Inc., 1986.

This history of the Christian and Missionary Alliance--an early evangelical faith mission and higher Christian life association--is non-critical and written in popular style. Directed toward the Alliance constituency it is nonetheless valuable as a succint introduction to Alliance history, objectives and programs. The early chapters by John Sawin chronicling founder A. B. Simpson's vision for evangelism constitute the best assessment of Simpson available to date.

1322. Padilla, C. Rene, ed. The New Face of Evangelism. Downers Grove, IL: InterVaristy Press, 1976.

A symposium on the Lausanne Covenant, reflecting third-world and some American evangelical concerns for an identity that made room for social justice and cultural integrity.

1323. Pomerville, Paul. The Third Force in Missions. Peabody, MA: Hendrickson, 1986.

An assessment of the contributions of the pentecostal movement to foreign missions by a one-time Assemblies of God missionary.

1324. Speer, Robert. Christ and Life. New York: Fleming H. Revell, 1901.

Secretary of the Presbyterian Board of Foreign Missions for 46 years and an active layman, Speer was also prominent in launching the Student Volunteer Movement for Foreign Missions. An evangelical deeply committed to evangelism, Speer was also a prolific author. This book summarizes his understanding of the Christian faith and life.

1325. Stott, John R. W. Christian Mission in the Modern World. Downers Grove, IL: InterVarsity Press, 1975.

Examines the biblical meaning of key words in contemporary debates about Christian mission in an attempt to move beyond stalemate to reconciliation around the biblical text.

1326. Taylor, Howard and Geraldine Taylor. Hudson Taylor's Spiritual Secret. London: China Inland Mission, 1932.

A condensed and adapted version of the authors' two-volume biography of Taylor. The book is inspirational as well as informative, detailing practical ways in which the spirituality that nurtured Taylor shaped the China Inland Mission.

1327. Taylor, Mary. Borden of Yale '09: The Life That Counts. London, Philadelphia, Toronto: China Inland Mission, 1926.

A classic, tracing the story of a young missionary who died en route to his station. Captures the pulse of the pre-World War I student missionary movement and has devotional power as a depiction of higher life spirituality.

1328. Taylor, Mary and Frederick Howard Taylor. By Faith: Henry Frost and the China Inland Mission. Philadelphia: China Inland Mission, 1938.

A biography of the North American secretary of the China Inland Mission, this book details his remarkable spiritual pilgrimage and therefore offers insights into the dynamics of "higher Christian life" views and their implication for missions. This book is a classic that is at once narrative and inspirational in style.

1329. Taylor, Mary and Frederick Howard Taylor. Hudson Taylor and the China Inland Mission: The Growth of a Work of God. Edinburgh: R & R Clarke, Limited, 1912.

A well-written and fascinating survey of how Taylor's vision for China gave form to the China Inland Mission. The authors, Taylor's son and daughter-in-law, also convey the spirituality which characterized Taylor. The book is a classic, revealing details about a major evangelical voluntary association, the personality of a widely revered evangelical leader, and the spirituality of the "higher Christian life" and Keswick movements.

1330. Taylor, Mary Guiness. The Triumph of John and Betty Stam. Philadelphia: China Inland Mission, 1935.

An evangelical classic describing the martyrdom in China of two missionaries serving under the China Inland Mission. Reveals the practical power of the "higher Christian life" teaching which the Stams and their mission embraced.

1331. Thomas, T. V., Murray W. Downey and Ken Draper. "A. B. Simpson and World Evangelization." In The Birth of a Vision, eds. David F. Hartzfeld and Charles Nienkirchen. Beaverlodge, Alberta: Buena Book Services, 1986.

An examination of the sources of the Christian and Missionary Alliance foreign missions agenda, detailing the Alliance founder's understanding of the task, his method and his goals.

1332. Tucker, Angeline. He is in Heaven. New York: McGraw-Hill, 1965.

A missionary biography describing evangelical outreach in the Belgian Congo and the heroic death of Assemblies of God missionary J. W. Tucker during the political turmoil that followed independence. Typical of a genre.

1333. Tucker, Ruth. From Jerusalem to Irian Jaya: A Biographical History of Christian Missions. Grand Rapids: Zondervan, 1983.

Tucker uses biography to recount the history of missions. Her book, Guardians of the Great Commision: A History of Women in Modern

Missions (Zondervan, 1988) studies the impressive contributions of women to the missionary enterprise.

1334. Zwemer, Samuel M. "Into All the World": The Great Commission, A Vindication and an Interpretaion. Grand Rapids: Zondervan, 1943.

Zwemer, Professor of the History of Religion and Christian Missions at Printecton Theological Seminary, was an evangelical missions authority, founder of a journal, The Muslim World, and premier representative of a scholarly evangelical approach to missions theology.

CHAPTER 21
RELIGIOUS EDUCATION

Twentieth-century evangelicals are deeply concerned about some aspects of religious education and less certain about others. Deploring the alleged secular humanism of public school systems, they have created thousands of Christian schools which, some scholars argue, are functioning as civilizing instruments in the evangelical world. On the other hand, Sunday schools--which were once perceived as evangelistic outreaches--are regarded as nurseries of the church, and although they remain popular in many places, declining commitment to the Sunday school is a marked feature of much recent evangelical life. Supplemented (and sometimes replaced) by life groups, home Bible studies and cell groups, Sunday schools have suffered in both enrollment and support.

The following books represent both classic evangelical approaches to Christian education and scholarly studies of evangelical educational institutions. They document changing approaches and abiding values.

1335. Baldwin, Ethel May and David V. Benson. Henrietta Mears and How She Did It. Glendale, CA: Regal Books, 1966.

An inspirational look at the life of an influential Christian educator whose work in Sunday school curricula led to the founding of Gospel Light Publications.

1336. Benson, Clarence. The Sunday School in Action. Chicago: Moody Press, 1941.

As director of the Moody Bible Institute's Christian education program, Clarence Benson exerted a wide influence on evangelical Sunday schools. An active promoter of graded Sunday school lessons and vacation Bible schools, Benson was also instrumental in the founding of Scripture Press, a major evangelical publisher of Christian education materials. This book summarizes his views on the Sunday school. These helped define an evangelical alternative to the progressive education strategies adopted by mainstream Protestant Sunday school agencies early in the twentieth century.

1337. Boylan, Anne M. Sunday School: The Formation of an American Institution. New Haven, CT: Yale University Press, 1989.

Boylan shows convincingly that the nineteenth-century Sunday School was a complex institution, important both for spreading evangelical faith and for promoting a synthesis of Christian and American values.

1338. Brigham, Judith. A Historical Study of the Educational Agencies of the Southern Baptist Convention, 1845-1945. New York: Columbia University Teachers College. Contributions to Education Series: No. 974. Reprint of 1951 ed. AMS Press.

1339. Carper, James C. and Thomas C. Hunt. Religious Schooling in America. Birmingham: Religious Education Press, 1984.

This collection of essays by 11 contributors examines both historical insights and contemporary concerns in religious elementary education. A chapter by James Carper on Christian day schools offers a penetrating analysis of a burgeoning movement.

1340. Cully, Iris V. and Kendig Brubaker Cully, eds. Harper's Encyclopedia of Religious Education. New York: Harper and Row, 1990.

1341. Davis, Billie. Teaching to Meet Crisis Needs. Springfield, MO: Radiant Books, 1984.

Directed especially to those involved in local church education programs, this book urges evangelicals to come to grips with the social crises that people in local congregations face.

1342. Eavey, C. History of Christian Education. Chicago, IL: Moody Press, 1964.

A sympathetic overview of the broad spectrum of Christian education from its Jewish roots to such American forms as vacation Bible schools and Protestant day schools.

1343. Gaebelein, Frank E. Christian Education in a Democracy. New York: Oxford, 1951.

This book by a prominent evangelical educator calls for standards in Christian education and addresses the challenge to integrate faith and learning.

1344. Gangel, Kenneth and Warren Benson. Christian Education: Its History and Philosophy. Chicago, IL: Moody Press, 1982.

In this survey of Christian education from the Hebrew academies to current settings, the authors stress the Jewish backgrounds, the early church and the eighteenth and nineteenth centuries to demonstrate the historical currents that have influenced contemporary views.

1345. Hakes, J. Edward, ed. An Introduction to Evangelical Christian Education. Chicago: Moody Press, 1964.

Hakes surveys Christian education in evangelical settings and analyzes its methodology and challenges.

1346. Hefley, James. Textbooks on Trial. Wheaton, IL: Victor Books, 1976.

A chatty and sympathetic account of Mel and Norma Gabler's surprisingly successful crusade to rid the Texas public schools of "objectionable textbooks." Their criteria for disapproving texts and the extent of their political activities are covered in detail.

1347. Hunt, Thomas C., James C. Carper and Charles R. Kniker. Religious Schools in America: A Selected Bibliography. New York: Garland Publishing, 1986.

This is a definitive bibliography which offers general coverage of subjects related to religion and schooling. It considers faith traditions separately.

1348. Joy, D. Meaningful Learning in the Church. Winona Lake, IN: Light and Life Press, 1969.

This readable, popular guide for Sunday school teachers and other church educators is typical of the spate of literature produced by evangelical presses to equip lay workers.

1349. Kennedy, William Bean. "Toward Reappraising Some Inherited Assumptions About Religious Education in the United States." Religious Education 76:5 (September-October, 1981): 476-481.

Analyzes longheld assumptions and urges their adaptation and/or replacement by new models and strategies that address contemporary realities.

1350. LeBar, Lois. Education That is Christian. Westwood, NJ: Fleming H. Revell Company, 1958.

This philosophy of Christian education by a woman who played a prominent role in the post-World War II evangelical Sunday School resurgence remains popular among evangelicals for its creative, insightful approach to the teaching/learning process. It has been widely used as an example of the evangelical approach to Christian education.

1351. LaHaye, Tim. The Battle for Public Schools. Old Tappan, NJ: Fleming H. Revell, 1983.

LaHaye, a best-selling fundamentalist sage, argues that secular humanism, the rejection of discipline, the collapse of moral values and the spread of sex education have all betrayed American youth. Public education must be retrieved from the hands of the humanists, and strong values and healthy competition restored to the schools.

1352. Lynn, Robert W. and Elliott Wright. The Big Little School: 200 Years of the Sunday School. 2nd rev. ed. Nashville: Abingdon, 1980.

Written originally to commemorate the 200th anniversary of the Sunday school movement, this small book by two able historians is informative and well documented. It offers insights into the reasons for widespread evangelical impatience with the direction of the national Sunday school agencies dominated by mainstream denominations and helps explain the proliferation and growth of evangelical Sunday school agencies in the twentieth century.

1353. Mason, Harold. Abiding Values in Christian Education. Westwood, NJ: Fleming H. Revell, 1955.

Mason's book remains popular for its statement of the principles and purposes of church education programs, a task Mason considered further in his The Teaching Task of the Local Church (Light and Life Press, 1960).

1354. McMillan, Richard C. Religion in the Public Schools: An Introduction. Macon, GA: Mercer University Press, 1984.

Comprehensive review of the relationship of religion and government as it pertains to the public schools. Concludes that the study of religion is an important secular, as well as spiritual, pursuit, which should not be neglected in the public schools curricula.

1355. Menendez, Albert J. School Prayer and Other Issues in American Public Education: A Bibliography. Garland Reference Library of Social Science, Vol. 291. New York: Garland Publishing, Inc., 1985.

1356. Moore, Richard and Dorothy. Homegrown Kids. Waco, TX: Word Publishing House, 1984.

Representative of evangelical literature advocating home schooling to assure the preservation of Christian values.

1357. Parsons, Paul F. Inside America's Christian Schools. Macon, GA: Mercer University Press, 1987.

Written in anecdotal style, this is a journalist's look at the reasons for the rapid growth in the number of Christian schools and the rationales that sustain them.

1358. Peshkin, Alan. God's Choice: The Total World of a Fundamentalist Christian School. Chicago: University of Chicago Press, 1986.

Peshkin writes with an anthropologist's sensitivity about the Christian school he studied for well over a year. He analyzes the moral and polemical values that led parents to select this education for their children and that children came to express in response to their schooling.

1359. Pride, Mary. The Big Book of Home Learning: The Complete Guide for Everything Educational for You and Your Child. Westchester, IL: Crossway, 1986.

In recent decades, evangelicals have opted in growing numbers for home schooling. This handbook is typical of the genre of literature supporting that trend.

1360. Richards, Lawrence. A Theology of Christian Education. Grand Rapids: Zondervan, 1975.

Larry Richards has been an imposing figure in evangelical Christian education since the 1970s. Forsaking earlier formal models for Christian education, he urges a discipleship model rooted in his emphasis on renewal. His practical advice on educational strategies for local churches has given him a large evangelical following. He has written extensively on many facets of local church ministry: A Theology of Children's Ministry (Zondervan, 1985); Creative Bible Teaching (Moody Press, 1970); Youth Ministry: Its Renewal in the Local Church (rev. ed., Zondervan, 1985).

1361. Rose, Susan D. Keeping Them Out of the Hands of Satan: Evangelical Schooling in America. New York: Routledge, 1988.

Part of the Critical Social Thought series edited by Michael W. Apple, this book focuses on two evangelical groups--a fundamentalist Baptist congregation and an independent charismatic fellowship--to examine both the innovative and reactionary elements in the Christian school movement. Contains a helpful bibliography.

1362. Seymour, Jack L. From Sunday School to Church School: Continuities in Protestant Christian Education in the United States, 1860-1929. Washington, DC: University Press of America, 1982.

An examination of the functions and interpretations of the role of Sunday schools in American culture. Traces the Sunday school's course from missions outreach to nursery of the church. The notes provide excellent bibliographical direction.

1363. Steward, David S. "Doctoral Dissertation Abstracts in Religious Education, 1878-1979." Religious Education 75 (July-August, 1980): 474-494.

1364. Wagner, Melinda Bollar. God's Schools: Choice and Compromise in American Schools. New Brunswick, NJ: Rutgers University Press, 1990.

Wagner's fascinating study of the culture within Christian schools takes issue with Peshkin's thesis that such schools are exclusivist "total institutions" and argues instead that they blend elements of popular culture, professional education culture and Christian culture.

1365. Wolterstorff, Nicholas P. Educating for Responsible Action. Grand Rapids: Eerdmans, 1980.

A penetrating assessment of theory and practice in moral education in an effort to determine responsible Christian ways to shape how children act.

1366. Wood, James E. Jr. "The Battle Over the Public School." Journal of Church and State 28 (Winter 1986): 5-14.

Wood argues that anger over secular humanism and the teaching of evolution mask a misplaced attack on the schools themselves as a cause of spiritual decline among youth. The author insists that installation of religious values should take place in the private sectors of society.

CHAPTER 22
REVIVAL AND RENEWAL

The wistful yearning, "revive us again," has characterized most evangelicals throughout the century. The longing for national revival as well as for personal renewal has found expression in the movement's hymnody and devotional literature. The holiness, pentecostal and charismatic segments of evangelicalism regard themselves as revival movements, and their understanding of the Holy Spirit has prompted debate about appropriate manifestations of revival. Nonetheless, the desire for renewal permeates all evangelical sectors. It manifests itself in a wide variety of literary forms, some of which are noted below. Inspirational books, biographies and stories of past revivals motivate evangelicals to hope for renewal. The list also includes studies of renewal and revival movements by historians and sociologists.

1367. Bennet, Dennis. Nine O' Clock in the Morning. Plainfield, NJ: Logos International, 1970.

In 1959, an Episcopalian rector, Dennis Bennet, spoke in tongues. Before long, both Time and Newsweek reported his experience and thus helped give visibility to the emerging charismatic renewal. This book recounts Bennet's transforming encounter with pentecostal teaching and examines the practical implications of the experience. A valuable primary source on the emergence of the charismatic movement, this achieved wide circulation.

1368. Blumhofer, Edith L. "Pentecost in My Soul": Explorations in the Meaning of Pentecostal Experience in the Early Assemblies of God. Springfield, MO: Radiant Books, 1989.

Examines early pentecostal spirituality, and introduces excerpts from primary sources describing the personal and public meaning of pentecostal experience. Pentecostals first perceived their movement as end-times revival that would sweep the church in preparation for Christ's second coming.

1369. Blumhofer, Edith L. and Randall Balmer, eds. Modern Christian Revivals. Urbana: University of Illinois Press, 1990.

This collection of essays on modern revivals is a volume presenting the proceedings of a conference on revivals sponsored by the Institute for the Study of American Evangelicals at Wheaton College. It includes among others contributions by Randall Balmer (Pietism); Gerald Moran (Puritan America); John Boles (the South); David Bebbington (England); Edith Blumhofer (Pentecostalism); David Edwin Harrell (Graham to Robertson); Daniel Bays (China); Everett Wilson (Latin America).

Cairns, Earle E. An Endless Line of Splendor: Revivals and their Leaders from the Great Awakening to the Present. Wheaton, IL: Tyndale, 1986.
(see 428)

1370. Christenson, Larry, ed. Welcome Holy Spirit: A Study of Charismatic Renewal in the Church. Minneapolis, MN: Augsburg, 1987.

Christenson is a Lutheran charismatic whose extensive preaching and writings have gained him a prominent place in the charismatic renewal. In this book he and others examine apsects of renewal, discussing its extent, theology and challenges.

1371. Criswell, W. A. The Baptism, Filling and Gifts of the Holy Spirit. Grand Rapids: Zondervan, 1973.

Presents a standard anti-charismatic view of such common pentecostal practices as tongues speech and healing. An excellent introduction to basic differences between large segments of evangelicalism.

1372. DuPlessis, David J. The Spirit Bade Me Go. Rev. ed. Plainfield, NJ: Logos, 1970.

A collection of papers--both autobiographical and theological--by a prominent figure in the charismatic renewal. Offers insights into the encounter between classical and charismatic pentecostals and reveals the tensions that characterized early encounters between pentecostals and ecumenists.

1373. Dupuis, Richard and Garth Roselle, eds. The Memoirs of Charles G. Finney: The Complete Restored Text. Grand Rapids: Zondervan 1988.

This classic, for the first time available in its original unabridged form, has inspired and motivated revivalistic evangelicals of all sorts for over a century.

1374. Enroth, Ronald M., Edward E. Ericson and C. Breckenridge Peters. The Jesus People: Old-Time Religion in the Age of Aquarius. Grand Rapids: Eerdmans, 1972.

Comprehensive and insightful, this work documents the mores, roots, faith and culture of the Jesus People movement with photographs and descriptions of specific churches and sects.

1375. Finney, Charles G. Lectures on Revivals of Religion. New York: Leavitt, Lord & Co., 1835.

The most widely published and influential collection of Finney's writings, these lectures have both motivated evangelicals to anticipate and work toward revival and provided a standard for measuring spirituality and effective witness.

1376. Finney, Charles G. The Promise of the Spirit. Timothy L. Smith, ed. Bethany House Publishers, 1980.

A representative collection of Finney's writings on the Holy Spirit, with an introduction by historian Timothy L. Smith. Smith traces the evolution of Finney's language to describe Spirit baptism showing how it shifted from describing the purifying experiences to an emphasis on empowering.

1377. Hamilton, Michael, ed. The Charismatic Movement. Grand Rapids: Eerdmans, 1975.

Here are ten thoughtful, well-researched essays on the theology, history, ecclesiastical effects, and American expressions of the charismatic gifts, edited by an Episcopal canon. Some of the contributors are charismatic, some are not, but all are judicious in their interpretations. Of particular interest are chapters on the history of tongues speech (George Williams and Edith L. Waldvogel); black pentecostals (Lawrence N. Jones) and the holiness movement in Southern Appalachia (Nathan L. Gerrard).

1378. Harrell, David Edwin Jr. All Things Are Possible: The Healing and Charismatic Revivals in Modern America. Bloomington: Indiana University Press, 1975.

Explores a little-studied segment of evangelicalism that has thrived through much of this century. This study offers penetrating insights into the personalities, issues and appeal of twentieth-century healing movements. Meticulously documented, it introduces the reader to the vast array of popular literature and theology spawned by charismatic healing revivalists.

1379. Harrell, David Edwin Jr. Oral Roberts: An American Life. Bloomington: Indiana University Press, 1985.

A major scholarly biography of one of America's best-known evangelicals, this book offers valuable insights into the character of popular rural pentecostal evangelicalism between the world wars as well as the rise of pentecostals and charismatics to prominence in the past forty years.

1380. Hughes, Richard T. and Leonard C. Allen. The Worldy Church. Abilene, TX: Abilene Christian University, 1988.

Critical look at the contemporary state of Churches of Christ and a call for renewal through mature reappropriation of heritage.

1381. Lovelace, Richard F. Renewal as a Way of Life: A Guidebook for Spiritual Growth. Downers Grove, IL: InterVarsity Press, 1985.

Historical and theological reflections on spiritual renewal, its preconditions, religious and social affects, and potential pitfalls.

1382. MacArthur, John. The Charismatics. Grand Rapids: Zondervan, 1980.

Anti-charismatic polemic by a leading independent fundamentalist; this book is an example of one brand of evangelical opposition to the mushrooming pentecostal movement.

1383. McLoughlin, William G. Billy Graham: Revivalist in a Secular Age. New York: Ronald Press, 1960.

This early serious biography of Graham attributes his huge popularity to the American propensity for revivalism and Graham's own attractiveness as a symbol of traditional, moderately conservative, American values.

1384. McLoughlin, William G. Billy Sunday Was His Real Name. Chicago: University of Chicago Press, 1955.

This was one of the earliest "outsider" accounts of Sunday, probably the best-known figure in American religion during the first third of the twentieth century, and certainly one of the most active itinerant revivalists. McLoughlin has solid material on Sunday as a cultural phenomenon, but sheds less light on the spiritual motives that drove Sunday and his audiences.

1385. McLoughlin, William G., Jr. Modern Revivalism: Charles Grandison Finney to Billy Graham. New York: Ronald Press Company, 1959.

An early attempt to chart continuities in the tradition of northern revival, McLoughlin writes with appreciation concerning the energy, the dedication, and the savvy of his subjects, but with less attention to the spiritual dynamics affecting their work.

1386. McLoughlin, William G. Jr. Revivals, Awakenings, and Reform: An Essay on Religion and Social Change in America, 1607-1977. Chicago and London: University of Chicago Press, 1978.

This important essay applies Anthony F.C. Wallace's definition of "revitalization movements", in which a culture seeks to adjust its ideology to match new behavioral norms, to the periodic upheavals of religious feeling in the United States. McLoughlin examines four great awakenings, the last one consisting of the radical youth movement that started in the 1960s. He dismisses the coeval resurgence of Protestant revivalism as a "traditionalist and backward-looking" (p. 187) movement that offers no innovative answers to a new age.

1387. Nash, Ronald, ed. Evangelical Renewal in the Mainline Churches. Westchester, IL: Crossway Books, 1987.

This book introduces evangelical renewal movements that are currently active among Presbyterians, Methodists, Episcopalians, Congregationalists, and other "old-line" Protestant denominations.

1388. Orr, James Edwin. "Evangelical Awakenings in Collegiate Communities." Ph.D. diss., University of California at Los Angeles, 1971.

1389. Orr, James Edwin. The Flaming Tongue: The Impact of Twentieth Century Revivals. Chicago: Moody Press, 1973.

Orr, an academic, an itinerant evangelist, and an indefatigable chronicler of revival, surveys the many and varied Christian awakening movements; The Flaming Tongue chronicles those of the twentieth century throughout the world, most of them evangelical or pentecostal in some form or the other.

1390. Poloma, Margaret M. The Charismatics: Is There a New Pentecost?. Boston: G. K. Hall, 1982.

This fine book by a sociologist and renewal participant analyzes the charismatic renewal. Well written and amply documented, it offers perceptive insights.

1391. Quebedeaux, Richard. The New Charismatics II: How a Christian Renewal Movement Became Part of the American Religious Mainstream. New York: Harper and Row, 1983.

This book, a thorough revision of Quebedeaux's New Charismatics (1976), details the process by which the expression of charismatic gifts moved from the margins of American religion among pentecostals, then to an uncertain status impinging upon other Protestants, and finally to a place of prominence in the life of American Protestantism.

1392. Ravenhill, Leonard. Why Revival Tarries. Minneapolis: Bethany House, 1979.

A call to revival that has sold hundreds of thousands of copies. Written in popular style and interspersed with biblical references, this book attempts to arrest spiritual apathy and prod evangelicals toward spiritual authenticity. Revival "tarries," says Ravenhill, because evangelism is commercialized and grace is cheap. An advocate of the "inner life," Ravenhill endorsed a spirituality similar to A. W. Tozer's.

1393. Revival in Our Time: The Story of the Billy Graham Evangelistic Crusades. Wheaton, IL: Van Kampen Press, 1950.

Accounts of early Graham crusades by prominent evangelicals who participated at various levels. Includes six of Graham's sermons.

1394. Roberts, Richard Owen. Revival. Wheaton, IL: Tyndale House Publishers, Inc., 1982.

This brief popular analysis of the meaning and experience of revival includes a valuable selected bibliography.

Schaeffer, Francis. The Church at the End of the Twentieth Century. Downers Grove, IL: InterVarsity Press, 1970.
(see 1502)

1395. Sherrill, John. They Speak With Other Tongues. Old Tappan, NJ: Fleming H. Revell, 1966.

Traces Sherrill's encounter with the charismatic movement through his own experiences of baptism with the Holy Spirit. Useful as both a primary and a secondary source.

1396. Sims, Patsy. Can Somebody Shout Amen!: Inside the Tents and Tabernacles of American Revivalists. New York: St. Martin's Press, 1988.

This fascinating look at the lives and beliefs of seven revivalists is culled from the author's experiences journeying through the back roads of the South to participate in revivals. The book is a revealing account of the ethos and nature of popular revivals as well as of the personalities who dominate them.

1397. Trueblood, Elton. The Company of the Committed. New York: Harper and Row, 1961.

This book by a well-known Quaker calls for Christians to move from the pews into the world as a "valiant band for Christ" to undertake the renewal of the church and society.

Wallis, Jim. The Call to Conversion and Recovering the Gospel for These Times. San Francisco: Harper & Row, 1981.
(see 1505)

Warner, Wayne E., ed. Touched by Fire: Eyewitness Accounts of the Early Pentecostal Revival. Plainfield, NJ: Logos, 1978.
(see 682)

1398. Weisberger, Bernard A. They Gathered at the River: The Story of The Great Revivalists and Their Impact upon Religion in America. Boston and Toronto: Little, Brown and Company, 1958.

A look at the modernization of revivalistic techniques from the turn of the 19th century through Billy Sunday. Although writing in the late 1950s, Weisberger wonders if revivalism can find a new voice geared to "modern" America or, if its day was over...hadn't he heard about Billy Graham?

CHAPTER 23
PROPHECY

Speculation about eschatological topics such as death, judgment, heaven, the Second Coming, and the Kingdom of God are universal within the Christian experience. Among American evangelicals, however, these reflections have tended to focus more narrowly around the anticipation of Christ's Second Coming. From the prophecy conferences of the late 19th century to the phenomenal sale of books like the Late Great Planet Earth in the 1970s, the evangelical enthusiasm for the apocalyptic has been a vital *leitmotif* in evangelical theology and life, strengthening its constituency in both numbers and resolve. One of the most noteworthy and distinctive prophetic viewpoints among modern evangelicals is dispensational premillennialism, a position first systematized by John Nelson Darby (1800-1882), an Irish Plymouth Brethren Bible teacher. The doctrines began to influence American evangelicals after the Civil War and as the years followed, premillennialism played a growing role in the evangelistic and devotional life of the subculture. The doctrine has experienced fluctuations in its popularity over the years--often coinciding with times of national and international crisis--with its most recent upswing occurring during the 1960s and 1970s. However, as one might expect with such a diverse movement, there are a wide variety of beliefs on prophetic matters. Not all, or maybe even most, contemporary evangelicals adhere to dispensational premillennialism or know it well as a system. Still, its advocacy by some of the movement's most visible spokespersons, denominations, and institutions has made many outsiders, and not a few insiders, automatically associate the belief as characteristic of all evangelicals. The works cited below, most of a popular nature, are a sampling of the extensive literature on both dispensationalism and other significant viewpoints represented within the wider evangelical movement.

1399. Anderson, Robert. The Coming Prince, or, the Seventy Weeks of Daniel With an Answer to the Higher Criticism. 5th ed. London: Hodder & Stoughton, 1895.

Written by a British barrister and one-time Assistant Commissioner of Police for London, The Coming Prince's complicated mathematical and astronomical analysis of the prophecy of the "Seventy Weeks" in Daniel 9:25-27 has been cited as conclusive proof of the Bible's, and dispensationalism's, supernatural accuracy by generations of evangelical authors dealing with prophetic themes.

1400. Armstrong, Herbert W. The United States and British Commonwealth in Prophecy. Pasadena, CA: Ambassador College, 1967.

Although he is viewed as a cultist by both evangelicals and fundamentalists, the late Herbert W. Armstong's British-Israelism, if not the aberrant theology of his Worldwide Church of God, represent a tie to a few within the subculture. This volume is representative of his views.

1401. Bass, Clarence B. Backgrounds to Dispensationalism: Its Historic Genesis and Ecclesiastical Implications. Grand Rapids: Eerdmans, 1960.

A Calvinist critic of dispensationalism, Bass traces the system's origins, claiming its teachings are an un-historic departure from the Church's traditional views and a cause of needless separatism.

1402. Bauman, Louis S. Light From Bible Prophecy. New York: Fleming H. Revell, 1940.

Distilled from a popular series of articles in the Sunday School Times, this book provides a good look at fundamentalist prophetic speculation about the likes of Hitler, Mussolini and Stalin.

1403. Blackstone, William E. (W.E.B.). Jesus is Coming. New York: Fleming H. Revell, 1898.

W.E. Blackstone played a key role in the promotion of both U.S. and World Zionism among gentiles at the turn of the century. What spurred him on, however, were his premillennial beliefs. His most significant achievement was the small volume Jesus is Coming. This book, translated into dozens of languages, was perhaps the most widely-read dispensationalist work of the early 20th century and was instrumental in spreading evangelical beliefs and dispensational teaching at the popular level.

1404. Branson, Roy. The End of the World. 2 vols. Lancaster, CA: Landmark Publications, 1988.

Provides a revealing look at contemporary eschatological speculation among today's ultra-conservative fundamentalists. Sensational chapters include conjectures about such topics as the "Resurrected Brains of the Unsaved Dead."

1405. Boyd, Frank M. Ages and Dispensations. Springfield, MO: Gospel Publishing House, 1935.

Aimed at the laity as part of the Assemblies of God's Christian Worker's Training Course, Ages and Dispensations is illustrative of the traditionally dispensational teachings of this increasingly important pentecostal denomination.

1406. Cantelon, Willard. The Day the Dollar Died. Plainfield, NJ: Logos Publishing, 1974.

Drawing upon the public's concern in the late 60s and early 70s over such issues as runaway inflation, the centralization of credit records, the impact of computerization, the population explosion and food and fuel shortages, this popular bestseller interpreted world events in light of biblical prophecies foretelling one-world government and the rise of the AntiChrist.

1407. Davis, John Jefferson. Christ's Victorious Kingdom: Postmillennialism Reconsidered. Grand Rapids: Baker, 1986.

Davis, an associate professor of systematic theology and Christian ethics at Gordon-Conwell Theological Seminary, reintroduces the concept of postmillennialism, a viewpoint that was anathema for decades, to a popular evangelical audience. Davis' interest in the subject, spurred by the growth of the Church in the Third World as well as his own respect for earlier postmillennial evangelicals such as Edwards and Warfield, is indicative of a growing trend within the ranks of the evangelical elite which may well filter down to the popular level.

1408. De Haan, M. R. The Jew and Palestine in Prophecy. Grand Rapids: Zondervan, 1950.

The establishment of the state of Israel in 1948 created much excitement among evangelicals. The return of the Jews to their ancient homeland, it was believed, was the final missing piece of the dispensationalist prophetic puzzle needed before the Rapture. This book by Dr. De Haan, the "beloved physician" who founded the widely-syndicated "Radio Bible Class," is typical of the literature on this topic at that time. For further examples see William L. Hull, The Fall and Rise of Israel (Zondervan, 1954); and Louis T. Talbot and William W. Orr, The New Nation of Israel and the Word of God! (Bible Institute of Los Angeles, 1948).

1409. Feinberg, Charles L., ed. Prophecy and the Seventies. Chicago: Moody Press, 1971.

This volume is an inclusive, and represenative, sampling of dispensationalist prophetic analysis at the beginning of the 1970s. Drawn from the Diamond Jubilee Congress on Prophecy of the American Board of Missions to the Jews held in May 1970 in New York, the book highlights four major topics: Christ and the prophetic scriptures, the Church and the prophetic scriptures, Israel and the prophetic scriptures, and the nations and the prophetic scriptures. Featured authors include Feinberg, Stephen F. Olford and John F. Walvoord.

1410. Gaebelein, Arno C. The Conflict of the Ages: The Mystery of Lawlessness, Its Origin, Historic Development and Coming Defeat. New York: "Our Hope" Publishing Office, 1933.

Arno C. Gaebelein, a prominent missionary to the Jews and editor of Our Hope magazine, was a prolific author on prophetic themes. In this book he traces the satanic line of descent running through the Illuminati, the French Revolution, Marx and the Bolsheviks. Takes a special look at Communist activities in America and the alleged complicity of mainline liberals.

1411. Graham, Billy. Approaching Hoofbeats: The Four Horseman of the Apocalypse. Waco, TX: Word Books, 1983.

Graham's book on the Four Horsemen of the Apocalypse spent months on both The New York Times and Christian Bookseller Association's best-seller lists. His analysis and sermonizing reflect not only the growing concern of evangelicals over issues of social responsibility including the environment, nuclear proliferation, and world hunger; but also the decreased emphasis on explicitly dispensational teachings within the movement.

1412. Gundry, Robert H. The Church and the Tribulation. Grand Rapids: Zondervan, 1973.

Amid the flood of bestselling dispensationalist literature that inundated evangelical bookstores in the early 1970s, Gundry's The Church and the Tribulation was a serious attempt to argue the merits of posttribulationism. Borrowing some of its hermeneutical and exegetical methods from mainstream biblical scholarship, it was the first important evangelical book to tout the posttrib position since George Eldon Ladd's 1956 volume, The Blessed Hope (see below).

1413. Hoekema, Anthony A. The Bible and the Future. Grand Rapids: Eerdmans, 1979.

Written by a former professor of systematic theology at Calvin Theological Seminary, this study is a thorough interpretation of biblical prophecy from a Reformed amillennial perspective. For other examples see Jay E. Adams, The Time Is At Hand (Presbyterian & Reformed, 1970); William E. Cox, Amillennialism Today (Presbyterian & Reformed, 1972); and Philip E. Hughes, Interpreting Prophecy (Eerdmans, 1976).

1414. Horton, Stanley. Welcome Back Jesus. Springfield, MO: Gospel Publishing House, 1975.

Originally published in 1967 as The Promise of His Coming, this book by an Assemblies of God theologian argues at the popular level for a pre-tribulational, premillennial prophetic viewpoint without reliance on dispensationalism.

1415. Kirban, Salem. 666. Wheaton, IL: Tyndale House Publishers, 1970.

A brisk seller in Christian bookstores in the early and mid-70s. This pre-trib "novel" set in the Last Days, provides a glimpse at some of the wide-spread theories and speculation concerning the practical details surrounding the Apocalypse.

1416. Kraus, C. Norman. Dispensationalism in America: Its Rise and Development. Richmond, VA: John Knox Press, 1958.

Kraus, a Mennonite minister, sees dispensationalism as a reactionary movement that sought to preserve the status quo and protected itself from liberalizing tendencies through its heightened supernaturalism. Views dispensationalist teachings as a detriment to the social dimension of the Gospel.

1417. Ladd, George Eldon. The Blessed Hope. Grand Rapids: Eerdmans Publishing Company, 1956.

A significant book in its day indicative that many of the "New Evangelicals" were to break away from the rigid premillennial dispensationalism of their fundamentalist forebears. Ladd, professor of New Testament and Biblical Theology at Fuller Theological Seminary, argues that "the Blessed Hope" is the Second Coming, not a pre-trib "Rapture," and stresses the recent origins of pre-tribulationism.

1418. Larkin, Clarence. Dispensational Truth, or, God's Plan and Purpose in the Ages. Philadelphia: Rev. Clarence Larkin, 1918.

An exhaustive look at prophecy by the DaVinci of dispensational chart-makers. Pictorial symbols and elaborate diagrams guide the student of prophecy step-by-step through the unfolding drama of the ages.

1419. Lindsey, Hal. The Late Great Planet Earth. Grand Rapids: Zondervan, 1970.

The single bestselling book of the 1970's, Hal Lindsey's The Late Great Planet Earth reinforced the dominance of traditional dispensationalist teaching within evangelical ranks and introduced its intricate arguments to a much wider audience. The tenor of the times and Lindsey's breezy, good-natured style and persona not only made his book a bestseller, but made him a popular guest on the lecture and talk show circuit. Other volumes followed on generally eschatological topics including There's a New World Coming (Vision House, 1973), and The 1980s: Countdown to Armageddon (Westgate Press, 1980). All sold well but could not match the phenomenal sales of his first book.

1420. MacPherson, Dave. The Incredible Cover-Up: The True Story of the Pre-Trib Rapture. Plainfield, NJ: Logos International, 1975.

The Incredible Cover-Up by journalist Dave MacPherson is, at the popular level, probably the most widely-read attack on premillennial dispensationalism. MacPherson underscores the recent origins of the doctrine as well as some of the eccentricities of its earliest major proponents. See also the author's The Great Rapture Hoax (New Puritan Library, 1983).

1421. Mathews, Shailer. Will Christ Come Again?. Chicago: American Institute of Sacred Literature, 1917.

Part of a sustained WWI-era trumpet blast against premillennialists by liberal scholars. This booklet, by Shailer Matthews of the University of Chicago Divinity School, was distributed by the thousands and was one of several books and articles that attacked dispensationalism as an anxious, unpatriotic reaction to war-time conditions that undermined the war effort and hindered the social gospel. For other examples of this literature see Shirley Jackson Case, The Millennial Hope: A Phase of War-Time Thinking (U. of Chicago, 1918); Case, "The Premillennial Menace," (Biblical World, LII July 1918, 16-23); and George Preston Mains, Premillennialism: Non-Scriptural, Non-Historic, Non-Scientific, Non-Philosphical (Abingdon, 1920).

1422. Mauro, Philip. The Seventy Weeks and the Great Tribulation. Toronto: Hamilton Brothers, 1923.

Mauro, a New York attorney and contributer to The Fundamentals was a dispensationalist who disavowed its teachings. Here he advocates an alternative framework of fundamentalist prophetic interpretation from the dominant dispensational teachings on Israel, the Seventy Weeks of Daniel, the Rapture and the Tribulation. See also his Gospel of the Kingdom (Hamilton, 1928).

1423. McCall, Thomas and Zola Levitt. Satan in the Sanctuary. Chicago: Moody Press, 1973.

This book gives a glimpse into contemporary evangelical views concerning Israel's place in the Last Days and in particular the belief that a modern Temple will rise again in Jerusalem.

1424. McKeever, Jim. Christians Will Go Through the Tribulation And How to Prepare For It. Medford, OR: Omega Publications, 1978.

An example of the recent emergence of a survivalist strain within fundamentalism. McKeever's book is both a prophetic sermon and a survivalist handbook for his readers. Practical tips for those who will refuse the Mark of the Beast include how to build a bomb shelter, store provisions, raise food, etc.

1425. Myland, D. Wesley. The Latter Rain Covenant and Pentecostal Power. Chicago: Evangel Publishing House, 1910.

A classic pentecostal statement on prophecy. This book draws parallels between the return of the Jew, patterns of increasing rainfall in Palestine and the pentecostal revival: the "latter rain."

Rausch, David A. Zionism Within Early American Fundamentalism, 1878-1918: A Convergence of Two Traditions. New York: Edwin Mellen Press, 1979.
(See 664)

1426. Ryrie, Charles C. Dispensationalism Today. Chicago: Moody Press, 1965.

A definitive statement by today's foremost theological interpreter of the dispensationalist position. See also his best-selling Ryrie Study Bible (Moody Press, 1976) which has begun to supplant the venerable Scofield Reference Bible (see below).

Sandeen, Ernest R. The Roots of Fundamentalism: British and American Millenarianism, 1830-1930. Chicago: University of Chicago Press, 1970.
(See 667)

1427. Scofield, C. I. The Scofield Reference Bible. New York: Oxford University Press, 1909.

This study Bible with cross-references and notes from a strictly dispensationalist viewpoint has become a trusted, devotional companion for many American evangelicals down through the years. Revised and updated several times, its notes, by being in such close proximity to the sacred text, have often tended to bask in a reflected aura of infallibility for many in the evangelical-fundamentalist sub-culture. For a more concise example of Scofield's views see his Rightly Dividing the Word of Truth (Bible House of Los Angeles, n.d.).

1428. Simpson, A. B. The Coming One. New York: Christian Alliance Publishing Co., 1912.

In the late 19th and early 20th centuries premillennial dispensationalism was a major goad to evangelical missionary efforts to "Bring Back the King." In this book the founder of the Christian & Missionary Alliance presents dispensationalist teachings and lauds their practical benefits for the missions crusade.

Smith, Wilbur M. 55 Best Books On Prophecy, in Good Books and the Good Book: Reading Lists by Wilbur M. Smith, Fundamentalist Bibliophile. Fundamentalism in American Religion, ed. Joel A. Carpenter. Volume 1. New York: Garland Publishing, 1988.
(See 55)

1429. Smith, Wilbur M. The Atomic Bomb And The Word of God. Chicago: Moody Press, 1945.

This pamphlet appeared immediately after the Second World War. Selling some 50,000 copies and excerpted in several fundamentalist periodicals, it was representative of reactions to the apocalyptic implications of the Nuclear Age and the Cold War. See also Smith's longer works This Atomic Age and the Word of God (W. A. Wilde, 1948), and World Crises and the Prophetic Scriptures (Moody Press, 1951).

1430. Trumbull, Charles G. How I Came to Believe in Our Lord's Return and Why I Believe The Lord's Return is Near. Chicago: Bible Institute Colportage Association, 1934.

The editor of the influential Sunday School Times collects the personal dispensationalist testimonies of some of the era's most influential pastors, evangelists, and leaders with an eye to events in Europe and Asia. Other popular books on prophecy in this time period include Harry Ironside, The Lamp of Prophecy (Zondervan, 1940) and Harry Rimmer, Palestine, The Coming Storm Center (Eerdmans, 1940).

1431. Walvoord, John F. and John E. Walvoord. Armageddon: Oil and the Middle East Crisis. Grand Rapids: Zondervan, 1974.

Emanating from the citadel of American premillennial dispentionalism, Dallas Theological Seminary, this book is an interesting example of how evangelicals often adapt contemporary events and trends, in this case the Energy Crisis of the early 70s, into their prophetic framework.

Weber, Timothy P. Living in the Shadow of the Second Coming: American Premillennialism, 1875-1982. New York: Oxford University Press, 1979; enlarged ed., Grand Rapids: Zondervan, 1983.
(See 458)

1432. Whisenant, Edgar. 88 Reasons Why The Rapture Will Be In 1988. Nashville: World Bible Society, 1988.

Evangelicals have usually been loathe to set dates for Christ's Second Coming. 88 Reasons, however, was an embarrassing exception. Written by a retired NASA engineer, it caused a commotion in some circles with its prediction that the Rapture of the Church would occur on Rosh Hashanah, 1988. Eventually, nearly 4 million copies were sold or distributed. Not surprisingly, his apologetic sequel, The Final Shout: Rapture Report 1989 (World Bible Society, 1989), sold only 30,000 copies.

1433. Wilkerson, David. The Vision. Old Tappan, NJ: Spire Books, 1973.

Written by the author of The Cross and the Switchblade (see 1294) and the founder of Teen Challenge, this volume appeared at the height of the 70s' prophecy mania detailing Wilkerson's personal vision of the impending apocalypse. Caused a short-lived stir in the evangelical subculture, especially in its pentecostal/charismatic sectors.

1434. Williams, Ernest. Systematic Theology. Vol. 3. Eschatology. Springfield, MO: Gospel Publishing House, 1953.

An example of a pentecostal "adjustment" of classic dispensational theology to correlate with the movement's teachings and emphasis on latter-day miracles.

1435. Wilson, Dwight. Armageddon Now? The Premillenarian Response to Russia and Israel Since 1917. Grand Rapids: Baker, 1977.

This monograph by an ordained Assemblies of God minister and Ph.D. in history takes a critical look at premillennialist writings citing past errors in speculation on specific events and world trends, and a disturbing tendency of the movement to produce a disinterest in social concern and a latent anti-Semitism among its followers.

SECTION VI: SPIRITUALITY AND PERSONALITY

Edith L. Blumhofer

CHAPTER 24
DEVOTION AND DISCIPLESHIP

Twentieth-century evangelicals are nurtured by a wide variety of devotional writings, some of which are widely acclaimed Christian classics like Thomas Kempis' The Imitation of Christ. Others stem from periods of renewal and reform in Protestant history. Thus evangelicals sense affinities with the spirituality of John and Charles Wesley, Nicholas von Zinzendorf, David Brainerd and Mary Fletcher. They thrill to biographical accounts of a common set of heroes--often missionaries like William Carey and Adoniram and Ann Judson whose stories they read for devotional benefit as well as for information. Other of their inspirational writings derive directly from their own experience as participants in an Anglo-American movement since the Civil War. British evangelicals of the past century like Hudson Taylor, William and Catherine Booth, Charles Haddon Spurgeon, George Mueller and F. B. Meyer still motivate an American constituency toward personal piety. Nineteenth-century revivalist Charles G. Finney remains a towering figure to evangelicals who long for personal and national renewal.

Such people have helped mold American evangelical expectations about the inner life and the meaning of discipleship. Religious biographies as well as devotional books and inspirational exhortations proliferate, offering models and advice to millions of Americans who yearn for a vital relationship with God. Those cited below have been selected to represent the range of evangelical devotional literature, from daily readings to book-length admonitions to "higher" or "deeper" Christian experience. Some of these--like Daily Light and Vance Havner's writings--have had enormous influence. Others have had more limited circulation. They have been selected as well with the theological preferences their authors in mind. They represent pentecostal, charismatic, fundamentalist Baptist and other evangelical persuasions and thus suggest something about the scope of emphases addressed by the vast literature to which evangelicals turn for spiritual nurture and direction.

1436. Bonhoeffer, Dietrich. The Cost of Discipleship. New York: MacMillan, 1963.

This work became popular among evangelicals of the 1960s, inspiring those concerned about the social issues of the period. Its critique of "cheap grace" and its call for a life of obedience ("costly grace") and social involvement was well suited to evangelicals who were beginning to recover their heritage of reform and activism.

1437. Brengle, Samuel L. Heart Talks on Holiness. Atlanta: Salvation Army, Southern, 1978.

This prolific early Salvation Army author offers insight and instruction about holiness that illumine the spirituality encouraged by holiness groups like the Salvation Army.

1438. Bright, Bill. The Holy Spirit: The Key to Supernatural Living. San Bernardino, CA: Campus Crusade for Christ, 1980.

Insights about the role of the Holy Spirit in daily Christian living. Bright, the founder and president of Campus Crusade for Christ, during the 1980s responded to the growing charismatic movement by affirming the necessity of a dynamic relationship between evangelical believers and the Holy Spirit.

1439. Carmichael, Amy. Gold by Moonlight. Ft. Washington, PA: Christian Literature Crusade, 1970.

Amy Carmichael was an Irish missionary to India from 1895-1951. Deeply influenced by the Keswick movement, she wrote extensively on the inward life and on coping with suffering. Founder of the Dohnavur Fellowship and of homes for children, she devoted much of her life to rescuing Indian girls from a life as temple prostitutes. Most of her devotional books were written during the last 20 years of her life when she was invalid.

1440. Carothers, Merlin R. Power in Praise. Plainfield, NJ: Logos International, 1972.

A charismatic leader during the 1960s and 1970s, Merlin Carothers gained acclaim for his two books, Prison to Praise and Power in Praise, both of which urge Christians to discover the liberating effects of obedience to biblical injunctions to praise God.

1441. Chambers, Oswald. My Utmost For His Highest. New York: Dodd, Mead, 1935.

A widely read best-selling collection of daily devotional readings culled from the works of a prominent British evangelical.

1442. Colson, Charles W. Life Sentence. Lincoln, VA: Chosen Books, 1979.

Since he wrote his first book, Born Again, recounting his conversion, Richard Nixon's former special assistant has been a popular evangelical author and speaker. His books challenge evangelicals to ethical reflection, unselfish obedience and unstinting Christian service.

1443. Daily Light on the Daily Path. New York: American Tract Society, n.d.

A collection of Bible verses arranged in 365 sections that has long enjoyed immense popularity among evangelicals.

1444. Day, Richard Ellsworth. Breakfast Table Autocrat: The Life Story of Henry Parsons Crowell. Chicago: Moody Press, 1946.

A sympathetic biography of the founder of Quaker Oats Company who was a prominent player in the extension of evangelical witness through institutions and outreaches sponsored by D. L. Moody and his successors, especially Moody Bible Institute.

1445. Dillard, Annie. Pilgrim at Tinker Creek. New York: Harper's Magazine Press, 1974.

A personal narrative, highlighting the author's year-long observations of the sights and sounds of nature in her immediate neighborhood. Well-received in evangelical literary circles.

Elliot, Elisabeth. Shadow of the Almighty: The Life and Testament of Jim Elliott. New York: Harper & Brothers, 1958.
(see 1305)

Elliot, Elisabeth. Through Gates of Splendor. New York: Harper & Brothers, 1957.
(see 1306)

1446. Friesen, Garry. Decision Making and the Will of God. Portland, OR: Multnomah Press, 1980.

A guidebook to Christian discipleship, this book is part of Multnomah Press' Critical Concern series.

1447. Gordon, S.D. Quiet Talks with World Winners. New York: A. C. Armstrong & Son, 1908.

Gordon's "Quiet Talks" series enjoyed wide popularity for their devotional reflections and advocacy of deeper religious experience. This lecturer and author was a sought after speaker at Bible conferences missionary conventions, and in YMCA work.

1448. Graham, Billy. Peace with God. Garden City, NY: Doubleday & Co., Inc., 1953.

A classic statement of the evangelical perception of the human problem (sin); the solution (the new birth); and the results (a new life of peace with God).

1449. Havner, Vance. Day by Day. Grand Rapids: Baker, 1984.

A book of daily devotional readings by an acclaimed evangelical devotional writer. These selections represent a form of evangelical spirituality that is popular among such widely divergent groups as pentecostals and independent Baptists.

1450. Hayford, Jack. Worship His Majesty. Waco, TX: Word Publishing Co., 1989.

Hayford, a towering figure in the charismatic movement during the 1980s, wrote one of the decades most popular worship songs--"Majesty." This call to worship is representative of emphases in the charismatic orb of which Hayford, pastor of a congregation affiliated with the International Church of the Foursquare Gospel, is part.

1451. Ironside, Harry A. Holiness: The False and the True. New York: Loizeaux Brothers, n.d.

This book by a well-known fundamentalist pastor examines the premises of the holiness movement, details the movement's theological errors and proposes another view of sanctification. Ironside, once a participant in the Salvation Army, begins the book with an autobiographical section and then proceeds to discuss relevant doctrines. His observations on the holiness movement reveal some of that movement's ethos and appeal.

1452. Jones, E. Stanley. Abundant Living. Nashville: Abingdon, 1942.

A collection of daily devotional readings by a noted Methodist missionary evangelist and author.

1453. Lea, Larry. Could You Not Tarry One Hour? Learning the Joy of Prayer. Altamonte Springs, FL: Creation House, 1987.

Pastor of an 11,000 member charismatic church in Rockwell, Texas and popular teacher and author, Lea has made prayer the focus of his ministry. He mobilizes hundreds of thousands of his TV audiences to exorcise demons and assert spiritual authority over the public arena as well as in the private sphere. He produces best-selling seminars and courses and has also written The Hearing Ear and Listening to God.

1454. MacDonald, Gordon. Ordering Your Private World. Chicago: Moody Press, 1984.

A popular pastor, author and former president of InterVarsity Christian Fellowship shares thoughts on spiritual discipline based on the assumption that a disciplined inner life issues in personal development and effective Christian witness. MacDonald's other writings include (Re)Discovering Yourself and Rebuilding Your Broken World.

1455. Marshall, Catherine. Something More: In Search of a Deeper Faith. New York: McGraw-Hill, 1974.

A well-known author describes her spiritual quest and struggles in living out her faith in a changing world.

1456. Meyer, F. B. The Present Tenses of the Blessed Life. New York: Fleming H. Revell, 1892.

Meyer's many writings uniformly urge readers to discover a "full" salvation. This British Baptist pastor, prominently identified with Keswick and D. L. Moody, gained a considerable following in the United States. His books have consistently been popular among evangelicals, both for the spirituality they describe and the sensitivity they convey.

1457. Miller, Keith. The Taste of New Wine. Waco, TX: Word Books, 1965.

Miller, a layman, discussed his spiritual quest in this popular book. While the book is about witnessing to Christian faith, it is in the form of an update on Miller's progress in translating his faith into action.

1458. Murray, Andrew. With Christ in the School of Prayer. New York: Fleming H. Revell, 1895.

Murray's many books achieved popularity in America during the late nineteenth century when this elderly South African Dutch Reformed pastor and author traveled to Great Britain and the United States. Identified with the Keswick movement in England as well as with D. L. Moody's Northfield Conferences, Murray reveled in intense, Christ-centered spiritual experience that found expression in books describing a spirituality craved by participants in various "higher life" holiness and pentecostal movements.

1459. Nee, Watchman. The Normal Christian Life. Wheaton, IL: Tyndale House, 1977.

Nee, a Chinese evangelical leader, originally wrote this book in Chinese in 1937. It outlines the nature of New Testament Christianity with special attention to local church life and the corporate dimensions of early Christian experience. Nee's many books emphasize a spirituality rooted in the experience of the cross, the power of the resurrection and new life in the Spirit.

1460. Packer, J. I. Knowing God. Downers Grove, IL: InterVarsity Press, 1973.

Presents the knowledge of God as the purpose of creation, the aim of life and life's most pleasurable experience. Packer, a prominent evangelical scholar, examines God's attributes and relationship to humankind in readable, devotional style.

1461. Redpath, Alan. Victorious Christian Faith. Old Tappan, NJ: Fleming H. Revell, 1984.

A well-known statement of the Keswick-influenced evangelical view of Christian spirituality. Redpath presents the Christian life as a process of surrender which results in "full salvation" and is analogous to a steady climb, energized by the gifts and graces of the Holy Spirit, culminating in face-to-face fellowship with God.

1462. Rice, John R. Prayer...Asking and Receiving. Wheaton, IL: Sword of the Lord Publishers, 1942.

A widely distributed book geared toward building faith and encouraging prayer. Rice had a large fundamentalist following that avidly read his instructions about prayer, healings and miracles.

1463. Ryrie, Charles Caldwell. Balancing the Christian Life. Chicago: Moody Press, 1969.

A prominent evangelical educator urges Christians to pursue balance rather than emotion and to chart a steady course rather than covet extraordinary experiences.

1464. Sheldon, Charles. In His Steps. Chicago: Advance Publishing Co., 1899.

An enduring classic that challenges Christians to respond in practical ways to the question "What would Jesus do?". This novel also offers insights into the ethos of turn-of-the-century Protestantism.

1465. Shelley, Bruce, ed. A Call to Christian Character. Grand Rapids: Zondervan, 1970.

Eleven evangelical scholars discuss the importance of piety, applying the concept in practical ways to the home, preaching, theology and mission.

1466. Smith, Hannah Whitall. The Christian's Secret of a Happy Life. New York: Garland, 1984; orig. 1870.

Several million copies of this evangelical classic have been published since it first appeared in the 1870s, and it remains in print. It aptly describes in practical terms the "higher Christian life" teaching that Hannah, a Quaker, and her husband, Robert Pearsall Smith, helped popularize in western Europe and the United States.

1467. Smith, Robert Pearsall and Hannah Whitall Smith. The Devotional Writings of Robert Pearsall Smith and Hannah Whitall Smith, ed. Donald W. Dayton. New York: Garland, 1984.

The books reprinted in this modern edition are Robert Smith's Holiness Through Faith and Hannah Smith's immensely influential The Christian's Secret of a Happy Life. The Smiths were important promoters of holiness teachings in the States before ministering in England in the 1870s, where they exerted a formative influence on the Keswick movement. Their emphasis on the baptism of the Holy Ghost, as in a key chapter of Hannah's book, anticipated some aspects of the later pentecostal movement.

1468. Swindoll, Charles. Growing Deep in the Christian Life: Returning to Our Roots. Portland, OR: Multnomah, 1986.

Advice from a popular pastor, author and broadcaster on the importance of biblical basics for true discipleship.

1469. ten Boom, Corrie. Marching Orders for the End-Times Battle. Fort Washington, PA: Christian Literature Crusade, 1969.

This beloved evangelical survivor of a Nazi concentration camp had enormous appeal as a speaker and author in the United States. Her several books--including The Hiding Place and A Prisoner and Yet revealed her simple, stalwart confidence in God.

1470. Tozer, A. W. The Pursuit of God. Camp Hill, PA: Christian Publications, 1948.

The writings of A. W. Tozer, a Christian and Missionary Alliance minister, are staple evangelical devotional fare. This challenge to a vibrant spiritual life is typical of Tozer's devotional books.

1471. Trueblood, Elton. The Common Ventures of Life: Marriage, Birth, Work and Death. New York: Harper & Bros., 1949.

A Quaker philosopher explores Christian views of marriage, birth, work and death and offers a framework for coping with these universal experiences. Rooted in a philosophy of wholeness, Trueblood's work assumes the sacramental nature of the universe.

1472. Wiersbe, Warren. Why Us? When Bad Things Happen to Good People. Old Tappan, NJ: Fleming H. Revell, 1985.

A popular evangelical pastor, teacher and radio speaker adresses tough questions and points readers to the strength he finds in his faith. Wiersbe's many inspirational books--including such titles as Walking with the Giants and Real Worship--enjoy wide circulation.

1473. Yancey, Phillip. Disappointment with God. Grand Rapids: Zondervan, 1988.

This noted author and editor-at-large at Christianity Today wrestles with the questions: Is God unfair? Is God silent? and Is God hidden? Offers an evangelical perspective on suffering and pain. A best-seller.

CHAPTER 25
MOTIVATION AND SELF-HELP

In recent years, evangelical efforts to make Jesus relevant to their culture have issued in motivational literature addressing a wide range of topics. From Free to be Thin to Twelfth Man in the Huddle, evangelical books urge readers to discover for themselves the liberating, motivating dynamic of Christ-focused living. Pat Boone's Pray to Win: God Wants You to Succeed is typical of the view that God wants believers to be achievers--that Christians need to be taught to attain and enjoy prosperous living and this-worldly success. In the view of large numbers of evangelicals, Christianity offers power and prosperity. Success (often measured in secular terms) is deemed the believer's right. Christian books advised readers how to succeed; how to climb the corporate ladder; how to combat eating disorders; how to shed guilt and greed. Preoccupied with self-fulfillment, some evangelicals give the impression that evangelical Christianity assures health, wealth and happiness. From Robert Schuller to Tim and Bev LaHaye, evangelicals motivate one another to bigger and better endeavors. From Pat Boone to Orel Hershiser, evangelical celebrities model success stories that prove that evangelical faith is compatible with popular acclaim. Such self-help, motivational books offer rewards in the here and now and have enormous appeal among a constituency that is inclined to demand immediate results.

Most of the books listed below are primary sources. Others are critical analyses of some of the tendencies and implications in the popular health-and-wealth gospel.

1474. Anderson, Ann Kiemel. I'm Running to Win. Wheaton, IL: Tyndale House, 1980.

Anderson's books have sold well over one million copies. She reflects on such basic human realities as pain, frienship, sexuality, depression, love and change in brief motivational books like Hi, I'm Anne; I'm Out to Change My World; And With the Gift Came Laughter.

1475. Barron, Bruce. The Health and Wealth Gospel: A Fresh Look at Healing, Prosperity and Positive Confession. Downers Grove: InterVarsity Press, 1987.

A sympathetic popular, but also somewhat critical, analysis of issues agitating in the charismatic movement about the "name it and claim it" gospel. Notes departures from traditional evangelical views on faith, sin and suffering.

1476. Barton, Bruce. The Man Nobody Knows. New York: Bobbs, 1925.

This best-seller of the mid-1920s helped redefine the evangelical faith in masculine terms. It offered a new look at Jesus who, Barton alleged, was a muscular outdoorsman with remarkable charisma and unparalleled organizational abilities. Appropiating the rhetoric of the era's "rugged individualism" this book sought to replace stereotypes of Jesus as meek, unattractive, weak and effeminate.

1477. Bright, Bill. How to Experience God's Love and Forgiveness. Campus Crusade for Christ, 1981.

A practical study guide, typical of Campus Crusade for Christ's use of the "how to" and "transferable concepts" approach to motivate people to a Christian lifestyle.

1478. Dobbins, Richard D. Your Spiritual and Emotional Power. Old Tappan, NJ: Fleming H. Revell, 1984.

An examination of religion and mental health by a pentecostal therapist. Dobbins directs EMERGE Ministries, Inc., a treatment center for Christian mental health care. This book explores a link between spiritual experience and emotional and mental well-being and urges the therapeutic value of prayer in achieving healthy feelings.

1479. Engstrom, Ted W. The Pursuit of Excellence. Grand Rapids: Zondervan, 1982.

President of several evangelical parachurch agencies over a long career and popular leader of seminars on time management, Engstrom enjoys high visibility within evangelicalism. Like other evangelical motivational books, this one urges Christians to achieve excellence by reaching beyond their limitations. A how-to manual, with specific strategies for excellence in daily life.

1480. Farah, Charles. From the Pinnacle of the Temple. South Plainfield, NJ: Bridge Publishing, Inc., 1979.

During the 1970s, many participants in the pentecostal and charismatic movements became enamored of faith teaching which stressed believers' rights to health and material affluence. Farah, a professor of theology at Oral Roberts University (a bastion of such views) wrote this book after closely observing the theological and practical implications of such teaching. It addresses the subject of presumption in the contemporary faith healing movement.

1481. Hagin, Kenneth. Turning Helpless Situations Around. Tulsa, OK: Hagin Ministries, 1981.

Typical of the motivational literature issuing from Hagin's Tulsa-based pentecostal ministries. Hagin urges the power of faith and especially of faith expressed in the spoken word.

1482. Hill, Harold and Irene B. Harrell. How to Live Like a King's Kid. Plainfield, NJ: Logos, 1974.

One of the first of the "name it and claim it" genre, this book greatly extended the popular charismatic message that believers had a right to health, wealth and happiness and told them how to obtain it.

1483. Hunt, Dave and T. A. McMahon. The Seduction of Christianity. Eugene, OR: Harvest House, 1987.

An attack on many popular evangelical spokespersons that became a big seller after it was endorsed and expanded upon by Jimmy Swaggart. Alleging that popular evangelical preachers and writers advocate human deification and--subtly--the New Age, these authors attempt to expose views they consider erroneous.

1484. McConnell, D. R. A Different Gospel: A Historical and Biblical Analysis of the Modern Faith Movement. Peabody, MA: Hendrickson Publishers, 1988.

A critical analysis of the "faith movement" which maintains that faith is a tool for achieving health and wealth. McConnell charges that it is both cultic and heretical. See also Charles Farah's From the Pinnacle of the Temple (1480), which represents an early evangelical challenge to charismatic faith teaching.

1485. McDowell, Josh. Building Your Self-Image. Wheaton, IL: Tyndale House, 1986.

Part of the diversification of the ministry and message of a widely known college lecturer from apologetics to popular issues. Urges the importance of a healthy self-image and offers practical advice.

1486. Peale, Norman Vincent. The Power of Positive Thinking. Englewood Cliffs, NJ: Prentice-Hall, Inc., 1952.

Published just before Graham's Peace with God, this popular book addresses similar concerns from a different perspective. Urging the power of prayer, self-confidence and a peaceful mind, this best-seller maintains that people who expect the best will experience it. This influential book spawned innumerable others, but it remains the enduring classic of this genre of self-help literature.

1487. Price, Eugenia. A Woman's Choice: Living Through Your Problems. Grand Rapids: Zondervan, 1983.

Urges women to choose to work through their problems and take control of their lives by receiving Christ's mind, using theirs and facing issues squarely. Accepts basic assumption that most women are ruled by emotions rather than reason.

1488. Roberts, Oral. Seed Faith Guide to the Holy Bible. Tulsa, OK: Oral Roberts Evangelistic Association, 1978.

"Seed faith"--or giving with the belief that the giver will reap more in return--is the basic principle that has supported Oral Roberts' charismatic outreaches since he left the sawdust trail for a university, medical complex and televangelism. This book is a revealing look at how Roberts uses scripture. It moves through the Bible, book-by-book, and identifies "seed faith texts" in each.

1489. Roberts, Oral. Three Most Important Steps to Your Better Health and Miracle Living. Tulsa, OK: Oral Roberts Evangelistic Association, 1976.

A succinct, fast-reading statement of the capacity of faith to bring health and miracles into the realm of daily living. Typical of popular literature spawned by charismatic televangelist ministries. A more recent variation on this theme of the ability of faith to provide health and wealth is Roberts' How I Learned Jesus Was Not Poor (1988).

1490. Schuller, Robert H. Move Ahead with Possibility Thinking. Garden City, NY: Doubleday & Co., Inc., 1967.

Presents Schuller's popular theme: facing life with positive attitudes--emphasizing possibilities rather than impossibilities--restores youthful energy, and produces happiness, success and peace. Schuller expanded on this theme in It's Possible (Old Tappan, NJ: Fleming H. Revell, 1978).

1491. Schuller, Robert H. You Can Become the Person You Want to Be. Old Tappan, NJ: Fleming H. Revell, 1976.

Succinct statement of Schuller's practical advice on problem solving and self-confidence. Like such other Schuller books as The Be-Happy Attitudes [1985]; Discover Your Possibilities [1980], this one is based on the assumption that prayer plus possibility thinking produces success.

1492. Shoemaker, Samuel M. How You Can Find Happiness. New York: E. P. Dutton & Co., 1947.

This motivational book is one of a long list of titles by this Episocpalian rector, counselor and radio speaker. Shoemaker supported the Oxford Movement; his writings stress the necessity of evangelism and of practical Christianity.

1493. Tilton, Robert. God's Law of Success. Tulsa, OK: Harrison House, 1986.

Tilton is a televangelist whose popularity is on the rise. Prone to prophesy and promise miracles, Tilton attracts a diverse following. This book is representative of the charismatic stress on material success as the right of all Christians. Reveals the rationalistic approach to believing and obtaining that attracts hundreds of thousands of evangelicals.

1494. Voskuil, Dennis. Mountains Into Goldmines: Robert Schuller and the Gospel of Success. Grand Rapids: Eerdmans, 1983.

Robert Schuller is a minister of the Reformed Church in America who, with a vision skillfully woven together from Norman Vincent Peale, Dale Carnegie and the Bible, has created a large and influential ministry in California. Voskuil's objective study is one of the better books avaliable on contemporary leaders of what might be called "feel-good evangelicalism." It includes a revealing chapter that traces this emphasis back through the past 150 years.

CHAPTER 26
LIFESTYLE AND STEWARDSHIP

During the 1970s, evangelicals were challenged by some within their ranks to reevaluate their priorities and lifestyles. Jim Wallis, editor of Sojourners magazine and John Alexander, editor of The Other Side, were prominent among those who argued that evangelicalism was too closely identified with the values of capitalist society. Urging the church to adopt a prophetic stance toward culture, such evangelicals shared the concerns of many of their contemporaries about the environment, world hunger and nuclear holocaust. Mounting evangelical discussion about lifestyle was influenced as well by an international evangelical gathering in Lausanne in 1974. There prosperous western evangelicals encountered resistance from representatives of the two-thirds world who criticized the western idiom of much of the discussion. Sensitized to the reality of poverty and suffering everywhere, some American evangelicals returned home committed to rethinking values and lifestyle.

Several other sections of this bibliography deal with specific aspects of lifestyle concerns. The writings listed below suggest some of the evangelical approaches to the concept of life as stewardship.

1495. Baker, Robert A. "The Story of the Southern Baptist Foundation." Baptist History and Heritage 21:1 (January 1986): 40-47.

This article is part of a dedicated issue that addresses stewardship in a Southern Baptist context. Other articles are by Bill Leonard (stewardship promotion); Louise Lorentzen (Lifestyle Concerns); Albert McClellan (denominational allocation); Alvin Shackleford (patterns of giving); William White (local church promotion).

1496. Campolo, Anthony, Jr. The Success Fantasy. Wheaton, IL: Scripture Press, 1980.

Analyzes evangelical assumptions about success and the will of God. Argues that God's measure of success differes radically from that of society and challenges evangelicals to measure their lives by biblical standards. See also The Power Delusion (Victor, 1983), Who Switched the Price Tags? (Word, 1986) and Twenty Hot Potatoes Christians are Afraid to Touch (Word, 1989).

1497. Dayton, Edward R. and Ted W. Engstrom. Strategy For Living: How to Make the Best Use of Your Time and Abilities. Glendale, CA: Regal Books, 1976.

Stressing Christian living as God's demand on Christians, the authors offer practical instructions, augmented by diagrams and charts, to facilitate right choices and reveal wrong priorities. See also Ted Engstrom and David Juroe's The Work Trap (1979).

1498. Dayton, Edward R. Tools for Time Management. Grand Rapids: Zondervan, 1974.

Suggestions about Christian integration to address overwork, indecision and stress. Popularly written, this advice manual deals with over 50 problem areas in typical day-to-day living.

1499. Eller, Vernard. The Simple Life: A Chritian's Stance Toward Possessions. Grand Rapids: Eerdmans, 1973.

Written in popular style, this book moves from Jesus to Paul and the early church and then examines Soren Kierkegaard's views on the meaning of the simple life. Eller offers concluding observations, noting that acceptable simplicity cannot be acheived by legalisms: it is, rather, characterized by joy and freedom.

Halteman, Jim. Market Capitalism and Christianity. Grand Rapids: Baker, 1988.
(see 979)

1500. Henry, Carl F. Such as I Have: The Stewardship of Talent. New York and Nashville: Abingdon-Cokesbury Press, 1946.

A brief exhortation to responsible Christian living by a prominent evangelical theologian who insists that stewardship should be at the core of the Christian life.

Mouw, Richard. Called to Holy Wordliness. Philadelphia: Fortress Press, 1980.
(see 1145)

1501. Pinnock, Clark. "A Call for Liberation of North American Christians." Sojourners 5 (May, 1976): 23-25.

An urgent call to evangelicals to recognize the gospel's message of radical, life-changing discipleship. Indicts American consumerism and challenges evangelicals to sensitivity toward human need and social justice.

Rifkin, Jeremy. The Emerging Order: God in the Age of Scarcity. New York: Putnam's 1979.
(see 1163)

1502. Schaeffer, Francis. The Church at the End of the Twentieth Century. Downers Grove, IL: InterVarsity Press, 1970.

An analysis of contemporary pressures on the church, focusing on form and freedom, on threats to freedom and on ecological issues. Schaeffer offers advice about genuine biblical communities and a program for individual and institutional reform to generate what he calls "revolutionary Christianity."

Sider, Ronald J., ed. The Chicago Declaration. Carol Stream, IL: Creation House, 1973.
(see 1172)

Sider, Ronald J. Christ and Violence. Scottdale, PA: Herald Press, 1979.
(see 1173)

Sider, Ronald J. Cry Justice. Mahwah, NJ and Downers Grove, IL: Paulist Press and InterVaristy Press, 1980.
(see 1174)

Sider, Ronald J., ed. Evangelicals and Development: Toward A Theology of Social Change. Philadelphia: Westminster, 1981.
(see 1175)

1503. Sider, Ronald J. Rich Christians in an Age of Hunger. Downers Grove, IL: InterVarsity Press, 1979.

Sider, a radical evangelical of Anabaptist heritage, has written and lectured widely urging evangelicals to reconsider their lifestyle and to live simply as stewards of God's creation and agents of justice.

1504. Sine, Tom. The Mustard Seed Conspiracy. Waco, TX: Word Books, 1981.

Using the biblical parable of the mustard seed as a model of God's intentions, Sine predicts that the most lowly among us will change the world. He invites Christians and the church to participate by rejecting materialism in favor of social action and creative simple living.

1505. Wallis, Jim. The Call to Conversion and Recovering the Gospel for These Times. San Francisco: Harper & Row, 1981.

Examines two questions: What is conversion? and How can we heed the call to conversion today? Wallis, founder of Sojourners, argues that attitudes toward economic injustice and nuclear holocaust measure the depth of conversion. Urging a new, gospel-rooted social vision, Wallis calls for renewal in worship and spiritual discipline.

White, John. Eros Defiled: The Christian and Sexual Sin. Downers Grove, IL: InterVarsity, 1977.
(see 1190)

1506. Wilkinson, Loren, ed. Earth Keeping: Christian Stewardship of Natural Resources. Grand Rapids: Eerdmans, 1980.

Produced by the Calvin Center for Christian Scholarship at Calvin College, this book resulted from studies on Christian stewardship and natural resources. Approaches environmental questions from a framework provided by biblical principles.

Wirt, Sherwood Eliot. The Social Conscience of the Evangelical. New York: Harper and Row, 1968.
(see 1193)

CHAPTER 27
MARRIAGE AND FAMILY

Recent evangelical preoccupation with advice literature has generated many titles about family living. Many evangelicals have looked with dismay at apparent disorder in the culture and have responded by reasserting the importance of stable, biblically-structured relationships in the Christian family. During the 1970s, the hierarchical paradigm renewed its appeal as the biblical way to understand parent-child and husband-wife relationships.

Female submission was urged with creative variations in Marabel Morgan's Total Woman, the single best-selling book of 1974. Morgan's book both reflected and stimulated changing attitudes among evangelicals toward sex. The change was apparent as well in a spate of sex manuals that issued from evangelical presses after Tim and Bev LaHaye published The Act of Marriage: The Beauty of Sexual Love. While Morgan and the LaHayes urged submission of women to men, others argued for recognition of the personhood of women and prodded evangelical women to pursue "total womanhood." Still others wrestled with scripture and opted for feminism.

The Christian family is central to the evangelical vision for Christian culture. Books related to family life have sold millions of copies and provided impetus for the emergence of a Christian counseling industry. Those listed below offer a sampling of the various points of view that thrive--and sometimes clash--under the evangelical umbrella.

1507. Adams, Jay. Christian Living in the Home. Phillipsburg, NJ: Presbyterian and Reformed Publishing Co., 1972.

Practical advice from a popular evangelical counselor on family life, communication and discipline.

1508. Baehr, Ted. The Movie and Video Guide for Christian Families. Nashville, TN: Thomas Nelson, 1987.

Summaries and ratings of several hundred videos evaluated from an evangelical perspective. Informative both for what the commentaries suggest about evangelical tastes and for its assumptions about evangelical family values.

1509. Bromiley, Geoffrey W. God and Marriage. Grand Rapids: Eerdmans, 1980.

An evangelical theology of marriage, focusing on the Trinity as a paradigm for marriage and examining such issues as adultery, incest, celibacy, and remarriage.

Bryant, Anita. The Anita Bryant Story: The Survival of Our Nation's Families and the Threat of the Militant Homosexuality. Old Tappan, NJ: Fleming H. Revell Co., 1977.
(see 1210)

1510. Burkett, Larry. The Complete Financial Guide for Young Couples. Wheaton, IL: Victor Books, 1989.

Typical of a recent spate of marriage advice literature. On the assumption that financial problems aggravate other marital difficulties, this financial counselor and popular evangelical author offers advice on finances and stewardship.

1511. Christenson, Larry. The Christian Family. Minneapolis, MN: Bethany Fellowship, 1970.

This book by a prominent Lutheran charismatic pastor maintains that recent widespread problems in Christian families derive from ignoring divinely established order. He discusses relationships of order and authority in the family and challenges each family member to accept a God-ordained place. Advocates an hierarchical model, urging men to rule, women to submit and children to obey.

1512. Dobson, James. Dare to Discipline. Wheaton, IL: Tyndale House, 1979.

A best-selling manual urging evangelical parents to assert authority and leadership in the home. One of the all-time evangelical bestsellers by the founder of Focus on the Family, this is typical of the evangelical family literature of the past two decades which is rooted in the assumption that the Christian family is the bulwark of national morality.

1513. Ellisen, Stanley A. Divorce and Remarriage in the Church. Grand Rapids: Zondervan, 1977.

In response to rising divorce rates within the church as well as in the secular sphere, Ellisen offers biblically based counsel to those embarking on a marriage, suffering through its decline, or contemplating remarriage. In his view, couples must work hard to avoid divorce through the application of Christian principles. However, if it is too late to save the marriage, God offers forgiveness to the penitent through spiritual renewal.

1514. Fairchild, Roy W. Christians in Families: An Inquiry into the Nature and Mission of the Christian Family. Richmond, VA: The Covenant Life Press, 1964.

Examines the nature and mission of the family. Develops Christian views of sex, marriage and parenthood and offers resources to assist families in cultivating identity as a Christian unit.

1515. Gaither, Gloria and Shirley Dobson. Let's Make a Memory. Waco, TX: Word Books, 1983.

Advice from the spouses of two widely-known evangelicals. Encourages families to strengthen family identity through the creation of traditions and customs. Part of the recent strong emphasis on the family among evangelicals.

1516. Gore, Tipper. Raising PG Kids in an X-Rated Society. Nashville: Abingdon Press, 1987.

The wife of Tennessee Senator Albert Gore gained noteriety for urging censorship in rating of rock music. Here she offers general guidelines for child rearing.

1517. Gundry, Patricia. Heirs Together. Grand Rapids: Zondervan, 1980.

Maintains that the Bible offers mutual submission as a principle to guide the marriage relationship. This replaces hierarchical marriage customs which, Gundry argues, derive from medieval theologians rather than from scripture. An important contribution by an active evangelical feminist whose other works include Woman Be Free.

1518. Hadden, Jeffrey K. "Televangelism and the Mobilization of a New Christian Right Family Policy." In Families and Religion, eds. William V. D'Antonio and Joan Aldous. Beverly Hills/London/New Delhi: Sage Publications, 1983.

An informative probe into the relationship between televangelism and New Right family policies by a prominent sociologist.

1519. Hargrove, Barbara. "Family in the White American Protestant Experience." In Families and Religion, eds. William V. D'Antonio and Joan Aldous. Beverly Hills/London/New Delhi: Sage Publications, 1983.

An excellent essay which provides a broader context for understanding evangelical family issues. Hargrove, a respected sociologist, offers a well-documented overview.

1520. Howe, Claude L. "Family Worship in Baptist Life." Baptist History and Heritage 8:3 (October, 1986): 45-55.

Evangelicals have historically encouraged family devotions as essential in the model Christian home. This informative article traces the custom and its function in one large segment of evangelicalism.

Keysor, Charles W., ed. What You Should Know About Homosexuality. Grand Rapids: Zondervan, 1979.
(see 1123)

1521. LaHaye, Tim. Spirit-Controlled Temperament. Wheaton, IL: Tyndale House Publishers, 1967.

Advice on how to overcome character faults by understanding your own and others' psychological temperaments. LaHaye and his wife, Bev, have published numerous popular books on family life, stressing male headship and female submission and offering practical suggestions as well as scripture. They include How to be Happy Though Married, Spirit-Controlled Family Living, and The Battle for the Family. The two also authored the first bestselling evangelical sex manual, The Act of Marriage: The Beauty of Sexual Love, which maintained that married Christians should enjoy sex more than do nonreligious couples.

1522. Morgan, Marabel. The Total Woman. Old Tappan, NJ: Fleming H. Revell, 1973.

Chipper homilies and practical advice fill both this book and its sequel, Total Joy (1976). These books, both of which sold millions of copies, guide the reader to marital, sexual and personal fulfillment with both explicit suggestions and relevant scripture. Morgan advises evangelical wives to follow the "four A's": Accept, Admire, Adapt, and Appreciate.

1523. Narramore, Bruce. Help! I'm a Parent. Grand Rapids: Zondervan, 1972.

A challenge to proper biblical and psychological orientation for parenting, this guide and an accompanying how-to manual by a prominent evangelical psychologist reflect a growing evangelical fascination with popular counseling and advice manuals.

Rekers, George A. Growing Up Straight. Chicago: Moody Press, 1982.
(see 1161)

1524. Rice, John R. The Home: Courtship, Marriage and Children. Wheaton, IL: Sword of the Lord Publishers, 1946.

John R. Rice was a prolific fundamentalist figure whose writings addressed a wide range of issues. This book was one of the first evangelical manuals for family relationships, a precursor of later works by people like Tim LaHaye and Ed Wheat.

Scanzoni, Letha and Virginia Ramey Mollenkott. Is the Homosexual My Neighbor? San Francisco: Harper & Row, 1978.
(see 1166)

1525. Schaeffer, Edith. What is a Family? Old Tappan, NJ: Fleming H. Revell, 1975.

A chronicle of the family experiences of this wife, mother and grandmother. She maintains that the family is a formation center for human relationships and happy memories. This popular evangelical author deals as well with late-twentieth-century challenges to Christian families.

1526. Sell, Charles M. Family Ministry: The Enrichment of Family Life Through the Church. Grand Rapids: Zondervan, 1981.

Part of the multi-volume Ministry Resources Library, this book argues the importance of local church ministry to families and education in family living. Includes valuable bibliography.

1527. Smalley, Gary and John Trent. The Language of Love. Pomona, CA: Focus on the Family, 1988.

An evangelical best-seller popularizing the marriage counseling associated with James Dobson's well-known efforts.

1528. Smedes, Lewis. Sex for Christians. Grand Rapids: Eerdmans, 1976.

Evangelical ethicist Lewis Smedes maintains that the Bible offers perspective on human sexuality and that, since God has created and redeemed the human body, sexual pleasure is morally appropriate within biblical guidelines.

1529. Spitzer, Walter O. and Carlyle L. Saylor, eds. Birth Control and the Christian: A Protestant Symposium on the Control of Human Reproduction. Wheaton, IL: Tyndale House Publishers, 1969.

A collection of papers presented to a Symposium on the Control of Human Reproduction (jointly sponsored by the Christian Medical Society and Christianity Today) offers a range of evangelical views on medical ethics, societal realities and biblical passages.

1530. Wheat, Ed and Gloria Perkins Wheat. Love-Life for Every Married Couple. Grand Rapids: Zondervan, 1980.

Best-selling authors provide an evangelical marriage manual similar to Wheat's other popular writings. These include Intended for Pleasure and Sex Technique and Sexual Fulfillment in Christian Marriages. These are among the best known and widely acclaimed evangelical sex counseling books.

CHAPTER 28
WOMEN'S ROLES

In 1888, Frances Willard expressed confidence that the time would come when "woman's heavenly ministries shall find their central home within God's house." Over the past century, evangelicals have inched toward Willard's hope while wrestling with gender-related issues in both church and society. Many evangelical traditions support women's participation in voluntary associations and missionary outreach; fewer offer women unequivocal partnership in church and denominational leadership.

The long--and sometimes heated--discussion of gender roles has spawned a rich literature, both popular and scholarly, which reveals assumptions about women nurtured both in specific denominations and in evangelical movements more generally. Recent studies offer historical perspective and document the relationship between evangelical attitudes and the larger culture. Key primary sources have recently been republished, both in reprint series and individually. The selections listed below offer guidance to those who want to recover a neglected aspect of the evangelical past and to understand current issues. They propose insights into the complex role religion has played in evangelical women's lives and suggest how religious perceptions influenced cultural assumptions about gender. They also provide a sense of the terms of the ongoing discussion. From A. J. Gordon and Uldine Utley to John R. Rice, Elizabeth Elliot and David Scholer, they reveal the diversity, hope and frustration about gender roles that characterize the evangelical mosaic.

1531. Andrew, Leslie. "Restricted Freedom: A. B. Simpson's View of Women in Ministry." In The Birth of a Vision, eds. David Hartzfeld and Charles Nienkirchen. Beaverlodge, Alberta: Buena Book Services, 1986.

Albert B. Simpson, founder of the Christian and Missionary Alliance, shaped turn-of-the-century evangelical "higher life" and missionary outreaches that depended heavily on the efforts of women. While he welcomed women as "fellow laborers," he restricted their participation in administrative leadership. Andrews' analysis of Simpson's writings and practice offers valuable insights into the diminished public presence of women in the denomination since Simpson's death in 1919. It is also a case study in the ambiguities and hesitations that shaped attitudes toward women in similar turn-of-the-century evangelical contexts.

1532. Barfoot, Charles H. and Gerald T. Sheppard. "Prophetic vs. Priestly Religion: The Changing Role of Women Clergy in Classical Pentecostal Churches." Review of Religious Research 22 (September, 1980): 2-17

Pentecostalism is often cited as a religious movement that has historically affirmed ministering women. In this sociological study, Barfoot and Shepard analyze statistics from four pentecostal denominations to support their thesis that alleged early pentecostal receptivity toward women in leadership was rooted in the social dislocation of pentecostal adherents. As the symbolic function of ministry shifted from prophet to priest, women were officially marginalized.

1533. Bass, Dorothy C. and Sandra Hughes Boyd. Women in American Religious History: An Annotated Bibliography and Guide to the Sources. Boston: G. K. Hall & Co., 1986.

Though it is weak on women in evangelical movements, this annotated bibliography is an invaluable guide to the broader subject of women in American religion.

1534. Bendroth, Margaret L. "Fundamentalism and Femininity." Evangelical Studies Bulletin 5 (March 1988): 1-4.

In a brief but stimulating essay, Bendroth documents how male fundamentalist leaders in the 1920s marginalized women. Sensing a loss of cultural authority, they both berated women for their alleged loss of virtue and asserted their own masculinity by identifying their faith in masculine terms.

1535. Bendroth, Margaret L. "The Search for 'Women's Role' in American Evangelicalism, 1930-1980." In Evangelicalism and Modern America, ed. George Marsden. Grand Rapids: Eerdmans, 1984.

This well-documented chapter offers the most penetrating analysis to date of women's place in modern evangelicalism. Although it virtually ignores attitudes toward women in such segments of evangelicalism as Wesleyan and pentecostal movements, it is essential reading which helps place continuing evangelical discussions in context.

1536. Bilezikian, Gilbert. Beyond Sex Roles. Grand Rapids: Baker, 1986.

A persuasive argument for believers' oneness in Christ. Bilezekian offers a comprehensive perspective on biblical teaching on male/female relationships that supports nondiscrimination in church and family life.

1537. Blevins, Carolyn DeArmond. "Patterns of Ministry Among Southern Baptist Women." Baptist History and Heritage 22 (July 1987): 41-49.

A brief overview of the ministry activities in which Southern Baptist women have engaged in the past, with consideration of the sources of opposition to their public roles.

1538. Blumhofer, Edith L. "A Confused Legacy: Reflections on Evangelical Attitudes Toward Ministering Women in the Past Century." Fides et Historia 22 (1990).

This survey maintains that evangelical attitudes toward ministering women were shaped in part by the cultural milieu. It also asserts that pentecostal movements never wholeheartedly endorsed ministering women, and it traces the role of evangelical voluntary associations in affirming expanded leadership roles for evangelical women.

1539. Blumhofer, Edith L. "Evangelical Ministering Women." Evangelical Studies Bulletin 5 (March 1988): 6-9.

This bibliographical essay offers orientation for those who wish to study scholarly writings on women in American evangelicalism.

1540. Blumhofer, Edith L. "Women in the Evangelical and Pentecostal Traditions." The Ecumenical Decade of Women, ed., Melanie May, Grand Rapids: Eerdmans, 1990.

This chapter is part of a book that looks at women's public roles in major American Christian traditions. It challenges evangelicals and pentecostals come to terms with changing roles of women in the church and society.

1541. Boyer, Paul. "Minister's Wife, Widow, Reluctant Feminist: Catherine Marshall in the 1950's." In Women in American Religion, ed., Janet Wilson James. Philadelphia: University of Pennsylvania Press, 1980.

As the wife and then biographer of the well-known Presbyterian pastor, Peter Marshall, and finally as a best-selling author in her own right, Catherine Marshall was a genuine evangelical success story. The meaning of such success for a movement that has offered both enhanced opportunities and tightly defined gender definitions is the subject of this interesting piece.

1542. Brumberg, Joan Jacobs. "The Ethnological Mirror: American Evangelical Women and Their Heathen Sisters, 1870-1910." In Women and the Structure of Society, eds. Barbara J. Harris and JoAnn K. McNamara. Durham: Duke University Press, 1984.

A well-written and well-researched chapter detailing the rise of women's missionary societies and their assumptions about the emancipatory role of Christianity and the oppression of women in non-Christian religions. Examines how reports of women's place in non-western societies molded the goals of the women's missionary movement.

1543. Buckingham, Jamie. Daughter of Destiny. South Plainfield, NJ: Bridge Publications, 1976.

Charismatic evangelist Kathryn Kuhlman crisscrossed America preaching a message of hope and healing that drew huge crowds to large stadiums wherever she went. This sympathetic, popular biography by a fellow participant in the charismatic movement offers insights into Kuhlman's ministry. It is useful as both a primary and a secondary source on the personalities and message of the charismatic movement.

1544. Dirksen, Carolyn Rowland. "Let Your Women Keep Silence." In The Promise and Power, ed. Donald Bowdle. Cleveland, TN: Pathway Press, 1980.

The role of women in the Church of God, Cleveland (TN) has been ambiguous from the start. In this book of essays about the denomination, Dirksen, a member of the denomination, discusses the prominence of women in the denomination's early evangelism and foreign missions efforts, their diminished contemporary presence in the pulpit, and their exclusion from the denomination's administrative structure.

1545. Dodson, Jualyne E. and Cheryl Townsend Gilkes. "Something Within: Social Change and Collective Endurance in the Sacred World of Black Christian Women." In Women and Religion in America, eds. Rosemary Radford Ruether and Rosemary Skinner Keller. Volume 3. San Francisco: Harper & Row, 1986.

This essay in an important multi-volume anthology on women in American religion analyzes the changing roles of women in twentieth-century black experience and then offers primary sources documenting women's participation and perceptions.

1546. Elliot, Elisabeth. Let Me Be a Woman. Wheaton, IL: Tyndale House Publishers, 1976.

Elliot, an influential evangelical author and speaker, defends the hierarchical paradigm that characterizes large segments of evangelicalism. Elliot maintains that woman's place is in the home in submission to her husband; that women were created for men; and that contemporary feminism is fundamentally unchristian. Written in popular, readable style, it is essential reading for anyone wanting to understand the popular appeal of this viewpoint.

1547. Flora, J. R. "Ordination of Women in the Brethren Church: A Case Study from the Anabaptist-Pietist Tradition." Journal of the Evangelical Theological Society 30 (December, 1987): 427-440.

Flora concentrates on an overview of the Brethren Church from the 18th century to the present but makes general observations about other free church groups as well. He traces the practice of ordaining women in the

Brethren Church from the nineteenth century and notes that it peaked in the World War I era and has declined steadily since.

1548. Gilkes, Cheryl Townsend. "'Together and Harness': Women's Traditions in the Sanctified Church." Signs: Journal of Women in Culture and Society 10 (Summer, 1985): 678-699.

This well-written article is essential reading for anyone interested in the role of women in black holiness and pentecostal churches.

1549. Gundry, Patricia. Woman, Be Free. Grand Rapids: Zondervan, 1979.

A well-written introduction to the biblical issues on which evangelical discussion of women's roles hinges, this book maintains that the hierarchical paradigm should be replaced by one that stresses partnership. Gundry participated prominently in the emerging evangelical feminist movement of the 1970s and her work reflects her thorough understanding of the issues on both sides of the debate.

1550. Hassey, Janette. No Time for Silence: Evangelical Women in Public Ministry Around the Turn of the Century. Grand Rapids: Zondervan, 1986.

Hassey combined her interests in history and theology in this thoroughly documented study of the ministry roles played by evangelical women between 1870 and 1930. She takes issue with both those who insist that support for ministering women is incompatible with views of biblical inerrancy and those who perceive evangelical feminism as a recent innovation sparked by secular feminism. The appendices offer reprints of significant--and sometimes rare--affirmations of ministering women by key evangelical leaders.

1551. Hestenes, Roberta and Lois Curley, eds. Women and the Ministries of Christ. Pasadena: Fuller Theological Seminary, 1979.

In 1978, Fuller Theological Seminary cosponsored a conference with the Evangelical Women's Caucus. This book compiles the conference papers which covered such topics as biblical foundations; women and the evangelical movement; women and the call to justice. It includes a helpful basic bibliography. Contributors include Virginia Ramey Mollenkott, Becky Manley Pippert and Paul Jewett.

Hill, Patricia R. The World Their Household: The American Women's Foreign Mission Movement and Cultural Transformation, 1870-1920. Ann Arbor: University of Michigan, 1985.
(see 1311)

1552. Hull, Gretchen Gaebelein. Equal to Serve. Old Tappan, NJ: Fleming H. Revell, 1987.

Argues that equality for women both within the church and in society is a Christ-serving, as opposed to self-serving, mandate. Clearly written, and full of biblical references, this anecdotal manifesto is intended for the popular audience.

1553. Jewett, Paul K. Man As Male and Female. Grand Rapids: Eerdmans, 1975.

This book caused something of a stir when published, with its argument that biblical comments on the character and role of women were sometimes culturally distorted. By the end of the 1980s, it had taken its place toward moderately left of center in the wide spectrum of evangelical views on the subject.

1554. Jewett, Paul K. The Ordination of Women: An Essay on the Office of Christian Ministry. Grand Rapids: Eerdmans, 1980.

This important study by a noted evangelical scholar makes a case for women in ministry. Thorough discussion of biblical texts relating to woman's nature and the nature of ministry is followed by consideration of masculine references to God and of the Pentecost event that, Jewett maintains, opened Christian ministry to women. Jewett offers suggestions for changes in both evangelical practice and language.

1555. Johnston, Robert K. "The Role of Women in the Church and Home: An Evangelical Testcase in Hermeneutics." Scripture, Tradition and Interpretation, W. Ward Gasque and William S. LaSor, eds. Grand Rapids: Eerdmans, 1978.

Johnston, a noted evangelical New Testament scholar, argues that evangelicals need to pay more attention to hermeneutical questions in their discussions of women's roles. He calls for reevaluation of exegetical method on the assumption that a critical look at relevant scriptures will clarify and unite.

1556. Keller, Rosemary Skinner, Louise L. Queen and Hilah F. Thomas, eds. Women in New Worlds: Historical Perspectives on the Wesleyan Tradition. 2 vols. Nashville: Abingdon, 1982.

The essays included in these volumes offer valuable insights into both issues and experiences relating to women in the Wesleyan tradition. They comprise an excellent general introduction that covers a broad time frame.

1557. LaHaye, Beverly. I Am a Woman By God's Design. Old Tappan, NJ: Fleming H. Revell, 1980.

Counsels women to accept their foreordained position as man's social subordinate, but moral equal. According to LaHaye, feminism endangers God's plan by rejecting His designation of woman as man's auxiliary, a privileged position that involves bearing and caring for children, and maintaining a good home and happy family. Calls for women to exercise their influence by demanding morality in both the civic and domestic arenas.

1558. Liftin, Duane A. "Evangelical Feminism: Why Traditionalists Reject It." Bibliotheca Sacra (July-September, 1979): 258-271.

In this brief article, Litfin aptly summarizes the theological reasons antifeminist evangelicals use to reject evangelical feminism. Maintaining that feminists distort biblical passages in their effort to eliminate hierarchy, he argues that evangelical feminists are motivated rather by the spirit of the age than by the spirit of the New Testament.

1559. McBeth, Leon H. Women in Baptist Life. Nashville: Broadman, 1979.

This study by a prominent Southern Baptist historian is essential reading for a grasp of attitudes toward and experiences of women in one vast segment of American evangelicalism.

1560. McPherson, Aimee Semple. The Story of My Life. Waco, TX: Word Books, 1973.

During the 1920s, Aimee Semple McPherson was a colorful, controversial presence on the American religious scene. The founder of the International Church of the Foursquare Gospel, she based her ministry in Los Angeles but traveled around the world. The best-known pentecostal evangelist of her day, McPherson was also a pastor, editor, radio preacher and Bible school founder. She wrote several autobiographies, of which this offers the shortest but most complete narrative of her life.

1561. Mickelsen, Alvera, ed. Women, Authority and the Bible. Downers Grove, IL: InterVarsity Press, 1986.

In 1985, an Evangelical Colloquium on Women and the Bible convened such prominent evangelicals as Clark Pinnock, Patricia and Stanley Gundry, David and Jeannette Scholer, J. I. Packer and Nicholas Wolterstorff to discuss the equality of the sexes and women's ministries. This book compiles the papers and responses and offers a sampling of evangelical support for ministering women.

1562. Mollenkott, Virgina Ramey. Women, Men and the Bible. Nashville: Abingdon, 1977.

Mollenkott played a prominent role in the emergence of a self-conscious evangelical feminist movement during the 1970s. Her book introduced theological and practical arguments for equality, urging each Christian individual to submit to all others. She took issue with antifeminists in evangelical ranks, basing her call for equality in the teachings and actions of Christ.

Morgan, Marabel. The Total Woman. Old Tappan, NJ: Fleming H. Revell, 1973.
(see 1522)

1563. Penn-Lewis, Jessie. The Magna Charta of Woman. Minneapolis: Bethany House, 1975.

Penn-Lewis, a well-known turn-of-the-century Welsh conference speaker and author, was prominently associated with the Keswick movement. Her book on women in ministry was an attempt to popularize the earlier work of Katherine Bushnell, an able advocate. Penn-Lewis roots woman's right to preach in the Pentecost event.

1564. Rice, John R. Bobbed Hair, Bossy Wives and Women Preachers; Significant Questions for Honest Christian Women Settled by the Word of God. Wheaton, IL: Sword of the Lord Publishers, 1941.

John R. Rice, founder and editor of The Sword of the Lord, was an influential separatist fundamentalist who strenuously opposed the "new women" of the post-World-War I era for flaunting their departure from what he understood to be specific biblical commands. This little book is a classic statement of the stance toward women of one large segment of evangelicalism at midcentury.

1565. Scanzoni, Letha and Nancy Hardesty. All We're Meant to Be: A Biblical Approach to Women's Liberation. Waco, TX: Word Books, 1974.

Claims that the traditional Christian relegation of women to the role of homemaker and child-bearer is a culturally rooted rather than biblical ideology. Offers a scriptural basis for sexual equality and encourages women to exercise all their God-given gifts, both intellectual and reproductive.

1566. Scanzoni, Letha and Susan Setta. "Women in Evangelical, Holiness and Pentecostal Traditions." In Women and Religion in America, eds. Rosemary Radford Ruether and Rosemary Skinner Keller. Volume 3. San Francisco: Harper & Row, 1986.

The three volumes of Ruether's and Keller's Women and Religion in America offer chapter-length essays that serve as introductions to selections from primary sources. This chapter and the documents that follow offer insights into the varied roles women have played in twentieth-century evangelical movements. Reliance on secondary sources, especially about pentecostal and holiness women, limits the usefulness of the introduction.

1567. Scholer, David M. "Feminist Hermeneutics and Evangelical Biblical Interpretation." Journal of the Evangelical Theological Society 30 (December, 1987): 407-420.

Scholer is a noted evangelical New Testament scholar whose careful research on women in ministry has made him a staunch advocate of full equality of women and men in the church. This article offers a sampling of his views.

1568. Stanley, Susan. "Alma White: Holiness Preacher with a Feminist Message." Ph.D. diss., Iliff School of Theology and the University of Denver, 1987.

Among the colorful, lesser known figures in American religious history is Alma White, a Methodist minister's wife who became a holiness preacher and bishop of the denomination she founded, the Pillar of Fire. Stanley's dissertation documents White's feminist stance in the context of her holiness theology and introduces this forceful woman whose story provides insights into the holiness and pentecostal movements as well as documentation about the potential for a nurturing relationship between holiness theology and feminism.

1569. Starr, Lee Anna. The Bible Status of Women. Women in American Protestant Religion Series, ed. Carolyn DeSwarte Gifford. New York: Garland Publishing, 1986.

This classic statement (1926) summarizes turn-of-the-century evangelical women's advocacy of woman's right to preach, insisting that male biblical scholars misinterpreted scripture and consequently restricted women. Starr also opposed the radical feminist view that cited the Bible as the source of woman's oppression. An essential primary source, this book was recently reprinted as part of a Garland Publishing series.

1570. Utley, Uldine. Why I am a Preacher: A Plain Answer to an Oft-Repeated Question. Women in American Protestant Religion, 1800-1930 Series, ed. Carolyn DeSwarte Gifford. New York: Garland Publishing, 1986.

Uldine Utley, a popular child evangelist of the 1920s, had a large following among working-class Americans across the country. Fundamentalist leader John Roach Straton wrote a spirited defense of her ministry in New York's Madison Square Garden, and Chicago's Methodist bishop authenticated her ministry gifts. This autobiography (1931) is valuable for its insights into popular religion in the 1920s as well as for its information on Utley. It includes several of her sermons.

1571. Warner, Wayne E. The Woman Evangelist: The Life and Times of Charismatic Evangelist Maria B. Woodworth-Etter. Metuchen, NJ: The Scarecrow Press, 1986.

From the 1880s until her death in 1924, Maria B. Woodworth-Etter was a familiar figure on the sawdust trail. Warner's biography documents her struggles as a woman as well as her evolving teaching on charismatic phenomena and healing. This book is especially useful for students of the holiness, healing and pentecostal movements.

1572. Willard, Frances E. Woman in the Pulpit. Boston: D. Lothrop, 1888.

Willard, leader of the Women's Christian Temperance Union, responds to popular objections about ministering women, urges them to active public roles and offers them encouragement from well-known male pastors. A sprightly, informative book.

INDEXES

AUTHOR INDEX

INSTITUTIONAL AND ORGANIZATIONAL INDEX
(Excluding Denominations)

SUBJECT INDEX

CONTRIBUTORS

RANDALL BALMER received his Ph.D. from Princeton University. He is assistant professor of religion at Columbia University.

EDITH L. BLUMHOFER received her Ph.D. from Harvard University. She is associate professor of history at Wheaton College and Project Director at the Institute for the Study of American Evangelicals.

JOEL A. CARPENTER earned his Ph.D. at the Johns Hopkins University. He is Program Officer for religion at the Pew Charitable Trusts in Philadelphia and former director of the Institute for the Study of American Evangelicals.

LARRY K. ESKRIDGE received his M.A. at the University of Maryland, College Park in American history. He is on the staff of the Institute for the Study of American Evangelicals.

KENNETH D. GILL is Collection Development Librarian at the Billy Graham Center Library at Wheaton College. He received a Ph.D. from the University of Birmingham.

MARK A. NOLL is professor of history at Wheaton College. He received his Ph.D. from Vanderbilt University.

ROBERT D. SHUSTER received an M.A. in American history from the University of Wisconsin, Madison and an M.A. in library science from Northern Illinois University. Since 1975 he has been director of the Archives of the Billy Graham Center at Wheaton College.

JAMES D. STAMBAUGH is director of the Billy Graham Center Museum at Wheaton College. He earned an M.A. at Cooperstown.

FERNE L. WEIMER earned an M.A. in library science at Northern Illinois University. Since 1980 she has been director of the Billy Graham Center Library at Wheaton College.